# Cultural Validity in Assessment

W9-ABN-521

What is assessment and how is it a cultural practice? How does failure to account for linguistic and cultural variation among students jeopardize assessment validity? What is required to achieve *cultural validity* in assessment? This resource for practicing and prospective teachers—as well as others concerned with fair and valid assessment—provides a thorough grounding in relevant theory, research, and practice. The book lays out criteria for culturally valid assessment and recommends specific strategies that teachers can use to design and implement culturally valid classroom assessments.

*Cultural Validity in Assessment: Addressing Linguistic and Cultural Diversity*:

- Explores the role of culture and language in assessment, not only as it relates to English language learners but to all students
- Gives teachers the necessary tools to develop a thorough understanding of cultural validity in assessment as well as practical knowledge of ways to maximize cultural validity in classroom assessment
- Examines every step in the assessment process, from assessment selection and design to administration, scoring, and score interpretation, with a view to identifying ways of maximizing fairness and validity for all students
- Offers examples from field-based work of the authors and others to illustrate constructive practices and policies that promise to yield more authentic accountability than present practices provide

Assessment plays a powerful role in the process of education in the U.S. and has a disproportionately negative impact on students who do not come from mainstream, middle-class backgrounds. Given the significance of testing in education today, cultural validity in assessment is an urgent issue facing educators. This book is essential reading for addressing this important, relevant topic.

**María del Rosario Basterra** is Independent Educational Consultant, Washington, DC, specializing in issues related to English language learners, language minority students, multicultural education, and preschool education.

**Elise Trumbull** is Independent Educational Consultant, Oakland, CA, specializing in issues related to language and culture in schooling, and Lecturer, California State University, Northridge, Department of Educational Psychology and Counseling.

**Guillermo Solano-Flores** is Associate Professor, Bilingual Education and English as a Second Language, University of Colorado at Boulder.

# Language, Culture, and Teaching
Sonia Nieto, Series Editor

Visit **www.routledge.com/education** for additional information on titles in the Language, Culture, and Teaching series.

# Cultural Validity in Assessment

## Addressing Linguistic and Cultural Diversity

Edited by
**María del Rosario Basterra**
**Elise Trumbull**
**Guillermo Solano-Flores**

NEW YORK AND LONDON

First published 2011
by Routledge
270 Madison Avenue, New York, NY 10016

Simultaneously published in the UK
by Routledge
2 Park Square, Milton Park, Abingdon, Oxon OX14 4RN

*Routledge is an imprint of the Taylor & Francis Group, an informa business*

© 2011 Taylor & Francis

The right of the editors to be identified as the authors of the
editorial material, and of the authors for their individual chapters,
has been asserted in accordance with sections 77 and 78 of the
Copyright, Designs and Patents Act 1988.

Typeset in Minion by Wearset Ltd, Boldon, Tyne and Wear
Printed and bound in the United States of America on acid-free
paper by Walsworth Publishing Company, Marceline, MO

*Library of Congress Cataloging in Publication Data*
Cultural validity in assessment : addressing linguistic and cultural
diversity / editors, María del Rosario Basterra, Elise Trumbull,
Guillermo Solano-Flores. – 1st ed.
p. cm. – (Language, culture, and teaching series)
1. Educational tests and measurements–United States–Evaluation.
2. Test bias–United States. 3. Minority students–United States–
Examinations. 4. Linguistic minorities–United States–
Examinations. 5. Multiculturalism–United States. I. Basterra, María
del Rosario. II. Trumbull, Elise. III. Solano Flores, Guillermo.
LB3051.C85 2011
371.26'013–dc22                                        2010025347

ISBN13: 978-0-415-99979-3 (hbk)
ISBN13: 978-0-415-99980-9 (pbk)
ISBN13: 978-0-203-85095-4 (ebk)

# Dedications

We dedicate this book to all the teachers who are seeking ways to promote excellence and equity in their classrooms. The authors also want to give special dedications to the following:

María del Rosario Basterra: To my husband Carlos and my daughter Lucía for their unconditional support and love.

Elise Trumbull: To my ever-patient husband, Jerry Salzman, who will solve a computer glitch for me any time, day or night.

Guillermo Solano-Flores: To María Araceli Ruiz-Primo (Ayis-Ayis), my wonderful wife and great colleague.

# Contents

# Foreword

*Eugene E. García*

Cognitive and linguistic abilities and the performance of children are generally assessed by measuring specific skills—typically through standardized testing. Several concerns and problematic issues (including litigations) have come to bear over the past few decades in relation to test development and assessment practices for culturally and linguistically diverse students. Efforts continue to be made to develop appropriate measures and procedures that take into account children's cultural and linguistic backgrounds so as to not penalize those who fall outside the cultural mainstream in the U.S. The goal of these efforts, in general, is to create culturally and linguistically relevant measures that accurately portray the abilities and concurrent performance levels for a diverse body of children.

This volume brings together a set of colleagues who collectively help us address the challenge of achieving this important goal, contributing at the theoretical, empirical, policy, and best-practice levels. Conceptually and theoretically, issues related to the key roles of culture and language are addressed in a substantive manner, laying the framework for understanding the complexity of assessment with diverse populations. At the best-practice level, specific guidance with regard to content-level assessment in reading, mathematics, and science are very useful to a field in need of this proper guidance. The specific and general overview of policies in this field is both informative and most helpful in understanding how future policy must be more responsive to diverse populations. By attending to these important issues, the volume addresses in the most comprehensive aggregate that I am aware of the complex yet growing concern regarding cultural validity of our assessments. In so doing, it adds a rich contribution to this ever-growing field of inquiry.

Although important strides have been made in the development of appropriate tests and assessment procedures for culturally and linguistically diverse students, much research and development is still needed. Tests are still limited in terms of their overall number as well as the domains and skills they cover. Moreover, several tests developed for specific language minority groups are merely translations of original English versions, which tend to be based on Euro-American cultural values. Their view of competence, in many cases, is simply not applicable to other groups with different backgrounds. As such, the content and construct validity of an English measure may not be the same when translated into another language. Furthermore, tests with appropriate psychometric properties should contain enough items to assess an identified skill and be standardized with representative samples of children from diverse ethnicities, national origins, language backgrounds, and socioeconomic conditions.

As noted throughout the volume, the National Research Council along with professional associations, such as the American Psychological Association, the American Education Research Association, and the National Association for the Education of Young Children, have addressed the set of issues relevant to the task of assessing diverse children and students with psychometrically sound attention to issues of validity and reliability. This volume provides more clarity yet resonates a major theme that assessments be guided by specific purposes with appropriate applications to meet the needs of the child. Contributions to this volume make it very clear that assessments and screenings should be used to offer better services and to develop more informed interventions. As this volume argues, this approach would encourage the inclusion of all students in accountability systems and the provision of meaningful measures that improve learning outcomes, allowing useful accommodations where appropriate.

Contributors to the volume also assert that instruments used to assess children and students should align with the specific cultural and linguistic characteristics of the child being assessed. This means that the cultural and linguistic content and context of the tests are congruent with the child's background, with the main purpose of assessment being to improve children's learning and development. In order for this to occur, multiple methods, measures, and informants should be incorporated in an assessment of the child's ongoing performance, given the curricular content and instructional approaches used in class. Moreover, the use of formal standardized assessments should be done with a clear understanding of the intent of each assessment and its limitations. Formal assessments may be appropriate to identify disabilities, evaluate programs (for accountability purposes), and/or to monitor and improve individual learning. However, test developers, evaluators, and decision-makers should be aware of the limitations and biases many of these tests introduce. Of course, those conducting assessments should have cultural and linguistic competence, knowledge of the child being assessed, and specific assessment-related knowledge and skills. It is important to remember that assessments are more likely to be valid for bilingual/bicultural students when carried out by teams of professionals who are bilingual/bicultural, and who are also knowledgeable about first- and second-language acquisition.

I would add a significant feature of this assessment challenge: Families of children or students should play critical roles in the assessment process. Parents (or legal guardians) should be queried as sources of data and should be involved in the process of interpreting comprehensive assessments. In addition, parents (or legal guardians) should always be aware of reasons for assessment, the procedures involved, and the significance of the outcomes. Their voices should be sought out and should influence program placement and other intervention strategies. Too often, families are left out of the process of assessment of their children in ways that hinder achievement of the overall purpose of those assessments.

As this volume makes clear, it is also important that conceptual and empirical work on student assessment move beyond the individual level. A vast majority of discussions in the assessment literature focuses on processes and outcomes within the individual—assessing language, cognitive development, academic learning, and so forth. With this knowledge-base, teachers and schools are expected to adjust aspects of the environment to improve learning. While it has become clear that processes outside the individual—including within the classroom (e.g., teacher–student interactions, peer-to-peer interactions), the home (e.g., frequency of words spoken, amount of books), and within the school (e.g., language instruction policies)—affect learning, the assessment field currently lacks conceptual frameworks and the measures necessary to move research forward to systematically improve assessment for student learning. This volume makes an important contribution by providing frameworks and explaining the role of context in learning and development and how assessment can take contextual variables into consideration.

We still have a long way to go before educators and families have the technical, educational, and cultural *confianza* in the way we assess and utilize assessments for the growing number of children who represent the U.S. diversity at every level of our education stream. This volume moves us in the right direction.

# Preface

Assessment plays a powerful role in the process of education in the U.S., and it has a tremendous negative impact on the lives of students who do not come from White, European-American, middle-class backgrounds. In response to this challenge, this book is intended to serve as a research-based resource for educators who are attempting to ensure valid, fair, and useful assessment for linguistically and culturally diverse students. It provides educators with the knowledge needed to be critical users of large-scale assessments as well as designers of culturally valid classroom assessment.

We were motivated to write this book because we believe that a multidisciplinary perspective is necessary to understand the complex relation between culture and student performance on assessments. The book casts a wide but carefully crafted net in assembling contributions intended to provide the kind of foundation that teachers and other educators need in order to understand and address cultural validity in their contexts. The book's editors and contributors represent a mix of researchers, teacher-educators, professional developers, bilingual experts, educational psychologists, applied linguists, policy experts, and psychometricians with ample experience doing multidisciplinary work in the field of assessment for linguistically and culturally diverse populations. This combined expertise makes it possible to create a unique resource for supporting the teaching force to better address equity and fairness in assessment. To our knowledge, the scope of content and the framework of cultural validity we propose are not addressed in other publications.

*Cultural Validity in Assessment: Addressing Linguistic and Cultural Diversity* is designed primarily for teachers but is also useful to teacher educators, professional developers, administrators, and state- and national-level policy experts concerned with improving the educational assessment of the diverse U.S. population. It should also be of interest to test developers who want to understand the issues entailed in testing diverse populations. The book introduces the construct of cultural validity as an organizing principle for addressing the issues entailed in ensuring the fair and valid assessment of students from ethno-linguistic minority group backgrounds.

Each chapter of the book highlights a specific area of assessment that is critical for understanding how to maximize fairness and validity in assessment for all students. Examples and field-based work are presented to show the way to practices and policies that are constructive and have the promise of yielding more authentic accountability than current practices can do.

The book provides teachers with the necessary tools for developing a thorough understanding of cultural validity in assessment as well as practical knowledge of ways to develop and use assessments in their classrooms. The book features a clear and easy-to-follow format and is written in a style that makes it accessible to anyone concerned with improving educational assessment policies and practices. While some chapters discuss quantitative aspects of testing, a sophisticated knowledge of statistics or psychometrics is not needed to be able to understand the concepts discussed. The book is organized in four Parts, described below.

## Part I: Cultural Validity in Assessment—Basic Concepts

Part I introduces the reader to the roles of culture and language in assessment as well as the social and policy contexts in which current assessment practices are carried out. Chapter 1, written by Solano-Flores, provides a general introduction to the concept of cultural validity in assessment. Key questions addressed include: What is assessment and how is it a cultural practice? How is cultural validity in assessment defined? What are the current challenges of translating the notion of cultural validity into fair assessment practices? What should I look for in tests or testing programs to know if appropriate actions have been taken to address students' linguistic and cultural diversity?

How is assessment dependent on language? What is the relationship between language and culture? How are language skills and/or knowledge confounded with other skills/knowledge, when language is used as a vehicle for assessment? What are their roles in assessment? How can the language of the testing interfere with test validity? Chapter 2, written by Trumbull and Solano-Flores, addresses these questions and provides recommendations on how teachers and other educators can reduce "language interference" as a threat to assessment validity.

## Part II: Assessing Students of Linguistically and Culturally Diverse Backgrounds

Part II deals with what teachers need to know in order to meet the assessment needs of the diverse populations they teach. In Chapter 3, Abedi focuses on such issues as: How is language addressed in large-scale assessment for English language learners? What factors need to be taken into consideration when assessing ELL and/or bilingual students? What are the challenges that professionals who specialize in testing and measurement face when they try to ensure that standardized tests are valid and reliable for both the mainstream population and the population of ELLs? What are the issues that educators and test users need to consider when they make decisions concerning the use of tests with ELLs?

In Chapter 4, Basterra addresses the following questions: What is the relation between cognition, culture, language, and assessment? How do cultural and language differences permeate the ways in which students respond to assessment tasks? The chapter presents an overview of key research findings related to these questions and provides ways to promote equitable and valid assessments in the classroom, taking into consideration students' cultural and linguistic backgrounds.

Kopriva and Sexton, in Chapter 5, focus on how teachers and students from diverse cultural and linguistic backgrounds might collect information about how ELLs think, understand, and develop skills in mathematics, science, and other academic content areas. Key aspects of classroom assessment are presented and discussed. The premise of this chapter is that classroom assessment is primarily about informing instruction based on understanding how students think—an endeavor that should involve and benefit both teachers and students.

In Chapter 6, Durán focuses on the different types of test scores and scoring methods, and key issues associated with them. The central question of this chapter is: How can educators interpret scores on achievement or language proficiency assessments so that they can accurately gauge the capabilities, learning needs, and learning progress of ELL students in the domain assessed? Durán explains how scores on standardized tests are derived and how the scores attained by ELLs must be interpreted through the lens of student background. He suggests questions that educators can pose to evaluate the appropriateness of assessments used with ELLs.

Chapter 7, examines cultural validity in the assessment of bilingual students who have been identified as having special needs. The authors, Hoover and Klingner, present an overview of the response to intervention (RTI) model and selected research results concerning its use with ELLs. They discuss the over-representation of bilingual students in programs for students with disabilities and its possible causes. The chapter provides recommendations for educators that will enable them to best understand and address cultural differences in making eligibility and referral decisions.

In Chapter 8, Lara and Chia present an overview of the No Child Left Behind assessment and accountability requirements that pertain to ELL learners and reviews concerns that have been expressed regarding the impact of these provisions on ELLs and the schools they attend. The chapter outlines outcomes of the law relative to ELLs, presents a brief discussion of accountability and assessment approaches offered as alternatives to the current system, and makes recommendations culled from the various reports that examine issues of assessment, accountability, and ELLs.

## Part III: Field Efforts to Increase Cultural Validity in Assessment

Part III reports on several promising routes to creating culturally valid assessments based on knowledge and experience from current research and development practices. In Chapter 9, Trumbull and Koelsch explain how teachers' knowledge of their own student population and instructional strategies appropriate for ELLs transitioning to English-only classrooms were the basis for a collaboration with researchers that resulted in reading assessments tailored to the district's context. Questions addressed include: How did a medium-sized district in California with a large population of ELLs create a reading assessment appropriate for fifth-grade students transitioning to English? What issues arose in designing, administering, scoring, and interpreting performance on the resulting assessment?

In Chapter 10, Trumbull and Solano-Flores introduce a framework for broadening teachers' approaches to analyzing the linguistic (formal and functional) and cultural properties of assessments. The framework is used to discuss lessons learned from research projects on developing mathematics assessments for ELLs. The chapter also addresses the question: How should teachers participate in the process of assessment development to properly address culture and language in mathematics assessment?

Chapter 11 focuses on promising practices in science and cultural validity. As high-stakes testing and accountability in science loom on the horizon, science educators are facing the dilemma of identifying effective educational practices to maximize achievement for all learners. A crucial issue is how to effectively address linguistic and cultural factors to ensure valid and equitable science assessments for all students. Drawing on research and development efforts in a large urban school district, Lee, Santau, and Maerten-Rivera address valid and equitable assessment of both science and literacy achievement of ELLs.

## Part IV: Conclusion

This section consists of Chapter 12, written by the editors Trumbull, Basterra, and Solano-Flores. It is a brief synthesis of the main themes across the chapters and some final reflections about the challenges and future implications of implementing cultural validity in the assessment of diverse students.

The authors acknowledge the complexity of the issue and hope that this book will provide teachers and educators with additional knowledge and tools that will help improve the design and implementation of culturally valid assessments for our growing linguistically and culturally diverse populations.

# Acknowledgments

As editors, we are grateful to have been able to collaborate with our exceedingly talented colleagues who have authored chapters in this book. We thank them profoundly for their excellent contributions. We also want to thank Eugene García for writing the Foreword of the book. Many others deserve recognition and thanks. Among these are Elizabeth VanderPutten, Larry Suter, Finbarr Sloane, Sharon Nelson-Barber, Min Li, Melissa Kwon, Chun-Wei (Kevin) Huang, Maria Araceli Ruiz-Primo, Henriette Langdon, Beverly Farr, David (Ludi) van Broekhuizen, Maria Pacheco, Rosalinda Quintanar-Sarellano, Susan Shaffer, Liz Wolfe, and Erin Bougie. A special thanks to Kate Farbry who provided excellent support in the preparation of the manuscript.

# Part I

# Cultural Validity in Assessment—Basic Concepts

Chapter 1

# Assessing the Cultural Validity of Assessment Practices

## An Introduction

*Guillermo Solano-Flores*

## Defining Cultural Validity

As with any other product of human activity, tests are cultural artifacts. They are a part of a complex set of culturally established instructional and accountability practices; they are created with the intent to meet certain social needs or to comply with the mandates and legislation established in a society; they are written in the language (and the dialect of that language) used by those who develop them; their content is a reflection of the skills, competencies, forms of knowledge, and communication styles valued by a society—or the influential groups of that society; and they assume among test-takers full familiarity with the contexts used to frame problems, the ways in which questions are worded, and the expected ways to answer those questions.

Viewing tests as cultural artifacts (see Cole, 1999) enables us to appreciate that, to a great extent, the ways in which students interpret test items and respond to them are mediated by cultural factors that do not have to do necessarily with the knowledge assessed. This is a matter of validity—scores obtained by students on a test should not be due to factors other than those that the test is intended to measure (Messick, 1995). This is as true of classroom assessments as it is of large-scale assessments.

While key normative documents on testing (e.g., AERA, NCME, & APA, 1999; Hambleton, 2005) recognize the importance of factors related to culture and language as a source of measurement error, current testing practices address culture as a threat to validity rather than the essence of validity. Culture is part of the discourse on test validity but is not viewed as the essence of a form of validity in its own right.

In 2001, we (Solano-Flores & Nelson-Barber, 2001, p. 555) proposed the concept of cultural validity, which can be defined as:

> the effectiveness with which [...] assessment addresses the socio-cultural influences that shape student thinking and the ways in which students make sense of [...] items and respond to them. These socio-cultural influences include the sets of values, beliefs, experiences, communication patterns, teaching and learning styles, and epistemologies inherent in the students' cultural backgrounds, and the socioeconomic conditions prevailing in their cultural groups.

Along with this definition, we contended that the cultural factors that shape the process of thinking in test-taking are so complex that culture should not be treated as a factor to correct or control for, but as a phenomenon intrinsic to tests and testing. We argued that both test developers and test users should examine cultural validity with the same level of rigor and attention they use when they examine other forms of validity.

The notion of cultural validity in assessment is consistent with the concept of multicultural validity (Kirkhart, 1995) in the context of program evaluation, which recognizes that cultural factors shape the sensitivity of evaluation instruments and the validity of the conclusions on program effectiveness. It is also consistent with a large body of literature that emphasizes the importance of examining instruction and assessment from a cultural perspective (e.g., Ladson-Billings, 1995; Miller & Stigler, 1987; Roseberry, Warren, & Conant, 1992). Thus, although cultural validity is discussed in this chapter primarily in terms of large-scale assessment, it is applicable to classroom assessment as well. This fact will become more evident as the reader proceeds through the book.

In spite of its conceptual clarity, translating the notion of cultural validity into fair assessment practices is a formidable endeavor whose success is limited by two major challenges. The first challenge stems from the fact that the concept of culture is complex and lends itself to multiple interpretations—each person has their own conception of culture yet the term is used as though the concept were understood by everybody the same way.

As a result of this complexity, it is difficult to point at the specific actions that should be taken to properly address culture. For example, the notion of "cultural responsiveness" or "cultural sensitivity" is often invoked by advocates as critical to attaining fairness (e.g., Gay, 2000; Hood, Hopson, & Frierson, 2005; Tillman, 2002). However, available definitions of cultural sensitivity cannot be readily operationalized into observable characteristics of tests or their process of development.

The second challenge has to do with implementation. Test developers take different sorts of actions intended to address different aspects of cultural and linguistic diversity. Indeed, in these days, it is virtually impossible to imagine a test that has not gone through some kind of internal or external scrutiny intended to address potential cultural or linguistic bias at some point of its development. Yet it is extremely difficult to determine when some of those actions are effective and when they simply address superficial aspects of culture and language or underestimate their complexities. For example, the inclusion of a cultural sensitivity review stage performed by individuals from different ethnic backgrounds is part of current standard practice in the process of test development. While necessary, this strategy may be far from sufficient to properly address cultural issues. There is evidence that teachers of color are more aware than white, mainstream teachers of the potential challenges that test items may pose to students of color; however, in the absence of appropriate training, teachers of color are not any better than white teachers in their effectiveness in identifying and addressing specific challenges posed by test items regarding culture and language (Nguyen-Le, 2010; Solano-Flores & Gustafson, in press).

These challenges underscore the need for approaches that allow critical examination of assessment practices from a cultural perspective. While assessment systems and test developers may be genuinely convinced that they take the actions needed to properly address linguistic and cultural diversity, certain principles derived from the notion of cultural validity should allow educators and decision-makers to identify limitations in practices regarding culture and language and ways in which these practices can be improved.

This chapter intends to provide educators, decision-makers, school districts, and state departments of education with reasonings that should enable them to answer the question, "What should I look for in tests or testing programs to know if appropriate actions have been taken to address culture?" These reasonings are organized according to four aspects of cultural validity: theoretical foundations, population sampling, item views, and test review.

In discussing these aspects, I share lessons learned and provide examples from three projects funded by the National Science Foundation (for a discussion of the methodological aspects of these projects, see Solano-Flores & Li, 2006, 2008, 2009; Solano-Flores & Trumbull, 2008). The first project, "Assessing the Cultural Validity of Science and Mathematics Assessments," investigated cultural influences on test-taking. Grade 4 students from 13 cultural groups (each defined by a unique combination of such factors as ethnicity, geographical region, ancestry, socioeconomic status, and linguistic influences) verbalized their thinking as they responded to the NAEP items shown in Figure 1.1 (see National Assessment of Educational Progress, 1996) and responded to interview questions on the ways in which they interpreted them.

The second project, "Cognitive, Sociolinguistic, and Psychometric Perspectives in Science and Mathematics Assessment for English Language Learners," examined how scores obtained by English language learners vary when they are tested in English or in their native language or in the local or standard dialects of those languages. The third project, "Teacher-Adapted Versus Linguistically Simplified Items in the Testing of English Language Learners" investigated the advantages of using language adaptations made by teachers on tests as a form of testing accommodation for English language learners (ELLs) tested in English. These two projects addressed language from a sociolinguistic perspective that takes into consideration the social aspect of language and the fact that language use varies across social groups. More specifically, these projects examined the extent to which the scores of ELL students in tests vary due to language and dialect variation (Solano-Flores, 2006). As a part of the activities for these two projects, we worked with teachers from different linguistic communities with the purpose of adapting tests so that their linguistic features reflected the characteristics of the language used by their students.

For discussion purposes, throughout this chapter, language is regarded as part of culture. However, when appropriate, language or linguistic groups are referred to separately when the topics discussed target language as a specific aspect of culture. Also, the terms "assessment" and "test" are used interchangeably.

**Mountains item:**
The pictures below show the same river and mountains, but one picture shows how they looked millions of years ago, and the other picture shows how they look now. Circle the letter under the picture that shows how the river and mountains look now. Explain how you can tell this.

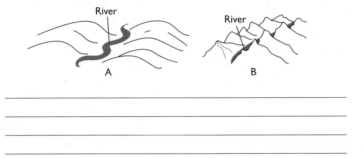

A                                      B

_____

_____

_____

_____

**Lunch Money item:**
Sam can purchase his lunch at school. Each day he wants to have juice that costs 50¢, a sandwich that cost 90¢, and fruit that costs 35¢. His mother has only $1.00 bills. What is the least number of $1.00 bills that his mother should give him so he will have enough money to buy lunch for 5 days?

**Metals item:**
Many things are made of metal, such as pots, pans, tools, and wire. Give two reasons why metals are used to make many different things.

**Gumball Machine item:**
Think carefully about the following question. Write a complete answer. You may use drawings, words, and numbers to explain your answer. Be sure to show all of your work.

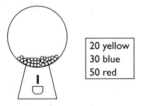

20 yellow
30 blue
50 red

The gum ball machine has 100 gum balls; 20 are yellow, 30 are blue, and 50 are red. The gum balls are well mixed inside the machine.
Jenny gets 10 gum balls from this machine.
What is your best prediction of the number that will be red?

*Figure 1.1* Items used in the project (source: National Assessment of Educational Progress, 1996. *Mathematics Items Public Release*. Washington, DC: Author).

## Theoretical Foundations

Testing practices should be supported by theories that address cognition, language, and culture. Regarding cognition, testing practices should address the fact that cognition is not an event that takes place in isolation within each person; rather, it is a phenomenon that takes place through social interaction. There is awareness that culture influences test-taking (Basterra, Chapter 4, this volume). Indeed, every educator has stories to tell on how wording or the contextual information provided by tests misleads some students in their interpretations of items. However, not much research has been done to examine the ways in which culture influences thinking during test-taking.

There is a well-established tradition of research on the cognitive validation of tests that examines students' cognitive activity elicited by items (Baxter, Elder, & Glaser, 1996; Hamilton, Nussbaum, & Snow, 1997; Megone, Cai, Silver, & Wang, 1994; Norris, 1990; Ruiz-Primo, Shavelson, Li, & Schultz, 2001), as inferred from their verbalizations during talk-aloud protocols in which they report their thinking while they are engaged in responding to items, or after they have responded to them (Ericsson & Simon, 1993). Surprisingly, with very few exceptions (e.g., Winter, Kopriva, Chen, & Emick, 2006), this research does not examine in detail the connection between thinking and culture or has been conducted mainly with mainstream, white, native English speaking students (see Pellegrino, Chudowski, & Glaser, 2001).

Regarding culture and language, testing practices should be in accord with current thinking from the culture and language sciences. Unfortunately, many actions taken with the intent to serve culturally and linguistically diverse populations in large-scale testing are insufficient or inappropriate. For example, many of the accommodations used by states to test ELLs do not have any theoretical defensibility, are inappropriate for ELLs because they are borrowed from the field of special education, or are unlikely to be properly implemented in large-scale testing contexts (Abedi, Hofstetter, & Lord, 2004; Rivera & Collum, 2006; Solano-Flores, 2008).

In attempting to develop approaches for ELL testing that are consistent with knowledge from the field of sociolinguistics, we (Solano-Flores & Li, 2006, 2008, 2009) have tested students with the same set of items in both English and their first language and in two dialects (standard and local) of the same language. Dialects are varieties of the same language that are distinguishable from each other by features of pronunciation, grammar, and vocabulary, among others (see Crystal, 1997; Wolfram, Adger, & Christian, 1999). Rather than testing these students with bilingual formats, the intent is to determine the extent to which ELL students' performance varies across languages or dialects. Generalizability theory (Brennan, 1992; Cronbach, Gleser, Nanda, & Rajaratnam, 1972; Shavelson & Webb, 1991, 2009)—a psychometric theory of measurement error—allows examination of language as a source of measurement error and, more specifically, the extent to which student performance varies across languages or dialects.

An important finding from our studies is that, contrary to what simple common sense would lead us to believe, ELLs do not necessarily perform better if they are tested in their native languages. Rather, their performance tends to be unstable across languages and across items. Depending on the item, some students perform better in English than in their native language, and some other students perform better in their native language than in English. Our explanation of this finding is that each item poses a unique set of linguistic challenges in each language and, at the same time, each ELL has a unique set of strengths and weaknesses in each language.

Another important finding from those studies speaks to the complexity of language. If, instead of being tested across languages, students are tested across dialects of the same language (say, the variety of Spanish used in their own community and the standard Spanish used by a professional test-translation company), it can be observed that their performance across dialects is as unstable as their performance across languages.

These findings underscore the fact that no simple solution exists if we are serious about developing valid and fair assessment for linguistic minorities (Solano-Flores & Trumbull, 2008). Testing ELLs only in English cannot render valid measures of achievement due to the considerable effect of language proficiency as a construct-irrelevant factor. The same can be said about testing ELLs in their native language. Valid, fair testing for ELLs appears to be possible only if language variation due to dialect is taken into consideration.

Our findings also speak to the fact that, even within broad linguistic groups (e.g., native Haitian-Creole speakers or native Spanish speakers), every group of ELLs is unique as to the sensitivity to the language or dialect in which it is tested. We have observed that the minimum number of items needed to obtain dependable scores may vary with dialect (i.e., more items are needed to obtain dependable scores if students are tested in one dialect than in another). Also, we have observed that groups of students within the same group (e.g., ELLs, native Spanish speakers who live in different regions in the United States), may vary considerably on the number of items needed to obtain dependable measures of their achievement.

Notice that the studies described were the first to use generalizability theory with ELLs. Appreciating the possibilities of using this theory in the testing of ELLs was possible because we were aware that sociolinguistic theory and research point to the importance of linguistic variation. We reasoned that, because bilingual populations are heterogeneous and dynamic rather than homogenous and static, better ELL testing approaches could be developed by using this theory, since it allows examination of multiple sources of score variation. This experience illustrates the notion that testing practices should be in accord with theories on content and knowledge. As the findings from the studies discussed show, the instability of student performance across languages (or dialects) and items is consistent with the well-known notion in sociolinguistics that the use of a first language or a second language among bilingual individuals is shaped by context and content (Fishman, 1965).

## Population Sampling

Statistically appropriate samples of students from different cultural and linguistic groups should participate at all stages of the process of test development. "Inclusion" is a term used these days to refer to the fact that ELL students are included in large-scale testing programs. However, inclusion itself does not ensure fairness or validity if it is limited to test administration and does not involve the entire process of test development. Sampling is key to ensuring cultural validity in testing practices.

Three aspects of sampling need to be discussed: population specification, population representation, and community participation. Population specification is critical to identifying the types and sizes of samples of culturally and linguistically diverse students that should be included in the process of test development. It refers to the ways in which cultural groups are defined and, therefore, the criteria used to determine when an individual belongs to a certain cultural group. A sufficient number of relevant attributes, such as ethnicity, first language, locale, socio-economic status, etc., should lead to proper population specification. Serious threats to the validity of tests for ELLs arise when cultural groups are defined in terms of irrelevant attributes or relevant but insufficient numbers of attributes (see Solano-Flores, 2009). Examples of population misspecification are: defining a cultural group based on race; inferring the proficiency of individuals in the predominant language based on their national origin; collapsing ELLs and special education students in the same category; and using one broad linguistic group of ELLs (e.g., those who are native Spanish speakers) as representative of all the broad linguistic groups of ELLs.

Population representation refers to the extent to which appropriate samples of diverse cultural groups are used in the process of testing. The samples of individuals from different cultural groups used in the process of testing (e.g., as pilot students) should reflect the cultural make-up of the target population (e.g., the population of fourth-grade students in a state) and the sizes of these samples should be consistent with their proportions in that population.

Unfortunately, culturally and linguistically diverse students are usually included only in the terminal stages of the process of test development, or not included at all. For example, it is not customary practice to include ELLs in the samples of pilot students who are asked about the ways in which they interpret draft versions of the items and how these items should be worded so that students understand them as intended. Test developers may wrongly believe these students do not have much to contribute as pilot students, due to their limited proficiency in English. However, a large segment of the ELL population has sufficient communicative skills in non-academic English. Indeed, there is evidence that, as many as two-thirds of ELL students chose to use English in the talk-aloud protocols and interviews conducted to determine how they interpret items; they communicate in English sufficiently well to allow the interviewer to obtain valuable information on their thinking and test-taking strategies (Prosser & Solano-Flores, 2010).

Community participation refers to the fact that decisions concerning the linguistic features of test items (e.g., their wording) should be sensitive to language usage among the communities. Items can be thought of as samples of the features of the language (and the dialect of that language) in which they are written (Solano-Flores, 2006; Solano-Flores & Li, 2006; Solano-Flores & Trumbull, 2003). By ensuring that communities participate in the process of testing, we can ensure that the ways in which language is used in their communities are properly represented in tests.

Traditionally, a panel of experts makes decisions about the ways in which tests should be written or the ways in which their wording should be modified to ensure that ELLs gain access to the content of items. While useful, this approach may not suffice to ensure that language factors are properly controlled for, especially because, as discussed above, the performance of ELL students in tests may be extremely sensitive to the dialect of the language in which tests are administered (Solano-Flores & Li, 2006, 2008, 2009).

We (Solano-Flores, Li, Speroni, Rodriguez, Basterra, & Dovholuk, 2007; Solano-Flores, Speroni, & Sexton, 2005) have investigated the advantages of using a sociolinguistic approach in the linguistic modification of tests. In this approach, teachers modify the linguistic features of test items based on their knowledge of the characteristics of the language used in their own schools. This approach takes into consideration the fact that language use and language usage vary across social groups (Wardhaugh, 2002). According to this sociolinguistic perspective, to minimize language as a source of measurement error, the process of language adaptation must be sensitive to differences in the ways language is used by different communities. Critical to this approach is the notion of localization, which we use to refer to the process of adapting the linguistic features of test items to the local English dialects used by the students' communities. Frequently used in the context of translation, the notion is also applicable in the context of dialects within a language. It refers to the "process of adapting text and cultural content to specific target audiences in specific locations" (World-Lingo, 2004). Originating in the jargon of globalization economy, the concept of localization recognizes that every location is unique by virtue of a series of linguistic and cultural factors. Thus, efforts to adapt text to a given target group must go beyond the pure formal level (Muzzi, 2001).

To examine the possibilities and limitations of using teacher adaptation as an approach to facilitating ELLs gain access to the content of items, we (Solano-Flores et al., 2007) conducted a study that compared teacher adaptation and linguistic simplification as forms of testing accommodation for ELLs. We converted the original version of a test into two test versions, teacher-adapted and linguistically simplified. Using a design that controlled for the effects of sequence, we gave ELL students the same set of test items in two test version combinations, teacher-adapted and original version or teacher-adapted and linguistically simplified. The teacher-adapted version of the items was created by using the approach described above. The linguistically simplified version of the items was created by using linguistic simplification procedures similar to those used by Abedi and his associates (e.g., Abedi, Lord, Hofstetter, & Baker, 2001).

A comparison of the teacher-adapted and linguistically simplified versions revealed that, in terms of their psychometric properties, the two forms of modified tests (internal consistency reliability and mean score differences) were similar. Mean score differences between test versions were either not statistically significant, or their effect sizes were small. In addition, we observed a negligible score variability across test versions, which indicates that teacher adaptation allows modification of test items in ways that do not alter their technical properties. However, we found that the two forms of accommodation are effective for different reasons. The teacher-adapted approach allowed specialists to focus more on the functional aspects of language; in contrast, the linguistically simplified approach allowed specialists to focus more on formal aspects of language.

We concluded that both the teacher adaptation and linguistic simplification approaches are effective in minimizing proficiency in the language of testing as a form of testing accommodation for ELLs. These results speak to the advantages of including teachers from the communities of the ELL populations in the process of ELL testing. Teacher adaptation-based approaches can be successfully used in combination with or as an alternative to linguistic simplification as a form of accommodation in the testing of ELL students.

## Item Views

As part of the process of test development, the views that students from different cultural groups have of items should be carefully examined. Item views can be thought as ways in which students tend to make sense of items and which are influenced by their cultural experience (Solano-Flores, 2001). The notion of item views is an extension of the notion of worldviews—culturally determined ways of making sense of experience (see Lee, 1999).

To examine the item views of different cultural groups, we (Solano-Flores, 2001; Li, Solano-Flores, Kwon, & Tsai, 2008) asked students to examine one of the four items shown in Figure 1.1. Then we asked them the following two questions intended to probe their item views: "What is this item about?" and "What do you have to know or be able to do to answer it?"

A conceptual framework for examining the observed students' responses to these questions is shown in Figure 1.2. According to this conceptual framework, students' views of test items can be characterized along two dimensions and four resulting quadrants. The dimension, content–context (vertical axis) refers to whether a student's view of the item is based on either the content addressed by the item or the contextual information provided by it. For example, when asked what the Gumball Machine item is about, some students identify a broad knowledge domain (e.g., *the item is about math*) whereas others focus on the characters and situations included in the items with the intent to make them meaningful (e.g., *the item is about a gumball machine*).

The dimension, specificity–generality (horizontal axis) refers to the level of specificity with which students think about the skills or knowledge assessed by an item. For example, when asked what they have to know or what they are able to do to answer the Gumball Machine item correctly, some students relate the item to a specific topic (e.g., *you need to know about probability*) whereas others invoke general skills they think are critical to responding to the item (e.g., *you need to be smart*).

**Focus on textual information.** Item is viewed in terms of how it reads. Student repeats or briefly summarizes the prompt or rephrases it with scant elaboration. For example, when thinking about the Mountains item, a student may say: [*The item is about*] *mountains and stuff like that.*
**Focus on personal experience.** Item is viewed in terms of recollections of experiences from personal life that are related to the topic of the item. Student provides examples or mentions specific objects or events from first-hand experience. For example, in reasoning about the Metals item, a student says: [*The item is about*] *bikes, Honda cars, and snow goes.*

**Focus on contextual information.** Item is viewed in terms of the information included in it by item writers with the intent to make it meaningful. Student focuses on things, characters, situations, or illustrations used in the item to provide a context for the exercise. For example, in thinking about the lunch money item, a student says: *It's about Sam, trying to get her lunch, but her mom only has one dollar.*
**Focus on general academic skills.** Item is viewed in terms of highly-valued academic skills inherent to taking tests. Student mentions basic knowledge, skills, or qualities that are needed to solve any exercise but are not sufficient to solve the item at hand. For example, when asked what students need to know and do to be able to answer an exercise, a student responds: [*I need to*] *understand the problem ... and to read the question.*

Context

I | II

**Specificity**                                      IV | III                                      **Generality**

**Focus on concepts related to the item.** Item is viewed in terms of the concepts and facts related to the assumed concept addressed by the item. Student may also mention processes, principles and facts that are related to the content of the item but are not mentioned explicitly in it. For example, a student says the following about the Mountains item: *You have to know about limestone, how it flows with water ... and about hard rock.*
**Focus on actions taken.** Item is viewed in terms of the actions taken by the student when responding to the item. Student describes the answer given or the reasonings or strategies used, or identifies formal characteristics that a successful response should have. For example, a student says the following about the Lunch Money item: *I subtracted.*

**Focus on knowledge domain.** Item is viewed in terms of the assumed content area addressed by the item. Student mentions a broad content or problem area or a topic addressed by the item. For example, when asked what students need to know to answer the Gumballs exercise, a student states: [*I need to know*] *about mathematics.*
**Focus on skills addressed.** Item is viewed in terms of specific skills or knowledge needed to respond to it correctly. Student describes a goal or task, or the operations needed to respond to the item. For example, a student says the following about the Gumballs exercise: *The item is asking me to guess how many gumballs there are in the machine.*

Content

*Figure 1.2* Item Views Quadrants that Result from the Combination of Two Dimensions of Student Item Views: Specificity–Generality and Content–Context. I. Context-Oriented, Specific; II. Context-Oriented, General; III. Content-Oriented, General; IV. Content-Oriented, Specific.

Figure 1.3 shows the percentage of students whose responses were coded as belonging to each of the four quadrants for a sample of cultural groups (Solano-Flores, 2001). For example, 53% of the responses given by Painas[1] students to the two questions above were coded as belonging to Quadrant 1 (Specific, Context-Oriented).

In addition to the percentages of responses coded by quadrant, the table shows the percentages of responses coded by dimension. Two facts stand out.

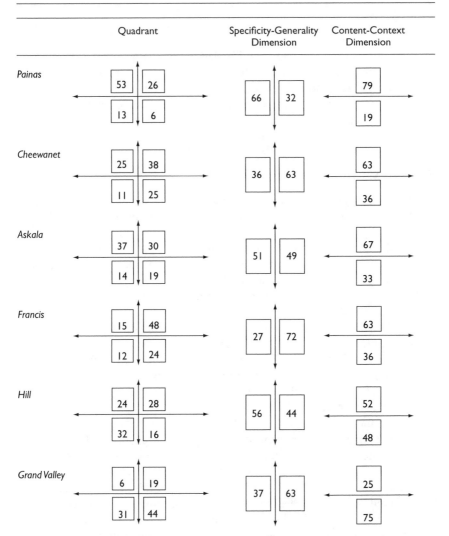

*Figure 1.3* Test Views Quadrant Case Frequencies in Percentages for Six Cultural Groups (Percentages Do Not Add Up to 100 in All Cases Due to Rounding).

First, each group seems to have either predominantly specific or predominantly generic item views. The only exception is Askala (51% and 49% respectively for the specific and generic components of the dimension). Second, as the third column in Figure 1.3 shows, the item views of students from Painas, Cheewanet, Askala, and Francis are predominantly context-oriented; the percentages of responses coded on the context component of the dimension for these groups range from 63% to 79%. In contrast, the students from Hill have comparable percentages of responses on content and context (48% and 52%, respectively), and the students from Grand Valley are predominantly content-oriented (with 75%

and 25% of responses coded respectively on the content and context components of the dimension).

The students from Hill and Grand Valley can be characterized as white, high socio-economic status, suburban. Students from both cultural groups obtained the highest average scores on the four NAEP items used in this study. These facts suggest that there is an important link between academic performance and content-oriented reasonings. They also suggest that the items reflect and favor content-oriented, de-contextualized thinking.

## Test Review

The review of test items with the purpose of examining their cultural and linguistic appropriateness should take into consideration multiple sources of information. Two aspects of test review are discussed here: the use of judgmental and empirical procedures for reviewing the cultural appropriateness of test items, and the use of alternatives of form of representation of data with the purpose of comparing multiple cultural groups on their interpretation of items.

Regarding the use of judgmental and empirical procedures, while teachers who belong to ethnic/cultural minorities are more aware of cultural issues in testing, they do not necessarily make more accurate judgments than their mainstream counterparts about the cultural appropriateness of test items. Rather, the two types of teacher tend to address only superficial features of the items when they are asked to propose ways of minimizing the likelihood for an item to be culturally or linguistically biased against their students (Nguyen-Le, 2010; Sexton & Solano-Flores, 2001).

To examine this issue more carefully, we have evaluated the challenges that a specific item may pose to students due to linguistic or cultural factors. We used the Lunch Money item (see Figure 1.1), whose correct solution involves addition, multiplication, and rounding. We used this item because we have evidence that several interpretation and reading errors observed for this item can be attributed to four kinds of linguistic features: vocabulary (meaning of individual words), semantics (meaning of words in a sentence), syntax (grammatical structure of sentences), and pragmatics (interpretation of words and sentences in context) (Solano-Flores & Trumbull, 2003). Also, the written responses and computations produced by some students who live in poverty suggest that they interpret the item as if they were asked, "What can Sam buy with $1.00?" For example, students wrote solutions such as, "He should buy only the sandwich" or "He can buy only the juice and the fruit" (Solano-Flores & Trumbull, 2003).

We examined how consistently four review approaches identified vocabulary, semantics, syntax, pragmatics, meaningfulness, and appropriateness issues as critical to addressing the linguistic and cultural appropriateness of the Lunch Money item. Two of these four review approaches were judgmental, the judgment of a linguist and whether the issue had been identified by at least 20% of the teachers who reviewed the item. The other two approaches were empirical, whether the issue had been observed among at least 20% of the students who read the item aloud (and whom we interviewed about their interpretations of the item) and whether statistically significant differences were observed between groups on the issues identified by the other criteria.

The results showed that the item features that may have a negative impact on student performance due to linguistic or cultural bias are difficult to anticipate based solely on judgmental procedures. Teachers produced a review of the Lunch Money item that did not reflect entirely the difficulties their own students had in interpreting the item.

These results speak to the need for revising current test development practices, which depend heavily on teachers' judgment for test review. Teachers' judgments are necessary but not sufficient to identify subtle ways in which items may be biased due to language. Teachers' judgments should be used in combination with empirical review procedures that examine the psychometric properties of items.

Regarding the use of alternative forms of representation of data, pattern charts (Solano-Flores, 2008b) illustrate ways in which different forms of information can be used in combination to examine cultural influences in test-taking. Pattern charts can be defined as devices for visually representing and linking information with different levels of statistical power on information obtained with different cultural groups.

Figure 1.4 shows an example of pattern charts. They display the relative standing of each cultural group with respect to the others in terms of the number and direction of statistically significant differences with other groups. The chart at the top of the figure shows group performance differences on the item, Gumball Machine; the chart below shows group differences on item meaningfulness, a concept advanced by Brenner (1998) when she examined how students relate school mathematics and everyday life. In our investigation, item meaningfulness was defined as the tendency of students to relate the content and/or context of an item to activities in which they are actors,[2] as reflected by the response to the question, "How do you see [the content of the item] as part of what you do when you are not at school?" This interview question was included with the intent to determine if students from different cultural backgrounds vary in their ability to relate the content of the item to activities that take place out of the school context in which they are actors.

The length of the bars with respect to the zero vertical line for a given cultural group indicates the number of instances that a statistically significant difference was observed between that group and another group on the construct measured. The orientation (to the left or to the right) of each bar indicates whether the statistically significant differences are in favor of or against the cultural group.[3] For example, in the pattern chart for the Gumball Machine item the length and the orientation of the bars for Grand Valley and the two mainstream, high socioeconomic status cultural groups that participated in the comparison indicate that each of these two groups had statistically significantly higher scores than nine of the eleven cultural groups included in the comparison. At the bottom of this chart is the group, Askala, which ranks the lowest; its performance on the item was statistically significantly lower than five of the other groups.

The brackets on the right of the charts show statistically significant score differences between sub-sets of groups. For example, the bracket on the right of the

**Gumball Machine item score differences**

| Site | −5 | −4 | −3 | −2 | −1 | 0 | 1 | 2 | 3 | 4 | 5 | 6 | 7 | 8 | 9 | 10 |
|---|---|---|---|---|---|---|---|---|---|---|---|---|---|---|---|---|
| Grand Valley | | | | | | | | | | | | | | | | |
| Hill | | | | | | | | | | | | | | | | |
| Francis | | | | | | | | | | | | | | | | |
| Saint Giacommo | | | | | | | | | | | | | | | | |
| Lynnbrook | | | | | | | | | | | | | | | | |
| Cheewanet | | | | | | | | | | | | | | | | |
| Decewash | | | | | | | | | | | | | | | | |
| East High Stick | | | | | | | | | | | | | | | | |
| Painas | | | | | | | | | | | | | | | | |
| Biltmore | | | | | | | | | | | | | | | | |
| Askala | | | | | | | | | | | | | | | | |

**Item meaningfulness score differences**

| Site | −5 | −4 | −3 | −2 | −1 | 0 | 1 | 2 | 3 | 4 | 5 | 6 |
|---|---|---|---|---|---|---|---|---|---|---|---|---|
| Grand Valley | | | | | | | | | | | | |
| Hill | | | | | | | | | | | | |
| Cheewanet | | | | | | | | | | | | |
| Biltmore | | | | | | | | | | | | |
| Decewash | | | | | | | | | | | | |
| Saint Giacommo | | | | | | | | | | | | |
| Francis | | | | | | | | | | | | |
| Lynnbrook | | | | | | | | | | | | |
| East High Stick | | | | | | | | | | | | |
| Painas | | | | | | | | | | | | |
| Askala | | | | | | | | | | | | |

*Figure 1.4* Number and Direction of Statistically Significant Item Score Differences with Other Groups: Score on the Gumball Machine and Item Meaningfulness on The Interview Question, "How Do You See [the Content of the Item] as Part of What You Do When You are Not at School?" Subsets for Alpha = 0.05. Tukey Post-Hoc Multiple Comparisons Indicated By Brackets.

chart for Gumball Machine distinguishes one sub-set comprising two groups, Grand Valley and Hill, from the rest of the groups.

A comparison of the two pattern charts reveals similar rank orderings of the cultural groups. Overall, the cultural groups with higher item meaningfulness scores in the interview question tended to score high in the Gumball Machine item; the cultural groups with low item meaningfulness scores in that interview question tended to score low in the Gumball Machine item. The similarity of these patterns supports the notion that socio-cultural factors that take place outside the formal instruction environment are a powerful influence that shapes performance on tests. Or, put in another way, the similarity of patterns suggests that the Gumball Machine item reflects contexts that are more familiar to mainstream, white, high socio-economic status students than students from any other cultural group.

Altogether, these results underscore the major role that informal, culturally determined experience plays as a factor that shapes student performance on test items. Also, they show the value of using alternative forms of visual representation of data and quantitative and qualitative information in combination to compare multiple cultural groups.

## Summary and Conclusion

I have written this chapter with the intent to support test users (teachers, decision-makers, school districts, and state departments of education) in their reasonings about how effectively cultural validity is addressed in tests and testing practices. The chapter responds to the need for tools for objectively examining the extent to which tests and testing practices are sensitive to issues of language and culture. Four main aspects of cultural validity are discussed: theoretical foundations, population sampling, item views, and test review.

Throughout the chapter, I have shared lessons learned from National Science Foundation funded projects which have examined cultural influences in test-taking and the relationship between language variation and score variation. Findings from those projects illustrate ways in which culture can be addressed in testing practices.

As a summary, in examining tests and testing practices from the perspective of cultural validity, test users have four questions to ask:

1. To what extent are the testing practices consistent with current thinking in the culture and language sciences?
2. How accurately are culturally and linguistically diverse populations specified, and how properly are they represented throughout the entire process of test development?
3. To what extent does the process of test development take into consideration ways in which students from different cultural backgrounds interpret items?
4. To what extent are test review practices based on multiple sources of information, and how well are various forms of data analysis and data representation used in combination to examine how culture influences student performance?

Test users interested in examining the cultural validity of tests and testing programs are strongly encouraged to try to answer these questions when they examine the supporting documentation provided by test developers. Also, readers are encouraged to ask these questions as they read each of the chapters included in this book.

## Author's Note

The research reported in this chapter was funded by the National Science Foundation, Grants REC-9909729, REC-0126344, REC-0336744, and REC-0450090. My sincere thanks to Elizabeth VanderPutten, Larry Suter, and Finbarr Sloane for their support. Also, thanks to my colleagues Elise Trumbull, María del Rosario (Charo) Basterra, Min Li, and Melissa Kwon. The opinions expressed here are not necessarily those of my colleagues or the funding agency.

## Notes

1. To meet confidentiality requirements, the real names of the sites in which the investigation was conducted are not disclosed. Fictitious names are used instead.
2. Rogoff's (1995) theory of social participation establishes that activities in which individuals engage within a group take place in one of three planes of social participation—apprenticeship, guided participation, or participatory appropriation—which imply different levels of involvement in sociocultural activity. Being an actor corresponds to the level of participatory appropriation. It involves contributing to an activity and a substantial understanding of the activity.
3. In order to properly interpret the chart for the interview question, one must bear in mind that, due to practical limitations, it was not possible to interview all students on their interpretations of each of the four items shown in Figure 1.1. As a consequence, the number of students interviewed on their interpretations of Gumball Machine for each cultural group is small. To circumvent this limitation, the chart was constructed by aggregating the information on item meaningfulness, regardless of which of the four items shown in Figure 1.1 any given student was interviewed about. This form of aggregating data assumes exchangeability of the four items used as stimulus materials. That is, we assume that, for a given group, the cultural influences on the students' interpretations of items are the same for any of the four items.

## References

Abedi, J., Hofstetter, C.H., & Lord, C. (2004). Assessment accommodations for English language learners: Implications for policy-based empirical research. *Review of Educational Research*, 74(1), 1–28.

Abedi, J., Lord, C., Hofstetter, C., & Baker, E. (2001). Impact of accommodation strategies on English language learners' test performance. *Educational Measurement: Issues and Practice*, 19(3), 16–26.

AERA, NCME, & APA (1999). *Standards for Educational and Psychological Testing*. Washington, DC: Author.

Baxter, G.P., Elder, A.D., & Glaser, R. (1996). Knowledge-based cognition and performance assessment in the science classroom. *Educational Psychologist*, 31(2), 133–140.

Brennan, R.L. (1992). *Elements of generalizability theory*. Iowa City, IA: The American College Testing Program.

Brenner, M.E. (1998). Meaning and money. *Educational Studies in Mathematics*, 36, 123–155.

Cole, M. (1999). Culture-free versus culture-based measures of cognition. In R.J. Sternberg (Ed.), *The nature of cognition* (pp. 645–664). Cambridge, MA: MIT Press.

Cronbach, L.J., Gleser, G.C., Nanda, H., & Rajaratnam, N. (1972). *The dependability of behavioral measurements*. New York, NY: Wiley.

Crystal, D. (1997). *A dictionary of linguistics and phonetics* (4th edition). Cambridge, MA: Blackwell.

Ericsson, K.A., & Simon, H.S. (1993). *Protocol analysis: Verbal reports as data*. Cambridge, MA: MIT Press.

Fishman, J.A. (1965). Who speaks what language to whom and when? *La Linguistique*, 2, 67–88.

Gay, G. (2000). *Culturally responsive teaching: Theory, research, & practice*. New York, NY: Teachers College Press.

Gay, G. (2001). Preparing for culturally responsive teaching. *Journal of Teacher Education*, 53(2), 106–116.

Hambleton, R.K. (2005). Issues, designs, and technical guidelines for adapting tests into multiple languages and cultures. In R.K. Hambleton, P.F. Merenda, & C.D. Spielberger (Eds.), *Adapting educational and psychological tests for cross-cultural assessment*. Mahwah, NJ: Lawrence Erlbaum Associates, Publishers.

Hamilton, L.S., Nussbaum, E.M., & Snow, R.E. (1997). Interview procedures for validating science assessments. *Applied Measurement in Education*, 10, 181–200.

Hood, S., Hopson, R., & Frierson, H. (2005). *The role of culture and cultural context: A mandate for inclusion, the discovery of truth, and understanding in evaluative theory and practice*. Greenwich, CT: Information Age Publishing Inc.

Kirkhart, K.E. (1995). Seeking multicultural validity: A postcard from the road. *Evaluation Practice*, 16(1), 1–12.

Ladson-Billings, G. (1995). Making mathematics meaningful in multicultural contexts. In W.G. Secada, E. Fennema, & L.B. Adjian (Eds.), *New directions for equity in mathematics education* (pp. 126–145). Cambridge: Cambridge University Press.

Lee, O. (1999). Science knowledge, world views, and information sources in social and cultural contexts: Making sense after a natural disaster. *American Educational Research Journal*, 36(2), 187–219.

Li, M., Solano-Flores, G., Kwon, M., & Tsai, S.P. (2008). "*It's asking me as if I were the mother*": *Examining how students from different groups interpret test items*. Paper presented at the annual meeting of the National Association for Research in Science Teaching, Baltimore, MD, April.

Megone, M.E., Cai, J., Silver, E.A., & Wang, N. (1994). Validating the cognitive complexity and content quality of a mathematics performance assessment. *International Journal of Educational Research*, 21(3), 317–340.

Messick, S. (1995). Validity of psychological assessments: Validation of inferences from persons' responses and performances as scientific inquiry into scoring meaning. *American Psychologist*, 50, 741–749.

Miller, K.F., & Stigler, J.W. (1987). Counting in Chinese: Cultural variation in a basic cognitive skill. *Cognitive Development*, 2, 279–305.

Muzzi, A. (2001). Challenges in localization. *The ATA Chronicle*, 30(11), 28–31.

National Assessment of Educational Progress (1996). *Mathematics items public release*. Washington, DC: Author.

Nguyen-Le, K. (2010). Personal and formal backgrounds as factors which influence linguistic and cultural competency in the teaching of mathematics. Doctoral dissertation, Educational Equity and Cultural Diversity Program, University of Colorado at Boulder.

Norris, S.P. (1990). Effect of eliciting verbal reports of thinking on critical thinking test performance. *Journal of Educational Measurement*, 27(1), 41–58.

Pellegrino, J.W., Chudowsky, N., & Glaser, R. (2001). *Knowing what students know: The science and design of educational assessment*. Washington, DC: National Academy Press.

Prosser, R.R., & Solano-Flores, G. (2010). *Including English language learners in the process of test development: A study on instrument linguistic adaptation for cognitive validity*. Paper presented at the Annual Conference of the National Council of Measurement in Education, Denver, Colorado, April 29–May 3.

Rivera, C., & Collum, E. (Eds.) (2006). *State assessment policy and practice for English language learners: A national perspective*. Mahwah, NJ: Lawrence Erlbaum Associates.

Rogoff, B. (1995). Observing sociocultural activity on three planes: participatory appropriation, guided participation, and apprenticeship. In J.V. Wertsch, P. del Río, & A. Alvarez (Eds.), *Sociocultural studies of mind*. New York, NY: Cambridge University Press.

Roseberry, A., Warren, B., & Conant, F. (1992). *Appropriating scientific discourse: Findings from language minority classrooms* (Working paper 1–92). Cambridge, MA: TERC.

Ruiz-Primo, M.A., Shavelson, R.J., Li, M., & Schultz, S.E. (2001). On the validity of cognitive interpretations of scores from alternative concept-mapping techniques. *Educational Assessment, 7*(2), 99–141.

Sexton, U., & Solano-Flores, G. (2001). *A comparative study of teachers' cultural perspectives across different cultures.* Poster presented at the annual meeting of the American Educational Research Association, Seattle, WA, April 2–6.

Shavelson, R.J., & Webb, N.M. (1991). *Generalizability theory: A primer.* Newbury Park, CA: Sage.

Shavelson, R.J., & Webb, N.M. (2009). Generalizability theory and its contribution to the discussion of the generalizability of research findings. In K. Ercikan & W.M. Roth (Eds.), *Generalizing from educational research* (pp. 13–32). New York, NY: Routledge.

Solano-Flores, G. (2001). *World views and test views: the relevance of cultural validity.* Paper presented at the European Association of Research in Learning and Instruction, Fribourg, Switzerland, August 28–September 1.

Solano-Flores, G. (2006). Language, dialect, and register: Sociolinguistics and the estimation of measurement error in the testing of English-language learners. *Teachers College Record, 108*(11), 2354–2379.

Solano-Flores, G. (2008a). *Cultural validity and student performance on science assessments.* Paper presented at the Symposium, Culture and Context in Large-Scale Assessments: Obstacles or Opportunities? organized by Sharon Nelson-Barber and Larry Sutter. Annual meeting of the American Educational Research Association, New York, NY, April 24–28.

Solano-Flores, G. (2008b). Who is given tests in what language by whom, when, and where? The need for probabilistic views of language in the testing of English language learners. *Educational Researcher, 37*(4), 189–199.

Solano-Flores, G. (2009). The testing of English language learners as a stochastic process: Population misspecification, measurement error, and overgeneralization. In K. Ercikan & W.M. Roth (Eds.), *Generalizing from educational research* (pp. 33–50). New York, NY: Routledge.

Solano-Flores, G., & Gustafson, M. (in press). Assessment of English language learners: A critical, probabilistic, systemic view. In M. Simon, K. Ercikan, & M. Rousseau (Eds.), *Handbook on large-scale assessments and secondary analyses.*

Solano-Flores, G., & Li, M. (2006). The use of generalizability (G) theory in the testing of linguistic minorities. *Educational Measurement: Issues and Practice, 25*(1), 13–22.

Solano-Flores, G., & Li, M. (2008). Examining the dependability of academic achievement measures for English-Language Learners. *Assessment for Effective Intervention, 333,* 135–144.

Solano-Flores, G., & Li, M. (2009). Language variation and score variation in the testing of English language learners, native Spanish speakers. *Educational Assessment, 14,* 1–15.

Solano-Flores, G., Li, M., Speroni, C., Rodriguez, J., Basterra, M.R., & Dovholuk, G. (2007). *Comparing the properties of teacher-adapted and linguistically-simplified test items for English language learners.* Paper presented at the annual meeting of the American Educational Research Association, Chicago, IL, April 9–13.

Solano-Flores, G., & Nelson-Barber, S. (2001). On the cultural validity of science assessments. *Journal of Research in Science Teaching, 38*(5), 553–573.

Solano-Flores, G., Speroni, C., & Sexton, U. (2005). *The process of test translation: Advantages and challenges of a socio-linguistic approach.* Paper presented at the annual meeting of the American Educational Research Association, Montreal, Quebec, Canada, April 11–15.

Solano-Flores, G., & Trumbull, E. (2003). Examining language in context: The need for new research and practice paradigms in the testing of English-language learners. *Educational Researcher*, 32(2), 3–13.

Solano-Flores, G., & Trumbull, E. (2008). In what language should English language learners be tested? In R.J. Kopriva (Ed.), *Improving testing for English language learners*. New York, NY: Routledge.

Tillman, L.C. (2002). Culturally sensitive research approaches: An African-American perspective. *Educational Researcher*, 31(9), 3–12.

Wardhaugh, R. (2002). *An introduction to sociolinguistics* (fourth edition). Oxford: Blackwell Publishing.

Winter, P.C., Kopriva, R., Chen, C.S., & Emick, J. (2006). Exploring individual and item factors that affect assessment validity for diverse learners: Results from a large-scale cognitive lab. *Learning and Individual Differences*, 16, 267–276.

Wolfram, W., Adger, C.T., & Christian, D. (1999). *Dialects in schools and communities*. Mahwah, NJ: Lawrence Erlbaum Associates.

WorldLingo (2004). *Glossary of terms*. www.worldlingo.com/resources/glossary.html. Retrieved May 24, 2004.

# Chapter 2

# The Role of Language in Assessment

*Elise Trumbull and Guillermo Solano-Flores*

---

**Chapter Overview**

In this chapter, we consider the role that language plays in assessment and how teachers can work towards minimizing the likelihood that the language used in classroom assessment activities affects the proper interpretation of students' responses or the proper interpretation of test scores.

---

Language is the primary human tool for appropriating knowledge (Mantero, 2002) and for sharing what we know or think we know (Bronkart, 1995). It is the most powerful means by which human beings gain understanding of what is in each other's minds—what Bronkart calls "intercomprehension." And language is the symbol system through which humans construct new knowledge, ideas, hypotheses, plans, and poetry.

It is of critical importance that teachers understand relationships between language and assessment because their assessment practices are—quite naturally—based on their "perceptions and understanding" (Jia, Eslami, & Burlbaw, 2006, p. 425). Language is so much a part of the processes of teaching, learning, and assessment that we—as educators—rarely stop to examine its role in these processes unless we are trying to teach English language learners (ELLs) or those who have language-based learning disabilities. In those cases, we become aware of how important language is to students' academic success and the nature of the linguistic skills necessary to such success.

We see that both basic and specialized vocabulary are essential. We observe that students may not have mastered certain grammatical forms necessary for understanding typical test questions; and we recognize that spelling, reading, and writing make particular demands that may not be so daunting to the native English-speaking student but do present problems for the English language learner. We know that for these students, assessments are often more of a test of language than of academic content-learning and may tell us little about what students actually know and can do (American Educational Research Association, American Psychological Association, & National Council on Measurement in Education, 1999; Heubert & Hauser, 1999; Valdés & Figueroa, 1994).

In our discussion, we address the fact that most of the research and recommended practice related to assessment appear to be based on the premise that language in assessment is only an issue for students who are English language learners. Although language issues are of greatest concern for these students, the fact is that language plays a critical role in the validity of assessment for every single student. There is a "spectrum of language difference," that includes not only ELLs, but also students who speak a dialect of English other than the one spoken in the classroom and students who speak a language other than English at home, who may be classified as "fully English proficient."

Teachers' perceptions of language and their interpretations of their students' responses to such assessment demands—formal or informal—no doubt influence their teaching decisions. In fact, for teachers, one of the primary purposes of assessment is to make decisions about what students need in the way of further instruction (cf., Herman, Gearhart, & Aschbacher, 1996; McKay, 2006; Murphy & Camp, 1996).

## The Dependence of Assessments on Language

It is almost impossible to design a meaningful academic assessment that does not depend on language in some way. The majority of assessments, no matter what the subject area, depend upon language in both their administration and the way in which students give their responses. Directions—oral or written—are given via language. Students often have to read one or more questions per test item and may have to respond in writing. Accurate problem representation is a prerequisite for accurate problem-solving (Durán, 1985; Lager, 2006), and in order to represent a problem to themselves, students inevitably use language.

There is no way around it: Human reasoning and learning depend upon language, as do classroom instruction and assessment. Advanced language skills are associated with higher-order thinking and ability to give high-level answers to thought-provoking essay questions (Scarcella, 2003). The question is: Can we minimize unnecessary language dependence of assessments? Our view is that this can be accomplished, as long as test writers and teachers are provided with the conceptual tools and the time needed to examine and discuss at length the characteristics of items and assessment tasks (see Solano-Flores & Trumbull, 2003).

## Classroom Assessment and Large-Scale Testing

Large-scale tests are "distal" from what goes on in classrooms and in students' lives. Classroom assessment is usually more "proximal" or close to students' own experiences. It often has the following features:

1. Parallels between assessment formats and procedures and instructional formats and procedures;
2. Opportunities for clarification of directions and prompts; and
3. Better matching of the language of assessment to students' own language (vocabulary, syntax, discourse).

Reasons 2 and 3 are both related to language. With regard to parallels between assessment formats and procedures in instruction and assessment, there are numerous possibilities. For instance, teachers may use the same kinds of graphic organizers to support language comprehension (see Trumbull & Koelsch, Chapter 9, this volume); they may refer students to a classroom checklist for reviewing answers, which they cannot do when administering a standardized test. Teachers may read instructions aloud, repeat or rephrase them, or—for ELLs—translate them (or have another student translate). They may help students collectively or individually with understanding the meaning of a question in ways that standardized administration does not permit. In the case of reason 3 above, teachers are in a better position than test developers to judge the level of language students are likely to comprehend. The fact that teachers can create assessments and tests that are more proximal to students' language and experience is probably one reason that many students get better grades than their large-scale test scores would predict (cf., Ruiz-Primo, Shavelson, Hamilton, & Klein, 2002).

Another language issue affecting students has to do with the decontextualized nature of the language of assessments, especially standardized tests. In the course of face-to-face instruction, teachers and students can clarify for each other what they mean through questions, repetition, visual supports, and the like. Similar clarifications are often permitted in relation to teacher-designed or other classroom assessments. When it comes to the vast majority of standardized tests, students are left to depend upon their language knowledge alone to follow directions; read and comprehend test items; and formulate answers or solutions to problems. On paper-and-pencil assessments, students have to make sense of language out of meaningful context. In a sense, students have to supply their own extra-linguistic context. In contrast, when an assessment task is meaningful and well-contextualized, its language demands are somewhat reduced.

## Assessing the Linguistic Demands of Assessments

We will use the term "linguistic demands" to refer to the language proficiency assumed by tests that is unrelated to the knowledge or skills being assessed. Linguistic demands may be a matter of unknown vocabulary. For example, contrary to what many would think, the terms that make it difficult for students to understand science texts are not exclusively terms that refer to scientific concepts (e.g., *thermodynamics, radioactivity*). Many challenging terms are those having different meanings in everyday language versus technical language (e.g., *mass*) or those that do not refer to scientific concepts but ensure precision in scientific reasoning (e.g., *likely, allegedly, significant*) (see Wellington & Osborne, 2001).

Linguistic demands also may be a matter of sentence or text complexity that gets in the way of comprehension and performance. For instance, many mathematics test items pose reading demands that are different from the reading demands posed by any other forms of text. Among other reasons, these different reading demands derive from the fact that mathematics test items contain not only many technical terms and but also decontextualized information in short sentences (see Ferguson, 1985).

Authors of a recent large-scale research project on standardized achievement tests concluded that the higher the "language load" of an assessment, the greater the gap in performance between native English speakers and English language learners (Abedi, 2003). However, poor readers and students with lower oral proficiency than their peers also struggle with language-heavy assessments (Kiplinger, Haug, & Abedi, 2000; MacGregor & Price, 1999). In fact, as suggested earlier, the potential for any assessment to be ultimately a test of language proficiency instead of subject-matter knowledge exists for *all* students, though it is magnified when students are being assessed through the medium of a second or third language or dialect.

### Vocabulary, Syntax, and Discourse

Figure 2.1 lists three sources of linguistic demands that researchers have identified as causing problems for not only English language learners but other students as well. Since these language demands are unrelated to the knowledge and skills that are being assessed, they can be eliminated without reducing the level of difficulty of the content of the assessment item.

Often, several of these language demands co-exist and interact in one assessment item; sometimes, a single word presents both vocabulary and syntactic problems. Abedi et al. (2000/2005) give an example of this phenomenon in a sample science item they constructed to examine the potential effects of high language demands. One sentence reads, "The biologist concluded that lack of protein had reduced the immune systems of these mice to a level subject to disease" (p. 96). Here, the word "subject" is used in a sense students may or may not be familiar with. They are probably used to hearing the word "subject" mean "content area course" or, perhaps, "topic of a sentence." In this case, "subject to" means "susceptible to" or "vulnerable to."

In addition, "subject" is not used as a noun but as part of an adjectival phrase ("subject to") that modifies "level." The sentence itself is complex in that it contains an embedded sentence ("[that] lack of protein had reduced the immune systems of these mice to a level subject to disease"). Within that embedded sentence are also two prepositional phrases ("of these mice" and "to a level subject to disease")—adding to processing difficulty. One might say that this is a very "adult" sentence. But, then, many such sentences are created for young students by test developers who are neither teachers familiar with student language nor linguists, or language-development experts.

### Idiomatic Language

An idiom is any "sequence of words that is a unit of meaning." One may think of examples such as "kick the bucket" (to die), "fly the coop" (to escape), "throw in the towel" (give up), "be on cloud nine" (be elated), "throw for a loop" (confuse or surprise), "pie in the sky" (unrealistic hope), "hot-button issue" (a highly inflammatory topic), "fly-by-night scheme" (a deceptive proposition) or "get on someone's nerves" (be annoying). Most teachers would tend to avoid such

**Vocabulary**
- *False cognates*: Words that are very similar in a student's home language (L1) or dialect (D1) and the language of school (L2/D2) but are different in meaning (e.g., *actual* in English means "real," in Spanish, it means "present-day").
- *Unfamiliar words and phrases*: Vocabulary that the student has not encountered (e.g., "ream" for 500 sheets of paper) or non-literal language (see "Idiomatic Language," below).
- *Long words*: Multisyllabic words, such as "fortuitousness" and "serendipity" when "luck" would suffice.

**Syntax (Grammar)**
- Long phrases in questions (without a question word at the beginning): "Within approximately what period of months could the swimming pool be constructed by the six men?"
- Compound sentences (two clauses connected by a conjunction): Jerry completed his homework, but he was interrupted several times.
- Logical connectors: If the water is to boil, it will have to be heated to F212° because that is the boiling point of water.
- Unfamiliar tenses: Dinosaurs might have succeeded in surviving, if they had had enough time to escape the comet.
- Long noun phrases: ... the first director of the newly developed organization
- Relative clauses (usually beginning with "who/whom," "that," "which"): the young man whom Charles had met; the triangle that is below the square; the missing gun, which was now at the bottom of the river.
- Unclear or missing antecedents of pronouns: Charles and Diana talked with Queen Elizabeth and Prince Philip. They were upset by all the negative publicity. It meant that life would continue to be difficult.
- Negative terms: Which of the following is NOT a property of gases? Under what conditions is it not impossible to float a lead canoe? (This is a double negative semantically.)
- Prepositional phrases, when there are many of them or when they come between subject and predicate: Scott's shirt in the top drawer of the bureau in his bedroom; Abi's textbook on top *of the shelf* threatened to topple.

**Discourse**
- *Lengthy problem statements or multiple steps of instructions; extra language that is not needed.*
- *Passive voice instead of active voice*: e.g., [passive] Six planks were placed over the stream by the farmer; versus [active] The farmer placed six planks over the stream.
- *Poor cohesion across paragraphs*: e.g., omission of transition words such as "then," or "next," abrupt changes in style.

*Figure 2.1* Three Sources of Extraneous Language Burden (source: Based in part on Abedi, Hofstetter, Baker, & Lord (2001)).

language on an assessment except when it is part of an existing reading passage on a literacy test, or if they were using it in a context where it can be explained. However, many of us would not necessarily realize that numerous common phrases are idiomatic and need to be learned apart from the vocabulary of which they are composed.

Consider such phrases as the following: "in and of itself," "through and through," "in short," "at length," "in good time," "up and about," "in tune with," "get over it," "wind down," "stir things up," "put one over on," "on top of," and "get to the bottom of." Even a phrase such as "from time to time" (meaning "now and then") does not translate directly to other European languages. The French "de temps en temps" is about as close as one gets, but literally it means "from time in/into time." The Spanish equivalent "de vez en cuando" literally translates as "from time in/into when."

In addition, the ways words work together in different languages are somewhat arbitrary and highly conventional. For example, in English we say that we "face problems" and "interpret dreams." Speakers of modern Hebrew say they "stand in front of problems" and "solve dreams" (Crystal, 1997, p. 105). In Spanish, you "make questions" and "take decisions." In Japanese, the same verb, "nomu" (which is usually translated "to drink") is used for not only consuming liquids but also for swallowing pills and smoking (Crystal, 1997, p. 105). So, English learners need to learn the particular so-called "collocations," or pairs of words that are often used together—in these cases, "drink/milk," "swallow/pills," and "smoke/cigarettes."

Many collocations may have counterparts in other languages, but as the examples above show, one cannot make "logical" assumptions about how words collocate. Consider these English collocations: "tender/resignation," "burning/desire," "fair/hair," "fair/deal," "fair/weather," "broker/agreement," "sink/swim," "pins/needles," "amicable/divorce," "threaten/(to) rain," "incur/debt," "pose/question," "harbor/resentment," and "level/accusation." All are based not on logic but on convention. It may be difficult for teachers to imagine that collocations such as these could present considerable linguistic demands for English language learners. Students whose home dialect of English is different from that of school may also be less familiar with collocations accepted as common by teachers or test developers.

## The Intersection of Language and Culture in Assessment

"[T]he language, language variety, or dialect one speaks is culture made manifest" (Nieto, 1999, p. 60). It is impossible to examine language in any depth without consideration for the culture that has created it, nor is it possible to gain deep understanding of a culture without knowing something about its language. Cultural assumptions reflected in language can affect a student's inferences about the intent of an assessment question or task as well as familiarity with its language (see Basterra, Chapter 4, this volume). In effect, an assessment can be thought of as a "cultural script" (Emihovich, 1994).

Developers of standardized tests do attempt to deal with differences among students that arise from differences in experience. For instance, they may recognize that urban and rural life provide access to different kinds of knowledge: Urban students may not know much about farm animals or harvesting crops; rural students may not have learned about escalators and high-rises. But many culture-based assumptions are less evident. A child asked to write an essay describing herself may describe her entire family. Is it because she did not read the directions accurately, or is it because in her culture of origin it is unthinkable to talk about oneself to the exclusion of one's family?

Some items on standardized reading tests have been shown to be answerable on the basis of middle-class dominant culture experience rather than reading

You are going to make a salt-water aquarium with your class. You have $100 to spend. The chart below shows the prices for different kinds of fish and equipment. Choose the items you want, being sure to keep your total expenses to no more than $100. Show your work.

| Item | Price |
|------|-------|
| 12-gallon tank | $29 |
| Water pump and filter | $12 |
| Damselfish | $4 each |
| Clown goby fish | $5 each |
| Angel fish | $3.50 each |
| Yellow tang fish | $5.25 each |
| Blue tang fish | $4.50 each |
| Box of tropical fish food | $3.50 |

*Figure 2.2* The Aquarium Task (source: Adapted from Kane & Mitchell 1996).

comprehension (Popham, 2001). "However, the problem becomes more complex when the items involve not just knowledge of cultural objects, but also a reasoning process that requires the student to accept underlying assumptions about the meaning of the item in question" (Emihovich, 1994, p. 40). An example of this phenomenon arose in a research project with which the first author was associated. American Indian teachers from the Western region of the U.S. evaluated performance tasks for appropriateness with their students. Figure 2.2 shows an approximation of one of the fourth-grade tasks.

The teachers judged that their students would be able to handle the mathematics in the task successfully, but the context—which could be motivating and interesting to children in White, middle-class families—would be unfamiliar to them. They explained that for their students, who lived in American Indian communities in the West and Southwest, fish were for eating. The concept of keeping fish for pets would be quite alien to them, and that might make the task unappealing. So, here is an example of how the linguistic and cultural assumptions underlying an assessment item would not be applicable to a particular cultural group of students, and perhaps to others as well (e.g., children from poor backgrounds, immigrant children from certain parts of the world). What is an "aquarium?" for instance. "Are the fish for eating?" "How big is a blue tang? Will it feed four people." "Should I stick to the angel fish because they are the cheapest?"

### Culture and Sociolinguistic Knowledge

As in any social situation, there are expectations for how language is to be used, whether it is the teacher or the student who is using it. It takes not only syntactic and semantic knowledge to participate but also sociolinguistic knowledge (Emihovich, 1994; Heath, 1983; Hymes, 1972). Students need to know how to talk to each other inside and outside the classroom—what the different norms of communication are for those two settings (Rothstein-Fisch, Trumbull, Isaac, Daley, & Pérez, 2003). They need to be aware of how to take turns in a discussion, how to gain the floor when they want to ask a question, when it is acceptable to interrupt someone and when not. Depending upon their cultural backgrounds, students may be comfortable with the communicative conventions of the classroom or not. For example, children from numerous Asian backgrounds may have been socialized to listen more than talk; whereas U.S. teachers tend to expect a lot of student participation in discussions (cf., Ho, 1994; Ryu, 2004).

### Oral Questioning as a Form of Assessment

U.S. teachers commonly use orchestrated discussions to teach, but they also assess student learning by questioning students within the context of such discussions (Edwards & Davis, 1997). The Socratic method, for example, depends largely on the teacher's posing questions to students, presumably to lead them to increased understanding of a topic (or to reduction of false belief, as Socrates would have it) through deeper and deeper probing. Many educational reformers have called for Socratic teaching (e.g., Adler, 1982; Postman & Weingartner, 1969; Sizer, 1992). Yet teacher questioning is fraught with the potential for misunderstanding, particularly when there are linguistic and cultural differences between teacher and student.

Just as it is assumed that a test question directly gets at the desired content or construct, teachers often assume that their questions are clear and that students know what kinds of answers are to be forthcoming. Nevertheless, it must be remembered that younger students and those new to the language or culture are in the process of learning the tacit rules of such discourse. By age eight—and beginning much earlier—most children are able to make inferences about the intentions of another speaker (Nelson, 2007); however, cultural knowledge of the context must be available to the student for accurate inferences to be made about such things as the intent of a teacher's question. So-called "known-answer questions," such as "Hayden, what color is this truck?" are notoriously unproductive for some young students. They are not accustomed to being asked something to which the questioner knows the answer and may not realize an answer is genuinely expected (Heath, 1983).

Students may miss important cues in the questions of teachers as to the type of answers they are expecting (Edwards & Davis, 1997), as illustrated by the vignette below (Figure 2.3; see Oswald & Oswald, 2002).

The teacher's goal with a question such as, "How are a banana and a pear alike and different?" is most likely to draw attention to "scientific" facts about fruits. She hopes to elicit the kind of language that is informative, or "essay-like" in its construction (Gee, 1990; Trumbull, Diaz-Meza, & Hasan, in press). It is likely that she has used this form of question before and perhaps even used the term "compare and contrast." She may be thinking that the form of the question gives

The first-grade class is beginning a science unit on fruits and vegetables. The teacher begins a lesson as follows.

Question: *How are a banana and a pear alike and different?*
Teacher's Mental List of Expected Answers
- Both are fruits.
- Both have seeds inside.
- Both grow on trees.
- They are different shapes. Pears are oval or "pear-shaped." Bananas are long and slender, and crescent-shaped.
- Sometimes bananas and pears are the same color. Pears can be yellow like bananas and green like unripe bananas.
- Pears are juicier than bananas.
- Bananas grow in warmer climates than pears.
- The seeds of the banana are tiny and can be swallowed without noticing; the seeds of a pear are bigger, and you wouldn't want to swallow them.
- You can eat the peel of a pear, but you can't eat the peel of a banana.

Children's Answers

Some of the same answers as those on the teacher's mental list, particularly if the class has been studying different kinds of fruits, but also:
- My mom gives me both bananas and pears for lunch sometimes.
- I like bananas. They taste better than pears. My brother doesn't like pears either, but he likes bananas … and so does my sister. My dad likes apples … (and more description of family likes and dislikes).
- I go shopping with my mother, and she lets me pick out bananas, but she says pears cost too much.
- I eat bananas on my cereal, but I don't eat pears on my cereal.
- My mama gave me a big old pear yesterday, but I didn't eat it because it was too hard. I ate a banana today, though, because it was soft and ripe.
- You can make banana bread, but you can't make pear bread. Can you?

*Figure 2.3* Comparing Bananas and Pears.

students cues about the expected form of response—factual and to-the-point. But now, she is hearing answers that are not on-target. Do the children have the knowledge she is trying to elicit? Does she know some children have probably learned to use language in their homes in ways that embed the "factual" within personal, social narratives (cf., Greenfield & Cocking, 1994).

## *Common Pitfalls: Misunderstanding and Misjudgment*

Researchers working in an Appalachian town with a mixed population of relatively poor White, African-American, and Southeast Asian families noted the following: "Teachers did not know what to do when students remained silent, gave an answer that appeared to be unrelated to the question, or told rather long personal stories when they anticipated focused information in a short response" (Edwards & Davis, 1997, p. 475). As Edwards and Davis note, "Teachers can misconstrue the content of an answer, based on their expectations about the purpose of the question, which can contribute to confusion about how well-formed or how appropriate the answer might be" (p. 493).

Effective questioning and discussion in culturally mixed classrooms depends upon considerable teacher knowledge and skill. Interpreting students' responses requires an equal degree of cultural understanding about various discourse styles and norms. Teachers who are expecting particular school-like discourse patterns may make negative judgments about responses that deviate from their expectations. A common pitfall is equating a student's proficiency with school-like language with his or her overall cognitive ability (Edwards & Davis, 1997; Minami & Ovando, 1995).

## Dialect and Register

Analyses of language issues in assessment or testing tend to focus on students' degree of proficiency with English. A student's overall proficiency with English is of importance, certainly. One who has "intermediate" proficiency cannot be expected to perform as well on an assessment as one with "advanced" proficiency, all other things being equal. However, to understand the relationship between language and assessment one must take into consideration two other levels of language: *dialect* and *register* (Solano-Flores, 2006).

### Dialect

Within any broad classification of English language learners—as first-language speakers of Spanish, Hmong, or Chinese—there are sub-groups of learners who speak various dialects of those languages. "Dialect" is usually defined as a variant of a language that can be understood by other speakers of the same language, despite some differences in vocabulary, syntax, pronunciation, and discourse norms related to how language is used. All dialects are rule-governed systems that appropriately serve the needs of their speakers; and no single dialect of a language is superior to another in any linguistic sense, though some have greater social status than others (Wolfram, Adger, & Christian, 1999). Languages spoken by large numbers of people, such as English and Spanish, have many mutually intelligible variants.

Speakers of the several dialects of British English can readily communicate with speakers of the several dialects of United States English—and of Australia, Canada, and other English-dominant nations. Likewise, the Spanish dialects spoken in Mexico, Central America, South America, Spain, and elsewhere are all mutually intelligible forms of Spanish. These different versions of Spanish have been enriched by the inclusion of words from other languages, particularly the Indian languages of Latin America such as Quechua (Peru), Nahuatl (Mexico), and the Mayan languages (Mexico, Belize, and Guatemala), among many others. A plausible argument—supported by some research with English language learners—can be made for taking dialect into consideration when evaluating the appropriateness of a given assessment or test item for any particular student: The linguistic demands of assessments are magnified when a student's home dialect is different from the dialect represented in the assessment (Solano-Flores & Li, 2006). Young students are still developing linguistically and cannot be assumed to have developed familiarity with more than one dialect or to have the kind of ability to make inferences about dialect differences that an adult speaker might be able to make.

This observation applies both to English speakers of dialects not privileged in the classroom and speakers of other languages for whom native-language tests have been constructed in a dialect different from the one they speak at home (cf., Wolfram et al., 1999). It is not only the comprehension of a teacher's question that is of concern: Teachers' interpretations or judgments of the correctness of students' spoken or written responses produced in a non-school dialect are also at risk of being wrong (Beaumont, de Valenzuela, & Trumbull, 2002; Wolfram et al., 1999).

### Register

Just as languages have numerous dialects, they also have numerous registers. A "register" is a variety of language that serves a particular purpose. Common examples are the legal register, the medical register, and the mathematics register. Whereas dialect is associated with a group of speakers, usually on the basis of geographic or social group, register is associated with the context of use. On a formal assessment or test, a student is faced with what has been called "the test register."

The test register is characterized by "dense text and scant contextual information" (Solano-Flores, 2006, p. 2364), as well as overly complex syntax and vocabulary that needs to be understood quite precisely if the student is to understand instructions and respond correctly. Typical of the test register are phrases like "Which of the following …?" "In the figure below, what does 'X' refer to?" "Use the information above to determine …," "Compare and contrast …" Test register discourse may take the form of "if–then" statements such as the following: "There are some rabbits and some hutches. If one rabbit is put in each hutch, then one rabbit will be left without a hutch. If two rabbits are put in each hutch …" (National Council of Teachers of Mathematics, n.d.).

All of these forms of test language are associated with particular sets of meanings. The student completing a test needs to be proficient with the test register as well as the content knowledge being assessed—and the particular register of the discipline in question. The mathematics register (see below, pp. 35–36) is quite different from the social studies register. In the assessment situation, the student needs to be able to navigate these intersecting and mutually influencing registers.

The test register is a particular form of academic language. Academic language is the language "required for success in public schooling and career advancement," in all modes—reading, writing, speaking, and listening (Scarcella, 2003). Theorists disagree as to whether academic language should be explicitly defined, or whether it should be more broadly characterized to include the multiple ways people use language that are different from the language currently accepted in schools as appropriate (Scarcella, 2003). Nevertheless, the current reality is that to succeed academically and professionally, people need proficiency with the "power codes" (Delpit, 1995), or the forms and uses of language that are privileged in classrooms and boardrooms. Most educators concerned with improving English language learners' schooling outcomes advocate explicit instruction in academic language (e.g., Chen & Mora-Flores, 2006; Feldman & Kinsella, 2008). Bailey, Butler, Stevens, & Lord (2007) have developed a framework for understanding and applying the concept of academic language to instruction and assessment.

## Language in Mathematics Assessment

Many people believe that mathematics is the one academic subject area exempt from language demands (see Trumbull & Solano-Flores, Chapter 10, this volume). This may be largely the case in a straightforward computational problem such as the one in Figure 2.4. On the surface, solving this problem does not require language.[1] Certainly, it does not require English. The student may use mental language to solve it ("Five and eight are 13, carry the one …"). Nevertheless, the language demands are minimal. And, in fact, research shows that English language learners tend to do as well as their native English-speaking peers on such mathematics problems (Kiplinger et al., 2000). They may be using their native language at times to engage in the mental problem-solving necessary.

### Language and Mathematical Reasoning

Mathematical reasoning is dependent on language (Kauffman, 2001; Oller, 1991). In current notions of mathematical competence this fact is highlighted, and language is accorded a prominent role. The "communications" standard of the National Council of Teachers of Mathematics (2000) states that students will:

- Organize and consolidate their mathematical thinking through communication;
- Communicate their mathematical thinking coherently and clearly to peers, teachers, and others; and
- Use the language of mathematics to express mathematical ideas precisely.

Once the student moves beyond computation, language is involved in reading and comprehending directions and formulating the solution to problems. Consider the test item in Figure 2.5. Some students may be able to solve the problem just by looking at the array of figures. However, if a student needs to read the directions, he or she is faced with a relatively complex English sentence that requires knowledge of vocabulary related to spatial position (above, below),

$5.65
+7.58
———

*Figure 2.4* Addition Problem.

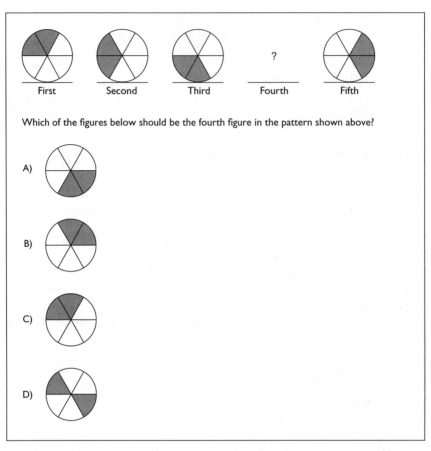

*Figure 2.5* Pattern Recognition (source: NAEP Mathematics Practice Test 3—Grade 8, Manipulatives (N.D.), p. 4, http://wvde.state.wv.us/oaa/pdf/naeptestlests/Math_Gr8_Test3.pdf).

ordinal numbers (fourth), and the terms "figure" and "pattern." The syntax itself involves a complex noun phrase, "which of the figures below ..." This phrase can be analyzed as the interrogative determiner "which" modified by a prepositional phrase serving as an adjective ("of the figures below"). This is followed by a complex verb tense (should be) followed by another complex noun phrase ("the fourth figure in the pattern") modified by a reduced relative clause ("shown above" = [the pattern that] is shown above).

The test item in Figure 2.6 is an efficient way to find out what a student knows about prime numbers—at least from the test developer's point of view. But the way it is written introduces the possibility of student error on the basis of language and not mathematical knowledge. In the case of the item in Figure 2.6, the student has only the linguistic context in which to make sense of the mathematical construct in question (prime numbers). The item introduces linguistic complexity by phrasing the stem in the negative. Negative phrasing like this is known

---

Which of the following is NOT true about prime numbers? [Item stem]

   A.  They have exactly two factors. [answer]

   B.  One is a factor of every prime number. [distractor]

   C.  No prime numbers end in zero. [distractor]

   D.  All prime numbers are odd numbers. [distractor]

---

*Figure 2.6* Prime Numbers (source: NAEP, N.D. http://nces.ed.gov/nationsreportcard/itmrls/itemdisplay.asp).

to add comprehension demands, and some theorists recommend that it never be used (e.g., Haladyna, Downing, & Rodriguez, 2002). Haladyna's belief is that "negative stems put more pressure on short term memory and involve more cognitive strain which exacerbates test anxiety" (pers. comm., March 14, 2007). It is possible—even likely—that such constructions are yet more difficult for English language learners. So, even though the item is short, it presents language demands that could penalize some students who might get a lower score because of the language and not because of their mathematical knowledge.

The test item in Figure 2.7 magnifies the problem associated with negative stems by using three semantically negative terms (*fail, without, except*). In this sample item released by the U.S. Foreign Service, it almost seems as though test developers are explicitly trying to use tricky language to trip up test-takers.

---

All of the following are examples of United States products that would typically fail to be produced to optimal output without government intervention EXCEPT:

   A.  National defense products (distractor)
   B.  Light provided by lighthouses (answer)
   C.  New automobiles (distractor)
   D.  New highways (distractor)

---

*Figure 2.7* Foreign Service Test Question (source: Lewin, 2006).

### The Mathematics Register

The Illinois State Department of Education website (www.isbe.net) lists approximately 200 words as necessary for a full understanding of grade three mathematics. (The website cautions that this list is not exhaustive.) Many of these terms have meanings in the non-mathematical lexicon: e.g., angle, even, operation, mass, segment, variable, unit, steps, cup, face, area. All students must learn the mathematical meanings of these content words in addition to the precise ways that relational words such as "by," "per," "if ... then," "from," and others are used to express mathematical relations.

Approximate meaning clarified by context is not adequate in mathematics, as it often is in the natural speech of conversations or discussions. The same is true to some degree in any discipline, but in many ways the language of mathematics presents a unique challenge to the learner. Speaking of ELLs, Kessler, Quinn, and Hayes (1985) note:

> [P]rocessing mathematics successfully rests on the ability to utilize very precise language of mathematics in doing mathematical reasoning. The context reduced language of mathematics, the extensive use of logical connectors [and/but/or], the specialized vocabulary and syntactical structures, and appropriate discourse rules, all present a complex set of problems for LEP children engaged in mathematics discourse.
>
> (p. 152)

## Toward Enlightened Assessment Practices: What Can Be Done?

Teachers often intuitively know what kinds of assessment practices are most appropriate and effective for their students, but internal pressures (e.g., time limitations) and external pressures (district policies) may prevent them from acting according to their best professional judgment. A recent study (Jia et al., 2006) of 13 elementary and middle school ESL (English as a second language) language arts teachers revealed that teachers used the following kinds of assessments:

- Teacher-constructed quizzes and short tests;
- Essay assignments;
- Classroom performance in discussion and oral reading;
- Publishers' tests associated with curriculum materials, state-mandated tests; and
- Computer-based reading tests.

Teachers in the study valued their classroom-based assessments—which they designed, administered, graded, and interpreted—above those designed externally because they were linked to the curriculum and were less threatening than the outside tests. They believed they got a truer picture of student progress from these kinds of assessments, as well as useful information about what might need to be re-taught and how to alter their programs. However, the authors of the study note:

> Although the ESL teachers in the study did not feel formal paper and pencil tests were appropriate or helpful measurements of their students' learning, such tests were used in their classrooms because almost all districts or schools participating in this study require teachers to use them.
>
> (Jia et al., 2006, p. 417)

Our belief is that education systems at all levels need to support teachers in ways that allow them to use the assessment strategies they know are most appropriate and to continue to develop their understanding of what makes for culturally valid assessment practices. Culturally-valid assessment should result in more accurate information on student learning and—if that information is used well—instruction tailored to students' needs. It should also help students themselves feel that assessment is both fair and useful to them in helping them set learning goals.

### Provide Opportunities for Teachers to Learn about Language

Every teacher needs to be able to answer such questions as: "What does this assessment expect students to be able to do with language?" "What language proficiencies does the student need in order to proceed with this assessment task?" "How could I modify the language of this assessment question to make it more comprehensible to my students?"

To a large extent, teachers' capacity to answer these kinds of questions depends on their knowledge of language and how it is involved in the assessment process. Some educators have called for teachers to have "diagnostic competence" regarding language, meaning that they need to be able to analyze the language of their students on many levels in order to make judgments about students' language proficiency (Edelenbos & Kubanek-German, 2004). It is this kind of competence that is required for making informed judgments about the language forms and uses that should be reflected in assessments. (See Trumbull & Solano-Flores, Chapter 10, this volume, for further discussion of this topic.)

The same kind of competence is also necessary if teachers are going to try to foster students' continued language growth. Evaluating a student's language proficiency can be done as part of normal classroom activity. Case and Obenchain (2006) recommend doing so during social studies instruction, for instance: "The benefit of assessing students' language ability as a regular part of social studies instruction and of understanding the relationships among scaffolding, assessment, and language instruction is clear" (p. 47).

We cannot emphasize enough that "providing teachers with opportunities to learn about language" should not be interpreted as simply providing them workshops and seminars on language. There is evidence that even if teachers report an increase in their knowledge, their practices concerning linguistically and culturally diverse students do not necessarily change (Lee, Hart, Cuevas, & Enders, 2004). Establishing instructional congruence with principles learned from professional development experience is indeed "a gradual and demanding process requiring teacher reflection and insight, formal training, and extensive support and sharing" (Lee, 2004, p. 65). Integrating practice with reasoning about language is critical for significant improvements in assessment practices to occur. Ideally, teachers will have the chance to talk with each other about what they are learning and its implications for practice.

In ELL testing, we (Solano-Flores, Trumbull, & Nelson-Barber, 2002) have observed, for example, that even teachers who are bilingual, and have deep roots in the communities of their students and a good number of years teaching in bilingual programs are not able to address issues of language in tests beyond a superficial level of analysis (e.g., spelling, literal translation of words, simplistic assumptions about the characteristics of the students), unless they engage in detailed discussions about the linguistic properties of items. If teachers are provided with the opportunity to discuss at length the potential linguistic demands of test items for their own students, they are often able to bring deep knowledge about students' languages and cultures to the surface. As they participate in the process of test development and adaptation, teachers may recognize the importance of specific home and school contexts that relate to students' native and second language knowledge and use. It is this kind of opportunity to talk with outside professionals and other teachers in a setting that allows for reflection on one's own professional knowledge and experience that (a) helps teachers tap knowledge they already have and (b) build on it in meaningful ways.

In a similar venue, working with teachers of culturally diverse students not considered ELLs, we have observed that—while necessary—ethnic and linguistic diversity among the teachers involved in the development or review of tests does not suffice to ensure that the linguistic demands of tests are properly addressed. Teachers of ethnic/cultural minority students who have the same ethnic–cultural backgrounds tend to be more aware of cultural and linguistic issues in testing than mainstream teachers (those with European-American backgrounds). However, both kinds of teachers tend to address only superficial features of test items when they are asked to think of ways to reduce cultural bias (Sexton & Solano-Flores, 2002).

In addition, we (Solano-Flores & Gustafson, in press) have evidence that indicates that, when asked to identify sources of potential cultural bias that a specific item might pose to their own students, teachers do not necessarily anticipate the difficulties their students actually have when they interpret the items. For example, in some cases teachers may regard as challenging for their students a word that those students have no problem reading aloud or understanding. At the same time, teachers may fail to recognize excessively complex syntactical sentence structures that do cause problems for students.

It is clear that current notions of what is sufficient to properly address language in assessment need to be revised. Providing teachers with both formal training on issues of language and opportunities to participate in test development and review projects appear to be promising strategies for promoting improved assessment practices concerning language.

### Allow Teachers to Apply Their Knowledge

One issue that teachers can address far better than professional test developers is ensuring that assessments reflect the dialect used by their own students and classroom texts. An experienced bilingual educator made the following observation:

> In my own teaching experience with LAUSD [Los Angeles Unified School District], I participated in the first year of the administration of the APRENDA

standardized test for Spanish-speakers. The other first grade teachers and I discovered that the math vocabulary used on the test was very different from the vocabulary that our math series used and from that used by the children and their families. Children were confused by the test directions, and—consequently—the test results did not accurately represent what students knew about math. The differences in the dialects skewed the outcomes unfavorably.

(Sadler, 2007)

Several assessment development projects with which we have been involved have demonstrated how teachers' insights and specific knowledge related to the dialect of the school, students' home languages, and students' home dialects can be used to improve assessments. Development projects that bring teachers and researchers together provide excellent two-way learning experiences: Researchers gain important knowledge of the students and school context, and teachers learn more about how language and assessment intersect.

## Support the Use of Promising Forms of Assessment

Two of the forms of assessment that have been recommended for English language learners are learning journals (where students reflect on their learning) and portfolios (Hurley & Tinajero, 2001). Portfolios have been highlighted by educators for their adaptability to a wide range of cultural contexts and ability to involve students in evaluating their own learning (e.g., Klassen, 2006; Koelsch & Trumbull, 1996). Recent literature across several disciplines has referred to "assessment dialogues," during which teacher and student confer about a student's progress (Bond, Tierney, Bertelson, & Bresler, 1999; Carless, 2006). Sometimes journals and dialogues are combined (dialogue journals) (Fern, Anstrom, & Silcox, 1994), with teachers and students communicating in writing through student journals. All of these forms of assessment are also appropriate vehicles for improved communication between teacher and student in classrooms with students who speak various dialects of English.

A classroom assessment can include elements that scaffold student participation, much as they scaffold learning during instruction (Trumbull & Koelsch, Chapter 9, this volume). Graphic organizers such as "concept maps, advance organizers, outlines, semantic webs and others" are commonly used by teachers of ELLs "to illustrate structure and connections between concepts and vocabulary terms" (Hurley & Tinajero, 2001, p. 94).

Whereas alternative forms of assessment (such as portfolios and dialog journals) hold promise as part of a general strategy for addressing language, we have to note that not much research has been done on their use with linguistically and culturally diverse populations. Decision-makers see the potential of these forms of assessment in the testing of ELLs. However, many assessment systems do not have the expertise needed to develop, administer, and score such assessments properly for accountability purposes (General Accounting Office, 2006).

It is also important to note that no form of assessment is language-free. Indeed, in the same way that every form of assessment is sensitive to a different form of knowledge (Shavelson, Baxter, & Gao, 1993), every form of assessment and every item pose a unique set of linguistic demands (see Solano-Flores & Li, 2006). Rather than looking for the form of assessment that is language free, educators and developers of assessment systems should try to use multiple forms of assessment in combination. Together they stand to capture student learning more accurately than any single measure can.

### Implement Inclusive Assessment Development Practices

"Inclusion," in the context of testing and accountability, is frequently used to refer to evaluating the performance of schools based on the standardized test scores of virtually all students, even if those schools have high enrollments of students who are not proficient in English. The term is used also in the context of testing accommodations intended to reduce limited proficiency in English as a source of invalidity of test scores.

Whereas we do not contest these uses of the term, we believe that no genuine inclusion of ELLs can be accomplished if their participation is limited to the final stages of the process of testing (see Solano-Flores & Nelson-Barber, 2001). Take as an example a teacher who is not bilingual and who has several ELL students in her class. The teacher develops an assessment using a process in which the wording of items is refined based on trying it out with some of her students. This teacher may not see the value of including ELLs in these try-outs. Since they are limited in their proficiency in English, she may think that not much information can be obtained from interviewing them about their interpretations of the items or from examining their responses to the item. She may think that any form of accommodation intended to address the special needs of those students should be provided once the final form of the assessment is ready.

That approach would be exclusive of ELLs and ineffective. Trying out the assessment exclusively with mainstream students leads to producing an assessment that addresses only the linguistic needs and characteristics of mainstream students. No opportunity is left for the teacher to detect and address false cognates, idiomatic expressions, cultural influences, and issues of discursive style, among many other things, that could pose a challenge for her ELL students, and that should be worked out in a timely fashion. Limitations of the assessment derived from unclear or unfamiliar language usage will be carried over to further stages in the process of testing and may not be resolved with testing accommodations or other (late) attempts to address language.

As we can see, in order to effectively address language issues in assessment, we need to transform our views and practices, rather than simply learn a few new concepts or skills.

## Conclusion

We have discussed the role of language in assessment and the knowledge and skills that teachers need in order to properly address language in their assessment activities. Although most educators are aware of the fact that assessment depends on language to a large extent, not many are aware of the subtle ways in which this dependence operates. Wording, discourse style, the use of idiomatic expressions, and the structural complexity of sentences are among the many aspects of language that may increase the "linguistic demands" of assessment tasks and test items. These linguistic demands shape the ways in which students understand and interpret assessments and the ways in which they respond to them. They are relevant to the teaching and assessment of every student, but they are of special concern for students whose English home dialects are not the same as the English dialect used in the classroom and for students who are still developing English as a second language.

The first step toward more valid and equitable assessment and testing practices is for educators and test developers to recognize how irrelevant language demands may wrongly affect the scores obtained by students on tests or their responses to questions in classroom assessment activities. Teachers who have worked with English language learners are well aware of this fact. A second important step is to ensure that new knowledge about language is incorporated into teachers' and test developers' practices. Meaningful knowledge about issues of language and assessment is constructed only when teachers are allowed to participate in assessment development and assessment review endeavors that are related to the context of their practice.

We believe that schools of education and district professional development programs must take a stronger role in educating teachers about language—preparing them to be more comfortable examining language at the level of vocabulary, grammar, and discourse; analytical about its role in teaching, learning, and assessment; and more knowledgeable about the implications of language differences based on home language, culture, and dialect (cf., Wong Fillmore & Snow, 2000). In addition, teachers need to be supported explicitly to develop the knowledge necessary to identify and—when possible—reduce the linguistic demands of existing assessments.

Classroom teachers are in a special position with regard to being able to assess students' academic language proficiency and design or modify tests in order to tailor the linguistic demands of tests to their students' developmental levels and particular language experiences. If they are to do so, they must have knowledge of how language develops and what constitutes language proficiency, along with the skills needed to evaluate language complexity.

## Note

1. In Latin America, students are used to a slightly different format for addition. This problem would be written as: \$5.65+7.58.

## References

Abedi, J. (2003). *Impact of students' language background on content-based performance: Analyses of extant data* (CSE Report 603). Los Angeles: University of California, Center for the Study of Evaluation/National Center for Research on Evaluation, Standards, and Student Testing.

Abedi, J., Bailey, A., Butler, F., Castellon-Wellington, M., Leon, S., & Mirocha, J. (2000/2005). *The validity of administering large-scale assessments to English language learners: An investigation from three perspectives* (CSE Technical Rep. 663). Los Angeles, CA: National Center for Research on Evaluation, Standards, and Student Testing. Graduate School of Education and Information Studies, University of California.

Abedi, J., Courtney, M., Mirocha, J., & Leon, S. (2005). *Language accommodations for English language learners in large-scale assessments: Bilingual dictionaries and linguistic modification* (CSE Report 666). Los Angeles: University of California, Center for the Study of Evaluation/National Center for Research on Evaluation, Standards, and Student Testing. Graduate School of Education and Information Studies (GSEIS), University of California.

Abedi, J., Hofstetter, C., Baker, E., & Lord, C. (2001). *NAEP math performance and test accommodations: Interactions with student language background.* CSE Technical Report 536. Los Angeles: University of California, Center for the Study of Evaluation/National Center for Research on Evaluation, Standards, and Student Testing. Graduate School of Education and Information Studies (GSEIS), University of California.

Adler, M. (1982). *The paideia proposal.* New York, NY: Macmillan.

American Educational Research Association, American Psychological Association, and National Council on Measurement in Education (1999). *Standards for Educational and Psychological Testing.* Washington, DC: American Educational Research Association.

Bailey, A.L., Butler, F.A., Stevens, R., & Lord, C. (2007). Further specifying the language demands of school. In A.L. Bailey (Ed.), *The language of school: Putting academic English to the test* (pp. 102–156). New Haven, CT: Yale University Press.

Beaumont, C., de Valenzuela, J., & Trumbull, E. (2002). Alternative assessment for transitional readers. *Bilingual Research Journal,* 26(2), 241–268.

Bond, E., Tierney, R.J., Bertelsen, C., & Bresler, J. (1999). *Beneath the veneer of learner-centered assessments: A confluence of agendas and power relationships.* Presentation at the Annual Meeting of the American Educational Research Association, Montreal, April 20.

Bronkart, J.-P. (1995). Theories of action, speech, natural language, and discourse. In J.V. Wertsch, P. del Rio, & A. Alvarez (Eds.), *Sociocultural studies of mind* (pp. 75–91). Cambridge: Cambridge University Press.

Carless, D. (2006). Differing perceptions in the feedback process. *Studies in Higher Education,* 31(2), 219–233.

Case, R., & Obenchain, K.M. (2006). How to assess language in the social studies classroom. *The Social Studies,* 97(1), 41–48.

Chen, L., & Mora-Flores, E. (2006). *Balanced literacy for English language learners, K-2.* Portsmouth, NH: Heinemann.

Crystal, D. (1997). *Cambridge encyclopedia of language* (second edition). Cambridge: Cambridge University Press.

Delpit, L.D. (1995). *Other people's children: Cultural conflict in the classroom.* New York, NY: New Press.

Durán, R.P. (1985). Influences of language skills on bilinguals' problem solving. In S.F. Chipman, J.W. Segal, & R. Glaser (Eds.), *Thinking and learning skills* (pp. 187–207). Hillsdale, NJ: Lawrence Erlbaum Associates.

Edelenbos, P., & Kubanek-German, A. (2004). Teacher assessment: The concept of "diagnostic competence." *Language Testing,* 21(3), 259–283.

Edwards, B., & Davis, B. (1997). Learning from classroom questions and answers: Teachers' uncertainties about children's language. *Journal of Literacy Research,* 29(4), 471–505.

Emihovich, C. (1994). The language of testing: An ethnographic-sociolinguistic perspective on standardized tests. In K. Holland, D. Bloome, & J. Solsken (Eds.), *Alternative perspectives in assessing children's language and literacy* (pp. 33–52). Norwood, NJ: Ablex.

Feldman, K., & Kinsella, K. (2008). Narrowing the language gap: The case for explicit vocabulary instruction in secondary classrooms. In L. Denti & G. Guerin (Eds.), *Effective practices for adolescents with reading and literacy challenges*. New York, NY: Routledge.

Ferguson, A.M. (1985). Language experience for problem solving in mathematics. *Reading Teacher*, 38, 504–507.

Fern, V., Anstrom, K., & Silcox, B. (1994). Active learning and the limited English proficient student. *Directions in Language and Education*, 1(2). Washington, DC: National Clearinghouse on Bilingual Education. Retrieved from www.ncela.gwu.edu/pubs/directions/02.htm.

Gee, J. (1990). *Social linguistics and literacies, ideology in discourses*. London: Falmer.

General Accounting Office (2006). *No Child Left Behind Act: Assistance from Education could help states better measure progress of students with limited English proficiency*. GAO Report to Congressional Requesters, July, GAO-06-815.

Greenfield, P.M., & Cocking, R.R. (Eds.) (1994). *Cross-cultural roots of minority child development*. Hillsdale, NJ: Erlbaum.

Haladyna, T.M., Downing, S.M., & Rodriguez, M.C. (2002). A review of multiple-choice item-writing guidelines for classroom assessment. *Applied Measurement in Education*, 15(3), 309–334.

Heath, S.B. (1983). *Ways with words: Language, life and work in communities and classrooms*. Cambridge: Cambridge University Press.

Herman, J.L., Gearhart, M., & Aschbacher, P.R. (1996). Portfolios for classroom assessment: Design and implementation issues. In R. Calfee & P. Perfumo (Eds.), *Writing portfolios in the classroom: Policy, practice, promise and peril* (pp. 27–59). Mahwah, NJ: Erlbaum.

Heubert, J.P., & Hauser, R.M. (Eds.) (1999). *High stakes testing for tracking, promotion, and graduation*. Committee on Appropriate Test Use, Board on Testing and Assessment, Commission on Behavioral and Social Sciences and Education, National Research Council. Washington, DC: National Academy Press.

Ho, D.Y.F. (1994). Cognitive socialization in Confucian heritage cultures. In P.M. Greenfield & R.R. Cocking (Eds.), *Cross-cultural routes of minority child development* (pp. 285–313). Mahwah, NJ: Erlbaum.

Hurley, S.R., & Tinajero, J.V. (2001). *Literacy assessment of second language learners*. Needham Heights, MA: Allyn & Bacon.

Hymes, D. (1972). On communicative competence. In J.B. Pride & J. Holmes (Eds.), *Sociolinguistics* (pp. 269–293). Harmondsworth: Penguin Books.

Jia, Y., Eslami, Z.R., & Burlbaw, L.M. (2006). ESL teachers' perceptions and factors influencing their use of classroom-based reading assessment. *Bilingual Research Journal*, 30(2), 407–430.

Kane, M. B., & Mitchell, R. (1996). *Implementing performance assessment: Promises, problems, and challenges*. Mahwah, NJ: Erlbaum.

Kauffman, L.H. (2001). The mathematics of Charles Sanders Peirce. *Cybernetics & Human Knowing*, 8(1–2), 79–110.

Kessler, C., Quinn, M., & Hayes, C. (1985). Processing mathematics in a second language: Problems for LEP children. In A. Labarca and L. Bailey (Eds.), *Issues in L2: Theory as practice, practice as theory* (pp. 151–163). Delaware Symposium on Language Studies.

Kiplinger, V.L., Haug, C.A., & Abedi, J. (2000). *Measuring math—not reading—on a math assessment: A language accommodations study of English language learners and other special populations.* Paper presented at the Annual Meeting of the American Educational Research Association, New Orleans, April.

Klassen, S. (2006). Contextual assessment in science education: Background, issues, and policy. *Science Education*, 90(5), 820–851.

Koelsch, N., & Trumbull, E. (1996). Cross-cultural portfolios. In R.G. Calfee & P. Perfumo (Eds.), *Writing portfolios in the classroom* (pp. 261–284). Mahwah, NJ: Lawrence Erlbaum Associates.

Lager, C.A. (2006). Types of mathematics-language reading interactions that unnecessarily hinder algebra learning and assessment. *Reading Psychology*, 27(2–3), 165–204.

Lee, O. (2004). Teacher change in beliefs and practices in science and literacy instruction with English language learners. *Journal of Research in Science Teaching*, 41(1), 65–93.

Lee, O., Hart, J.E., Cuevas, P., & Enders, C. (2004). Professional development in inquiry-based science for elementary teachers of diverse student groups. *Journal of Research in Science Teaching*, 41(10), 1021–1043.

Lewin, T. (December 17, 2006). Rarely win at trivial pursuit? An embassy door opens. *New York Times*, Section 4, p. 4.

MacGregor, M., & Price, E. (1999). An exploration of aspects of language proficiency and algebra learning. *Journal for Research in Mathematics Education*, 30(4), 449–467.

McKay, P. (2006). *Assessing young language learners.* Cambridge: Cambridge University Press.

Mantero, M. (2002). Evaluating classroom communication: In support of emergent and authentic frameworks in second language assessment. *Practical Assessment, Research & Evaluation*, 8(8). Retrieved from http://PAREonline.net/getvn.asp?v=8&n=8.

Minami, M., & Ovando, C.J. (1995). Language issues in multicultural contexts. In J.A. Banks, & C.A.M. Banks (Eds.), *Handbook of research on multicultural education* (pp. 427–444). New York, NY: Macmillan.

Murphy, S., & Camp, R. (1996). Moving toward systemic coherence: A discussion of conflicting perspectives on portfolio assessment. In R. Calfee & P. Perfumo (Eds.), *Writing portfolios in the classroom: Policy, practice, promise and peril* (pp. 103–148). Mahwah, NJ: Erlbaum.

National Assessment of Educational Progress (n.d.) NAEP mathematics practice test 3—Grade 8, Manipulatives. Retrieved from http://wvde.state.wv.us/oaa/pdf/naeptestlests/Math_Gr8_Test3.pdf.

National Council of Teachers of Mathematics (2000). *Principles and standards for school mathematics.* Retrieved from http://standards.nctm.org/document/chapter3/comm.htm.

Nelson, K. (2007). *Young minds in social worlds.* Cambridge, MA: Harvard University Press.

Nieto, S. (1999). *The light in their eyes: Creating multicultural learning communities.* New York, NY: Teachers College.

Oller, J.W., Jr. (1991). *Language and bilingualism: More tests of tests* (with S. Chesarek & R. Scott). Lewisburg, PA: Bucknell University Press.

Oswald, J., & Oswald, D. (2002). Fruits galore. *Plant Based Nutrition: A Newsletter for all People Everywhere*, 5(3), 1–13. Retrieved from www.plantbased.org/plant_based_nutrition_2002–03.doc.

Popham, W.J. (2001). *The truth about testing: An educator's call to action.* Alexandria, VA: Association for Supervision and Curriculum Development.

Postman, N., & Weingartner, C. (1969). *Teaching as a subversive activity.* New York, NY: Dell Publishing.

Rothstein-Fisch, C., Trumbull, E., Isaac, A., Daley, C., & Pérez, A. (2003). When "helping someone else" is the right answer: Teachers bridge cultures in assessment. *Journal of Latinos and Education*, 2(3), 123–140.

Ruiz-Primo, M.A., Shavelson, R.J., Hamilton, L., & Klein, S. (2002). On the evaluation of systemic science education reform: Searching for instructional sensitivity. *Journal of Research in Science Teaching*, 39(5), 369–393.

Ryu, J. (2004). The social adjustment of three, young, high-achieving Korean-English bilingual students in kindergarten. *Early Childhood Education Journal*, 32(3), 165–171.

Sadler, N. (2007). Personal Communication, February 19.

Scarcella, R. (2003). *Academic English: A conceptual framework*. Santa Barbara, CA: University of California Linguistic Minority Research Institute.

Sexton, U., & Solano-Flores, G. (2002). *Cultural validity in assessment development: A cross-cultural study on the interpretation of math and science items*. Paper presented at the annual meeting of the American Educational Research Association. New Orleans, LA, April 1–5.

Shavelson, R.J., Baxter, G.P., & Gao, X. (1993) Sampling variability of performance assessment. *Journal of Educational Measurement*, 30(3), 215–232.

Sizer, T. (1992). *Horace's school*. New York, NY: Houghton Mifflin.

Solano-Flores, G. (2006). Language, dialect, and register: Sociolinguistics and the estimation of measurement error in the testing of English-language learners. *Teachers College Record*, 108(11), 2354–2379.

Solano-Flores, G., & Gustafson, M. (in press). Assessment of English language learners: A critical, probabilistic, systemic view. In M. Simon, K. Ercikan, & M. Rousseau (Eds.), *Handbook on large-scale assessments and secondary analyses*.

Solano-Flores, G., & Li, M. (2006). The use of generalizability (G) theory in the testing of linguistic minorities. *Educational Measurement: Issues and Practice*, 25, 13–22.

Solano-Flores, G., & Nelson-Barber, S. (2001). On the cultural validity of science assessments. *Journal of Research in Science Teaching*, 38(5), 553–573.

Solano-Flores, G., & Trumbull, E. (2003). Examining language in context: The need for new research and practice paradigms in the testing of English-language learners. *Educational Researcher*, 32(2), 3–13.

Solano-Flores, G., Trumbull, E., & Nelson-Barber, S. (2002). Concurrent development of dual language assessments: An alternative to translating tests for linguistic minorities. *International Journal of Testing*, 2(2), 107–129.

Trumbull, E., Diaz-Meza, R., & Hasan, A. (in press). Using cultural knowledge to inform literacy practices: Teacher innovations from the bridging cultures project. In P.M. Greenfield, A. Isaac, E. Trumbull, C. Rothstein-Fisch, & B. Quiroz (Eds.), *Bridging cultures in U.S. classrooms*. New York, NY: Sage Foundation.

Valdés, G., & Figueroa, R. (1994). *Bilingualism and testing: A special case of bias*. Norwood, NJ: Ablex Publishing Company.

Wellington, J., & Osborne, J. (2001). *Language and literacy in science education*. Buckingham: Open University Press.

Wolfram, W., Adger, C.T., & Christian, D. (1999). *Dialects in schools and communities*. Mahwah, NJ: Lawrence Erlbaum Associates.

Wong Fillmore, L., & Snow, C. (2000). *What teachers need to know about language*. Washington, DC: U.S. Department of Education, Office of Educational Research and Improvement.

# Part II

# Assessing Students of Linguistically and Culturally Diverse Backgrounds

# Chapter 3

# Assessing English Language Learners

## Critical Issues

*Jamal Abedi*

---

**Chapter Overview**

This chapter focuses on the challenges that professionals who specialize in testing and measurement face when they try to ensure that standardized tests are valid and reliable for both the mainstream population for which they are originally designed and the population of English language learners (ELLs). It also addresses the issues that educators and test users need to consider when they make decisions concerning the use of those tests with ELLs to ensure that content-based tests do not become tests of English language proficiency rather than the particular skills and knowledge they purport to assess.

## The ELL Performance Gap: The Role of Language

Research on the assessment of ELLs clearly shows that academic performance of these students is substantially lower than that of their native English speaking peers (Abedi, 2004, 2006; Gándara, Rumberger, Maxwell-Jolly, & Callahan, 2003; Grissom, 2004; Solano-Flores & Trumbull, 2003). Explaining such a performance gap requires a comprehensive review of the factors affecting this phenomenon.

ELL students face a dual challenge: developing English and learning the academic content of the curriculum in English. Developing English, and particularly academic English, as a second language is a long process that adds to the learning challenge that these students have to bear in their academic career. It is quite a difficult task for English learners to learn academic content in a language that they are still struggling to learn. For most ELLs, it takes five to seven years, and sometimes even more, to gain the mastery of academic English needed to join their English speaking peers in taking full advantage of instruction in English (Hakuta, Butler, & Witt, 2000). Limited proficiency in English affects both students' learning and their performances on assessments. Therefore, to help close the performance gap between ELL and non-ELL students, both learning and assessment conditions must be addressed.

The linguistic complexity of instructional material and assessments is a major factor contributing to the performance gap between ELL and non-ELL students (Abedi, 2006; Abedi & Herman, 2010; Abedi, Hofstetter, & Lord, 2004;

Solano-Flores & Trumbull, 2003). Low performance of ELL students on content-based assessments may be due to a lack of understanding of the language of the test rather than a lack of content knowledge. Researchers focusing on the assessment of ELLs believe that performance outcomes in content-based areas such as math and science are confounded with students' proficiency in English.

Standardized achievement tests that have been constructed for mainstream students, but do not take into account the special needs of English learners, can present a further challenge for these students and may not provide a good indication of what they know and can accomplish. Chapter 2 of this book (Trumbull & Solano-Flores) presents a comprehensive view of the role of language in the assessment of ELL students. This current chapter addresses technical issues in the assessment of these students, many of which are related to linguistic and cultural factors.

Discussing the technical issues regarding assessment of ELL students requires a complex technical language that may not be readily transparent to the general audience. The chapter provides, in plain language, explanations of the technical terms and interpretations of the psychometric data discussed. The reader does not need to possess a high level of measurement expertise in order to grasp the principal ideas discussed.

### Concerns Over Reliability and Validity of Assessments for ELL Students

In order to understand the technical aspects of assessment, we need to understand what a *valid* and *reliable* assessment is. A simple example will help to illustrate the reliability and validity of assessments. To obtain a driver's license, we expect to be tested on driving rules in our state. A test that asks questions about how to change a transmission or how to paint a car would not constitute a valid driving test because that test asks questions that are irrelevant (construct-irrelevant) to the knowledge of and experience in driving.

We also want tests to be reliable. If most of the people taking the driving test in the morning performed well and most of those taking the test in the afternoon performed poorly, that would not be a reliable test because time of day (as a source of measurement error) influences the outcome of the test.

Complex linguistic structure of assessment (or the complexity of the language of the test) negatively impacts the reliability and validity of assessments for ELL students. ELL students may do poorly on assessments conducted in English, not necessarily due to the lack of content knowledge that is the subject of assessment but due to lack of understanding of assessment questions per se. Research findings consistently suggest that ELL students perform substantially better on assessment with clear language. The results of studies indicate, for example, that the lower the level of language demands of test items, the smaller the performance gap between ELL and non-ELL students (see, for example, Abedi, 2009). We will discuss the impact of linguistic complexity of assessments on the reliability and validity of content-based assessment for ELL students later in this chapter.

## Number of Students Affected

The impact of language factors on the instruction and assessment of ELL students is of paramount importance, as language diversity in the U.S. is rapidly increasing. In 1990, 32 million people over the age of five in the U.S. spoke a language other than English in their home, comprising 14% of the total U.S. population. By 2000, that number had increased by 47% to 47 million, representing 18% of the population of the United States (U.S. Census Bureau, 2002). In 1999, the U.S. Census Bureau listed 70 different languages and dialects in their *Survey of Language Spoken at Home*, yet, without a doubt, many other languages not included on the census survey are spoken in the United States today as well.

These data suggest that the population of ELLs is the fastest growing population in the nation (Kindler, 2002) and now numbers about five million students, representing approximately 10% of all K-12 students nationally (GAO, 2006).[1] Consequently, the fairness and validity of their assessment must be among the top priorities of the national education agenda.

## Test Development: The Common Approach

Despite current research findings on the impact of language factors on the assessment of ELLs, most local, state, and national assessments are developed and field-tested for the mainstream student population for whom language factors may not have much impact on their assessment outcomes. The standard procedure in test item development is to write test items according to the plans specified in the test blueprint and make sure that the test has construct and content validity. Construct validity is attained when all of the test items measure the intended construct. For instance, a science item that purports to assess a student's understanding of the composition of Earth's atmosphere ought to do so without depending upon advanced reading skills that have less to do with the science construct (concept) being assessed. Content validity is attained when test items accurately address the content that is being tested. A test blueprint will include these and other important elements for the test. A typical test blueprint provides general guidelines for test development that are used for assessing all students, including sub-groups such as ELLs and students with disabilities (see Durán, Chapter 6, this volume). While many factors are incorporated into the test blueprint, language factors are not among them. Early versions of a test are administered to groups of students that may include students whose second or third language is English, but the specific language needs or characteristics of those students are not taken into account in the actual design of the test.

## Factors to Consider When Assessing ELL Students

Research literature suggests that the performance gap between ELL and non-ELL students can be explained by many different factors, including parent education level and poverty (Abedi, Leon, & Mirocha, 2003), the challenge of second language acquisition (Hakuta et al., 2000; Moore & Redd, 2002), and a host of inequitable schooling conditions (Abedi & Herman, 2010; Gándara et al., 2003). Other factors may also impact their achievement outcomes, such as gender and ethnicity (see Abedi, 2004; Grissom, 2004; Solano-Flores & Trumbull, 2003), dialect, and cultural experiences (Lipka & Adams, 2004; Solano-Flores & Trumbull, 2003). Solano-Flores introduced the concept of "cultural validity" as a form of test validity that links many linguistic and cultural factors to ELL students' assessment outcomes (Solano-Flores & Nelson-Barber, 2001).

Results of an event history[2] on a cohort of 1993–1994 grade 7 students (with a total number of 23,856 students) who were followed for a period of six years (12 semesters, fall 1993 to spring 1999) also demonstrate this notion. The study found that in addition to students' levels of language proficiency, family socio-economic status and background variables (such as ethnicity and culture) appear to be related to ELL classification (Abedi, 2008). The findings indicated that there was a large variation in time spent in ELL classification (Abedi, 2008) across racial/ethnic categories. For example, results of these analyses indicated that Hispanics had the smallest percentage of Reclassified Fluent English Proficient (RFEP), the language status required for a student to exit from special language programs and join the mainstream: Only 57% of Hispanics compared to 77% of Asians and 68% of Caucasians who spoke languages other than English were RFEP. It took almost 10 semesters for Hispanic students to be reclassified from ELL to RFEP, whereas it took half as much time for Asian and Caucasian students to be reclassified. This discrepancy between reclassification rate of Hispanic and others is most likely due to linguistic and cultural biases in assessment that may have more impact on the judgement of academic performance of Hispanic students than on students from other cultural backgrounds.

In a recent paper, Abedi and Gándara (2006) provided a summary of major factors that contribute to the performance gap between ELL and mainstream students. These included cognitive factors such as the development of reading skills, complex language that interferes with understanding content, and accommodations used in the assessment of ELL students. These factors relate directly to the methods by which we teach and assess ELLs. The non-cognitive factors were communicative competence and socio-cultural factors, as well as affective factors in learning and assessment. These factors are more strongly related to cultural sensitivity in the teaching and learning process. The authors concluded:

> It is important to consider that there are many other factors beyond the cognitive domain in general and language factors in particular that are affecting the academic achievement of ELL students. Cognitive factors (motivational and volitional aspects of learning) as well as affective factors can greatly impact students' performance in school. Lack of progress due to serious challenges that ELL students are faced with may seriously impact their level of motivation. Undue pressure to perform well in the nation's accountability system and other sources of pressure in the academic life of ELL students may cause frustration and impact their academic performance.
>
> (p. 44)

This short summary of research suggests that ELL students are not from a homogeneous population, and they differ from each other on many factors, including language and culture. In order to provide valid, reliable, and accessible assessments for these students, factors that impact performance outcomes of ELL students must first be identified and controlled.

## Should We Assess ELLs in their Home Language or in English?[3]

As indicated above, ELLs constitute a highly heterogeneous group in many aspects, including their level of proficiency in their native language (L1) and proficiency in English (L2). A major source of information for providing appropriate assessments for ELL students is the use of accurate assessments of their proficiency in both their L1 and L2. Only when students' relative language proficiency in both languages[4] has been assessed can an informed decision be made about the language of assessment. Language assessments ideally address not only discrete language skills and the ability to communicate but also a student's proficiency with academic language—the language associated with learning and demonstrating knowledge in school. For a student who is highly proficient in academic content using her native language, an assessment in the student's native language will provide a more valid outcome of what the student knows and is able to do. On the other hand, ELL students who have higher-level English proficiency and are instructed in English will benefit more from assessments in English (see Abedi et al., 2004). Before decisions are made regarding assessments for ELL students, it is critical to obtain reliable and valid estimates of students' levels of proficiency in both L1 and L2.

However, validity of many of the existing tests for measuring students' levels of proficiency in their native language and in English is questionable (see Abedi, 2007b, for a comprehensive review of the existing English language proficiency assessments). Many do not include a measure of academic language proficiency (defined in Chapter 2). To elaborate on some of the issues in measuring language proficiency, we will discuss measures of L1 proficiency and then address concerns in the assessment of English language proficiency (L2).

## Assessment of Students' Proficiency in L1

Assessment of students' native language proficiency poses many different challenges, the foremost being the ever-expanding variety of languages spoken in this country. As the number of non-native English speakers in schools increases, so does the need for valid and reliable assessments for these students. Despite this increasing need, assessments to measure primary language proficiency are not widely used in the United States. A literature search produced only a few articles that referred to assessments of primary language proficiency in the primary grades. For example, the California Department of Education (CDE) does not include any tests of non-English speakers' primary language proficiency in its database (CDE, 2006), and the assessment division of CDE does not provide any additional information regarding statewide language assessment beyond the California English Language Development Test (CELDT).

Oller (1992) claimed that some states have utilized the verbal component of intelligence tests to determine primary language proficiency, a practice that raises questions about the content and construct validity of L1 assessment, since such tests were not designed for this purpose. Several articles also referred to the use of an assessment called the Learning Record to document native and English oral and written language skills. Though it was used primarily in England, the Learning Record was adapted for use in California in the 1990s (renamed the "California Learning Record") (Barr, 2000).

One virtue of the Learning Record, from a teacher's perspective, is its ability to document student progress over time in the way that portfolios do and to provide a clear picture of student learning for both students and parents that is linked closely to language and literacy standards (E. Trumbull, personal communication, August 2, 2007). However, neither the British nor the California Learning Record examine language in the linguistic terms that formal language tests do. Among these formal language tests are the IDEA Proficiency Test (IPT) CELF-4® and the Bilingual Syntax Measure (Burt, Dulay, & Hernández-Chávez, 1980), which are available in English and Spanish versions. Many of these formal tests (e.g., the CELF) are administered and interpreted by a speech/language professional rather than a teacher. In the past, some districts that provided bilingual education used such tests (see Trumbull & Koelsch, Chapter 9, this volume). With the substantial discontinuation of bilingual education, there has been much less emphasis on evaluating a student's proficiency in any language other than English.

While the latest mandated tests of language development have a strong focus on the four language modes (reading, writing, listening, and speaking) (see Abedi, 2007b), they fall short in addressing deeper and more complex aspects of language that are critical to academic achievement and performance on assessments. Some of these neglected aspects, referred to by Farr and Trumbull (1997) as communicative competence, include discourse and the strategic use of language.

A body of research exists on the role of primary language in the development of literacy skills. For example, students with higher emergent Spanish language skills (that is, those whose skill level is high in their native language) are more successful in transitioning to English reading and speaking (see Langer, Bartolome, Vasquez, & Lucas, 1990; Reese, Garnier, Gallimore, & Goldenberg, 2000). Emergent literacy in both the primary language and the secondary language has a positive impact on the development of future literacy. However, no formal assessments to measure primary language or literacy proficiency in the school setting are evident.

The need to take into account primary language levels in assessment procedures for non-English speaking students is addressed by several educational researchers[5] (Butler & Stevens, 1997; Solano-Flores & Trumbull, 2003). There is growing recognition that testing only students' English language proficiency leaves out an important component of language and literacy development in ELLs which could be built upon to produce more appropriate learning outcomes

(Solano-Flores & Trumbull, 2003). Having a more accurate picture of a student's native language proficiency could inform designing and implementing classroom instruction as well as making placement decisions and the setting of more realistic instructional goals. Of course, assessment of students' native languages depends upon appropriate tests in those languages and professionals who are themselves proficient in those languages. However, it must be acknowledged at this point that, while a majority of ELL students (over 75%) are native Spanish speakers, the remaining 25% are from a variety of cultural and linguistic backgrounds. Therefore, it would be a major challenge to create tests that measure native language proficiency for these students.

## Assessment of Students' English Language Proficiency

Over the years, states have used commercially available "off-the-shelf" tests of English language proficiency. These assessments have been used to establish the baseline for the NCLB Title III assessments, and some states are currently using them to fulfill Title III requirements. However, many of these assessments lack construct and consequential validity—the defensibility of decisions based on test outcomes, such as program placement or graduation. For example, reviews of some of the most commonly used language proficiency tests reveal differences in the types of tasks the tests cover and the specific item content of the tests (Abedi, 2007b; De Ávila, 1990; Linquanti, 2001; NRC, 2000; Valdés & Figueroa, 1994; Del Vecchio & Guerrero, 1995; Zehler, Hopstock, Fleischman, & Greniuk, 1994). The reviewers indicated that these tests are based on different theoretical emphases prevalent at the time of their development, which suggests that the domain of English language proficiency is not clearly defined in many of these tests (see, for example, Abedi, 2007b; Del Vecchio & Guerrero, 1995; Katz, Low, Stack, & Tsang, 2004; Zehler et al., 1994). Furthermore, analyses of data from the administration of some of the existing language proficiency tests reveal problems with the reliability and validity, the adequacy of the scoring directions, and the limited populations on which field testing samples are based (Abedi et al., 2003; Zehler et al., 1994).

Due to content and technical issues with many of the existing English language proficiency tests, NCLB required changes in the state policy and practice in Title III assessments (No Child Left Behind, 2002). Specifically, NCLB Title III required states to (1) develop and implement English language proficiency standards suitable for ELL students' learning of English as a second language; (2) implement a single, reliable, and valid English language proficiency assessment aligned to ELP standards that annually measures listening, speaking, reading, writing, and comprehension; and (3) establish annual measurable achievement objectives (AMAOs) for ELL students that explicitly define, measure, and report on these students' expected progress toward and attainment of English language proficiency goals (see Title 1, Part A Section 1111 (b) and Title III, Part A Section 3102 (8) and Part A Section 3121 (a) (2) and (3)).

In response to the NCLB mandate, the U.S. Department of Education provided support to states for developing reliable and valid English language proficiency assessments through the Enhanced Assessment Grant under Section 6112b of the No Child Left Behind Act. Four different consortia of states have developed and are currently implementing English language proficiency assessments that attempt to address Title III assessment requirements while the remaining states are using either their own state-developed tests or some version of commercially available assessments, augmented or off-the-shelf (Zehler, 1994). The newly developed English language proficiency tests include four modalities (reading, writing, speaking, and listening), are aligned with the states' English language proficiency content standards, and focus on the concept of *academic English* (Abedi, 2007b). Although federal technical assistance and review of Title III has begun, many state policy-makers and education leaders have voiced the need for enhanced guidance as well as technical assistance and policy support in implementing these assessments and related accountability systems (GAO, 2006).

In addition to the states' efforts, several test publishers have been engaged in major development of assessments that are consistent with the requirements set forth by the NCLB Title III accountability mandate. These publishers significantly upgraded their existing English language proficiency tests or created new ones that address the NCLB Title III requirements. For example, the new version of Language Assessment Scales (LAS), LAS Links, addresses both academic and social language. LAS Links also measures each of four domains (reading, writing, listening, and speaking) separately, provides a comprehension score, and supplies a common vertical scale to facilitate comparisons across grade level clusters.

Stanford English Language Proficiency (SELP) measures English language proficiency of ELL students in grades PreK-12. This assessment identifies ELLs for language acquisition placements with five levels of proficiency, assesses both academic and social English, and determines instructional needs. SELP measures skills in the four language domains (listening, speaking, reading, and writing) and sets proficiency levels (Pre-Emergent, Emergent, Basic, Intermediate, and Proficient). The SELP publisher is conducting ongoing psychometric research on the validity of SELP tests used in many states, including analyses of: equivalence of test constructs across multiple forms of the SELP, dimensionality of the test and internal structure, external validity of SELP with state achievement tests for reading and writing, and comparisons of the performance of ELL students classified as proficient and non-ELL students on state achievement tests.

We now elaborate on some of these technical terms. "Construct equivalence" means that different forms of the same test measure the same content and the same construct. For example, two forms of a reading proficiency test should have the same number and type of items at the same level of difficulty, measuring the same reading ability in order to be considered as equivalent or parallel forms. "Dimensionality" refers to the number of distinct constructs that an item measures. For example, an item or a test intended to measure number sense may also be measuring reading skills due to its linguistic complexity. Internal structure refers to consistency between items on what they measure. For example, if different items in a test measure different constructs then they may not be internally consistent. For examining the internal structure of items, a principal components analysis model has been used. This concept of internal structure of items is similar to the internal consistency approach in reliability. Finally, the term "external validity" refers to consistency between what test items measure with an external criterion. For example, if a teacher-made reading test correlates highly with the score of a state-administered reading test (the state test used as external criteria) then this outcome may be used as validity evidence for the teacher-made test.

Despite all the advancements in the assessment of students' levels of English language proficiency, major concerns remain. For example, many states use pre-NCLB English proficiency tests for establishing the baseline for AMAOs. Given the content and psychometric concerns with these assessments, "comparability" across the different English Language Proficiency (ELP) assessments raises serious questions of accuracy. Furthermore, while the newly developed ELP tests are based on sound content and psychometric principles, there are not enough data yet to judge the quality of these assessments.

## Can a Test Designed for Native English Speakers Provide Valid Assessment Outcomes for Bilingual/ ELL Students?

Speakers of English as a second language who are mainstreamed before becoming proficient in English may not benefit from instructional materials and teachers' instructions at the same level as their native English language peers do. Similarly, unnecessary linguistic complexity can negatively affect the reliability and validity of assessments for ELL students. If linguistic complexity confuses students to the point that the items are misunderstood, then construct validity is in question.

The larger issue is the differential impact of language factors on the performance of ELL versus non-ELL students. Measurement theory establishes the same underlying model for all students, including ELL students, in order for academic achievement tests to be deemed reliable and valid. That is, all interfering variables, including unnecessary linguistic complexity of assessments, are assumed to have the same effect on all students. However, research findings clearly suggest that language factors have a much more profound effect on ELL students than on native speakers of English (Abedi, 2006; Abedi et al., 2003). Solano-Flores and Trumbull (2003) found that language factors interact with test items, such that linguistically complex items contribute largely to the measurement error for ELL students but not for native speakers of English. All nuisance variables that could cause inconsistencies in the outcome of assessments are called "measurement error." Measurement error comes from different sources, such as guessing on multiple-choice tests, subjective scoring of essay tests, error in interpreting observational data, and interpreting self-reported data (Linn & Gronlund, 1995). For ELL students the main source of measurement error comes from unnecessary linguistic complexity of assessments (Abedi, 2006; Solano-Flores, 2008). Therefore, assessments designed for native English speakers may not provide reliable and valid assessment outcomes for ELL students.

The literature has documented major differences between ELL and non-ELL in the measurement characteristics of content-based assessment. To illustrate this point, we will now focus on two principal characteristics of tests, reliability and validity, using actual data obtained from large-scale national assessment databases.

## Reliability

"Reliability" refers to the ability of a test to produce consistent measures or the ability of scorers or scoring machines to come up with the same scores for each item. To estimate the reliability of standardized achievement tests, a number of different approaches are used. Internal consistency is the most common approach.

Internal consistency examines whether all the items in a test are measuring the same construct. For example, if the test is measuring knowledge of *algebra* then all questions should be about some aspect of *algebra*. The literature suggests that the internal consistency approach assumes that the test measures a single construct, the construct that is the target of assessment. However, tests with complex linguistic structure measure language as an additional construct or dimension. Cronbach's alpha (a measure of internal consistency) is shown to be extremely sensitive to multi-dimensionality of test items (see Abedi, Lord, & Hofstetter, 1998; Cortina, 1993). That is, if test items contain content outside of the topic of the test, then the coefficient alpha will give a lower estimate of the reliability of the test. Earlier, we presented data suggesting that the linguistic complexity of test items might introduce another dimension into the assessment, i.e., the construct irrelevant dimension.

Table 3.1 summarizes the results of an internal consistency analyses. These data are from a study conducted by Abedi et al. (2003) from several locations nationwide. The results of analyses are reported for five content areas: reading, mathematics, language, science, and social sciences. Within each of these content areas, reliability (alpha) coefficients are reported by categories identified in the student population, such as different SES levels. Since the majority of ELL students are from lower SES families, some researchers argue that poverty is the main factor that explains the lower reliability coefficient for ELL students. The categories "free" and "reduced-price lunch program" provide a proxy for SES. The analyses indicate the importance of SES to the reliability of assessment outcomes. The table shows a lower trend of reliability for students in lower SES families, but the gap between high and low SES students is substantially smaller than the gap between ELL and non-ELL students. This suggests that SES is not the only or the most important variable in ELL achievement.

More specifically, internal consistency (alpha) coefficients are generally high for non-ELL students (particularly those at the higher level of SES). The average alpha over the five content areas for non-ELL students[6] at the higher SES level is 0.837 and at the lower SES level is 0.784, with a difference of 0.053. For native English speakers, the average alpha coefficient is 0.841, as compared with an average alpha of 0.685 for ELLs, with a difference of 0.156 between the two

*Table 3.1*  Stanford 9 Sub-Scale Reliabilities (Site 2 Grade 9) (Alpha Coefficients)

| Sub-scale (number of items) | Non-ELL, free lunch participation | | Average for all non-ELL | ELL |
|---|---|---|---|---|
| | No | Yes | | |
| **Reading** | | | | |
| Vocabulary (30) | 0.828 | 0.781 | 0.835 | 0.666 |
| Reading comprehension (54) | 0.912 | 0.892 | 0.916 | 0.833 |
| **Average reliability** | 0.870 | 0.837 | 0.876 | 0.750 |
| **Math** | | | | |
| Total (48) | 0.899 | 0.853 | 0.898 | 0.802 |
| **Language** | | | | |
| Mechanics (24) | 0.801 | 0.759 | 0.803 | 0.686 |
| Expression (24) | 0.818 | 0.779 | 0.823 | 0.680 |
| **Average reliability** | 0.810 | 0.769 | 0.813 | 0.683 |
| **Science** | | | | |
| Total (40) | 0.800 | 0.723 | 0.805 | 0.597 |
| **Social science** | | | | |
| Total (40) | 0.803 | 0.702 | 0.805 | 0.530 |
| **Average reliability across all areas** | 0.837 | 0.784 | 0.841 | 0.685 |

Source: Abedi, Leon, and Mirocha (2003).

groups. By comparing the differences in overall reliability coefficients between groups separated by SES and those separated by ELL status, it becomes quite clear that language factors have much greater impact than SES on the reliability of assessments. The fact that many ELL students come from lower SES families does not alone explain the gap in the reliability coefficients between ELL and non-ELL students. It is necessary to look to other factors to obtain a more comprehensive understanding of how to best assess the content knowledge of ELL students.

As indicated earlier, the main assumption underlying the internal consistency approach is unidimensionality of assessment; that is, the assessment is testing only one construct. When an assessment tests more than one dimension, then the internal consistency approach underestimates the reliability of the assessments. That is, using alpha as a measure of reliability may underestimate internal consistency of assessments that are designed to include a secondary construct. However, in the case of the assessment of ELL students, unnecessary linguistic complexity of test items may introduce a second and *unintentional* dimension—a so-called "construct-irrelevant" dimension. In other words, language can become an additional (and unwanted) dimension or construct of the assessment. Such assessments may, therefore, be unintentionally multi-dimensional in nature.

To illustrate the impact of unnecessary linguistic complexity on the assessment of ELL students, we present the following example. Below is an actual math test item used for grade 4 students:

A certain reference file contains approximately six billion facts. About how many millions is that?

A.  6,000,000
B.  600,000
C.  60,000
D.  6,000
E.  600

The operation behind this item is to identify how many millions are in "six billion." However, the test item was made complex by including unfamiliar vocabulary such as "certain," "reference," "approximately," and "facts." Below is a revised version of this item in which unnecessary linguistic complexity that may confuse ELL students was removed.

Mack's company sold six billion pencils. About how many millions is that?

A.  6,000,000
B.  600,000
C.  60,000
D.  6,000
E.  600

In this revision, unfamiliar vocabulary was replaced with words that may be more familiar to students.

To illustrate the concept of unidimensionality, we conducted a principal component analysis on the assessment outcomes from both ELL and non-ELL groups. Principal component analysis is used when there are many variables that correlate highly and may be measuring the same constructs. This analysis, sometimes described as a variable reduction procedure, allows identification of the unobserved variables that measure different constructs. A large number of factors as a result of the principal component analysis is an indication of multi-dimensionality. This investigation was done with assessments originally developed for and field tested with non-ELLs, then used with both ELLs and non-ELLs (for a detailed discussion of this study, see Abedi et al., 2003).

Table 3.2 summarizes the finding of these analyses. Test scores from ELL students show a stronger trend of multi-dimensionality than do those from non-ELL students. For example, in most of the cases, across different content and different grade levels, the data for non-ELL students fit in a two- or three-factor model, whereas the ELL data required at least a four-factor model. This suggests that the performance of ELL students was attributable to more dimensions (for example, cultural and linguistic biases) on the test than non-ELL students. The results also suggested that the data for non-ELL students shared a larger percentage of variance (over 50%) compared with ELL students (averaging 25%). Put simply, the assessment outcomes for ELL students appear to be affected by more sources of bias than do those for non-ELL students.

Table 3.2 Summary Results of Principal Components by ELL/Non-ELL

| Subsection/grade | Number of factors (Eigenvalue > 1) for non-ELLs | Number of factors (Eigenvalue > 1) for ELLs | Percent of variance of first component for non-ELLs | Percentage of variance of first component for ELLs |
|---|---|---|---|---|
| **Math problem-solving** | | | | |
| Grade 3 | 2 | 4 | 47.22 | 23.95 |
| Grade 6 | 2 | 5 | 46.45 | 21.72 |
| Grade 8 | 2 | 5 | 44.25 | 20.14 |
| **Math concepts** | | | | |
| Grade 3 | 2 | 4 | 55.22 | 29.34 |
| Grade 6 | 2 | 4 | 56.11 | 27.61 |
| Grade 8 | 3 | 5 | 52.10 | 28.41 |
| **Math estimation** | | | | |
| Grade 3 | 2 | 4 | 48.16 | 24.32 |
| Grade 6 | 3 | 4 | 45.12 | 22.26 |
| Grade 8 | 3 | 5 | 42.49 | 20.56 |
| **Math data interpretation** | | | | |
| Grade 3 | 2 | 3 | 51.89 | 26.25 |
| Grade 6 | 2 | 4 | 44.57 | 24.24 |
| Grade 8 | 3 | 5 | 53.22 | 20.16 |
| **Math computation** | | | | |
| Grade 3 | 3 | 3 | 58.48 | 31.79 |
| Grade 6 | 3 | 3 | 54.26 | 28.44 |
| Grade 8 | 3 | 4 | 55.29 | 22.14 |
| **Reading** | | | | |
| Grade 3 | 3 | 4 | 51.33 | 28.66 |
| Grade 6 | 3 | 4 | 48.29 | 26.54 |
| Grade 8 | 39 | 5 | 46.45 | 21.48 |

Source: Abedi, Leon, and Mirocha (2003).

## Validity

Validity concerns in the assessment of ELL students are twofold: (1) the construct being measured and (2) the structural relationship of assessment outcomes across students' ELL language status. "Structural relationship" refers to the way in which assessment outcomes can be explained or modeled, with reference to particular factors. For example, when a mathematics test has items with varying degrees of complex linguistic structure, then those items perform differently for ELL students. Test items with more complex linguistic structure would be more difficult for ELL students regardless of the level of content difficulty. Therefore, the correlation between items for ELLs and non-ELLs would be different because language becomes a major factor for ELLs and not so for non-ELLs. For monolingual students, the structural relationship is simpler than for ELLs: Student performance is largely attributable to their understanding of the construct being tested. The structural relationship between factors and outcomes is different for ELLs. Because language acts as a factor to influence assessment outcomes for ELLs, a more complex structural relationship exists.

## Construct Being Measured

Sometimes variables unrelated to the construct being measured may affect the outcome of the measurement. These variables – often referred to as "nuisance" variables (Abedi, 2006), "extraneous" variables (Linn & Gronlund, 1995), "contaminants" or "construct-irrelevant" variables (Haladyna & Downing, 2004; Messick, 1994) – may become threats to the reliability and validity of assessments. Linn & Gronlund (1995) suggest that test developers must attempt "to rule out extraneous factors that might distort the meaning of the scores" and conduct follow-up studies for verification (p. 71). Among the most influential nuisance variables in the assessment of ELL students are language factors not directly related to the construct being measured, which create unnecessary linguistic complexity in the assessment. The Standards for Educational and Psychological Testing (American Educational Research Association [AERA], American Psychological Association [APA], & National Council on Measurement in Education [NCME], 1999) reminds us that:

> Test use with individuals who have not sufficiently acquired the language of the test may introduce construct irrelevant components to the testing process. In such instances, test results may not reflect accurately the qualities and competencies intended to be measured. [Therefore] special attention to issues related to language and culture may be needed when developing, administering, scoring, and interpreting test scores and making decisions based on test scores.
>
> (p. 91)

Since language factors influence the performance outcomes of ELL students systematically, they may not be considered as a source of measurement error with a random distribution (Allen & Yen, 1979). For example, a major source of error is guessing in multiple-choice tests. Such a source of error is said to be random since, by guessing, sometimes students gain and sometimes lose score points. However, the language variable is not randomly distributed for all students taking the test but, rather, applicable in this case only to ELLs. In the case of linguistic complexity, this source of construct-irrelevant variance introduces a component to the ELL assessment model that distinguishes it from the model used for mainstream students.

### Structural Relationship of Assessment Outcomes Across the Students' ELL Status

As noted above, language factors as a source of construct-irrelevant variance may introduce another factor into the assessment model, making the assessment outcome for ELL students multi-dimensional. One dimension is the construct (concept) being measured; the other dimension is linguistic complexity.

To illustrate this point, we present the results of analyses of data from several different locations nationwide (Abedi et al., 2003). In the reliability section of this chapter, we presented the results of a principal components analyses, which showed that test scores from ELL students have a higher trend of multi-dimensionality than those from non-ELL students. To further investigate this result, we used a multiple-group confirmatory factor analysis model to compare ELL and non-ELL students on the structural relationships in their assessment outcome. The multiple-group confirmatory factor analysis (MGCFA) model provides the opportunity to test the hypothesis of impact of linguistic factors on content-based assessments such as mathematics and science. For example, if the language of the assessment influences its outcomes differently across ELL and non-ELL groups, then language becomes an additional dimension for ELL students. Thus, for ELL students, a two-dimensional model (language and mathematics) would better fit the data, while a single dimension would better fit the non-ELL data. In this way, we would be able to further test the hypothesis that language is, indeed, a factor in the assessment outcomes of ELLs. We also tested several hypotheses of invariance (similarities between correlational patterns between items and sub-scales) across the two groups, to find out whether the same pattern of score differences between ELLs and non-ELLs would prevail.

Table 3.3 summarizes the outcome of these analyses. Assessment outcomes for ELL students suffer from lower correlations between items with the sub-tests (items parcels) when compared with the outcomes from non-ELL students. For example, the average correlation between individual reading items with the reading sub-tests (item parcels 1 through 4) is 0.749 for ELLs and 0.847 for non-ELLs; in mathematics the average correlations is 0.724 for ELLs and 0.830 for non-ELLs; and in science the average correlation is 0.539 for ELLs and 0.708 for non-ELLs. These results clearly show that ELL assessment outcomes are not structurally as consistent as those for non-ELL students. The main reason for the lower level consistency between outcomes for ELL students is the impact of a language factor as a source of construct irrelevance. When students are presented

*Table 3.3* Stanford 9 Reading, Math, and Science Structural Modeling Results (Site 2, Grade 9)

| Content areas | Non-ELL factor loadings | ELL factor loadings |
|---|---|---|
| **Reading comprehension** | | |
| Parcel 1 | 0.852 | 0.719 |
| Parcel 2 | 0.841 | 0.739 |
| Parcel 3 | 0.835 | 0.779 |
| Parcel 4 | 0.858 | 0.760 |
| **Math factor** | | |
| Parcel 1 | 0.818 | 0.699 |
| Parcel 2 | 0.862 | 0.789 |
| Parcel 3 | 0.843 | 0.733 |
| Parcel 4 | 0.797 | 0.674 |
| **Science factor** | | |
| Parcel 1 | 0.678 | 0.477 |
| Parcel 2 | 0.679 | 0.531 |
| Parcel 3 | 0.739 | 0.532 |
| Parcel 4 | 0.734 | 0.614 |
| **Factor correlation** | | |
| Reading vs. Math | 0.782 | 0.674 |
| Reading vs. Science | 0.837 | 0.802 |
| Science vs. Math | 0.870 | 0.789 |
| **Goodness of fit** | | |
| Chi Square | 488 | 158* |
| NFI | 0.997 | 0.992 |
| NNFI | 0.997 | 0.993 |
| CFI | 0.998 | 0.995 |

Source: Abedi, Leon, and Mirocha (2003).

Notes
*Significant at the 0.05 nominal level.
NFI = Normed fit index.
NNFI = Non-normed fit index.
CFI = Comparative fit index.

with test items that are difficult to understand, they may not be able to provide a good indication of what they know and can do.

In summary, these results show important structural differences between the performance of ELL and non-ELL students (for a detailed description of these analyses, see Abedi et al., 2003). The assessments, originally developed for and field tested with mainstream students, appear less valid for ELL students.

## So, How *Can* Decisions Be Made About the Language Used to Test a Student Whose Home Language is Not English?

The decision as to which language to use for the assessment of non-native speakers is complex and dependent on many different factors, among which the language of instruction plays a very important role. Students who are instructed in English, even with a very high level of proficiency in their native language, are likely to perform better on assessments in English. (However, as Solano-Flores' Chapter, this volume, notes, this pattern may vary from item to item.)

Students' levels of proficiency in their native language is another critical factor, but the assessment of students' native language poses many different challenges. As mentioned earlier, the main problem is the variety of languages other than English spoken in this country. Whereas the majority of non-native speakers of English have a Spanish language background, there are many other languages spoken in the nation (Kindler, 2002), making it extremely difficult to provide the option of providing native language assessments to all individuals who are not native speakers of English.

There are also equity issues concerning assessments in the students' native language. One might propose the use of translated tests, but researchers caution about lightly assuming comparability of the original and the translated versions of the assessments (see Hambleton, 1994). It is very difficult to create assessments in two languages that are truly parallel, since each language has unique and distinct conceptual constructs with socially and culturally embedded meanings.

Various studies have examined the effectiveness of assessing students in their native language and found that ELL students function well under the condition that the languages of instruction and assessment are aligned. Hofstetter (2003) analyzed data from 849 eighth-grade students in Southern California and found that students perform best in tests in their native language when they are instructed in their native language (see also Duncan et al., 2005). Similarly, Dolan, Murray, and Strangman (2006) reviewed literature on mathematics instruction and assessment for ELL students and reported that, "Test translation and dual-language test booklets do not appear to be broadly beneficial to ELL students but may improve the scores of ELL students who receive mathematics instruction in Spanish" (p. 22).

Abedi et al. (1998) compared the performance of Spanish-speaking grade 8 students taking the Spanish version of the NAEP (National Assessment of Educational Progress) math test with those Spanish-speaking students taking the original English version of the test. To ensure that the results of the study were not confounded with the differences in the experiences students had in their classrooms, the Spanish and English versions of the same assessments were randomly assigned to students within classrooms. Spanish speaking students taking the original English version performed significantly better than Spanish speaking students taking the Spanish version of the test. One explanation for this difference is that the majority of students in the sample received mathematics instruction in English (sheltered English and Non-ELL), suggesting that ELL students perform best on mathematics tests where the language of the items matched their language of instruction. This finding was confirmed in additional sub-analyses with ELL students enrolled in mathematics classes where instruction was in Spanish. For these students, performance was significantly higher on the mathematics test in Spanish than the test in standard English or modified English. Although the numbers of students in this sub-sample are small, these findings further reinforce the contention that the language of instruction is an important consideration in identifying suitable test accommodations for ELL students. The study concludes that:

> Translating assessment tasks into the students' native language is frequently assumed to be a good accommodation strategy. Our data suggest otherwise. Translating test items from English to other languages may not necessarily accommodate [ELL] students when their language of instruction is English. In summary, the data suggest that students perform most effectively when the language of the math test matches their language of instruction.
>
> (p. 62)

Assessing ELL students in their native language seems an attractive option in the assessment of ELL students, and this is one of the most commonly used assessment forms by many states (Rivera & Collum, 2006). However, the summarized research presented above clearly supports native language assessment only if native language assessment is coupled with native language instruction.

## What Teachers Can Do to Improve the Quality of Assessment Outcomes for ELL Students

Teachers can contribute greatly toward improving the quality of assessment for ELL students. They need to understand the instructional and assessment needs of these students in general, and the main factors influencing assessment outcomes in particular. The process of developing skills in a new language is difficult and requires time and effort. Thus, it takes a long time for ELL students to become proficient enough in English to understand a teacher's instructions and test questions in a language with an unfamiliar structure and vocabulary.

A teacher's lack of a proper background in teaching ELL students and a lack of understanding ELLs' academic needs may negatively affect the instruction and assessment of ELLs. Unfortunately, literature suggests that ELL students are more likely to be taught by teachers without appropriate teaching credentials and with less classroom experience than other students (Rumberger & Gándara, 2004). A recent study of 4,800 teachers of ELL students in California responding to a survey about the challenges they faced in teaching ELLs in their classrooms found large percentages of these teachers expressing the concern that they were not prepared to teach these students (Gándara et al., 2003).

Understanding the impact of language factors on the instruction and assessment of ELL students is essential if teachers are to be able to provide highly needed linguistic assistance to their ELL students. Literature on the assessment and accommodations of ELL students clearly demonstrates that unnecessary linguistic complexity (unrelated to the construct being measured) impacts validity of assessments for these students (see Abedi, 2006; Solano-Flores & Trumbull, 2003). By fully understanding these issues, teachers can revise their instructional materials, to the extent that is practical, to reduce the level of unnecessary linguistic complexity in both their instruction and assessment, and can help their students become more familiar with the vocabulary and complex linguistic structure of the state-administered assessments. In the absence of more relevant diagnostic information, teachers' access to test questions and item level data can help them have a better understanding of the assessment questions that cause problems for their ELL students.

Based on the research literature presented in this chapter, and on our understanding of assessment issues for ELL students, the following recommendations are provided for teachers:

- Acquire more knowledge and experience related to ELLs' academic needs in both instruction and assessment;
- Have enough interactions with ELL students to understand the challenges they are facing when instruction and assessment are offered in English;
- Encourage ELL students to contact you when they have questions and concerns regarding their academic affairs;
- Discuss the content of academic English with your ELL students and encourage them to read more and learn more academic English;
- For illustration purposes, use the test items that are more challenging for ELL students to help them understand language issues;
- Provide more systematic instruction on academic English where instruction and assessment are provided only in English; and
- Recognize the limitations of what can be inferred about an ELL student's learning on the basis of a test designed for non-ELLs.

## Conclusions

Assessments have a strong influence on the academic careers of ELL students. Outcomes of these assessments can determine their classification (ELL versus non-ELL), affect the type of instruction they receive, and influence decisions made concerning accommodations. Therefore, assessments for ELL students should be viewed as "high-stakes," since problems in the validity of assessment outcomes could jeopardize ELLs' academic life in profound ways.

Unfortunately, studies on the assessment of ELLs raise major concerns with regard to reliability and validity. Nuisance variables such as unnecessary linguistic complexity and cultural factors often have negative impacts on the reliability and validity of these assessments. However, controlling for such factors is no easy task; each variable must be analyzed as to whether it negatively or positively influences the assessment outcomes for ELL students.

We discussed factors that affect assessment outcomes for ELL students, among which were language factors. Tests that are developed and field-tested for native speakers of English and the mainstream student population may not be relevant for ELL students. For native speakers of English, understanding the language of the assessment may not be an issue, but for ELL students the language of the assessment is critical. If assessment questions have a complex linguistic structure, the validity of the assessment may be compromised because unnecessary linguistic complexity that is unrelated to the content is measured in addition to the target content of the assessment. Thus, outcomes of assessment are confounded with factors that are irrelevant to the construct assessed.

In our summary of research on factors that have a major impact on the assessments for ELLs, we have shown that controlling for these factors is essential in developing and implementing reliable and valid assessments for these students. To reduce the impact of students' language background on the assessment of ELL students, some assessment experts suggest testing them in their native language. While this might seem a reasonable solution for some ELL students, it may not be good practice for students who are not proficient in their native academic language and may even provide invalid results. It may also not be good practice when instruction is delivered in English. This interaction requires that educators carefully and accurately assess ELL students' native language proficiency to make informed decisions about whether to provide instruction in English or a native language.

In this chapter we elaborated on the fact that tests which are designed for native English speakers may not provide a valid picture of what ELL students know and their capabilities. Assessments that are reliable and valid for native English speakers are not necessarily so for ELL students. In order to provide ELL students with appropriate placement and instruction, it is imperative *to accurately assess ELL students' language proficiency* and then examine the content and technical characteristics of assessments that are used for this rapidly growing population of students.

## Notes

1. Language factors may impact performance of all students, including bilingual students. Theorists and researchers point out that ELLs and bilinguals cannot be fairly or accurately compared to monolinguals on the same assessments: Their performance profiles will necessarily be different from those of their monolingual peers (Valdès & Figueroa, 1994).
2. An event history documents patterns in people's (or an organization's) lives and factors that are correlated with those events (Yamaguchi, 1991). In this case, the event history was conducted in order to attempt to understand relationships among students' background variables such as language and ethnicity, and their placement and retention in programs for ELLs.
3. In an ideal world, many ELLs/bilingual students would be assessed in *both* languages because assessment in only one of their languages cannot tap their complete knowledge base (cf., Solano-Flores & Trumbull, 2003; Valdes & Figueroa, 1994). In research conducted by Solano-Flores and Li (2006, 2009), some ELL students performed better on some mathematics items in English and better on others in their native language.
4. Some students may be learning or speaking three or more languages. For example, Mexican immigrants from Indigenous groups may have learned an indigenous language along with Spanish and now be faced with learning English.
5. Assessing the linguistic proficiency of bilingual individuals in both their first and their second language is common practice in other fields. For example, in the field of bilingual speech-language pathology, it is widely accepted that bilingual students should be examined in both languages in order to gain a reasonable understanding of their language development and to understand their school performance (Langdon, 2008).
6. This includes students who were formerly classified as ELL and native English speakers.

# References

Abedi, J. (in press). Classification system for English language learners: Issues and recommendations. *Educational Measurement: Issues and Practice.*

Abedi, J. (2004). The No Child Left Behind Act and English language learners: Assessment and accountability issues. *Educational Researcher,* 33(1), 4–14.

Abedi, J. (2006). Language issues in item-development. In S.M. Downing & T.M. Haladyna (Eds.), *Handbook of test development* (pp. 377–398). Mahwah, NJ: Lawrence Erlbaum Associates.

Abedi, J. (2007a). English language proficiency assessment and accountability under the NCLB Title III: An overview. In J. Abedi (Ed.), *English language proficiency in the nation: Current status and future practice.* Davis, CA: University of California, Davis.

Abedi, J. (Ed.) (2007b). *English language proficiency assessment in the nation: Current status and future practice.* Davis, CA: University of California, Davis.

Abedi, J. (2008). Classification system for English language learners: Issues and recommendations. *Educational Measurement: Issues and Practice,* 27, 17–31.

Abedi, J. (2009). Computer testing as a form of accommodation for English language learners. *Educational Assessment,* 14, 195–211.

Abedi, J., & Gándara, P. (2006). Performance of English language learners as a subgroup in large-scale assessment: Interaction of research and policy. *Educational Measurement: Issues and Practice,* 25(4), 36–46.

Abedi, J., & Herman, J.L. (2010). Assessing English language learners' opportunity to learn mathematics: Issues and limitations. *Teachers College Record,* 112(3), 723–746.

Abedi, J., Hofstetter, C., & Lord, C. (2004). Assessment accommodations for English language learners: Implications for policy-based empirical research. *Review of Educational Research,* 74(1), 1–28.

Abedi, J., Leon, S., & Mirocha, J. (2003). *Impact of student language background on content-based performance: Analyses of extant data* (CSE Tech. Rep. No. 603). Los Angeles, CA: University of California, National Center for Research on Evaluation, Standards, and Student Testing.

Abedi, J., Lord, C., & Hofstetter, C. (1998). *Impact of selected background variables on students' NAEP math performance* (CSE Tech. Rep. No. 478). Los Angeles, CA: University of California, Center for the Study of Evaluation/National Center for Research on Evaluation, Standards, and Student Testing.

Allen, M.J., & Yen, W.M. (1979). *Introduction to measurement theory.* Monterey, CA: Brooks/Cole.

American Educational Research Association, American Psychological Association, & National Council on Measurement in Education (1999). *Standards for educational and psychological testing.* Washington, DC: American Educational Research Association.

Barr, M.A. (2000). Looking at the learning record. *Educational Leadership,* 57(5), 20–24.

Burt, M., Dulay, H., & Hernández-Chávez, E. (1980). *Bilingual syntax measure [BSM].* San Antonio, TX: The Psychological Corporation.

Butler, F.A., & Stevens, R. (1997). *Accommodation strategies for English language learners on large-scale assessments: Student characteristics and other considerations* (CSE Tech. Rep. No. 448). Los Angeles, CA: University of California, National Center for Research on Evaluation, Standards, and Student Testing.

California Department of Education (2006). *State AYP report.* Retrieved June 6, 2006, from www.ayp.cde.ca.gov/reports.

Cortina, J.M. (1993). What is coefficient alpha? An examination of theory and applications. *Journal of Applied Psychology,* 78(1), 98–104.

De Ávila, E. (1990). *Assessment of language minority students: Political, technical, practical and moral imperatives.* Proceedings of the First Research Symposium on Limited English Proficient Student Issues.

Del Vecchio, A., & Guerrero, M. (1995). *Handbook of English language proficiency tests.* Retrieved from www.ncela.gwu.edu/pubs/eacwest/elptests.htm.

Dolan, R.P., Murray, E.A., & Strangman, N. (2006). *Mathematics instruction and assessment for middle school students in the margins: Students with learning disabilities, students with mild mental retardation, and students who are English language learners.* A literature review prepared for the Rhode Island Enhanced Assessment Grant.

Duncan, T.G., Parent, L., Chen, W., Ferrara, S., Johnson, E., Oppler, S., & Shieh, Y. (2005). Study of a dual-language test booklet in eighth-grade mathematics. *Applied Measurement in Education,* 18(2), 129–161.

Farr, B.P., & Trumbull, E. (1997). Assessment alternatives for diverse classrooms. Norwood, MA: Christopher-Gordon Publishers, Inc.

Gándara, P., & Rumberger, R., Maxwell-Jolly, J., & Callahan, R. (2003). English learners in California schools: Unequal resources, unequal outcomes. *Education Policy Analysis Archives,* 11(36). Retrieved June 14, 2006, from http://epaa.asu.edu/epaa/v11n36/.

GAO (2006). No Child Left Behind Act: Assistance from education could help states better measure progress of students with limited English proficiency. Washington, DC: United States Government Accountability Office.

Grissom, J.B. (2004). Reclassification of English language learners. *Education Policy Analysis Archives,* 12(36). Retrieved September 3, 2004, from http://epaa.asu.edu/epaa/v12n36/.

Hakuta, K., Butler, Y.G., & Witt, D. (2000). *How long does it take English learners to attain proficiency?* Santa Barbara, CA: University of California Linguistic Minority Research Institute.

Haladyna, T.M., & Downing, S.M. (2004). Construct-irrelevant variance in high-stakes testing. *Educational Measurement: Issues and Practice,* 23(1), 17–27.

Hambleton, R.K. (1994). Guidelines for adapting educational and psychological tests: A progress report. *European Journal of Psychological Assessment,* 10(3), 229–244.

Hofstetter, C. (2003). Contextual and mathematics accommodation test effects for English-language learners. *Applied Measurement in Education,* 16(2), 159–188.

Katz, A., Low, P., Stack, J., & Tsang, S.-L. (2004). *A Study of content area assessment for English language learners.* Prepared for the Office of English Language Acquisition and Academic Achievement for English Language Learners, U.S. Department of Education. Oakland, CA: ARC Associates.

Kindler, A.L. (2002). *Survey of the states' limited English proficient students & available educational programs and services, 2000–2001 Summary Report.* Washington, DC: National Clearinghouse for English Language Acquisition and Language Instruction Educational Programs.

Langdon, H.W. (2008). *Assessment & intervention for communication disorders in culturally & linguistically diverse populations.* Clifton Park, NY: Thomson Delmar Learning.

Langer, J.A., Bartolome, L., Vasquez, O., & Lucas, T. (1990). Meaning construction in school literacy tasks: A study of bilingual students. *American Educational Research Journal,* 70, 350–354.

Linn, R.L., & Gronlund, N.E. (1995). *Measuring and assessment in teaching* (7th ed.). Englewood Cliffs, NJ: Prentice-Hall, Inc.

Linquanti, R. (2001). *The redesignation dilemma: Challenges and choices in fostering meaningful accountability for English learners.* Policy Report 2001–1. Santa Barbara, CA: University of California Linguistic Minority Research Institute.

Lipka, J., & Adams, E. (2004). Culturally based math education as a way to improve Alaska Native students' math performance. The Appalachian Collaborative Center for Learning, Assessment and Instruction in Mathematics Series. Retrieved January 20, 2004, from http://acclaim.coe.ohiou.edu/rc/rc_sub/pub/3_wp/list.asp.

Messick, S. (1994). The interplay of evidence and consequences in the validation of performance assessments. *Educational Researcher*, 23(2), 13–23.

Moore, K.A., & Redd, Z. (2002). *Children in poverty: Trends, consequences, and policy options* (Research Brief No. 2002–54). Washington, DC: Child Trends, Inc.

National Research Council (2000). *Testing English-language learners in U.S. schools: Report and workshop summary.* Committee on Educational Excellence and Testing Equity. Kenji Hakuta and Alexandra Beatty, Editors. Board on Testing and Assessment, Center for Education. Washington, DC: National Academy Press.

No Child Left Behind Act of 2001, Pub. L. No. 107–110, 115 Stat. 1425 (2002).

Oller, J. (1992). Language testing research: Lessons applied to LEP students and programs. In *Proceedings of the second national research symposium on limited English proficient student issues: Focus on evaluation and measurement*, pp. 43–123. Volume 1. Washington, DC: U.S. Department of Education.

Reese, L., Garnier, H., Gallimore, R., & Goldberg, C. (2000). Longitudinal analysis of the antecedents of emergent Spanish literacy and middle-school English reading achievement of Spanish-speaking students. *American Educational Research Journal*, 37(3), 633–662.

Rivera, C., & Collum, E. (2006). *State assessment policy and practice for English language learners: A national perspective.* Washington, DC: Routledge.

Rumberger, R., & Gándara, P. (2004). Seeking equity in the education of California's English learners. *Teachers College Record*, 106, 2031–2055.

Solano-Flores, G. (2008). Who is given tests in what language by whom, when, and where? The need for probabilities views of language in the testing of English language learners. *Educational Researcher*, 37(4), 189–199.

Solano-Flores, G., & Li, M. (2006). The use of generalizability (G) theory in the testing of linguistic minorities. *Educational Measurement: Issues and Practice*, 25(1), 13–22.

Solano-Flores, G., & Li, M. (2009). Language variation and score variation in the testing of English language learners, native Spanish Speakers. *Educational Assessment*, 14, 1–15.

Solano-Flores, G., & Nelson-Barber, S. (2001). On the cultural validity of science assessments. *Journal of Research in Science Teaching*, 38(5), 553–573.

Solano-Flores, G., & Trumbull, E. (2003). Examining language in context: The need for new research and practice paradigms in the testing of English-language learners. *Educational Researcher*, 32(2), 3–13.

U.S. Census Bureau (2002). *State & county quickfacts: U.S.A.* Retrieved from http://quickfacts.census.gov.

Valdés, G., & Figueroa, R. (1994). *Bilingualism and testing: A special case of bias.* Norwood, NJ: Ablex Publishing Company.

Yamaguchi, K. (1991). *Event history analysis.* Applied Social Science Research Methods Series, 28. Newbury Park, CA: Sage Publications.

Zehler, A.M., Hopstock, P.J., Fleischman, H.L., & Greniuk, C. (1994). *An examination of assessment of limited English proficient students,* Arlington, VA: Development Associates, Special Issues Analysis Center.

# Chapter 4

# Cognition, Culture, Language, and Assessment

## How to Select Culturally Valid Assessments in the Classroom

*María del Rosario Basterra*

---

**Chapter Overview**

In order to be effective across the broad range of students in U.S. classrooms today, teachers must know how to accurately and equitably assess learning. To do so, they need to be aware of the role that cognition, language, and culture play in children's perception and understanding of the world and how they can use that knowledge to ensure culturally valid assessment practices in their classrooms. This chapter is divided into two main sections. The first section provides an overview of key research findings on the overall impact of culture and language on cognition and assessment. The second section discusses ways to promote equitable assessment in the classroom, taking into consideration the impact of students' cultural and linguistic backgrounds.

For the sake of simplicity, the terms "test item" and "assessment task" are used interchangeably.

---

## The Relationship Between Culture and Cognition

There is little doubt that, throughout the world, all children follow the same general pattern of cognitive development. However, it is important to acknowledge the cross-cultural variability among and within each culture. Most of the cultures research on child development has focused on Western patterns of human thought and only in children from certain socio-economic and cultural backgrounds. For example, in the U.S., most of the research is based on a standard population of children who are white, middle class, and urban. As Patricia Greenfield (2000) indicates, there is a need for a developmental framework that provides insight into the relationship between social and cognitive development and addresses cross-cultural variability.

According to Resnick (1991), every cognitive act must be viewed as a specific response to specific social and physical circumstances. In order to understand children's development, we need to be aware of the context in which children construct and acquire knowledge. Children grow and develop in specific cultural settings. Different ways of understanding and relating to objects and people influence the development of their cognition. Castagno and McKinley (2008) emphasize that "one's epistemology is fundamental to how he or she sees the world, understands knowledge, and lives and negotiates everyday experiences" (p. 952). A key question that needs to be addressed is, to what degree does culture influence cognition? What follows is a brief summary of research that highlights recent findings in selected areas.

The following example in the area of categorization illustrates how cross-cultural differences impact the way this concept is acquired and represented. Adopting a cross-linguistic, cross-cultural developmental perspective, Waxman, Medin, and Ross (2007) focused on the relationship between core knowledge, naming, and acquisition of the concept "alive," or "living things." Their research questions were: (1) What are the capacities young children bring to the tasks of acquisition of the concept? (2) How does the environment shape the process of acquisition? The concept of living things includes members of both plant and animal kingdoms. Developmental research reveals that this concept is difficult to master (Angorro, Waxman, & Medin, 2005; Hatano & Siegler, 1993; Piaget, 1954). Piaget observes that young children tend to believe that inanimate objects are alive because they appear to move on their own.

In order to understand how children from different cultural and language backgrounds address this concept, Waxman et al. (2007) gave two tasks to children of ages 4 to 10 from Indonesia, Mexico (Mayan), and the United States. In the first task, they showed them a picture of a person and asked them: "Could you call this an animal?" As in a previous study (Angorro et al., 2005), Indonesian and Tzotzil-speaking Mayan children responded categorically in the negative, suggesting that for them, people and animals are mutually exclusive categories. In contrast, 50% of English-speaking children responded in the positive, indicating that human beings are also animals, and 50% responded in the negative. On a separate task, children were asked to sort 17 cards, each depicting a living or non-living entity. Children were asked to sort the cards in different ways. Specifically, they were asked to sort on the basis of whether the entities: (1) were alive, (2) could die, or (3) could grow. The three possible sorting anticipated were: only animals, living things including animals and plants, and natural kinds (animals, plants, and other natural things that were not artifacts).

Important commonalities were found in the categorization, naming, and reasoning tasks of the three different communities of children. Regardless of their cultural background, all children were able to sort cards by LIVING THINGS, placing humans, animals, and plants in the same category. However, when they sorted on the basis of the predicate ALIVE, striking differences were found. While English and Indonesian children had similar patterns of development, with minor differences in reference as to how they used the term ALIVE to sort, Mayan children endorsed a broader interpretation of ALIVE to include natural phenomena such as the sun, clouds, and water. These natural kinds are considered inanimate in the English speaking and Indonesian communities. The sorting results illustrate the intimate connection between culture and conceptual organization in the developmental patterns. In the Mayan culture, it is not uncommon to give these entities (sun, clouds, etc.) a living power. Very likely, the developmental differences reflect the naming practices and the belief systems in each representative community.

Research has shown evidence of both similarities and differences in patterns of cognitive organization. For example, Saalbach and Imai (2007) conducted a study to determine whether Westerners organize object concepts around taxonomic relations, while Easterners organize them around thematic relations, as Nisbett (2003) has suggested. Saalbach and Imai tested the relative importance of three types of relations—taxonomic, thematic, and classifier—for Chinese and German speakers using a range of tasks, including categorization, similarity judgment, property inductions, and fast-speed word–picture matching. No significant differences were observed in the ways in which Chinese and German speakers organize everyday object concepts. However, minor differences were observed related to linguistic and cultural factors. For example, they found that Chinese preschoolers used shape similarity as a basis for non-verbal categorization at a higher rate than German preschoolers.

Greenfield (2000) indicates that we need to look very closely at the specific ways that children develop their cognitive abilities in different cultures. Also, she stresses the need for ensuring that the methods used to assess performance on cognitive tasks are in accord with the characteristics of the children's cultures. These issues are clearly highlighted in research conducted by Cole (1996, 2006), who argues that the common belief that all children reach a certain level of cognitive development at roughly equal ages across cultures is not necessarily true. When standardized Piagetian conservation tasks are given to children in different societies, widely varying results are obtained. This finding has led to two different, but not necessarily exclusionary, hypotheses. First, it is likely that some cultures promote more cognitive development than others; second, without certain kinds of cultural experiences (for example, formal schooling), more abstract ways of thinking, such as that involved in conservation, might not be attainable (Cole, 2006). However, the same research also implicates cultural differences in the interpretation of the children's performance on the tasks, not necessarily in logical development.

Two examples illustrate how performance on the same task is shaped by cultural factors. The first example involves the standard conservation procedure, as developed in Geneva, in which the participant is presented with two beakers of equal circumference and height filled with equal amounts of water. The water from one beaker is then poured into another taller beaker with a smaller circumference, and then the person is asked which of the two beakers contains more water. In the study described by Cole (1996), children and young adults from non-literate societies of a given age were significantly more likely than children from other societies to decide that the taller, thinner beaker contained more water. However, an experiment on the effects of modifying testing procedures to match local cultural knowledge revealed a different pattern of results. In the revised procedure, the participants were asked to solve the conservation task and then to explain their answers to the experimenter according to language usage in their communities. While these participants continued to wrongly indicate that the narrower beaker had "more" water, when asked to provide an explanation, they explained that although the level of the water was "more," the quantity was the same (Cole, 2006). In other words, the participants were aware that the quantity was the same, which is the correct answer. However, the format and the language of the testing procedure did not allow them to give their answers in a way in which they would be properly interpreted.

The second example involves procedures developed in Cambridge, Massachusetts, as an extension of Piaget's work in Geneva. Greenfield (1997) administered conservation of quantity tasks to unschooled Wolof children in Senegal. The children were instructed to transfer water from a short beaker to a long, thin one; and then, according to the Cambridge interview protocol, they were asked whether the quantity of water in the thin beaker was the same, more, or less in their native language. Questions such as: "Why do you *think* it is the same (or more, or less) amount of water?" or "Why do you *say* it is the same (or more, or less) amount of water?" were not responded to by the children. They were only able to respond when the question was changed to: "Why *is* the water the same (or more, or less)?" Greenfield explained that the reason the children did not answer the protocol questions was that the Wolof culture has an epistemology of mental realism. The children were not making a distinction between the nature of reality and their knowledge of it. Providing explanations of why they thought something happened was not relevant for them. It was the actual action that took place that was meaningful to them, not what they thought about it.

If the protocol had not been changed to further explore the children's lack of response, a wrong assumption about their knowledge would have prevailed. As Solano-Flores and Nelson-Barber (2001) indicate, because culture and society shape mental functioning in many ways, individuals have predisposed notions of how to respond to questions and solve problems. Therefore, it is important to design and use assessments that take in consideration the socio-cultural context of the people being assessed.

## The Relationship Between Language and Cognition

Language development in children is characterized by astonishing complexity and speed. By two years of age, children have learned many words and can put them together to form simple sentences. By age four, children have mastered a large portion of the grammatical components of their native language. There is, of course, variation in children's language development by the age they enter school; and many of the more complex syntactic forms as well as high-level vocabulary and phonological skills associated with reading and writing are yet to be learned over a period of years (Bowey & Tunmer, 1984; Flood & Menyuk, 1983; Owens, 2001; Snow, 1990). The sociocultural contexts of children's language learning have considerable impact on the nature of the language they have mastered by age four or five, particularly upon the ways children use language to interact with others, to show what they know, or to express themselves (cf., Heath, 1983; Schieffelin & Ochs, 1986).

The question of how language is developed has resulted in a longstanding controversy. Some scholars, like Chomsky (2002), hold the view that humans are equipped with innate language structures distinct from other cognitive capacities. Other scholars assert that language is developed through the interaction between the organism and its cultural environment through general cognitive mechanisms (Bates, Elman, Johnson, Karmiloff-Smith, Parisi, & Plunkett, 1998; Tomasello, 2008). The question about the influence of language on cognition has also been the center of many discussions among psychologists, linguists, and anthropologists. Although there is not one clear undisputed answer, there seems to be some agreement on the ways that cognition and language are influenced by one another.

There is consensus on the fact that language, cognition, and culture do not act independently of biological processes during the early years of development (Cole & Cacigas, 2010). It is also widely accepted that, in the early stages of development, children link linguistic forms directly to concepts and categories that they have already established in the course of their non-linguistic cognitive development (Bowerman, 2000). However, continuous disagreement continues to permeate theory and research on specific areas of language acquisition. One of these areas is semantic (meaning) development. The key question regarding semantic development is how children end up mastering the semantic patterns of their own language. Significant variation in semantic structuring has been documented for a variety of conceptual domains, including the notion of causality (Bowerman, 2000).

Choi and Bowerman (1991) found linguistic differences in children's ways of expressing spatial concepts at a very young age. Comparing early use of spatial words at ages one and three years in children speaking English, Korean, and Tzotzil, a Mayan language, they found that, from the earliest production of language, spatial words are associated with language-specific categories of events. It appears that, while there might be a universal sequence of word production of words related to spatial concepts, children use them to convey slightly different meanings in alignment with their native languages. One example is how children expressed the motion of falling. While English-speaking children used the terms "fall" or "fall down" for a broad range of uncontrolled motions downward, Korean-speaking children distinguished between falls from a higher to a lower place (e.g., a pencil falls from a table: *ttlelecita*) and falls onto the same surface (e.g., a child falls on the floor, a tower is knocked over: *nemecita*).

Bowerman (1996) and Choi (1997) conducted research to investigate the early development of special semantic categories in children who grow in cultures with different languages. Their study showed that children as young as two to two years and five months of age who are learning different languages classify spatial relationships differently for purposes of talking about them. The differences found were closely related to how the concept of space is used in different languages. Children who are in the process of developing English, Dutch, and Korean use different verbal classifications for actions like putting a block into a pan, putting a small book into a fitted case, putting a Lego piece on a stack of Legos, putting a ring on a finger, putting a cup on a table, putting a hat on someone's head, and putting a towel on a towel rack. While English speaking children use the words "in" and "on" to verbally classify all these actions, Dutch speaking children use four different terms ("in," "om," "op," and "aan") to show different concrete spatial relationships. Korean speaking children use five terms to show them. These outcomes show that, while children speaking different languages are learning spatial concepts at a similar age, they use different spatial words that represent different ways of thinking about those concepts. Language plays a critical role in how children categorize their world. Dutch speaking children, for instance, will be naturally disposed to make distinctions that English speaking children will not.

Additional research findings related to the variation in spatial terms and children's use of them are provided by de Leon (2001). She found that Tzotzil toddlers use different verbs that distinguish language-specific categories of position: "nuj" be located faced down/upside down, "kot" be located standing on all fours, "pak" be located on the ground, and "kaj" be located on a high surface.

Clearly, culture and language play a central role in cognitive development. While general patterns of cognitive and language development are found in children of all cultures, these patterns are influenced significantly by the culture and language of origin. As Nisbett and Norenzayan (2002) noted, societies differ in the cultural practices they promote by providing, through language, different sets of cognitive strategies to their young.

## Assessment and Cognition

Research conducted by Saalbach and Imai (2007) demonstrates that, depending on what task is used to tap knowledge, different patterns of response may emerge. When a child is asked to choose what object goes with another, he or she may make a different choice than when asked what object shares a property with the first or what objects share the same name as the first.

It is increasingly accepted by the measurement community that the method of assessment affects the outcome. Abstract thinking, for example, is considered a universal capacity. However, the domains of application may vary across individuals and cultures. A car mechanic may be able to use abstract thinking when fixing problems in cars. On the other hand, he/she may perform poorly when attempting to apply the same logical operations to other domains.

Another example, provided by van de Vijver (2006), highlights this situation in relation to mathematical thinking. In one experiment, a group of women were asked which of two cans of peanuts they would buy based on comparing their prices: Can A, weighing 10 oz. for 90 cents, or Can B, weighing 4 oz. for 45 cents. In another test, the same women were asked to compare the ratios 90/45 and 10/4. From a mathematical perspective, the two problems are equivalent; however, from a psychological perspective, they are perceived and solved differently. The former, concrete, version of the problem was correctly solved more frequently.

This phenomenon was also found with a group of Zinacanteco women in Mexico. These women can weave highly complex patterns. The women showed superior planning skills in a weaving task when they had to reproduce known patterns, but did not outperform non-weavers when the planning involved unfamiliar patterns. Planning skills acquired in the context of professional training did not generalize broadly across the cognitive spectrum (van de Vijver & Willemsen, 1993).

## Cognitive Development, Culture, and School Assessment

What impact do cognitive and language research findings have or should they have on school assessment? In close alignment with findings in the fields of cognitive development and overall assessment research, Solano-Flores and Nelson-Barber (2001) argue that, because socio-cultural groups create meaning from experience in culturally determined ways,

> individuals have predisposed notions on how to respond to questions, solve problems, and so forth. It follows that these predispositions influence the ways in which students interpret materials presented in tests and the ways in which they respond to test items.

Solano-Flores and Nelson-Barber (2001) indicate that the ways students make sense of science test items, for example, are influenced by the values, beliefs, experiences, communication patterns, teaching and learning styles, and epistemologies originating in their cultural background and socioeconomic conditions.

Solano-Flores and Nelson-Barber (2001) investigated how ways of thinking, communication patterns, and learning styles that permeate the cultures of students influenced the way in which they responded to standardized test items. They conducted a study with students from four different cultural groups included Chamorro and Carolinian students from the Commonwealth of the Northern Mariana Island, Yup'ik students from rural Alaska, and immigrant Latino students from rural Washington State. All students were administered one item from a set of two mathematics and two science items selected from a pool of released items of the National Assessment of Educational Progress issued in 1996. The study found that students' demonstrated competence depended on the match between the demands of a task, the context in which it is embedded, and the culturally developed skills of the learner (Solano-Flores & Nelson-Barber, 2001).

In a study conducted by Nelson-Barber, Huang, Trumbull, Johnson, and Sexton (2008), the authors show the influence of cultural beliefs on the way that students respond to standardized test items. Figure 4.1 shows a science item of the National Assessment of Educational Progress and the response of a Hawaiian eighth grader as described in the study.

---

Item:
Bacteria and laboratory animals are sometimes used by scientists as model organisms when researching cures for human diseases such as cancer. Describe one possible advantage and one possible disadvantage of using bacteria as models to help find cures for human diseases.

Response:

Advantage: *Closer to being humans*

Disadvantage: *There is no such thing as laboratory animals. All animals are our brothers and sisters and our spiritual teachers. We don't have the right to use or kill them unless it is for food.*

*Figure 4.1* Sample item and response (source: National Assessment of Educational Progress, 1996).

Very likely, the response to this item would be considered "incorrect," based on the possible "correct" responses provided by the item developers. The goal of the problem as stated in the NAEP Content Classification explanation is to engage students' "practical reasoning" by assessing their abilities to use and apply learned concepts in real-world applications. As Nelson-Barber et al. (2008) indicate, the students are prompted to respond to a "context-free" item. Therefore, they are free to imagine the setting for the item as well as to how best to respond to the question from their own perspective.

Culture permeates all aspects of assessment, including methods, choices, and attitudes towards assessment. In a comparative study of assessment in French and English infant schools, Raveaud (2004) examines two different approaches to teaching and assessment from a socio-cultural perspective, relating assessment to teachers' culturally situated practices and values. While in the English "emergent writing" approach "spelling mistakes" are considered to be a central part of the constructive learning process, in the French school system children are expected to spell words "correctly" as soon as they start writing them so that they do not memorize them with mistakes.

The study illustrates how English teachers guide students through the writing process by encouraging students to re-think their answers ("Are you sure about that?"), providing positive comments ("You were close"), and avoiding negative statements ("Good try"). French teachers, on the other hand, refer explicitly to the students' mistakes (e.g., "That is wrong," "There is a mistake").

Different approaches to actual assessments were also presented for both systems. In the English system, students were evaluated in relation to several factors and not limited to whether their work was "right" or "wrong." Factors taken into account included progress made, diligence, and neatness. In the French system, students' progress is based solely on academic attainment. While French teachers were aware of how hard their pupils were trying, the progress they were making, and where their difficulties lay, their final assessment was based on their performance.

Raveaud discusses how these assessment systems are tied not just to the different pedagogies, but to a broader national culture and values. The relevance of Raveaud's findings to this discussion is that assessment practices, while perceived as objective and accurate, are also unconsciously tied to a set of societal judgments as to what is considered "correct" or "incorrect," "appropriate," or "inappropriate." Raveaud indicates that, because English children are used to a more "nurturing" approach, they would probably have a negative reaction to a French teacher's comments. French children who are used to this system will not necessarily feel that the teacher is being harsh. A different impact was noted for immigrant children in French classrooms who were not used to this system.

In sum, there is evidence that culture and language permeate the ways in which we perceive reality, develop concepts, and create and respond to assessment tasks. Teachers need to make sure that, when they design, select, and use assessments, they provide students with the opportunity to demonstrate what they really know in culturally responsive and valid ways.

## Promoting Culturally Valid Assessment in the Classroom

### Cultural Competence

"Cultural competence" entails recognizing the differences among students and families from different cultural groups, responding to those differences positively, and being able to interact effectively in a range of cultural environments (Lindsey, Robins, & Terrell, 2003). Research indicates that, in order to promote high academic standards for all students, teachers must use an approach to mediate academic content with students' cultural experience to make such content accessible, meaningful, and relevant (Lee & Fradd, 1998; Ladson-Billings, 1995). Ladson-Billings (2001) states that cultural competence is present in classrooms where the teacher: (1) understands culture and its role in education; (2) takes responsibility for learning about students' culture and community; (3) uses students' cultures as a basis for learning; and (4) promotes the flexible integration of the students' local and global culture.

The first step in becoming culturally competent is to recognize that everyone has a culture or is a participant in a cultural community (Gutiérrez & Rogoff, 2003) and that culture plays a role in defining who we are, how we respond to each other, and how we learn. In the first section of this chapter we discussed how culture shapes cognition and language and how students from different backgrounds respond to assessment. Cultural competency encompasses being able to understand and appreciate how different cultures approach learning and how individual students interpret, react to classroom settings, instruction, and assessment. A culturally competent teacher is aware of his/her own culture as well as that of his or her students. Rather than imposing one way of approaching learning and assessment, he or she learns to identify students' different learning styles and uses the information to provide them with culturally responsive instruction and culturally valid assessments. The culturally competent teacher is also aware that not all members of a given culture approach learning in exactly the same way and does not stereotype or generalize his or her findings on individual students to all the students who belong to the same cultural group. These teachers are aware of their own prejudices and are constantly trying to learn more accurate information about their students' cultural backgrounds.

## What Teachers Can Do

### Selecting and Using Classroom Assessments to Promote Cultural Validity

In the previous section of this chapter we discussed the influence of culture and language on cognition. This section discusses some strategies teachers can use in the classroom to promote culturally valid assessments. What strategies can teachers use in the classroom to promote culturally valid assessments? What follows is a summary of selected strategies.

### Use Different Types of Assessment to Assess Student Knowledge

As a general rule, teachers should use a variety of assessment tools, choosing in each case the method that best captures intended knowledge and skills in their context of use. Teachers need to make sure that classroom assessments: (1) provide valid information about student learning for both teacher and student, so that they can adapt instruction and the students can set learning goals; (2) are flexible enough to accommodate differences in students' linguistic and cultural backgrounds; and (3) offer choices to students about how and when they will demonstrate what they have learned.

The value of using a wide variety of assessment techniques can never be underestimated, if these three conditions are to be met. Different learning goals might require different types of assessment, and the type of assessment interacts in complex ways with the very nature of what is being assessed. For example, being able to retell a story after reading might be fundamentally different learning from being able to answer questions about the story (Gredler & Johnson, 2004). Thus, even for the same learning objective, there are important reasons to assess learning in more than one way.

Also, it is important to select assessments based on the cultural preferences, characteristics, needs, and strengths of your students. For example, some common formats, such as multiple-choice and true/false, may be less preferred by American Indian/Alaska Native students because they force a single answer rather than reflection and respect for more than one perspective (Macias, 1989; Nelson-Barber & Trumbull, 2007). Individual classroom questioning in the class by teachers might inhibit American Indian students (Swisher & Deyle, 1992), Alaska Native students (Eriks-Brophy & Crago, 1993), and Native Hawaiian students (Au & Kawakami, 1994), who may have a preference for more collective approaches. English language learners (ELLs) might respond better to assessments that do not rely heavily on English language proficiency or on knowledge of specialized or sophisticated vocabulary that has not been taught or is not necessary.

Drawing or building models to represent complex relationships may allow students who are still learning English to demonstrate their understanding of concepts (Lee & Fradd, 1998). Of course, academic language proficiency is intimately intertwined with subject matter knowledge, so there is a tension between making assessments accessible to ELLs and using appropriate academic language on assessments (cf., Wolf et al., 2008).

Students should be allowed to demonstrate their competence using the particular conditions that show them to their best advantage (at least as one of the ways in which they are assessed) (Shepard, 2000). This could include selecting an oral presentation instead of a written exam for students who perform better orally or including writing topics that are familiar to the students. At the same time, students should not always rely on the format that is most comfortable or easiest to handle. Effective instruction should focus on both areas of weakness and strength and should have increased and robust knowledge as a goal. For example, ELLs should have the opportunity to demonstrate their mathematical knowledge without the confounding effects of language proficiency, and at the same time, should be working to improve their mathematical communication (Shepard, 2000).

### Conduct Classroom Observations

Observing student attitudes and performance during instruction and assessment is key to knowing the type of assessment that yields best results in depicting student knowledge. Gathering information about cultural preferences, individual styles, degree of understanding, and comfort level with different type of assessments can help teachers determine what assessments to use and how to best use them. All this information is very important to identify, document, and later use for improving culturally responsive instruction and culturally valid assessments.

The first step in conducting observations is to identify a specific purpose and setting for the observation. It is very important to ensure that selected contexts and situations provide adequate opportunities to observe how students respond to different assessment tasks. Opportunities to observe student responses to specific assessment tasks will arise in a variety of settings. For example, they may occur when a student is expressing his or her thoughts about how and why an approach or a solution makes sense, responding to the thoughts of fellow students, making choices about tasks or materials to use, or participating in class discussions. Brief records documenting teacher observations, along with related copies of the student's written work, provide important tools to aid in making decisions about assessments.

In order to provide systematic observations of students, it is important to use a method that helps identify, document, and track student responses or reactions in a consistent and uniform way. How do students express and perform on different assessment tasks? For example, in being assessed on a given concept, does a given student perform better on multiple-choice items, short-answer items, essays, or oral presentations? Does this student do better using graphic diagrams or writing paragraphs; presenting individually or as part of a group? Being able to observe and document these facts allows teachers to tap into students' preferred and most effective way to express and demonstrate knowledge. Table 4.1 shows an example of a format for recording student reactions and performance in relation to different types of assessments.

Table 4.1 Example of Observation Record

| Observations of individual students | Paper-and-pencil assessments | | | | Visual representations (webs, graphs, illustrations) |
| --- | --- | --- | --- | --- | --- |
| | Multiple-choice, true–false | Fill-in-the-blank | Short-answer (sentences or paragraphs) | Essays | |
| Luisa | Stared at questions but didn't answer them | | | | |
| Ya-han | | | | | |
| Pedro | | | | | Produced elaborate graph |

Note
Adapted from: Gredler and Johnson (2004).

Teachers can use anecdotal records to complete the matrix. Anecdotal records consist of brief, written descriptions of concrete actions or events observed by the teacher. They are factual, not inferential, and require that several examples are obtained before conclusions are reached about the student (Gredler & Johnson, 2004).

These are some examples of behavior that teachers could observe and document:

*Luisa stares at the multiple-choice questions and spends a significant amount of time without answering any of them.*

*Ya-Han, an ELL student, provides an elaborate graph about the concept of living things.*

*Pedro, a student with language-based disabilities, frequently asks the meaning of words in the "fill in the blank" assessment.*

It is important to emphasize that all notes should be concrete and factual, and not interpretations or evaluations. There are multiple ways of making observation notes using charts like the one above. Among the methods teachers have found to be useful include: using sticky notes to document individual students' specific responses to different types of assessments during the assessment and then transferring those observations to a chart; or inserting observations directly into the observation chart.

Teachers may choose any method that works well for them. However, it is important that, whenever they are using anecdotal records, they follow a guideline to ensure validity and reliability in their observations. The guidelines in Table 4.2 will help in the process of collecting and documenting observations.

It is important to conduct these observations throughout the year. However, it is critical to conduct them at the beginning of the school year so that teachers can develop an awareness of students' abilities and reactions to different types of assessments. Observations are always a first step in gathering information about students. Once a teacher has observed certain patterns of behaviors or responses, the next step is to try to understand what's behind a given response. Is a given response possibly influenced by a cultural characteristic of the student's background? Is the child experiencing difficulties because he/she is not English proficient? The next step is to find out more about these particular responses.

Observations combined with other forms of assessment contribute to a comprehensive view of students' strengths, weaknesses, strategies, styles, and attitudes toward different tasks and learning. Teachers may use a portfolio system to collect observations, student work exemplifying particular standards, and various forms of assessment in a single place (Tierney, Carter, & Desai, 1991). Portfolios can be a useful tool in classrooms with diverse populations because they have the flexibility to reflect the context in which students are learning and link to the actual curriculum taught—in any language (cf., Koelsch & Estrin, 1996). For a portfolio system to be valid, attention does need to be given to the

*Table 4.2* Guidelines for Using Anecdotal Records

| Steps | Examples |
| --- | --- |
| 1. Identify a purpose for the observation in advance. | 1. Student responses to different pen-and-pencil assessment tasks. |
| 2. Select the activity or situation, focusing on one type of assessment at a time. | 2. Multiple-choice, fill-in-the-blank, short-answer, essays, visual representations. |
| 3. Develop observational notes that provide information about a specific area of interest. | 3. Focus on observing and documenting target area. |
| 4. Develop a systematic record to keep track of observations. | 4. Use observation notebook, sticky notes, observation chart. |
| 5. Obtain adequate samples of a student's responses and behaviors prior to making an interpretation. | 5. Conduct observations of student responses to different assessment tasks on different days and different concepts. |

Source: Adapted from: Gredler and Johnson (2004).

criteria for selecting portfolio entries and judging student work (Kubiszyn & Borich, 2007).

### Use Cognitive Interviews and Think-Alouds

These techniques can also be used in the classroom to gain understanding of student responses or approaches to different types of assessments. Cognitive interviews can be defined as a process by which the teacher asks a series of questions to find out students' reasoning in completing a particular task. Think-aloud is one of the cognitive interview methods that prompts students to verbalize their thoughts as they solve a problem or respond to a test item (Ericsson & Simon, 1993). The focus in the think-aloud is to gain access to student processes while completing a task or an assessment. Think-aloud is considered a powerful method because it provides information about students' thoughts while they are still in short-term memory, with relatively minor interference with task requirements (Hamilton, Nussbaum, & Snow, 1997). Both techniques allow teachers to develop a better understanding of why and how students respond to particular questions and or assessment tasks.

Cognitive interviews are commonly used to: (1) assess students' comprehension of test items: (e.g., what does the student believe the item is about? What do specific words and phrases in the questions mean to the students:); and (2) help students retrieve relevant information (e.g. what information does the student need to recall in order to answer the question? What strategies does the student use to retrieve information?).

As mentioned above, providing students with the opportunity to explain their answers allows teachers to better understand the cognitive process by which students come up with an answer. In addition, teachers can learn what testing formats present more or less cognitive demands (Hamilton et al., 1997). For example: Do students have more difficulty explaining a particular concept using a multiple-choice format or using a short-answer format? Do students use methods taught in class to respond to the questions? What other methods do they use to respond? In addition, and most important, this technique also helps teachers to explore how socio-economic, cultural, and linguistic factors might influence or determine students' responses.

As previously discussed, all children bring to the learning process their own ways of interpreting the natural and social worlds, developed within their cultural environments, traditions, and personal circumstances. Therefore, their background might deeply influence the way they interpret questions and respond to them. Using cognitive interviews and think-aloud techniques helps teachers to have a clear idea of the students' understanding of the tasks, how students process questions, and how they come up with answers to those questions.

The following example from Solano-Flores and Trumbull (2003) illustrates how socio-economic background might influence how students might interpret and respond to test items. (This item is also discussed in Trumbull & Solano-Flores, Chapter 2, this volume, from a different perspective.) Solano-Flores and Trumbull analyzed the responses of students with multiple cultural backgrounds to items from the National Assessment of Educational Progress (1996) public release. This is one of the items used in their study:

> Sam can purchase his lunch at school. Each day he wants to have juice that costs 50 cents, a sandwich that costs 90 cents and fruit that costs 35 cents. His mother has only $1.00 bills. What is the least number of $1.00 bills that his mother should give him so he will have enough money to buy lunch for five days?

The researchers interviewed a low-income student about this item.

RESEARCHER (R): Now what do you think this question is asking from you? What is it about?

STUDENT (S): It's about Sam and he wants to buy his juice, his sandwich, and his fruits.

R: mm-hm.

S: For lunch. Maybe he was hungry. But, I think his mom didn't have enough money.

R: Why?

S: Because she only had one dollar bill.

(R asks a question that S does not understand; R rephrases)

R: So, what did you need to know to be able to answer this problem?

S: I had to know, um, do, um, I had to do the math problems, like, how much money needed, um, check how many money he needed for five days and how much, uh, juice and sandwich costs and his mother only, his mother only had one dollar bill and, and that's all.

Given his low socio-economic status, this student may have been more concerned about the "fact" (his interpretation) that the mother only had $1.00 (a situation that he was probably familiar with) than the rest of the information provided and the specific response requested in the item. This interpretation of the item made the student unable to respond to the item correctly. If the researchers had not interviewed the student about his understanding of the problem, they would not have been able to have insight on how the way the item was written influenced the student's interpretation and response.

### Check Prior Knowledge and Experience

Classroom practices should include assessment of students' relevant knowledge and experience to address the fact that new learning is shaped by prior knowledge and cultural background. The impact of using prior knowledge to elicit effective and culturally responsive learning has been documented (e.g., Alexander, 1996). Students become active learners and perform better on assessments that take into account their personal experience, prior knowledge, and cultural background (Au & Jordan, 1981; Nelson-Barber et al., 2008; Pressley, Wood, Woloshyb, Martin, King, & Menke, 1992).

As discussed earlier, students' socio-economic, language, and cultural backgrounds influence the way they relate to school as well as learning content and assessment. Knowing students' prior knowledge and experience can help teachers plan both instruction and assessment. Familiarity with the places and cultures in which students have been reared help teachers to integrate students' previous experiences in instruction to support their learning of new content. Knowing about students' backgrounds helps teachers to understand their preferences and learning styles, have an appropriate interpretation of their responses to test items, and, ultimately, to select valid assessment tools for use in the classroom.

The following example from *Toolkit98* by the Regional Educational Laboratories used by Kusimo, Ritter, Busick, Ferguson, Trumbull, and Solano-Flores (2000) shows how having information about a student's background can help to understand and clarify a student's answers.

Test item:

> Four birds were sitting on a fence. A farmer threw a stone that hit one of the birds. How many birds were left on the fence?

The anticipated correct answer was 3. However, it is possible that children who grew up on farms would respond differently. Farm children would know that if there was a stone thrown toward a fence, no matter how many birds were hit, *all* would fly. Based on their experience, the correct answer would be 0.

Without having information about a student's background, and using this information to review and score the responses, a teacher might penalize students for having the wrong answer although their rationale was correct.

Gredler and Johnson (2004) provide several strategies for accessing prior knowledge and experience. These include:

- Unstructured discussions: Teachers ask students about their experience with the topic. It relies on students' freely recounting their experience with a particular topic or knowledge about a concept or words.
- Free recall and word association: Teachers ask students to think of everything they can about the topic, concept, or word.
- Structured questions: Teachers develop questions on topics or concepts. They can then ask the questions orally or in writing; individually or in groups. For example, for the sub-topic "tropical forest," the questions may include: "How could you describe the tropical forest?" "What kinds of animals live in the tropical forest?" The importance of structured questions is that they can elicit information about student knowledge and thinking. Most important, they can yield information about how students perceive, relate to, and understand different topics.

The emphasis on using these strategies should be on gathering information about the student's knowledge as well as cultural background. Efforts should be made to go beyond the "correct" or "incorrect" answers in order to gain knowledge and understanding of the student's overall cultural background and style responding to test items. As Shepard (2000) recommends, it is essential that teachers become familiar with relevant experiences and discourse patterns in diverse communities.

Trumbull and Koelsch, Chapter 9, this volume, illustrate how a district assessment keyed to local standards failed to engage students, and how a revised assessment that connected the tasks to students' experiences and language proved to be successful.

### Assess Understanding of Key Terms Used in Different Subject Areas

An example provided by Luykx, Lee, Mahotiere, Lester, Hart, and Deaktor (2007) highlights how students might interpret science terms with reference to their everyday meanings or similarities to terms in their native languages rather than their specialized scientific meaning. (The issue of domain-specific registers is taken up in Trumbull & Solano-Flores, Chapter 2, this volume.)

Luykx et al. (2007) conducted a study that focused on cultural and linguistic interference in the open-ended responses of third- and fourth-grade students on paper-and-pencil science tests. They examined children's responses linked to: (1) linguistic influences in terms of phonological, orthographic, or semantic features from children's home languages; (2) cultural influences in terms of specific knowledge or beliefs deriving from children's homes and communities, and implicit cultural assumptions underlying student responses; and (3) language and cultural features of children's written discourse.

The researchers found that, for example, the common use in some Spanish speaking countries of the word *gaseosa* ("gaseous") refers to soft drinks (a liquid) and was a cause of confusion with the term "gas" in science. They also found that among Spanish speaking children, there was a confusion with the abbreviations F (Fahrenheit) and C (Celsius) with the Spanish abbreviations for frio = cold = Fahrenheit (F) and caliente = hot = Celsius (C).

These experiences show that, when assessing prior knowledge and experience, it is very important to assess students' knowledge of key terms used in the content areas or in specific courses. In developing and using assessment tasks, teachers need to ask, Do *all* my students have a common understanding of the key terms used? Does language or do cultural factors affect the ways in which my students use and understand the different terms?

### Make Sure Students Understand the Purpose of a Specific Assessment

In order to properly assess what students know, teachers need to be sure that students understand the main purpose of a given assessment; what is being specifically assessed; and why it is important. When teachers do not clearly explain what they are specifically looking for in students' answers, students might not be able to respond in the specific way teachers expect based on many factors, including their cultural backgrounds.

Solano-Flores (2008) asserts that certain characteristics of tests and the ways in which they are administered favor communication styles that are not necessarily universal. For example, using rubrics that highly value long written responses to open-ended questions may negatively affect the scores of children from cultural groups in which giving long responses to questions asked by adults is perceived as impolite (Heath, 1983).

Teachers' unspoken expectations in assessments might not be understood by students from cultural groups who may have different responses. Trumbull and Solano-Flores, Chapter 2 this volume, provide examples of how teachers' lack of explanation of their expectations can impact students understanding of tasks. It is important to help students bridge between the communication patterns in their home/culture and the expectations in the classroom. But the differences between home and school communication expectations may not be evident to students (Gee, 1996). We need to provide students with a clear idea of what the learning target is and what specific communication patterns or types of responses are expected in the assessments used.

Kopriva (2000) recommends that, in order to help students have clear expectations regarding assessment questions, teachers should do the following:

1. Clearly state student responses options. For instance, teachers should indicate and provide examples of acceptable types of responses (written responses, pictures, diagrams, charts, etc.).
2. Let students know how their answers will be evaluated. The evaluation criteria should be clear to the students through directions or in rubrics provided and discussed with the students prior to the assessment.

The best results are achieved when students are more involved in understanding and providing input about the assessments (Kusimo et al., 2000). Helping students understand expectations allows them to recognize how to improve their own performance. Clarifying what is expected helps students determine how to integrate and select components of their own cultural background to respond appropriately.

### Contextualize Assessment Tasks

In order to ensure culturally valid assessment, it is important to create and use assessment formats and frame and pose questions taking into consideration the culture and background of the student. Assessments that allow drawing upon personal experience and creating one's own meaningful contexts have been shown to be a successful method for eliciting knowledge of Navajo students (e.g., Shields, 1997). Similar successful results were obtained elsewhere when the assessments chosen emphasized local cultural contexts and the evaluation relied on the cooperation of the group rather than the performance of the individual (Nelson-Barber, Trumbull, & Wenn, 2000).

As we have mentioned earlier, cultural norms may influence the way in which students interpret and solve problems (Kopriva & Sexton, 1999). An example provided by *Making Assessment Work for Everyone* (Kusimo et al. 2000) helps clarify this issue:

> Students are asked to create a fair race. Students are expected to create a racecourse in which each contestant runs the same distance. Those from cultures that do not emphasize competition may interpret the word "fair" in a different way and create shorter distances for slower runners, as if the item asked them to create a racecourse in which all contestants have equal chances of winning.
>
> (p. 146)

The example shows how a teacher can anticipate the way in which students' culturally influenced values can influence the way in which they respond to the question posed. Consistent with this notion, Nelson-Barber et al. (2008) demonstrated, in their study with American Indians, how enriching the context of items allows all students to imagine or understand why the concept could be important in his/her life, or in someone else's situation; make a link between the concept that he or she was likely to be exposed to through reading, watching, or storytelling in class or at home; and actively think about, research, explore, or interact with the concept.

### Teach and Prepare Students as to How to Best Respond to Different Types of Assessments

While providing students from diverse backgrounds with culturally valid assessments, it is also important to prepare those students to be able to respond to different types of assessments. Teachers can help students bridge their cultural and school background by offering them options and teaching them how to respond to specific formats and types of questioning. As Hamilton et al. (1997) indicate, if students do not know that they are expected to respond in a certain way and using specific skills, the assessment may not yield a valid picture of their capabilities.

One of the main goals of learning is that students are able to have a deep understanding of concepts and to generalize and transfer knowledge to new situations. True understanding is flexible, connected, and generalizable (Shepard, 2000). Learning is more likely to be transferred if students have the opportunity to practice and apply their knowledge in different settings and ways (Bransford, 1979). Teachers need to help students to generalize and transfer their knowledge from one situation to another in a culturally responsive way. This applies both to instruction and to assessment. As Okhee Lee (2003) indicates, learning and achievement occur when students successfully participate in Western, mainstream approaches to science or other subjects, while also valuing alternative ways of knowing in their everyday worlds. This balanced orientation emphasizes academic achievement and cultural identity.

## Conclusion

Providing students from diverse backgrounds with equitable and valid assessments is a challenge that needs to be addressed in order to ensure that ALL students have an opportunity to succeed. There is no question that culture influences and impacts cognition and, therefore, the ways that students respond to assessment tasks. As the population in the nation's schools becomes more linguistically and culturally diverse, it is essential to promote culturally valid assessments in the classrooms. This chapter attempts to contribute to a better understanding on the importance of exploring learning and assessment from a developmental and socio-cultural perspective, and using research findings to promote equity and valid assessments in the classrooms. The chapter first provided a brief discussion and summary of the impact of culture and language in cognition resulting in the development of ways of knowing and understanding from a cross-cultural perspective. Second, based on these research findings, it emphasized the importance of conducting equitable and culturally valid assessments in the classroom. Finally, the chapter presented teachers with selected strategies to assess students from diverse cultural and linguistic backgrounds.

## References

Alexander, P. (1996). Special Issue: The role of knowledge in learning and instruction. *Educational Psychologist*, 31, 89–145.

Angorro, F.K., Waxman, S.R., & Medin, D.L. (2005). The effects of naming practices on children's understanding of living things. In B. Bara, L. Barsalou, & M. Bucciarelli (eds.) *Proceedings of the twenty-seventh annual meeting of the Cognitive Science Society*, 139–144. Mahwah, NJ: Lawrence Erlbaum Associates.

Au, K., & Jordan, C. (1981). Teaching reading to Hawaiian children: Finding a culturally appropriate solution. In H. Trueba, G.P. Guthrie, & K.H. Au (Eds.), *Culture in the bilingual classroom: Studies in classroom ethnography* (pp. 139–152). Rowley, MA: Newbury House.

Au, K.H., & Kawakami, A.J. (1994). Cultural congruence in instruction. In E.R. Hollins, J.E. King, & W.G. Hayman (Eds.), *Teaching diverse populations* (pp. 5–23). Albany, NY: State University of New York Press.

Bates, E., Elman, J., Johnson, M., Karmiloff-Smith, A., Parisi, D., & Plunkett, K. (1998). Innateness and emergentism. *A Companion to Cognitive* Science (pp. 590–601). Oxford: Basil Blackwell.

Bowerman, M. (1996). Learning how to structure space for language: A crosslinguistic perspective. In P. Bloom, M. Peterson, L. Nadel, & M. Garrett (Eds.), *Language and space* (pp. 385–436). Cambridge, MA: MIT Press.

Bowerman, M. (2000). Where do children's word meanings come from? Rethinking the role of cognition in early semantic development. In L. Nucci, G. Saxe, & E. Turiel (Eds.), *Culture, thought, and development* (pp. 199–230). Mahwah, NJ: Lawrence Erlbaum Associates.

Bowey, J.A., & Tunmer, W.E. (1984). Word awareness in children. In W.E. Tunmer (Ed.), *Metalinguistic awareness in children: Theory, research and implications* (pp. 73–92). New York, NY: Springer.

Bransford, J. (1979). *Human cognition: Learning, understanding and remembering.* Belmont, CA: Wadsworth.

Castagno, A., & McKinley, B. (2008). *Review of Educational Research,* December, 78(4), 941–993.

Choi, S. (1997). Language-specific input and early semantic development: Evidence from children learning Korean. In D.I. Slobin (Ed.), *The crosslinguistic study of language acquisition,* vol. 5. Expanding the Contexts (pp. 41–133). Mahwah, NJ: Lawrence Erlbaum Associates.

Choi, S., & Bowerman, M. (1991). Learning to express motion events in English and Korean: The influence of language-specific lexicalization patterns. *Cognition,* 41, 83–121.

Chomsky, N. (2002). *On nature and language.* Cambridge: Cambridge University Press.

Cole, M. (1996). *Cultural psychology: A once and future discipline.* Cambridge, MA: Harvard University Press.

Cole, M. (2006). *Culture and cognitive development.* New York, NY: John Wiley & Sons, Ltd.

Cole, M., & Cacigas, X. (2010). Cognition. In M. Bornstein (Ed.), *Handbook of Cultural Developmental Science.* New York, NY: Psychology Press.

De Leon, L. (2001). Finding the richest path: Language cognition in the acquisition of verticality in Tzotzil (Mayan). In M. Bowerman & S. Levinson (Eds.), *Language acquisition and conceptual development.* Cambridge: Cambridge University Press.

Ericsson, K., & Simon, H. (1993). *Protocol analysis: Verbal reports as data* (Revised edition). Cambridge, MA: MIT Press.

Eriks-Brophy, A., & Crago, M. (1993). *Transforming classroom discourse: Forms of evaluation in Inuit IR and Ire routines.* Paper presented at the American Education Research Association, Atlanta, Georgia, April 12–16.

Flood, J., & Menyuk, P. (1983). The development of metalinguistic awareness and its relation to reading achievement. *Journal of Applied Developmental Psychology,* 4, 65–80.

Gee, J.P. (1996). Vygotsky and current debates in education: Some dilemmas as afterthoughts to *Discourse, learning, and schooling.* In D. Hicks (Ed.), *Discourse, learning, and schooling* (pp. 269–282). New York, NY: Cambridge University Press.

Gredler, M., & Johnson, R. (2004). *Assessment in the literacy classroom.* Boston, MA: Pearson Education, Inc.

Greenfield, P. (1997). Culture as process: Empirical methods for cultural psychology. In

J.W. Berry, Y. Poortinga, & J. Pandey (Eds.), *Handbook of cross-cultural psychology* (2nd Edition), Vol. 1: Theory and Method (pp. 301–346). Needham Heights, MA: Allyn & Bacon.

Greenfield, P. (2000). Culture and universals: Integrating social and cognitive development. In L. Nucci, G. Saxe, & E. Turiel (Eds.), *Culture, thought and development.* Mahwah, NJ: Lawrence Erlbaum Associates.

Gutiérrez, K.D., & Rogoff, B. (2003). Cultural ways of learning: Individual traits or repertoires of practice. *Educational Researcher,* 22(5), 19–25.

Hamilton, L., Nussbaum, M., & Snow, R. (1997). Interview procedures for validating science assessments. *Applied Measurement in Education,* 10(2), 181–200.

Hatano, G., & Siegler, R.S. (1993). The development of biological knowledge: A multinational study. *Cognitive Development,* 8(1), 47–62.

Heath, S. (1983). *Ways with words: Language, life and work in communities and classrooms.* Cambridge: Cambridge University Press.

Koelsch, N., & Estrin, E.T. (1996). Cross-cultural portfolios. In R.G. Calfee & P. Perfumo (Eds.), *Writing portfolios in the classroom* (pp. 261–284). Mahwah, NJ: Lawrence Erlbaum Associates.

Kopriva, R. (2000). *Ensuring accuracy in testing for English language learners.* Washington, DC: Council of Chief State School Officers.

Kopriva, R., & Sexton, U. (1999). *Guide to scoring LEP students to open-ended science items.* Washington, DC: Council of Chief State School Officers.

Kubiszyn, T., & Borich, G. (2007). *Educational testing and measurement: Classroom applications and practices.* New York, NY: John Wiley & Sons.

Kusimo, P., Ritter, M., Busick, K., Ferguson, C., Trumbull, E., & Solano-Flores, G. (2000). *Making assessment work for everyone: How to build on student strengths.* Assessment Laboratory Network Project. Southwest Educational Development Laboratory (SEDL). Austin, Texas.

Ladson-Billings, G. (1995). Toward a theory of culturally relevant pedagogy. *American Educational Research Journal,* 32(3), 465–491.

Ladson-Billings, G. (2001). *Crossing over to Canaan: The journey of new teachers in diverse classrooms.* San Francisco, CA: Jossey-Bass, Inc.

Lee, O. (2003). Equity for linguistically and culturally diverse students in science education: A research agenda. *Teachers College Record,* 105(3), 465–489.

Lee, O., & Fradd, S. (1998). Science for all, including students from non-English language backgrounds. *Educational Researcher,* 27(4), 12–21.

Lindsey, R., Robins, K., & Terrell, R. (2003). *Cultural proficiency: A manual for school leaders.* Thousand Oaks, CA: Corwin Press, Inc.

Luykx A., Lee, O., Mahotiere, M., Lester, B., Hart, J., & Deaktor, R. (2007). Cultural and home language influences on children's response to science assessments. *Teachers College Record,* 109(4), 897–926.

Macias, C. (1989). The role of Indigenous learning strategies. *Journal of American Indian Education,* Special Issue, pp. 43–52.

National Assessment of Educational Progress (1996). *Mathematics items public release.* Washington, DC: Author.

Nelson-Barber, S., Huang, Ch., Trumbull, E., Johnson, Z., & Sexton, U. (2008). *Elicitry test design: A novel approach to understanding the relationship between test items features and student performance on large-scale assessments.* Paper presented at the annual meeting of the American Educational Research Association, New York, NY, March.

Nelson-Barber, S., & Trumbull, E. (2007). Making assessment practices valid for Indigenous American students. *Journal of American Indian Education,* 46(3).

Nelson-Barber, S., Trumbull, E., & Wen, R. (2000). *The Coconut Wireless Project: Sharing culturally responsive pedagogy through the World Wide Web*. Honolulu, HI: Pacific Resources for Education and Learning.

Nisbett, R. (2003). *The geography of thought: How Asian and Westerners think differently ... and why*. New York, NY: The Free Press.

Nisbett, R., & Norenzayan, A. (2002). Culture and cognition. In H. Pashler & D. Medin (Eds.), *Steven's handbook of experimental psychology: Memory and cognitive processes* (Vol. 2, pp. 561–597). Hoboken, NJ: John Wiley & Sons, Inc.

Owens, R. (2001). *Language development: An introduction*. Boston, MA: Allyn & Bacon.

Piaget. J. (1954). *The Construction of reality in the child* (M. Cook, Trans.). New York, NY: Basic Books.

Presslye, M., Wood, E., Woloshyb, V., Martin, V., King, A., & Menke, D. (1992). Encouraging mindful use of prior knowledge: Attempting to construct explanatory answers facilitates learning. *Educational Psychologist, 27*, 91–109.

Raveaud, M. (2004). Assessment in French and English infant schools: Assessing the work, the child or the culture? *Assessment in Education, 11*(2), 193–211.

Resnick, L. (1991). Shared cognition: Thinking as a social practice. In L. Resnick, J. Levine, & S. Teasley (Eds.), *Perspectives on socially shared cognition*. Washington, DC: American Psychological Association.

Saalbach, H., & Imai, M. (2007). Scope of linguistic influence: Does a classifier system alter object concepts? *Journal of Experimental Psychology, 136*(3), 485–501.

Schieffelin, B.B., & Ochs, E. (Eds.) (1986). *Language socialization across cultures*. Cambridge: Cambridge University Press.

Shepard, L. (2000). *The role of classroom assessment in teaching and learning*. CSE Technical Report 517. CRESST/University of Colorado at Boulder.

Shields, C.M. (1997). Learning about assessment from Native American schools: Advocacy and empowerment. *Theory into Practice, 36*, 102–109.

Snow, C. (1990). The development of definitional skills. *Journal of Child Language, 17*, 697–710.

Solano-Flores, G. (2008). Who is given tests in what language by whom, when, and where? The need for probabilistic views of language in the testing of English language learners. *Educational Researcher, 37*(4), 189–199.

Solano-Flores, G., & Nelson-Barber, S. (2001). On the cultural validity of science assessments. *Journal of Research in Science Teaching, 38*(5), 553–573.

Solano-Flores, G., & Trumbull E. (2003). Examining language in context: The need for new research and practice paradigms in the testing of English-language learners. *Educational Researcher, 32*(2), 3–13.

Swisher, K., & Deyhle, D. (1992). Adapting instruction to culture. In J. Reyhner (Ed.), *Teaching American Indian students* (pp. 81–95). Norman, OK: University of Oklahoma Press.

Tierney, R.J., Carter, M.A., & Desai, L.E. (1991). *Portfolio assessment in the reading–writing classroom*. Norwood, MA: Christopher-Gordon.

Tomasello, M. (2008). *Origins of human communication*. Cambridge, MA: MIT Press.

Valencia, S.W. (1990). A portfolio approach to classroom reading assessment: The whys, whats, and hows. *The Reading Teacher, 43*, 338–340.

Van de Vijver, F.J.R. (2006). *Cultural Differences in Abstract Thinking*. Retrieved from http://mrw.interscience.wiley.com/emrw/9780470018866/ecs/article/s00510/current/abstract.

Van de Vijver F.J.R., & Willemsen, M.E. (1993). Abstract thinking. In J. Altarriba (Ed.), *Culture and cognition* (pp. 317–342). Amsterdam: North Holland.

Waxman, S.R., Medin, D.L., & Ross, N. (2007). Folkbiological reasoning from a cross-cultural developmental perspective: Early essentialist notions are shaped by cultural beliefs. *Developmental Psychology*, 43(2), 294–308.

Wolf, M.K., Kao, J.C., Herman, J., Bachman, L.F., Bailey, A.K., Bachman, P.L., Farnsworth, T., & Chang, S.M. (2008). *Issues in assessing English language learners: Proficiency measures and accommodation uses. Literature review (Part 1 of 3)*. Los Angeles, CA: National Center for Research on Evaluation, Standards, and Student Testing. Graduate School of Education & Information Studies. University of California, Los Angeles.

Chapter 5

# Using Appropriate Assessment Processes

## How to Get Accurate Information about the Academic Knowledge and Skills of English Language Learners

*Rebecca Kopriva and Ursula Sexton*

---

**Chapter Overview**

This chapter focuses on approaches teachers can use to collect information about how students who are English language learners (ELLs) are thinking, understanding, and developing skills in mathematics, science, or other academic content areas. The chapter does not address how English language proficiency should be assessed. Rather, it addresses how English proficiency and emergent language skills should be taken into account when assessing academic content among ELLs, and the strategies and communication supports they need to have in order to demonstrate their understandings. Therefore, this chapter will discuss some key aspects of classroom assessment that may be particularly effective for this population, as well as provide an overview of best practice. Since the chapter is focused entirely on what teachers can do, there is no separate section on that topic, as is the case for other chapters in this volume.

---

The premise of this chapter is that classroom assessment is primarily about informing instruction and that it actively involves and benefits both teachers and students through the use of ongoing assessment activities that include:

- Developing promising instructional situations where inquiry into and exploration of the students' grasp of the content and concepts is embedded in learning;
- Developing effective ways of asking questions or otherwise obtaining information about the students' knowledge and skills at particular time points and, if possible, the specific reasons that hamper their learning;
- Implementing the situations and assessment opportunities in a manner that is likely to render reasonably accurate information; and
- Analyzing student responses to inform instruction and inform students about where they need to focus their efforts, what they need to think about differently, or otherwise take next steps in interacting with future learning opportunities.

Assumptions in this chapter are that students will be taught content that is at grade level (knowing that remediation may be part of the challenge) and that the state's (and perhaps also the district's) content standards will be specifying what is being taught in mathematics, science, and the other academic subject areas. These assumptions, then, put teachers of ELLs on the same page as what most other teachers are expected to teach to most of the students in their district. This parallel status can and should be used to keep communication lines open between teachers and between students from different classrooms.

## What Teachers Can Do

### What You Need to Consider Before You Start

#### Planning is Key

The process of designing an integrated and potentially successful classroom assessment system throughout the year requires a teacher's thorough analysis of the planning process and an integration of learning and assessment activities. This includes reflecting upon and planning from the beginning of the instruction unit about how to effectively develop assessment activities that produce information on how students are benefitting from instruction and how the teacher might adapt further instruction to respond to assessment results. It also includes how to evaluate the value of any existing, commercially available assessments and those included in textbooks being used in the program. All in all, effective planning is about how to bridge gaps between teaching practices, assessment practices, and teacher's adaptations based on student responses to the assessment queries.

As part of planning, through the use of grade level articulation and the guidelines in the state or district content frameworks, a teacher may take into consideration questions like the ones below, to guide the conceptual flow of a lesson or series of lessons, and to bring into focus the type of assessments and criteria that will be used. For instance:

- What was taught in the previous year, month, or week? What will be taught in the next year, month, or week?
- What concepts come before or after this concept is introduced?
- How can it be contextualized? How will I teach and assess meaningful content?

Having a clear picture of how a specific lesson or activity fits within the conceptual flow of the year-long academic curriculum entails looking more closely within each instructional unit and facilitating the effective placement of assessment activities within specific concepts. Teachers should address issues such as:

- How does a lesson or activity fit into the conceptual flow of ideas in the unit?

- What precedes it? What follows it? What knowledge do students have prior to beginning instruction?
- What should I expect to hear and see while a task is performed and a concept is addressed? Answers to this question become the criteria for scoring student responses.
- In order to verify if the task and its response format are effective as assessment tools, how can I plan to make use of student work to inform both instruction and students on their progress?

Another important part of planning is identifying the types of steps to take after the implementation of the lessons and assessment queries have been completed. Issues to address at this stage include:

- What should students know after a topic is taught?
- What have we (teacher and students) gained from the analysis of student work?
- Were the student assessment tasks and the scoring criteria adequate? (This topic is also addressed in Durán, Chapter 6, this volume.)
- Were assessment formats and approaches relevant and meaningful?
- Are my students involved in the development of assessment criteria and the feedback processes? How? When?
- What other student needs must be identified and reflected in adaptations for future instruction and assessment activities?

A discussion of some kinds of assessment tasks and queries, scoring guidelines, and what types of tasks to use to collect what types of information are outlined below. It is recommended that teachers use tips offered in this section when making planning decisions about how to integrate teaching and assessment activities within particular types of lessons.

### Plan to Teach and Assess the Full Range of Content Complexity

In many professional discussions surrounding ELLs, we hear: "Just because a child doesn't speak much English doesn't mean she is not thinking in complex ways." Nonetheless, as educators we seem to fall short in following this conversation with the necessary instructional preparation that provides opportunities in the classrooms for students to engage in and communicate complex thinking. This continues to be true when we consider the kinds of assessment opportunities we use in the classroom in order to assess actual student understanding and learning. Consequently, teachers need to seek and have tools that allow them to be the most effective facilitators of knowledge in their classroom instruction and ongoing assessment of student progress. The type and level of instructional opportunities that invite more cognitively complex learning and the types of questioning associated with the range of cognitive inquiry should be part of all lessons in all content areas. Bloom and Krathwohl's (1956) taxonomy, new Bloom's taxonomy (Anderson & Krathwohl, 2001), and the taxonomy of types of knowledge developed by Li, Ruiz-Primo, and Shavelson (2006), and shown in Table 5.1 on page 106 (with adaptations), may be helpful for that purpose.

Practices that encourage these kinds of learning occasions need to utilize a variety of participatory structures that promote delving into and exploring the complexity of problems during instruction and allow for frequent opportunities for students to engage in dialogue and self-analysis and to listen to the teacher.

## Plan for Diversity

One part of planning that is often overlooked and undervalued is a careful assessment of the strengths and challenges of individual students. The effectiveness of instruction and meaningfulness of assessment results are directly related to how well this step is carried out. Lesson and assessment planning that considers how the students will benefit from the material and the questions and assessment response criteria that guide thinking about what students mean when they respond in particular ways should prove to be more useful in sustaining learning. Such considerations include:

- How students' different cultural backgrounds affect how they interpret what is being taught (this topic is also addressed in Basterra, Chapter 4, this volume);
- The experiential knowledge associated with the lessons that the students bring into the classroom;
- The tools for delivery;
- The process and participatory structures for classroom interaction that best match students' socialization;
- Learning styles; and
- Students' input.

Educators encourage teachers to understand what prior knowledge and skills students bring to the instructional tasks in order to gain insight into the learning process. These include both knowledge and skills directly related to what is being taught and other types of information and expertise that could facilitate or hamper learning. Additional questions to consider when planning instruction and assessment alignment are:

- What do the students know about the targeted content?
- What level of language development do they have? What level of academic language do they use?
- Are there considerations that will act as barriers to their learning?
- How else might I be able to communicate content with them, and how else might they be able to communicate with me about what they know, without changing the rigor and cognitive complexity of what I want to teach and assess?

## A Note About Teacher Knowledge

A body of research emphasizes that their own expertise in a content area and a deep understanding from different perspectives of the information being taught have a substantial impact on teachers' ability to effectively and flexibly communicate with students. When teachers know the content so as to be able to establish cross-disciplinary connections, when they can map their expectations backwards and break down the cognitive demand into smaller "chunks" of information, their instruction often reflects their expertise (Ball & Bass, 2000). In contrast, when teachers are not as confident about their knowledge of the subject matter, they tend to depend solely on textbooks or materials not critically reviewed. Instruction is, then, watered down or weakened. This situation can serve as a self-assessment indicator that points to the need for additional support from mentors and professional development.

The same is true for assessment. When teachers lack expertise in assessment, they seem to more often rely on textbook-based tests and pre-packaged test items. They tend to not know what to do with their students' responses to these items, and further instruction seems detached from assessment results.

On the other hand, teachers who know the content deeply and have interest in communicating effectively with their students integrate many "mini-feedback loops" into their instructional tasks and keep on top of how students are hearing what they are trying to convey. Further, their teaching reflects their responsiveness based on what students are saying. Knowing that students communicate in varied ways, and that various levels of cognitive complexity in the targeted subject matter are often communicated differently as well, these teachers have and are able to use a large repertoire of practices when they assess their students (DiRanna et al., 2008; Basterra, Chapter 4, this volume; Lee et al., Chapter 11, this volume).

Finally, teachers who know the content deeply and have an interest in communicating effectively with their students are familiar with common misconceptions and naive and unsophisticated skills; and they have thought about optimal ways to interact with students in order to effectively facilitate future learning. As such, in addition to finding out whether a student meets certain target learning goals, these teachers have ways of finding out how their students are processing what is being taught (Darling-Hammond & Bransford, 2005) and integrate opportunities into instruction that allow students to learn from their mistakes.

## The Nuts and Bolts of an Effective Academic Classroom Assessment Program

### What Does an Effective Program Look Like?

The development of best practices in teaching most academic subjects (e.g., mathematics, science, and social studies) has been debated and shaped over the last 20 years. Most educators today believe that students learn best through first-hand experience and by being provided with ample opportunities to engage in discourse and connect new information to what they already know through social interaction. Solely listening to a teacher lecture or reading a textbook are not rich enough experiences that enable them to learn. Most educators today understand the importance of providing ample opportunities to engage in discourse and in iterative and interactive skill development to connect new information to what students already know. This applies not only to learning rote and factual knowledge, but also to the development of higher-order thinking and reasoning skills associated with various types of content (for example, see Bransford, Brown, & Cocking, 2000; Duschl, Schweingruber, & Shouse, 2007; Yager, 2005).

Recently, interest has surged in the use of learning progressions in assessment (see Shavelson, 2009). Serious efforts have been made to design test items in ways in which their features are linked to models of cognitive development for the constructs assessments are intended to measure. For example, each of the options of multiple-choice items can be designed to reflect different levels of development of knowledge and understanding of the construct being measured, which allows for proper interpretation of the cognitive correlates of student performance (see Briggs, Alonzo, Schwab, & Wilson, 2006).

This notion can be used by teachers in building lessons and assessment tools, and aligning them throughout the year. An example of the use of the notion of learning progressions in classroom assessment can be found in the FOSS science curriculum products developed by the University of California, Berkeley's Lawrence Hall of Science and in the work completed recently by the K-12 education arm of the American Association for the Advancement of Science (AAAS).

In alignment with these pedagogical advances, assessment experts encourage educators to design assessments that provide information about their students' thinking and problem-solving strategies and examine how teachers might track factual, reasoning, and processing skills in their students (e.g., Pellegrino, Chudowsky, & Glaser, 2001; Basterra, Chapter 4, this volume). Instructionally embedded items developed by teachers tend to focus on recall, rather than the application or development of ideas. Few of these items can elicit students' higher-order thinking. Figure 5.1 provides an example of how some teachers approached learning about their students' knowledge and skills at various levels of inquiry.

Sometimes, assessment tasks are developed to capture information about student learning from the students' errors as well as their successes. This diagnostic information can then be used to confirm that students appear to have learned particular pieces of knowledge and mastered certain concepts or skills. This information can also be used to inform future instruction in order to correct misconceptions that may be responsible for incorrect responses. Black, Wiliam, Stiggins, and Popham, among others, have written extensively about these kinds of classroom assessment tasks and provide many examples (e.g., see Popham, 2006; Stiggins, 2003). Ongoing classroom assessment opportunities that gauge the accomplishments and errors of individual students explicitly link feedback to student performance and provide students with strategies for improvement are called "formative assessment" (see Shepard, 2006).

The illustration below shows several organisms within an ecosystem.

1. **Use the illustration above and what you know about the food chain to complete the blanks below.**

Select one organism, and connect it to the food chain category. Briefly explain each category's function:

The _mushroom_ is a **decomposer** _that feeds off dead organisms_
   *(organism)*        *(category)*        *(function)*

The _____ is a **omnivore** _that eats plants and meat_
   *(organism)*         *(category)*        *(function)*

The _____ is a **carnivore** that _____
   *(organism)*         *(category)*        *(function)*

The _____ is a **producer** that _____
   *(organism)*         *(category)*        *(function)*

The _____ is a **herbivore** that _____
   *(organism)*         *(category)*        *(function)*

2. **Put each category of the food chain in sequential order.**

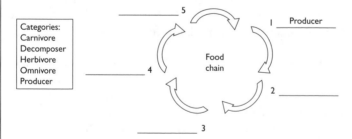

Categories:
Carnivore
Decomposer
Herbivore
Omnivore
Producer

3. **Using all of the previous information, what effect would it have in the ecosystem if one of the categories of the food chain was eliminated or destroyed? Explain in the space below using words or pictures.**

*Figure 5.1* An Example of a Multi-Step Assessment Task (source: Dual Language Concurrent Assessment Development for English Learners—Science; NSF: REC 0352148, SGER Grant).

Informal and formal formative assessment opportunities aimed at evaluating learning of the full range of concepts and skills should be integrated frequently into ongoing instruction (see Ruiz-Primo & Furtak, 2007). These assessments should be explicitly and purposefully considered and developed as part of the planning process. Teachers should plan these assessment activities based on:

- Deeply knowing the content (including pitfalls and students' common mistakes);
- Learning to anticipate what is expected of students through assessing students' prior knowledge and their communication strengths and challenges;
- Performing regular observations during and between lessons and making proper adjustments as they go; and
- Critically analyzing student work from current opportunities in order to adapt future instruction and assessment plans.

Well-designed and varied assessments of student learning can serve to reinforce effective instructional practices, as teachers begin to better understand how and when to use assessments as an integral part of the curriculum. Figuring out *what* to collect will be discussed briefly below. *How* to collect the proper data about students' knowledge and strategies is multifaceted and will be discussed in more detail. Different forms of assessment provide different kinds of information on student content knowledge, skills, and understanding. The same way as no single form of instruction provides the best way to teach all content and skills, no single form of assessment can provide all the evidence of student learning (Basterra, Chapter 4, this volume).

As is widely acknowledged, pre-packaged tests from textbooks, well-meaning curriculum companies, the Internet, and other teachers abound. In critiquing these tests or in developing your own, the focus should be on building tasks that fit your instruction and properly capture information about whether the student knows the content and the processes underlying incorrect responses. The issue is what type of task (e.g., multiple-choice items or embedded performance tasks) measures the targeted content or skills effectively.

There is great value in examining students' responses to assessment tasks with the purpose of determining how they can be improved to increase their effectiveness as formative assessment tools. In addition, asking a wide range of students about their interpretation of the tasks and the reasonings they use when they respond to them helps students become aware of their own learning, and helps teachers to improve their instruction (Bell & Cowie, 1999). In schools where teachers are encouraged and supported to work collaboratively in these activities, analyzing student work within grade levels becomes an excellent embedded professional development opportunity.

## Know What You Want to Assess

Assessment should not be an afterthought or take place as an experience isolated from the rest of the instruction (Stiggins, 2003). Thinking about how we want to evaluate students' needs should occur as a part of our instructional planning and should be integrated and aligned in purpose with what and how the students are supposed to learn. As educators, before we choose or develop any assessment task, we need to have a clear idea of the forms of knowledge we want to assess. Knowing what we want to assess comes directly from the desired student learning outcomes in the lesson plans which state what students are supposed to learn from instruction.

Because of the pervasive use of multiple-choice items in today's standardized tests, textbooks, and other materials, many of us may have been conditioned to believe that these kinds of items suffice to measure all the forms of knowledge or skills, or we may assume that published items are better than anything we could design. However, rarely will commercially available, off-the-shelf multiple-choice items fit our specific classroom assessment needs.

In deciding what we want to assess, we must focus on the knowledge and skills instruction is supposed to support. For instance, when students are engaged in science investigations, we may be interested in promoting among them the use of inquiry through social interaction. To measure these kinds of skills, we may want to learn how well students are able to organize, categorize, predict, or communicate information, how materials are handled, or how a problem is being approached and solved. Additionally, we may want students to learn specific scientific concepts used in their investigations. We may want to know about students' learning of specific content at a recall or declarative level; how students are interpreting systems of conceptual information; how well they can manipulate and interpret data within the context of the concepts; and how well they are making substantive connections within or across disciplines as they discuss, summarize, and record their findings.

It is important to remember that *all* students—not just older ones or native English speakers—should be challenged routinely with instructional and assessment activities that promote higher-order thinking skills. The examples in Figure 5.1 include measuring more complex or higher-order reasoning. In this instance, students are asked to predict what might happen to an ecosystem from their understanding of a given set of environmental conditions.

### What to Use When You Want to Assess Different Kinds of Knowledge and Skills

Assessment tasks range from traditional multiple-choice and short-answer items to essay and other constructed-response tasks that engage students in designing, conducting, and reporting the results of investigations, projects, or experiments. Formal and informal assessment may include protocols by which teachers observe students as they engage in solving problems, using arguments to build their cases or participating in discussions that involve student–student or teacher–student interactions. Performance is assessed according to certain criteria, according to scoring rubrics, which are familiar to many teachers. Assessment tasks that go beyond short answers require students to demonstrate what they know and are able to do—and how they can apply their content knowledge to new problems. Teachers may choose to use and adapt pre-packaged assessment tasks. Or, they may opt to develop their own tasks individually or collaboratively, which constitutes a valuable professional development activity.

Below is an example of a knowledge-based approach for measuring science learning (see Ruiz-Primo, 2007). The framework proposes the existence of four types of knowledge:

1. Declarative knowledge (D) includes facts, terms, and definitions that can be learned and held in memory as words, images, or sensory representations. It can also include statements such as "CO2 is carbon dioxide." Declarative knowledge can be described as "knowing that."
2. Procedural knowledge (P) entails if–then rules or sequences of steps such as in algorithms. Examples include reading data tables or designing experiments. Importantly, a central ingredient of procedural knowledge is that, with practice, individuals can convert it into automatic responses. Procedural knowledge can be described as "knowing how."
3. Schematic knowledge (Sc) typically entails the application of scientific principles or explanatory models and knowledge that guides actions, troubleshoots systems, or predicts the effect of changes. As examples of this form of knowledge, Li et al. (2006) mention "explaining why the moon generally rises about 50 minutes later each day or how a particular virus functions" (p. 292). Schematic knowledge can be described as "knowing why."
4. Strategic knowledge (St) entails the proper application of knowledge. Examples of this form of knowledge are strategies such as using skills to represent problems or deal with certain tasks unknown to the individual, general monitoring abilities or planning strategies—for example, dividing a task into sub-tasks or integrating different pieces of information. Strategic knowledge can be described as "knowing when, where, and how."

The framework, presented in Table 5.1, shows the link between type of knowledge and type of assessment task. The first and second columns show four basic types of tasks and their characteristics. The third column shows examples of specific activities corresponding to those tasks. The fourth column describes the types of knowledge to which those types of tasks are sensitive.

As an example, the first sub-category of task demands is "defining/using terms." This sub-category is best associated with measuring declarative knowledge. Declarative knowledge is also associated with the cognitive demand sub-category "recalling facts." As the table recommends, "selecting responses" under item openness is good for declarative knowledge as well.

The table *does not* tell us directly what question or task type (multiple-choice, true/false, extended constructed response, performing an experiment, etc.) is best for assessing which kind of knowledge. Rather, it allows the reader to think in terms of knowledge purpose, and then find or build an item that fits those task characteristics. For instance, if we are interested in assessing how well students can reason using models, we could build or find a multiple-choice item that

Table 5.1 Knowledge-Based Framework for Identifying Proper Questions or Task Types

| Aspects of tasks | Description | Selected examples of coding sub-categories | Possible links with knowledge type |
|---|---|---|---|
| Task demands | Task(s) that students are asked to perform | • Defining/using terms<br>• Providing explanations<br>• Designing an experiment<br>• Mathematical calculation | • D<br>• D/Sc<br>• P<br>• P |
| Cognitive demands | Inferred cognitive processes students likely act upon to provide responses | • Recalling facts<br>• Reading figures<br>• Reasoning with models<br>• Comparing and selecting strategies | • D<br>• P<br>• Sc<br>• St |
| Task openness | Degree of freedom students are allowed to have in shaping responses to an item or task | • Selecting vs. generating responses<br>• Stem presented as a complete question vs. an incomplete stem<br>• One vs. multiple correct answers<br>• Recipe directions | • Selecting good for D<br>• Incomplete stem good for D, but not good for Sc/P/St<br>• One good for D vs. multiple good for Sc/St<br>• Not good for St |
| Additional factors | Domain-general factors that influence the item difficulty | • Linguistic challenges<br>• Textbook vs. novel tasks<br>• Inclusion of irrelevant information | • Not good for any type<br>• Textbook good for D vs. novel good for St<br>• Good for St |

Source: Adapted from: Li Ruiz-Primo, and Shavelson (2006).

allows students to "select all that apply" of several options, as long as the options have been carefully designed to provide various kinds of partial information. Only certain combinations of selected responses would receive full credit, but partial credit could be given if the student selected certain other types of combinations.

The American Association of the Advancement of Science has a large pool of available items like these. You can build an open-ended question that requires students to show their reasoning by writing about it or drawing diagrams. If language is still needed, teachers of ELLs would need to think about how they could support their students in explaining themselves. For instance, they may be able to read the students' code-switching explanations, they may need these students to orally explain their diagrams until the teacher is satisfied, or the teacher can ask them to respond to other items to see if the student has a firm grasp on the targeted reasoning. This topic is also addressed in Trumbull and Koelsch, chapter 9, this volume. In each case, what would *not* be acceptable is a fact-finding item, as students could "differentiate" or "guess" their way through without necessarily having to demonstrate their grasp of the reasoning skills.

As borne out by research findings, the authors of this table argue that a given set of skills and competencies is best measured with a given, optimal combination of tasks. Also, improper use of certain tasks could restrict the students' ability to demonstrate knowledge. For ELLs, developing appropriate tasks would certainly entail consideration of the kinds of information found in Table 5.1. In addition, other factors need to be considered. One of them is the set of characteristics, such as language load or cultural references, that may hamper students' understanding of what the task is asking or the opportunity for them to respond in ways that accurately reflect their competencies (see Trumbull & Solano-Flores, Chapter 2; Abedi, Chapter 3, this volume).

So, what does all this look like in an ongoing classroom setting? Teachers are responsible for planning and implementing the instructional program, managing the dynamics of a classroom filled with students, and tracking and reporting the educational progress of both individual students and the class as a whole. Formative assessment of student learning in the classroom is an integral part of these complex responsibilities, but teachers have to understand how to make the most of each instructional activity and where the assessment component could often be integrated into the teaching.

Each type of task, whether it is a multiple-choice question, an open-ended task or a hands-on experiment, can only give partial information about the students' skills or knowledge. A vast array of approaches—including opportunities for students to "think aloud" during some activities, integrated sessions where students analyze their own work or other students' work, as well as informal and formal teacher-led questioning (both orally or on paper)—are all opportunities for teachers to systematically collect and subsequently evaluate information about pre-planned targeted knowledge and skills (Basterra, Chapter 4, this volume). Additionally, many teachers have found it useful to work aloud with students when they are developing their assessment criteria and scoring rubrics.

Several states, such as California, have put in place periodic Program Quality Review systems, which allow for reflective practices on behalf of teachers and administrators to come together in order to make meaningful and timely modifications in the school's curricular area of focus. School educators can use opportunities such as this to collectively think about assessment strategies associated with specific curricular goals or to analyze student work together. While time seems in very short supply, some experts suggest that the primary hurdle is learning how to evaluate individual students creatively, effectively, and frequently, and to do so in a way in which teachers learn not only what students know, but also identify misunderstandings or missing important knowledge or skills. As discussed above, this process, and how teachers adapt future instruction to reflect and to correct misunderstandings, are the ultimate goals of formative assessment.

### Tips for Measuring Content Knowledge in ELLs

#### BEFORE YOU START

Given that each content area and discipline has its own register (academic language, including vocabulary and discourse style), the teaching of content language and academic concepts and processes require attention to detail for all students, but especially for ELLs (Trumbull & Solano-Flores, Chapter 2, this volume). Teaching both language and content is key for understanding and using the discourse of the subject being learned. Capitalizing on teachers' passion for their subject matters, teachers who are experts in teaching ELLs could work with these teachers and educate them about the best ways to support their ELL students as they are learning academic language along with content. Thus, a first step in promoting effective assessment for ELLs consists of doing collaborative work that ensures that these students are included in each classroom discussion and take part in the wide range of formative assessment activities discussed above.

That said, it is vitally important to remember that teaching and assessing the *full range* of knowledge and skills *must* be available for ELLs as well as for non-ELLs. It is often easier to restrict the range of instruction and testing of ELLs to lower levels of knowledge because the language tends to be more concrete, simpler in structure, and more reliant on high-frequency words. However, doing this keeps these students from developing more complex thinking and reasoning skills, in general, and in each specific content area. Each school year that this occurs, ELLs fall further behind, making it harder, if not impossible, for them to catch up. Further, accountability systems (including classroom grades and school benchmark tests) that allow this to happen provide distorted and misleading information about these students' learning and ability to learn. A false sense of mastery will become evident later when students cannot compete in more challenging classes and end up being shunted into lower academic tracks or even special education (Garcia & Ortiz, 2006). The second objective, then, of assessing the knowledge and skills of ELLs is not to let these students "off the hook" but, instead, make sure they receive the full range of instruction and are held accountable for demonstrating their learning relative to that range.

## NOW WHAT?

How can formative assessment tasks be designed to retain the rigor and variation of the relevant content while still being accessible to ELLs? To date, most of the published assessment tasks being designed to collect these types of formative data on student learning tend to depend largely on the use of text to ask questions and communicate meaning and context. While some tasks let students demonstrate their responses in a limited number of alternative ways, for the most part they assume students can comprehend the nuances and subtle semantic distinctions in the principled but wordy multiple-choice options, or they require them to use expressive language skills to write textual responses that explain their thinking. This problem pertains to not only assessment tasks presented in static, paper-and-pencil tests but also most of the computer-based tasks that are presented in engaging and dynamic interactive environments.

So, how can formative assessment tasks be properly designed for ELLs? This question has many answers, depending on the students' challenges and strengths. Instead of avoiding the kinds of tasks being suggested in a good, forward-looking classroom where formative feedback is part of learning, the challenge is to figure out how to adapt these materials. First, an assessment of students' individual strengths (for instance, their primary language [L1] proficiency in general, literacy in L1 if available, compensatory learning styles, previous learning experiences, and even perhaps "street smarts") is essential and can be implemented across subject areas. An assessment of ELL students' challenges is also vital, for example, beyond their English proficiency in the four domains (speaking, listening, reading, and writing). For example, a full assessment would include inquiry about their home communities' assumptions about testing that may (or may not) be inconsistent with ongoing assessments used in the U.S., a restriction of assessment experiences in previous grades in the U.S. or in their home country, or a lack of previous instructional experiences related to particular curricula (Abedi, Chapter 3, this volume). Second, once these assessments are completed for each student (if possible by the ELL expert in the school) and explained to other teachers as relevant, the ELL expert can develop and use various adaptations that do not lessen the complexity of the content. If possible, this professional can work with the content-area teachers to share these adaptations and identify other suitable solutions. For instance, teachers can use:

- "Sheltered English";
- L1 resources from the community for oral help (for benchmarks, scripts should be reviewed by others, and then recorded and used that way, so that cueing is not an issue);
- Bilingual glossaries (if students are literate enough in either L1 or in English to benefit);

- Examples of ways students can demonstrate knowledge, so that they do not always have to write about it;
- Examples of ways to score responses that allow for pictures, code-switching, etc.

Often adaptations can be used in tandem. A few guidelines continue below:

1.  The simple act of providing an "opening" instructional activity that is engaging and that involves students in dialogue, discovery, and communication allows the teacher to monitor emergent language; to obtain a basal assessment of students' understanding of concepts; and to assess prior knowledge in context with the concepts at hand. By using a task-based engaging introduction, the teacher is able to tap into the students' linguistic and conceptual reservoirs, while listening attentively to their dialogue during the engaging task (i.e., monitoring, roving, probing, and recording key student ideas and language). Then, the teacher is able to bridge and provide tools (i.e., word/concept organizers) for learning, to clarify ideas, to model and apply the lesson's intended academic language, while providing contextualized cues, visuals, and ensuing multiple opportunities for their use.

2.  Contrary to popular opinion, ELLs do not necessarily like or do well with "language-less" assessment tasks. Rather, we recommend that teachers use context wisely, so that students can understand the meaning of what is asked. Word problems use context to measure if and how student apply concepts or skills; taking language out changes what the item is measuring. Some computer-based items for ELLs are using animation and simulation to provide context; think about how context can be put in items clearly, and think about how the language can be supported with student strengths. Additionally, more cognitively complex tasks in most subjects use language to communicate a level of precision, and this language is part of what needs to be conveyed to and from the student. It is important to know when this is so, or when the complexity of language can be reduced without jeopardizing conceptual and cognitive target goals. This may mean simplifying the structure of a sentence without substituting key academic language being measured. For example, in testing the "role" of consumers in an ecosystem, the term "role" implies a relational interaction that the word "job" does not have. Therefore, while during instruction, the targeted language can be amplified, with synonyms, clarifications, examples, and definitions, the key academic language needs to be applied frequently. Then, in the assessment, the academic terms can be used with the same rigorous academic meaning ELLs will need in order to develop effective academic discourse. Constructed responses may be easier for these students than trying to navigate the shorthand, nuanced language of multiple-choice or other forced-choice tasks. What is needed here is not so much changing how the student demonstrates what he or she knows, but improving how these kinds of responses are scored. Kopriva and Saez (1997) and Kopriva and Sexton (1998) provide good manuals for educating monolingual, English-speaking teachers about

how to score the constructed responses of ELLs, respectively in mathematics and science assessment. (These materials are available at www.ccsso.org.)

3.   Scaffolding questions is something often discussed as a way to adapt assessment activities for ELLs. Scaffolding can be supportive as long as it does not change what is being measured. For instance, cueing when the cueing in any way narrows down the possible responses or points towards one answer is an inappropriate use of scaffolding for assessment purposes. In addition, an essential component of more complex tasks is that they are measuring the students' skills in multi-step problem-solving. Leading the students through the steps destroys a fair amount of the complexity. But see Trumbull & Koelsch, Chapter 9, this volume, for a counter-example.) A serious critique of the targeted intent of tasks is needed before scaffolding is done.

4.   As noted above, sometimes teachers think that assessment information must be collected using trite multiple-choice, true/false, or fill-in-the-blank items. These question types may elicit informative student knowledge under certain conditions. However, there are multiple ways in which knowledge and skills can be evaluated that go beyond these methods, especially when more cognitively complex concepts are being measured. One of the best ways of assessing student progress is to utilize some of the tools used as part of instruction and learning. Properly implemented, the practice of using familiar materials reduces the gap between instructional and assessment practices, providing a basic scaffold of support without reducing the complexity of the intended questions. It also lowers the threshold of anxiety among ELLs and offers opportunities for them to demonstrate their understanding. For example, when recording tools are used during instruction, such as graphic organizers, charts, and tables, the same formats can be used effectively during formative assessment situations. Strategies such as Sentence Starters, and the use of multiple modes of representation (i.e., illustrations, matching cards, oral presentations) that are used routinely in content teaching for ELLs may be productive when certain kinds of knowledge and skills are being evaluated. (cf. Trumbull & Koelsch, Chapter 9, this volume.)

5.   There is an inherent value in performing a qualitative analysis of student work with students. This includes having students discuss their interpretations of content and their reasoning during and after assessment tasks. This feedback forms part of student self-assessment with guidance from the teacher. It also helps to address cultural diversity, as students from various other backgrounds are socialized in ways that encourages their active participation in self-assessment, observation, and reflective practices.

6.   Practice, practice, practice. Assessment methods most validly reflect student learning when they are asking the questions you want asked, and when they are used by students frequently throughout the year. This way, the methods, appropriately adapted to be accessible, facilitate the communication of desired knowledge and skills to and from the student, instead of being something that, in addition to the targeted content, acts as a hurdle or barrier for students to struggle with as they try to demonstrate what they know and can do.

Figure 5.1 (page 102) puts some of these ideas together to measure students' multi-faceted understandings of ecosystems. First, teachers who developed the example worked backwards, thinking about what is expected of students in fourth grade to conceptualize and understand about how food webs function. Second, the selection of images was contextualized according to the type of local habitat the students have experienced or have visited in field trips. Third, the format of the task allows for flexibility in levels of language. In other words, using "cloze" as a format with examples, prompt sentence frames, "word walls," and providing visual input with an illustration allows students at lower levels of English language development to demonstrate whether they know the content by using scaffolds embedded throughout without improperly cuing certain responses. Fourth, to ensure that the students had a thorough understanding of the content, the teachers decided to use three items within the task to measure conceptual knowledge from different perspectives. The first section of the item tells the teacher if the student has a general understanding of the content or not. The second section includes a cyclical image, which embeds a slightly more complex level of reasoning, while the use of a "word wall" provides support for students. The development team felt that giving them the first piece (Producers) as an entry would allow students to focus their attention on the interactions within the depicted ecosystem, while providing a degree of success for all students. Finally, the last section of the item is more open-ended and asks students to predict what might happen under certain future conditions. This section measures more cognitive complex reasoning than the earlier items. To support their current level of language development, students are encouraged to use whatever methods they need to successfully get their points across.

Setting up a good formative assessment program that uses a variety of methods repeatedly throughout the year is the goal. Building up the repertoire is the hard part. But, with the aid of suggestions such as those discussed here, ELLs can benefit from a rich learning environment and at the same time thrive with a range of assessment tools that they recognize and are comfortable with.

## Conclusion

Readers might think this chapter should begin with the last section, that is, specific tips and ideas for measuring content knowledge among ELLs. Actually, this is the end product. The first step is careful planning that identifies and interconnects the overarching constructs that embody various instructional units and also identifies the core ideas within each unit that teachers want their students to learn. These core ideas, as well as the overarching constructs that include the development of reasoning and strategic skills, become the focus for the ongoing assessments of students.

Each assessment task should have a purpose that is clearly and explicitly spelled out by the teacher *before* he or she makes a decision about how exactly to assess for that purpose. Some task methods work better for some kinds of knowledge and skills, and building a repertoire of diverse approaches is needed if certain techniques are to be considered for a specific purpose. Just as it is important to teach and assess the nuts and bolts of content, it is also important to evaluate more complex content and skills. Finally, of course, depth of teacher knowledge is key as well. All in all, the purpose of this chapter is to provide guidance on how to develop a thoughtful formative assessment program. Success in this task will certainly provide a strong foundation for ELLs, as they continue to learn and grow within each of the content domains.

# References

Anderson, L., & Krathwohl, D.A. (2001). *Taxonomy for learning, teaching and assessing: A revision of Bloom's Taxonomy of Educational Objectives*. New York, NY: Longman.

Ball, D.L., & Bass, H. (2000). Interweaving content and pedagogy in teaching and learning to teach: Knowing and using mathematics. In J. Boaler (Ed.), *Multiple perspectives on teaching and learning* (pp. 83–104). Westport, CT: Ablex Publishing.

Bell, B., & Cowie, B. (1999). *Formative assessment and science education, research*. Report of the Learning in Science Project (assessment), August.

Bloom, Benjamin S., & David R. Krathwohl. (1956). *Taxonomy of educational objectives: The classification of educational goals, by a committee of college and university examiners*. Handbook 1: Cognitive domain. New York, NY: Longmans.

Bransford, J.D., Brown, A.L., & Cocking, R.R. (Eds.) (2000). *How people learn: Brain, mind, experience, and school* (Expanded Edition). Washington, DC: National Academy Press.

Briggs, D.C., Alonzo, A.C., Schwab, S., & Wilson, M. (2006). Diagnostic assessment with ordered multiple-choice items. *Educational Assessment*, 11, 33–63.

Darling-Hammond, L., & Bransford, J. (Eds.) (2005). *Preparing teachers for a changing world: What teachers should learn and be able to do*. San Francisco, CA: Jossey-Bass.

DiRanna, K., Osmundson, E., Topps, J., Barakos, L., Gearhart, M., Cerwin, K., et al. (2008). *Assessment-centered teaching: A reflective practice*. Thousand Oaks, CA: Corwin.

Duschl, R.A., Schweingruber, H.A., & Shouse, A.W. (Eds.) (2007). *Taking science to school: Learning and teaching science in grades K-8*. Washington, DC: National Academy of Sciences. Retrieved December 30, 2007, from: www.nap.edu/catalog. php?record_id=11625.

Garcia, S.B., & Ortiz, A.A. (2006). *Preventing disproportionate representation: Culturally and linguistically responsive prereferral interventions*. National Center for Culturally Responsive Education Systems. Retrieved from: www.nccrest.org/Briefs/Pre-referral_Brief.pdf?v_document_name=Pre-Referral%20Brief.

Kopriva, R.J., & Saez, S. (1997). *Guide to scoring LEP student responses to open-ended mathematics items*. Washington, DC: Council of Chief State School Officers.

Kopriva, R.J., & Sexton U. (1998). *Guide to scoring LEP student responses to open-ended science items*. Washington, DC: Council of Chief State School Officers.

Li, M., Ruiz-Primo, M.A., & Shavelson, R.J. (2006). Towards a science achievement framework: The case of TIMSS 1999. In S.J. Howie and T. Plomp (Eds.), *Contexts of learning mathematics and science: Lessons learned from TIMSS*. New York, NY: Routledge.

Pellegrino, J.W., Chudowsky, N., & Glaser, R. (Eds.) (2001). *Knowing what students know: The science and design of educational assessment*. Washington, DC: National Academy Press.

Popham, W.J. (2006). Assessment for learning: An endangered species? *Educational Leadership*, 63(5), 82–83.

Ruiz-Primo, M.A. (2007). Assessment in science and mathematics: Lessons learned. In M. Hoehpl and M.R. Lindstrom (Eds.), *Assessment of technology education*. New York, NY: McGraw Hill.

Ruiz-Primo, M.A., & Furtak, E.M. (2007). Exploring teachers' informal formative assessment practices and students' understanding in the context of scientific inquiry. *Journal of Research in Science Teaching*, 44(1), 57–84.

Shavelson, R.J. (2009). *Reflections on learning progressions*. Paper presented at the Learning Progressions in Science (LeaPS) Conference, June, Iowa City, IA.

Shepard, L. (2006). Classroom assessment. In R. Brennan (Ed.), *Educational measurement* (4th edition, pp. 624–646). Westport, CT: Praeger.

Stiggins, R. (2003). *Student involved classroom assessment* (3rd edition). Upper Saddle River, NJ: Merrill Prentice Hall.

Yager, Peter. (2005). The effects of varied inquiry experiences on teacher and student questions and actions in STS classrooms. *Bulletin of Science Technology and Society*, 25(5), 426–434.

# Chapter 6

# Ensuring Valid Educational Assessments for ELL Students

## Scores, Score Interpretation, and Assessment Uses

*Richard P. Durán*

---

**Chapter Overview**

This chapter expands the exploration of how differences in students and assessments affect assessment performance. It focuses on the interpretation of ELL student scores earned on assessments that target students' knowledge and skills in academic domains such as reading, mathematics, science, and other subject matter areas taught in K-12 education. It also addresses the interpretation of ELL students' scores on language proficiency assessments. The central question that is the focus of the chapter is: "How can we interpret scores on achievement or language proficiency assessments so that we can accurately gauge the capabilities, learning needs, and learning progress of an ELL student in the domain assessed?" This is a fundamental question that underlies the "validity" of an assessment for ELL students and, for that matter, students at large.[1]

## The Design of Assessments, their Purpose, and Different Types of Assessment Scores

The meaning of an assessment score depends entirely on the design of the particular assessment and the ways that scores are compiled from the components of that assessment. Accordingly, it is essential that assessment users understand clearly the goals and purposes of an assessment and the nature of different assessment score types.

Every assessment is designed to have a purpose, regardless of whether it is developed as a large-scale assessment mandated by a state as part of its accountability system or whether it is a classroom assessment designed locally by a teacher, school, or school district to probe students' learning. In this chapter, the main focus is on large-scale assessments, such as state annual achievement assessments, given their prevalence and policy significance. From time to time, however, the discussion includes classroom based assessments as well.

Another important basic property of an assessment is that it can be characterized as being either a norm referenced or a criterion referenced assessment. The scores on these different kinds of assessments have different meanings. On a norm referenced assessment, a student obtains a numerical score that indicates his or her performance rank relative to other students who took the test as part of a norming sample when the test was developed. The goal of a norm referenced achievement assessment is to rank order students, from the least able to most able in a given domain. On the other hand, in a criterion referenced assessment, a student obtains a numerical score or descriptive label that is intended to reflect the degree to which he or she has demonstrated particular knowledge or skills relative to a set of standards or objectives—not relative to a norming group.

### Norm-Referenced Assessments and Scores

The norming sample on a norm-referenced assessment needs to be selected so that it is representative of students as a whole in the population being assessed. This principle applies, of course, to ELL students as well (see Solano-Flores, Chapter 1, this volume). For example, if ELL students are a large proportion of students in a state, then the norming sample used to develop a state achievement assessment should have a nearly equivalent, large proportion of ELL students randomly chosen from the population of ELL students in that state. In this way, we can be assured that comparing the scores of ELL students to students as a whole in a state is not biased by lack of representation of ELL students in the norming sample. Nationally and regionally, ELL students perform lower overall on achievement assessments. When such students are excluded from or only minimally included in a norming sample, the result is a higher average performance on a state assessment. Then, when such a norm referenced assessment is implemented on a regular basis as part of a large-scale assessment, the scores of ELL students as a group will be artificially lower than the average for students as a whole (see Solorzano, 2008, for an extended discussion). Fortunately, in recent times, the issue of not including sufficient numbers of ELL students in norming samples is not as serious a problem as in the past because of the heightened efforts to assure accuracy of assessment results for the growing number of ELL students in the country and the policy imperatives of NCLB (the No Child Left Behind Act, 2002).

The concern for adequately norming an assessment applies as much to locally developed classroom assessments as to large-scale assessments. Teachers and school staff developing local assessments to be used with ELL students need to be careful to develop and try out assessment items and scoring procedures with the full range of students targeted for assessment. Care needs to be taken that the heterogeneity of ELL students in terms of their language background, English learner status, educational history, etc., are taken into account in establishing expectations of how student performance scores will be interpreted. For example, assessment developers need to consider how a learner's history of instruction in English versus another language might affect his or her ability to respond to mathematics items in English.

### Criterion Referenced Assessments and Scores

The purpose of criterion referenced assessments is to yield information on whether students have mastered skills and knowledge that they were expected to have acquired based on previous instruction. Design and implementation of criterion referenced assessments raise related but somewhat different concerns than for norm-referenced assessments.

Criterion referenced assessments, such as state assessments established under NCLB requirements, target mastery of specific skills and knowledge that reflect state learning standards in a domain such as reading, math, or science for all students. Of course, this applies to all ELL students as well. While norm-referenced assessments yield scores that reflect knowledge and skills relevant to subject matter instructional outcomes as well, they are not designed to focus so specifically on skills and knowledge that *all* students are expected to have mastered by the time they are assessed.

Proficiency classifications used in criterion referenced assessments, such as those required under NCLB, are derived from numerical scores. In this instance, however, the developers of an assessment utilize a "standards setting" technique to determine cut-scores that separate individual student scores into those that meet or fall above the cut-point and those that fall below the cut-point for the different proficiency categories (see Cizek & Bunch, 2007, for a detailed overview and synopsis of different standard setting methods). Standards setting procedures for setting score cut-points for proficiency categories are used widely in state achievement assessments in various subject matter domains and in English language proficiency assessments for ELL students. The processes that are followed are inherently judgmental. They call upon teachers, instructional staff, concerned community members, and others to make judgments about how well students need to perform on an assessment in order to attain a higher or lower proficiency classification.

Further treatment of criterion referenced assessment and its implications for analyzing the learning status and learning needs of ELL students needs to incorporate a discussion of assessment stakes for learners (see below). In other words, what outcomes flow from the way a student performs on a given assessment? Can he or she be held back a grade? Will his or her teacher(s) modify instruction in an attempt to improve student performance? Will he or she be steered to either gifted or special education programs? Will he or she be referred for additional English language development? Accordingly, the issue of assessment stakes is also deeply connected to the notion of the consequential validity, the validity of inferences and decisions based on a given assessment score.

### Assessment Stakes and Assessment Scores

Another important characteristic of assessments that affects the interpretation of assessment scores is whether they have low stakes versus high stakes for students assessed—this is also a matter of consequential validity. Low stakes assessments provide information on what examinees know and can do but do not have a dramatic, impactful effect on what happens to a student subsequently based on his or her test score. For example, administration of an assessment such as a National Assessment of Education Progress (NAEP) assessment in mathematics at grade 4, 8, or 12 can provide states, the Federal Government, and some large city school districts with score information about how proficient ELL students and other students are in the domains of reading, mathematics, and sometimes other subject matter areas. However, these assessments come with no reporting of individual assessment scores or immediate consequences to the instruction of the students assessed on NAEP, their schooling status, or services provided them. On the other hand, high stakes criterion referenced assessments such as high school exit examinations or grade promotion assessments have important immediate consequences for students. Scores on such assessments are used to determine whether students are eligible to graduate with a diploma from high school or to move on to the next school grade.

State policies commonly assume that high stakes assessments are appropriate for judging whether students have met the standards established by the state and that the student scores reflect whether students have or have not met the standards. As implied earlier, such an assumption may be ill-founded. In fact, quite the contrary, there is reason to believe that educational assessments are not currently of the quality necessary to make valid and reliable judgments about the achievement of ELLs when they are treated as the sole evidence for achievement.

It should be noted that state assessments under NCLB that do not have individual, immediate high stakes for students—while classified as low stakes—can have immediate high stakes consequences for states, school districts, and schools. Those consequences can lead to practices and policies that result in high stakes consequences later on for ELL and other students. Under current NCLB provisions, state and school jurisdictions receiving federal funding under the law must have all students and key student sub-groups (including ELL students) attain "proficient" or above assessment scores in grades 3–8 reading and mathematics at percentage rates meeting Adequate Yearly Progress (AYP) goals, set by a state and accepted by the federal government.[2] (Science was added as a mandated assessment in 2007 at certain grade spans.) ELL students lag behind other students in attaining these goals and can contribute to schools and school districts being identified formally as in need of improvement. This designation leads schools to impose instructional remediation strategies for ELL students such as tutoring, thereby affecting the schooling experience and services received by such students—an example of a high stakes consequence that may or may not be positive.

## Teacher Classroom Assessments

Yet other assessments might be termed "teacher classroom" assessments. These assessments are designed locally by teachers or other instructional staff to yield practical, diagnostic information on what students know and can do in classroom settings. Some of the possible teacher classroom assessments are short-answer quizzes, end-of-unit tests, collections of student work (such as portfolios), individual and group performances or demonstrations, oral questioning, projects, and observational checklists.

Scoring and interpreting the scores of ELL students on such assessments can have immediate high stakes consequences in that teachers' use of score information can tie immediately and directly into instruction provided to students that can improve their mastery of knowledge and skills targeted by assessments. Such assessments may also be used to determine students' grades and contribute to decisions about retention or moving to the next grade.

## Assessment Goals, Blueprints, Task Formats, and Scores

Understanding whether assessments are norm-referenced or criterion referenced, and whether they are high vs. low stakes for ELL students, is important to setting the stage for understanding the meaning of ELL student scores on an assessment. There is one further important step, however. One needs to understand how the sub-scores of the components of an assessment are used to derive an overall summary score. As a starting point, it is important to remember that the main goal of any subject matter achievement or language proficiency assessment is to yield evidence of what a student knows and can do in a targeted learning domain. The interpretation of ELL students' assessment scores benefits immensely by "looking under the hood" at the make-up of an assessment and its scored components and how these scored components contribute to overall estimates of students' achievement. In order to address this point more concretely, as will be done below, it is first useful to consider how assessments are built around particular goals and how these goals are embodied in assessment items.

## Assessment Blueprints

Every formal assessment is expected to have a blueprint or explicit design (Cohen & Wollack, 2003).[3] The blueprint usually takes the form of a document and accompanying charts that provide a summary of the make-up of an assessment in terms of its measurement objectives and components that are scored separately. An example of such a blueprint is shown in Appendix 6.1 for the design of the California Standards Test in Grade 2 Mathematics for *Number Sense*. This is only one of six areas covered by the blueprint, but it helps make concrete the nature of one state's blueprint system. In the case shown, each blueprint entry corresponds to a California State Standard for mathematics knowledge that second-graders are expected to master prior to administration of the math assessment during the spring semester of the second grade.

The scores derived from students' performance on assessment items are then combined in various ways, following a formal procedure to yield an overall score (and sometimes strand sub-scores). It is not always the case that states will report strand sub-scores because of the measurement limitations of such scores, as will be described in a later section. Some states do report strand sub-scores, in terms of the proportion of items an examinee answered correctly within a strand.

### Assessment Strand Achievement Scores and Levels

It is common today to find that state assessments break out the overall scores of an assessment into strand or cluster scores (Ryan, 2006). For example, a score report for tenth-graders in mathematics may include sub-scores, and/or corresponding percentile levels, or proficiency levels earned in areas such as "number relationships," "geometry," "algebra," and "measurement." Characteristically, these strand areas reflect the blueprint of an assessment. The sub-scores and proficiency levels reported are derived from the performance of students on the particular form of the assessment administered to them. The sub-scores can provide useful information on strengths and weaknesses shown by students on the particular problem items they encountered in each different strand area on the particular assessment form they took.

There are many limitations to strand sub-scores that teachers need to be aware of. While this information has a "diagnostic" flavor, in that more intensive instruction or remediation would seem indicated on strands where students performed below expected levels, this assumption is not warranted, particularly on year-to-year comparisons. The assumption is unlikely to hold because every time a new form of an assessment is developed and administered, the difficulty of items in a particular strand area will not remain invariant across an old and new form—even though both assessments follow the assessment blueprint for strand areas that need to be present.

While assessment developers and psychometricians can construct two forms of an assessment so that they are, overall, of approximately equal difficulty and reliability, two important constraints make it unlikely that strand sub-scores will be as valid and accurate measures as the overall score of an examinee. The number of assessment items that can be sampled to represent a blueprint strand area will be relatively small—say, 4–8, or some similar number, compared to, say, 24–36 items for an assessment made up of two or more strands of items. In order to ensure that the overall difficulty of a new form of an assessment is comparable in difficulty and content to a previous form of an assessment, the assessment developers need to have the freedom to pick items for the new form that may not be of matched difficulty to items on previous forms for the same strand. The upshot of this situation is that items for, say, an algebra strand on a math assessment in a given year may turn out to be noticeably easier or harder than in a previous year, though the overall math assessment would be of very similar difficulty.

A second and related constraint regarding the utility of strand sub-scores is that the relatively small number of items representing a strand will result in a low reliability for the resulting sub-score scale. Thus, for example, while an overall assessment with, say, 36 or so items may show an acceptable internal consistency reliability in the 0.85–0.95 range, a sub-score scale may show a much lower reliability, say in the 0.4–0.6 range—see the section of this chapter entitled Assessment Score Validity and Accuracy (pp. 131–134). This lower reliability means there will be so many more examples of error of measurement in the strand sub-score that it cannot be counted on to report accurately what an examinee knows and can do in the isolated area targeted by an assessment strand.

When assessments are high stakes, as is the case with high school exit examinations, the foregoing means then, for example, that algebra items on one form of a math high school exit exam might turn out to be notably easier or harder on two different exams, though each exam is following the same assessment blueprint. Thus it is possible that students who concentrate on preparing for a math high school exit exam in only one strand area may not benefit as expected on the strand they concentrated on and possibly not as anticipated on the math exit exam as a whole as a result of strand targeted math remedial instruction.

One further caveat seems in order, however, regarding the performance of ELL students as revealed by strand scores. If a given strand features problem items or constructed-response tasks with a high English language load (e.g., math word problems or written reports) and the performance of ELL students is noticeably low on that strand, then this may indicate the importance of strengthening ELL students' verbal problem-solving, writing, or other expressive skills in English in the strand areas showing depressed sub-scores relative to other sub-scores. The problem may not lie with failure to provide opportunities for students to learn the content. This same caveat also applies when an assessment strand showing depressed scores utilizes item formats that are likely to be unfamiliar to ELL students from schooling and cultural backgrounds that have led to little or no experiences with these formats.

### Constraints of Blueprints

Assessment blueprints are not intended to specify everything a student is expected to learn and eventually master in an achievement domain. The intent of blueprints is, rather, to select problems or tasks from a target universe of skills and knowledge that are judged to be critical in a domain, e.g., those embodied in state learning standards. These target areas for achievement are further refined into specific task formats that can be used on an assessment to gather evidence of learning.

The fact that assessments and their blueprints cannot represent a target learning domain completely is an important point that cannot be emphasized enough (see Koretz, 2008, for a detailed discussion in the context of current state accountability assessments). Assessments, no matter how well-founded conceptually, can at best provide only partial evidence of the range of competence that a student has in a learning domain. This is true even for a very specific skill, such as applying the appropriate mathematical formula to calculate the area of a circle. The assessment item presents particular demands in a particular format (using particular language). Successful student performance depends on not only the student's knowledge but also on correct interpretation of what he or she is being asked to do (see Basterra, Chapter 4, this volume). This point is illustrated by the example in the following paragraphs.

### Students' Interpretation of Test Items

A state may specify a math learning standard at, say, the sixth-grade level, that states that students will learn and be able to apply the well known formula $A = \pi r^2$ to calculate the area of a circle. Accordingly, a math test item for sixth-graders may present an item as shown in Figure 6.1. Students may be allowed to use a calculator with $\pi$ and significant digits set to three decimal places.

Jack nails one end of a rope that is 5 feet long to the ground. He then attaches a piece of chalk to the other end of the rope and then draws a ring with the chalk. What is the area of the ring?

    a) 5 square feet
    b) 25 feet
    c) 78.125 square feet
    d) 38.828 feet

*Figure 6.1* Determining the Area of a Circle.

The test item in Figure 6.1 is just one sample from an open universe of ways that a problem item requiring knowledge of the underlying math objective targeted by the item could be stated. Further, in order for a student to solve this item correctly, he or she needs to understand the words and sentences making up the item, e.g., words such as "rope," "nails," "ring," "end," "draws," and "chalk." He or she also needs to understand the mathematical meanings of the words "area," "feet," and "square feet," as well as numerical expressions such as "5," "25," "78.125," and "38.28." Understanding of the term "ring" in the context of the problem also requires that an examinee infer that "ring" alludes to the mathematical concept of "circle." In addition, in order to solve this item with a calculator, an examinee would need to know how to use a calculator— not just any calculator, but the particular physical calculator available, with its particular layout of keys and screen display. Also at issue is the skill of a student to apply different strategies to eliminate or prioritize various multiple-choice responses, in case the correct option was not readily identified from working the problem.

The example in Figure 6.1 also makes evident the potential importance of accompanying visual information that may help a student interpret an item appropriately. Consider the presence of a figure such as that shown in Figure 6.2 in the presentation of the item in question. An examinee having this figure available would be given additional information supporting the interpretation of the item. The figure would likely reduce the language comprehension load imposed by the item because the student could use information represented by the figure to help interpret the meaning of the problem statement. Such figural information may support the comprehension of not only ELLs but also poor readers.

As has been previously discussed in this book and elsewhere (e.g., Lager, 2006), there may be many linguistic, cultural, and experiential characteristics of ELL students that block their intended interpretation of an item such as the one in Figure 6.2. The ultimate result can be misinformation regarding the student's mastery of the intended knowledge and skill targeted by an assessment item. An ELL student may not have had adequate familiarity with the English used in the item or cultural familiarity with the meaning of the concepts alluded to by the English words on the basis of past experiences in and out of U.S. contexts (see also, Chapter 2).

*Figure 6.2* Graphic Representation for Item on Determining Area of a Circle.

## Limitations in Sampling a Domain Through Given Formats

The issue of how well an assessment can sample and represent what ELL students are expected to know and do is yet more complex. What students actually do and accomplish in a classroom is richer and more complex than the limited sample of behavior represented by assessment task formats and performance on an assessment. After all, they are learning and demonstrating learning through a wide variety of activities in various formats over an extended period of time. The samples of behavior collected and then scored on an assessment reflecting competence in target knowledge and skills area are dependent on the formats utilized by an assessment to assess each targeted achievement proficiency domain. So, what can be discovered about students' learning is constrained—both by the limited number of questions that can be asked and the limited kinds of formats that tend to be used. Research by Solano-Flores (discussed in Solano-Flores & Trumbull, 2003) has shown that a larger number of assessment items may well be needed to obtain a reliable estimate of ELL students' learning than is required for native English speakers. Thus, the proper interpretation of ELL students' assessment scores requires considering whether the opportunities to show knowledge and skills on an assessment are adequate to reflect what students know and can do in authentic classroom learning settings.

To illustrate this point more concretely, we may come back to the example of the math item shown in Figure 6.1 and its graphic representation in Figure 6.2. Assessing a student's knowledge of the formula for the area of a circle via this item is not the same as assessing that same knowledge via an authentic instructional event that is part of the everyday life of math instruction in the classroom. Instruction about the formula for calculation of the area of a circle would occur most likely as part of a unit devoted to this topic, with a teacher's presenting materials and activities tied to learning and the use of the formula. A teacher might also ask students to solve problems involving mastery of the formula as part of homework or as part of an end-of-unit assessment. Both of these assessment conditions would be likely to be directly associated with the occurrence of an instructional unit and not as part of a "drop-out-of-the sky" multiple-choice problem a student encounters on an annual state assessment of math learning.

### Degree of Match Between Instruction and Assessment

The alignment of assessment items with classroom instruction may be more critical for ELLs than for native English speakers. ELLs may rely on familiar formats to scaffold their understanding of assessment questions, for instance (see, e.g., Trumbull & Koelsch, Chapter 9, this volume). Teachers and practitioners should ask, "How well does such an assessment item (and its knowledge and performance requirements) align with instruction on computing the area of a circle in the classroom?" A follow-on question is, "In what ways is instruction leading to anticipated mastery of a skill part of a systematic sequence of instructional activities to teach the concept of area of a circle as part of the math curriculum?" Another related and important question would be, "What kinds of evidence of mastery of a concept were collected, analyzed, and used by an instructor to guide instruction?" Given responses to these questions, it would then become possible to interpret how well the problems occurring on the assessment matched the content students had had opportunities to master.

Unfortunately, this ideal scenario is unlikely to arise readily in the real world because students and teachers seldom get an opportunity to examine the items administered on a large-scale assessment after the fact. This is because large-scale state assessment programs often reuse the same assessment items on future administrations of an assessment. Hence, keeping items secure is of practical value, so that teachers don't teach mastery of just such specific assessment items. That stated, however, many states release some assessment items used in the past. These can then be subjected to some of the foregoing questions as suggestive of the extent to which classroom instruction matches the demands of items found on assessments.

## Types of Formats Used on Assessments

Attention now turns to the broader question of the kinds of common formats in which assessment items occur. It is useful to keep in mind the previous discussion on the degree of alignment between items found on large-scale assessments and instruction. This matter comes up frequently at many points in the chapter.

The range of possible formats used in assessments can be broken down into two major categories: *on-demand* assessment items administered during a formal assessment session; and *student work samples* collected or observed outside of the constraints of a formal assessment session. On-demand items are administered in a standardized manner, according to a prearranged schedule, with a fixed order of item presentation. Student work samples may include: (1) administration of extended performance items in a regular, instructional classroom setting; (2) collection of portfolio samples of students' classroom work over time;[4] or (3) observer ratings of students' regular classroom performance during individual or group work.

A given assessment may rely on just one of these major formats, or intermix the two formats based on the blueprint for an assessment. When interpreting the scores of an ELL student on an assessment, it is important to understand the kinds of formats used by that assessment and how student performance, given these formats, might affect the scores of ELL students on the individual scored components of an assessment.

### On-Demand Selected Response Assessment Items

Most commonly, assessments are developed as stand-alone events wherein students are asked to respond to a number of items presented sequentially as separate, back-to-back problems. Students can respond selectively to items by choosing among multiple-choice answer options (the correct option is termed the "key," while the incorrect options are termed "distractors"). Responses to such items are usually scored dichotomously as either "correct" or "incorrect." It is possible in some assessment designs for there to be more than one acceptable answer, in which case the responses of a student would be weighted according to a scoring key. The most common scoring procedure used with large-scale state assessments is machine scanning of individual responses on answer sheets. At the classroom level, such assessments are commonly scored by a teacher or other staff person, such as a teacher's aide. Scores on selected response items are often termed "objective" because the score assigned by a machine or person is based solely on the multiple-choice response of the student and not on scorer judgment of the qualities of a student response.

With regard to the math item in Figure 6.1, ELL students' familiarity with the multiple-choice format in addition to understanding the problem task posed by the item are important to consider. The notion that a multiple-choice assessment item usually has only one correct answer option and that the other options are incorrect is learned through experience taking this form of assessment early on in formal schooling—whether in the U.S. or another country with a similar type of formal schooling. ELL students from some schooling backgrounds outside the U.S. may not be accustomed to this practice, however. They may not know strategies for increasing their chances of selecting a correct multiple-choice response, e.g., by eliminating unlikely or impossible response options as the solutions to an assessment item.

As another related issue, ELL students' problem in selecting a single correct response to a multiple-choice option is made all the more challenging when a reasonable interpretation of an unfamiliar term in an item can lead to the selection of a wrong answer option. Consider, for example, the released fifth-grade reading item drawn from the California Standards Test shown in Figure 6.3.

The term "extraordinary" could be taken to mean not "beyond normal" as intended, but rather "super-highly-ordinary"—a not unreasonable interpretation of the term "extraordinary" by someone new to learning the English language. Such an interpretation might lead a student to conclude that the answer is option A, "regular." And because there is no further context to illustrate the meaning of the target word, the student has to rely on his or her particular linguistic knowledge and experience to infer its meaning.

---

**Read this sentence.**
My dog, Tibbs, is a truly <u>extraordinary</u> animal.

**In this sentence, what does extraordinary mean?**

**A**  regular
**B**  amazing
**C**  imaginary
**D**  perplexed

---

*Figure 6.3* Fifth-Grade Reading Item (source: California Department of Education, 2003 Through 2008 CST Released Test Questions, Item
CSR10550.OSA).

The item in Figure 6.3 is intended to assess a student's knowledge of English
vocabulary. However, many items that purport to assess something other than
vocabulary knowledge may be couched in words that ELLs have less elaborated
understanding of than their native English speaking peers (August, Carlo,
Dressler, & Snow, 2005). Because individual items on an assessment are presented concisely, in a stand-alone manner, back-to-back, there is always a danger
that ELL students may not interpret a problem item and its multiple-choice
options as expected. The wording of assessment items will vary in terms of their
linguistic complexity and the cultural load of their content—an issue explored at
length in other contributions to the present volume. The upshot to this predica-
ment is that ELL students who do not understand a problem item adequately
may not respond to the item at all or respond by selecting an answer option randomly. Both of these outcomes can lower the overall score earned by an ELL
student by adding error to the estimate of his or her proficiency in the domain
under assessment (see Solani-Flores, Chapters 1, and Abedi, 3, this volume).

## On-Demand Constructed-Response Assessments Items

On-demand constructed-response (c-r) items can be *short, intermediate,* or
*extended* in length—the distinction being relative, as opposed to absolute. Short
c-r items present examinees with problems that might require just a one or two
word response or a brief phrase or sentence response. Alternatively, they might
require an examinee to place a mark, circle, or other inscription onto a figure or
piece of text shown in an item. Consider the item below (Figure 6.4) as an illustration of a short c-r item appropriate for a middle elementary grade student.
The item requires just a simple numerical entry response.

Intermediate demand c-r items might require more than one written sentence or phrase, or up to a very small number of written sentences for a
response to a problem. Such items, alternatively, might require the construction
of a diagram or figure in response to a problem question. Below (Figure 6.5) is
an example of such an item drawn from released items on the NAEP fourth-
grade Science Test.

Jim has many 2" tiles of the sort shown below.

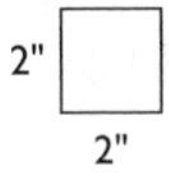

2" ☐
  2"

Jim arranges several of the tiles as shown below.

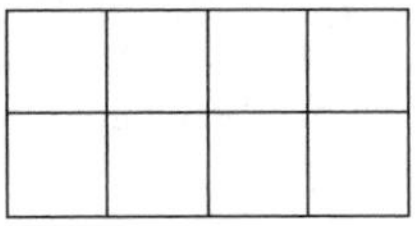

What is the area of the object that Jim constructs?

Write your answer here: _____ square inches.

*Figure 6.4* Middle Elementary-Grade Simple Constructed Response Mathematics Item.

Pat set up four different jars with a burning candle in each jar. He put the lids on jars 1, 2, and 3, as shown in the picture below.

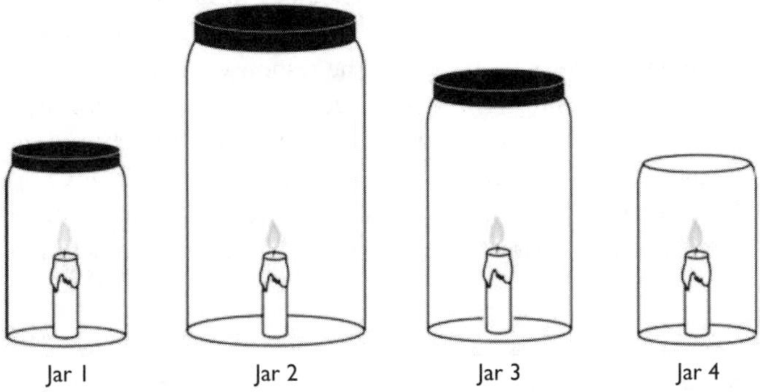

Jar 1             Jar 2             Jar 3             Jar 4

5. Pat did not put lid on jar 4. The candle in jar 4 burned for a very long time. Tell why this candle kept burning so much longer than the other candles.

_____

_____

_____

_____

*Figure 6.5* Fourth-Grade Constructed Response Science Item (source: U.S. Department of Education, Institute of Education Sciences, National Center for Education Statistics, National Assessment of Educational Progress (NAEP), Grade 4 Science, 2005).

Extended response c-r items are lengthier and may even require an essay length response. Scoring of c-r items is done by a designated scorer, applying a scoring rubric. A scoring rubric is a set of guidelines for interpreting the responses of examinees in terms of the quality of a response. Using these guidelines, the scorer assigns a score to the students' response. This score can range from simply "correct" vs. "incorrect" to a numerical score based on an integer rating scale, such as 0–1–2–3. Sometimes more than one rubric is applied to the scoring of a c-r item, reflecting different dimensions or qualities that are targeted for assessment by an item based on the assessment blueprint. This practice is common in writing assessment, for instance, where a single student performance can be evaluated vis-à-vis content, structure, mechanics, and other attributes. Figure 6.6 is an example of an extended response item adapted from a released item on the New England Common Assessment Program Grade 8 Writing Assessment.

Just as with on-demand selected response items, ELL students may not respond to on-demand constructed response items as intended, even if they have the knowledge and skills called for. This is because they must also understand the nature of the situation reflected in the statement of an item and the performance demands posed by the item. The same issues raised earlier apply: ELL students must have sufficient linguistic and cultural knowledge to orient to and interpret items and their demands as expected; otherwise their responses will lead to a lower performance score on an item and to greater error in their overall score. In addition, the score of an ELL student on an on-demand c-r item can be affected by the scorer's ability to interpret the response of an ELL student in the manner intended by the student.

Scorers need to be familiar with ways that the response of an ELL examinee to a c-r item may be affected by his or her language and cultural background, independent of the examinee's knowledge and skill in the target domain of an item (see especially chapters Kopriva & Sexton, Chapter 5; Lara & Chia, Chapter 8; and Trumbull & Solano-Flores, Chapter 10, this volume). For example, if a scorer does not realize that Spanish speakers often add a short "e" sound to the

---

*Read this passage and think about how you will continue it. Then write a response at the prompt below.*

**Can I Talk to You?**

My best friend and I always seem to be arguing about something. What happened last weekend is a perfect example.

"Listen, can I talk to you?" I asked.

**Prompt:** Continue this story, using dialogue to develop the plot/story line.

---

*Figure 6.6* Eighth-Grade Extended Constructed Response Item (source: New England Common Assessment Program. Released Items 2008 Grade 8 Writing).

beginning of words that begin with "st" and spell the long "e" sound (ee) in Spanish with the letter "i," he may not recognize a student's written word "estrit" as equivalent to the English word "street." In particular, if a c-r item is not intended to assess spelling, grammatical, or linguistic fluency, the rubric scoring of a response to a c-r item should not be based in any way on demonstration of these linguistic competencies.

As noted earlier, on-demand selected response and constructed response items might occur together on the same assessment. Teachers and other educational stakeholders need to keep this in mind in interpreting the overall scores earned by ELL students on an assessment and the degree to which an overall score (or sub-scores) on an assessment reflect a weighting of one item format over the other. This may be a highly idiosyncratic issue at the individual ELL student level. For example, some ELL students, because of their background, may be better prepared to handle the demands of c-r items as compared to other ELL students. Each type of item presents its own challenges that interact with student characteristics and preferences.

### Extended Response Tasks Administered in Classroom Contexts

Sometimes students are asked to complete assessment tasks as part of regular classroom instruction in a content area such as science (see, e.g., Koretz, 2008). The goal of such tasks is often to gain evidence of students' mastery of complex learning standards that require them to integrate knowledge and skills. These tasks may consist of a series of steps and take several hours or days to complete. In addition to a final product, en route to completing such a task, students may be asked to produce pieces of work that can be collected and scored using extended response rubric scoring techniques. Below are some prominent examples of extended response formats.

#### Portfolios

Portfolios constitute an assessment format through which evidence of competence in a learning domain is collected outside of an on-demand assessment activity. Portfolios typically involve aggregating and scoring pieces of student work collected over an extended time period. Portfolios usually include samples of authentic student classroom work, such as written assignments, project products, or even multi-media documentation of student performances. The tasks documented in portfolios are targeted at highly specific learning objectives such as those referenced by state standards. But they represent more, in that they occur as part of students' classroom sense-making as cultural practice—an issue that will receive further attention later in this chapter. Portfolio assessment has the potential for cultural validity for several reasons:

1.  It can document student performance in a meaningful context (i.e., situated within the usual instructional process).

2.  It can include many forms of evidence of learning—ranging from a teacher's checklist, to a test, to a student essay, to a video made by the student.
3.  It documents progress over time, from marking period to marking period and, as such, provides a view of a student's development.
4.  Teachers and students can annotate the entries within a portfolio to shed light on the meaning of a student's performance or product.
5.  Students can exercise judgment about what to include and how to interpret its importance to the learning process.
6.  Any language can be used by the student or teacher.

In using portfolio assessment, teachers need to consider what counts as a culturally valid way of using the portfolio overall. Practices such as students' evaluating their own performance, students' presenting their portfolios at parent conferences, and having students critique each other's work may be more or less easily adopted by students—depending upon their cultural norms and values (Trumbull, Greenfield, Rothstein-Fisch, & Quiroz, 2007). Teachers need to make decisions about how to ensure that rubrics are appropriate for students who are still learning English. Even those students who have been designated as fully English proficient, but who are not native speakers of English, should still be regarded as English language learners (cf., Linquanti, 2001).

### Observational Protocols

Observational protocols are sometimes used to rate or categorize students' learning performance and capabilities by having a trained observer/scorer watch a student in authentic classroom activity. The observer/scorer can be (but is not always) the teacher. He or she may use a checklist to document particular actions of a student, including ways of using language to engage in a discussion or apparent strategies a student is using to solve a mathematics problem. To come up with a score (or scores) for a particular performance, the observer often uses a rubric to rate a student's demonstration of target skills or knowledge.

### Critical Issues for ELLs

All three formats raise scoring issues for ELL students. Just as with rubric scoring of c-r on-demand items, the scores assigned to students based on rating of collections of their work via observational protocols are dependent on the ability of ELL students to understand the demands of such tasks and to respond as expected. As suggested earlier, the propensity to respond as expected is highly idiosyncratic. It is based not only on students' familiarity with the skills and knowledge they are expected to exercise but also their linguistic, cultural, and educational backgrounds. But, while caution is necessary in interpreting the performance of ELL students on such items, one important advantage these assessment formats have over an on-demand format is that they are embedded in regular, ongoing classroom contexts. Because of this feature, ELL students are more likely to draw on their understanding of the everyday social and cultural characteristics of classroom life and its academic linguistic and task demands in responding to tasks.

As with c-r on-demand assessment items, the scores assigned to students' work or observed performance on these assessment formats arising in authentic classroom contexts are entirely dependent on scorer judgment, given the rubric criteria for scoring. As with scoring of on-demand c-r items, the rubric ratings generated by scorers is affected by scorers' familiarity with the characteristics of ELL students and scorers' understanding of how students' work or observed performances indicate relevant versus irrelevant knowledge and skills, given the goals of the assessment at hand.

Assessments involving scoring of collections of student work or observed performances vary in their reliance on local scorers, such as teachers and local school staff, versus reliance on professionally hired scorers who are not immediately familiar with the students and their communities. For instance, some states, such as Vermont, have attempted to use portfolio assessment for accountability purposes (Koretz, Stecher, Klein, & McCaffrey, 1994). Large-scale assessment developers and implementers are professionally responsible for training scorers on the use of scoring rubrics and for monitoring the quality and reliability of scoring on an ongoing basis. It is much more challenging to propose and implement such systematic accountability with individual classroom teachers and local scoring personnel without extensive resources. However, because teachers and local staff are more likely to be familiar with ELL students and their knowledge, skills, and responsiveness to instruction on a day-to-day basis, their scores may be more accurate or valid than those of professionally trained outsiders.

## Assessment Score Validity and Accuracy: What to Look for When Assessing ELLs

Where does all the foregoing discussion take us with regard to teachers', educational stakeholders', and students' understanding of the *overall scores* of ELL students reported on an assessment? At this point, it is useful to recall that an important and fundamental property of an assessment score is that it is only and always an *estimate* of what an individual knows and can do in a domain under assessment. (See Koretz, 2008, for a lucid, commonsense, but technically sophisticated, discussion of why this is so.)

The estimate of achievement provided by an overall assessment score is influenced by the assessment's focus on some skill and knowledge areas in an assessment domain (and not others) and by the ways in which assessment items are able to capture evidence of this knowledge and these skills reliably. A further constraint is that every assessment weights the contributions of its scored components in the computation of an overall score (or sub-scores), following mathematical and statistical procedures. These procedures give more importance or less importance to different assessment components/items, based on the assessment blueprint and ways of treating the sub-scores statistically.

In this light, it is helpful to review some of the most basic properties of assessment scores that are used to summarize how well students performed on an assessment. We will look at key properties that are of greatest concern in evaluating the validity and accuracy of the test scores of ELL students relative to other student groups. For a more detailed and comprehensive coverage of contemporary assessment and measurement at an introductory level, see Payne (2002).

Overall assessment scores are typically reported on a numerical scale. They may also be reported as a proficiency classification based on scores earned by students (e.g., "basic," "proficient," "advanced"). Sometimes, both kinds of scores are reported together. Students' overall scores of either sort are based on an aggregation of their scores on the individual scored pieces of an assessment, based on the specifications of the assessment blueprint. Regardless of the numerical scale or "ruler" used on any assessment to report overall performance, almost without exception in the everyday world of assessment, the higher the reported overall score, the higher the estimated underlying proficiency of a student in the domain assessed.[5]

All numerically scored assessments yield a probability distribution of scores for a sample of students who have taken the assessment. That is to say, every individual score occurs with different frequency—i.e., each score is found to occur a certain number of times, ranging from occurring not at all to occurring the most frequently. If we divide the number of times a given score occurs by the total number of persons taking a test, we get the proportion of times a given score arose. If we add these proportions together across every possible score we get a total of 100%. Beyond examining the proportion of times each score occurs, we are interested in two other kinds of statistical indicators of overall performance on an assessment. The *mean* score is the average score earned by all examinees. A statistic known as the *standard deviation* provides a measure of how spread out scores are across their range, relative to their distance from the mean. Given knowledge of the relative frequency of different scores, we can compute the *percentile rank* for any given score. This is simply the percentage of students who attained a lower score, i.e., the sixtieth percentile means that 60% scored below the student in question. Score reports provided to schools usually include this information. Sometimes percentile scores are reported in units such as *stanines*, *quartiles*, or other related measures based on percentiles.

Students' overall assessment scores are only estimates of underlying skills and knowledge, and can reflect both construct relevant variability and construct irrelevant variability. Score variation actually has two components: (1) construct relevant variance, or the score differences based on variation in students' levels of proficiency with the knowledge and skills targeted by the assessment; and (2) construct irrelevant variance, or the score differences that are not related to differences in students' targeted knowledge and skills. These may include lack of familiarity with test format or limitations in vocabulary that have nothing to do with the subject domain. Despite the best efforts of assessment developers (psychometricians and teachers alike), some error of measurement is reflected in any assessment score. The issue is whether it is possible to limit the influence of factors that distort the interpretation of the scores of ELL students and that can thus distort our understanding of how to support ELLs' learning.

The *reliability* of an assessment is the degree to which such an estimate is judged to be accurate. Assessment developers have created various statistical techniques to estimate the reliability of quantitative assessment scores as well as ways to estimate the accuracy of proficiency classifications based on assessment scores.

In the ideal world, a student's overall score on an assessment would not fluctuate if the student took an assessment twice in close temporal proximity, or if a student were administered either of two perfectly parallel forms of an assessment. Not unexpectedly given our practical knowledge of the everyday measurement of natural phenomena, this ideal circumstance does not match reality. Some error of measurement is unavoidable. Two sorts of error arise in overall assessment scores: (1) random error that cannot be controlled or be easily controlled for; and (2) error of a systematic nature that affects both the validity and accuracy of scores and proficiency classifications and that, in principle, might be controlled for—this is captured by the notion of construct irrelevant variance mentioned above. The individual scoring elements of an assessment that contribute to an overall assessment score are the origins of both construct relevant and irrelevant variance reflected in an overall score. These scoring elements include scores (often called "sub-scores") earned on individual items that are administered in an "on-demand" manner, or scores derived from evaluation of student work samples.

To deal with these two sources of measurement error, psychometricians and measurement experts rely on alternative techniques to estimate and measure the reliability of overall assessment scores. Commonly used measures on state assessments used under NCLB include measures of internal consistency (the degree to which students perform better on easy items and less well on hard items) and scorer agreement rates (used to capture whether different scorers rate the same c-r items similarly for the same examinees).

The combined occurrence of both kinds of error in overall scores on an assessment is commonly captured by a statistic known as the standard error of measurement. This statistic estimates the average deviation of students' observed score from their predicted true score (Payne, 2002). The estimated standard error of measurement ought be very similar for ELL students and non-ELL students. When the estimated standard error of measurement is greater for ELL students, then there is the possibility that non-random factors are systematically leading ELL students to perform differently on an assessment compared to non-ELL students. In this case, evidence of possible construct irrelevant variance in assessment scores has emerged and deserves investigation. When ELL students only show a limited variability in their overall scores, this in itself may lower the reliability of their scores for statistical reasons. For instance, if a very large proportion score between the fifteenth and thirtieth percentile, the assessment may not be detecting important differences in students' learning that would be reflected were a broader range of students with a greater range of achievement assessed.

The reliability and standard error of measurement of an assessment are rarely, if ever, reported on score reports of state assessments. Nonetheless, educators are advised that professional testing standards (AERA, APA, & NCME, 1999) take the position that reporting and examination of this information is critical when evaluating the validity and accuracy of tests and educational assessments.

Estimating and reporting the accuracy of classifications of students into achievement proficiency categories is a technical topic beyond the scope of the present chapter (see Luecht, 2006). Suffice it to say that teachers, educational practitioners, and parents need to be aware that local school district assessment data experts should be held accountable for answering questions about whether the score cut-points to set proficiency categorizations lead to similar accuracy in classifying ELL and non-ELL students into proficiency categories.

## Interpreting the Validity of Overall Assessment Scores for ELL Students Given Student Background

One simple and important piece of advice is that interpreters of ELL student scores on an assessment should examine the mean, standard deviation, and percentile distribution of ELL students relative to non-ELL students in their local school jurisdiction and other related jurisdictions of interest. For example, a teacher or school administrator may want to know whether ELL students in certain grades in a school are performing not only like non-ELL students in the same grades locally, but also higher or lower than ELL and non-ELL students in the surrounding school district or state.

This information is useful for helping infer what underlying contextual demographic and curriculum/teacher issues may play a role in sensitizing instruction to the needs of local ELL students. Every educational jurisdiction, whether it is a classroom and grade, school district, geographical region, or state, has unique characteristics—even though it shares similarities with other jurisdictions. ELL students vary in terms of their background characteristics just as do schools, their teachers and instructional resources, and interpretations of policies and status within state regulatory processes (e.g., status in terms of compliance with state and NCLB policies). Also important are the racial and sociodemographic characteristics of communities. These ELL student demographic and contextual factors all co-vary and have been found to interact with assessment indicators of ELL student achievement (Fry, 2007, 2008). Accordingly, it is important that every jurisdiction places value on formulating its own investigation of factors influencing the assessment performance of its ELL students, where there is will and motivation to do so on equity and policy grounds. It is unwise to specify a single rationale or strategy for doing so; each strategy must be tailored to the needs and motives of a given jurisdiction, though it is fair to state that NCLB and state policies consistent with NCLB will mandate such attention in most jurisdictions.

For example, if local ELL students perform well below ELL students at the state level, this should trigger concern for more intensive exploration of demographic and educational background characteristics of local ELL students and how these may vary from state statistics in this regard. Important factors that might emerge, include, e.g., the possibility that local ELL students tend to be from highly transient, low-income families with low parent educational attainment backgrounds. Or it could be that in the upper grades there is an exceptionally high concentration of longstanding ELL students in an urban community who are U.S. born and who show a pattern of increasingly lower mean assessment scores relative to non-ELL students as they progress through the school grades. It could, of course, be that programs and instruction provided to ELLs are inferior to those in other districts or are not well-matched to the needs of students. Those responsible for the education of ELLs need to be careful not to fall into the trap of assuming that deficiencies in student performance are caused by deficits in students themselves (cf., Valencia, 1997).

If the scores of some ELL students are higher than the average for other ELL students locally or at other jurisdictional levels, this too deserves an examination in terms of student characteristics or educational practices. It could be, e.g., that a high incidence of ELL students from particular non-English language groups, coupled with a high incidence of parents with advanced educational and professional attainment, is associated with higher assessment scores—perhaps more so in an achievement area such as math or science than in language arts and reading.

## Going Beyond Understanding ELL Aggregate Scores: Understanding ELL Student Classroom Achievement

Scores and proficiency classifications resulting from scoring on an assessment will necessarily yield incomplete information about what students know and can do in the knowledge and skill domains targeted for assessment. As discussed earlier, ELL students' assessment performance and their resulting scores derived from their performance may be affected by factors that were not intended as measurement targets but that arise because of unfamiliar or construct irrelevant demands of assessment items and their formats. Hence, the credence placed by the public and policy-makers in ELLs' scores on large-scale assessments is quite likely unmerited.

ELL students' instruction and learning occur in the day-to-day activities of classroom life and in the development of students' identities as learners and participants in the classrooms as cultures (Green, Yeager, & Castanheira, 2008; Basterra, Chapter 4, this volume). Teachers, instructional staff, and students themselves are engaged in constantly creating and extending classroom life in ways that shape students' capacity to acquire and apply new knowledge and skills based on earlier experiences in and out of classroom life. Classrooms can be said to have "cultures" in that they are places where particular expectations for particular ways of interacting, using language, demonstrating knowledge, and the like occur as practices, beyond just beliefs about how to think and act. These expectations and practices reflect underlying values—such as cooperation or independence—that are often implicit and most often aligned with the mainstream culture of the U.S. (Hollins, 1996). When teachers recognize the cultural underpinnings of their students' behaviors and approaches to learning in the classroom, they can best capitalize on students' strengths (cf., Gutiérrez, Baquedano-López, & Tejeda, 1999; Rothstein-Fisch & Trumbull, 2008).

Interpreters of ELL students' scores on assessments would be well advised to consider teachers' and students' understanding of what performances and standards of performance are expected in authentic classroom learning activities in subject matter domains such reading/language arts, mathematics, science, and others targeted by standards and standards informed assessments. Assessment scores provide only one channel of information into these concerns.

Attention needs to be given to instructional goals set for students by teachers as well as to policies and instructional practices that might enable ELL students to reach goals—both immediate local goals and policy goals. The goals of an assessment represented by the sampling of behaviors on that assessment and the scores earned may not match what individual ELL students are actually expected to know and do in a classroom. A push–pull tension arises as a result. On the one hand, teachers are expected to have students master skills and knowledge represented on assessments and reflected to varying degrees of accuracy in assessment scores. On the other hand, classroom instruction in its most effective form is tailored to assisting students to achieve new skills and knowledge just ahead of their present capabilities (Tharp & Gallimore, 1988). Existing state assessments in subject matter areas, with their implications for accountability and high stakes for students and schools, are not going to go away in any foreseeable future. So what can be done?

One matter that needs careful attention is improving schools' and teachers' timely interpretation of ELL students' state assessment achievement scores, with proper attention to individual students' background, schooling experiences, and forthcoming curriculum and learning intervention opportunities. Nationwide, a serious dilemma has arisen because state achievement assessment information used for school accountability is not well synchronized with students' academic programming at the time scores are made available to local educators—e.g., last year's spring test scores aren't available until the start of a new school year when students have a new instructor who is unfamiliar with them. A related problem is that teachers and school staff have limited capacity and time to devote to understanding the meaning of individual ELL students' assessment scores in depth.

The upshot of the foregoing tension between assessment scores and the true diagnostic information needed by teachers to guide instruction is that the score of a student on a large-scale assessment has important, though constrained, value. Such scores can be used for understanding what students have learned in the past and can inform how teachers might improve instruction for a new group of students at the same grade level. Or, the assessment scores of a given student can be used to measure or predict the learning progress of the student in the following year when new instruction or remedial instruction is provided. However, this use raises many technical and conceptual issues of the sort cited in this chapter tied to the reliability and validity of assessment, the non-equivalence of assessments across years, and the importance of other achievement evidence beyond assessment evidence.

## What Teachers Can Do

### Final Points for Teacher and Practitioner Reflection and Action

As this chapter has shown, making sense of ELL students' assessment scores is a challenging endeavor. While it is impossible to expect that any list of points suffices, it is possible to enumerate and put in order some guiding questions that every teacher and practitioner should attend to in order to understand and make use of ELL student assessment scores. Here is my candidate list:

1.  What is the purpose of an assessment, and do I understand what skills and knowledge are targeted by the assessment? Am I gauging the meaning of student scores with these issues in mind?
2.  What are the kinds of items and performance demands of items on an assessment whose scores I receive? Do I understand how these items and their performance demands, such as language requirements and item format requirements, relate to the learning objectives and instruction in my classroom?
3.  What do I know about the language background, schooling, and instruction received previously by the ELL students I serve at present in my classroom; and how can that knowledge help me understand student performance?
4.  When I am given the scores resulting from an assessment, what do I know about how the assessment was scored and how these scores are based on the assessment blueprint tied to item types and based on learning standards that students are expected to master? How are scores supposed to inform judgments about what students are expected to know and do? Are scores designed to be measures of competence, or are they just norm-referenced measures?

Do my answers to (1)–(4) add up so that I can have some confidence in my ability to make appropriate use of the assessment scores of the ELL students I serve? Am I able to make valid inferences about my students' learning and needs, given my best understanding of how their ELL status and their individual characteristics interact with the demands of assessments?

5.  In particular, how confident am I that my ELL students have had the opportunity to learn the skills and knowledge represented on state and local assessments?
6.  As a related, but important, factor, are the scores on an assessment reported to me in a timely manner, so that I can connect their meaning to the instruction I provide to support students' mastery of skills and knowledge systematically related to learning standards and the outcomes of an assessment?
7.  Do I understand the limitations of assessment scores, particularly strand sub-scores?
8.  Do I have non-large-scale assessment evidence of achievement based on my own classroom tests, instruction, and evaluation/observation of student

work that supports or supplants the information provided by scores and assessment in order for me to improve the instruction given to students?

Of necessity, this list is incomplete and schematic. Nonetheless, it represents essential questions for all teachers and instructional staff to consider and discuss with other stakeholders. Only by addressing these questions can educators have confidence in their interpretation of the scores of ELL students on large-scale assessments such as state achievement tests. Collaboration among educators with various kinds of expertise—knowledge of language, assessment, human development, culture, educational curriculum and standards—is essential if ELL students are to be well-served. Educators can also benefit from reading and discussing other recent publications that explore these concepts in an in-depth and accessible manner (see, e.g., Kopriva, 2008).

## Conclusion

Understanding ELL students' performance on assessments requires examining the correspondence between the assessment goals, assessment blueprint, and scores on an assessment, and how these affect interpreting the meaning of scores for ELL students, given their individual profiles. Given the heterogeneity in the linguistic, cultural, and educational backgrounds of students, an appropriate strategy might be to work with profile clusters of students (see research by Winter, Kopriva, Chen, & Emick, 2006, as an example). For example, educators could cluster individual ELL students clinically into profiles classifying students as "high vs. low" in areas such as:

- English language oral proficiency (listening and speaking);
- English language reading proficiency;
- English language writing proficiency;
- Length of schooling in U.S. ("more than 2 years vs. less");
- Ability to perform complex tasks independently;
- Familiarity with formats encountered on an assessment (based on prior schooling); and
- Classroom performance in the content area of an assessment.

The goal of such a strategy would be to identify clusters of ELL students whose assessment scores are better interpreted with reference to (1) special challenges they face, given their profiles and (2) the demands of an assessment that might detract from accurate and valid assessment of the skills and knowledge targeted by that assessment.

Such information could be used to better prepare students for assessments. But this would not be an optimal goal. A more important strategy would be to have teachers, educators, parents, students, and other stakeholders realize improved ways to strengthen local instructional practices so as to attain classroom learning goals for individual students, given their background, schooling, and language profile characteristics. The current move towards formative assessments based on teachers' implementation of explicit subject matter learning progressions can help implement this strategy (Bailey & Heritage, 2008). Learning progression strategies require that instruction in subject matter skills and knowledge be tied explicitly to learning activities and materials logically ordered and sequenced so as to provide students and teachers with assessment feedback on progress toward learning goals. In such an approach, teachers and students would negotiate and elaborate their common understanding of instructional goals, activities, and benchmark accomplishments embedded in formative assessments that are designed to provide alternative evidence of students' progress toward learning goals.

One of the most important ramifications of a learning progression instructional strategy for ELL students is the possibility of a careful monitoring of students' understanding of the format, purpose, and detailed practices of learning activities and assessments. This monitoring could be coupled with close-in—if not immediate—feedback to students about whether they are understanding what was expected of them and how well they are performing. Elsewhere, I have argued that ELL student assessment would be well served by coupling feedback of this sort to efforts to foster students' sense of self as agents and participants in their own learning (Durán, 2008). Current large-scale state achievement assessments are not designed or intended to accomplish these ends, and the interpretation of their scores cannot adequately serve to inform close-in instructional practices. However, such scores might legitimately capture the gross achievement characteristics of students, subject to limitations cited in this chapter.

# Appendix 6.1

| California Content Standards: Grade 2 | Number of items | % |
|---|---|---|
| By the end of grade two, students understand place value and number relationships in addition and subtraction, and they use simple concepts of multiplication. They measure quantities with appropriate units. They classify shapes and see relationships among them by paying attention to their geometric attributes. They collect and analyze data and verify the answers. | | |
| **Number sense** | 38 | 58 |
| **Standard Set 1.0 Students understand the relationship between numbers, quantities, and place value in whole numbers up to 1,000** | | |
| 1.1* Count, read, and write whole numbers to 1,000 and identify the place value for each digit. | 3 | |
| 1.2 Use words, models, and expanded forms (e.g., 45 = 4 tens + 5) to represent numbers (to 1,000). | 1 | |
| 1.3* Order and compare whole numbers to 1,000 by using the symbols <, =, >. | 4 | |
| **Standard Set 2.0 Students estimate, calculate, and solve problems involving addition and subtraction of two- and three-digit numbers** | | |
| 2.1* Understand and use the inverse relationship between addition and subtraction (e.g., an opposite number sentence for 8 + 6 = 14 is 14 − 6 = 8) to solve problems and check solutions. | 2 1/2** | |
| 2.2* Find the sum or difference of two whole numbers up to three digits long. | 4 | |
| 2.3 Use mental arithmetic to find the sum or difference of two-digit numbers. | **NA*** | |
| **Standard Set 3.0* Students model and solve simple problems involving multiplication and division** | | |
| 3.1* Use repeated addition, arrays, and counting by multiples to do multiplication. | 2 | |
| 3.2* Use repeated subtraction, equal sharing, and forming equal groups with remainders to do division. | 3 | |
| 3.3* Know the multiplication tables of 2s, 5s, and 10s (to "times 10") and commit them to memory. | 3 | |

Source: California Mathematics Standards Grade 2, 1997.

## Notes

1. Many of the concepts and terms used in this chapter have been introduced in Chapter 1, and readers may want to refer to explanations in that chapter for amplification.
2. AYP goals are decided uniquely by each state, although they are reviewed for their appropriateness by the U.S. Department of Education. These goals typically specify the percentage of students attaining proficiency in a subject matter area of an assessment—this figure increasing until a goal of 100% is attained by the 2013–2014 year under NCLB legislation effective as of the time of the writing of this chapter.
3. The blueprint is sometimes referred to as a *set of specifications*, especially when it includes an explicit description of how the assessment is administered.
4. Both (1) and (2) are scored subsequently.
5. This directionality is a convention rather than a necessary way of orienting an assessment measurement scale.

## References

American Educational Research Association, American Psychological Association, The National Council on Measurement in Education (1999). *Standards for educational and psychological testing*. Washington, DC: American Psychological Association.

August, D., Carlo, M., Dressler, C., & Snow, C. (2005). The critical role of vocabulary development for English language learners. *Learning Disabilities Research and Practice*, 20(1), 50–57.

Bailey, A.L., & Heritage, M. (2008). *Formative assessment for literacy instruction: Developing academic language and reading proficiency in diverse learners*. Thousand Oaks, CA: Corwin/Sage Press.

Cizek, G.J., & Bunch, M. (2007). *Standard setting: A practitioner's guide*. Newbury Park, CA: Sage.

Cohen, A., & Wollack, J. (2003). Helpful tips for creating reliable and valid classroom tests: Getting started—the test blueprint. *The Learning Link*, 3(4), 1–2.

Durán, R.P. (2008). Assessing English Language Learners' achievement. In J. Green, A. Luke, & G. Kelly (Eds.), *Review of research in education*, Vol. 32. Washington DC: American Educational Research Association, pp. 292–327.

Fry, R. (2007). *How far behind in math and reading are English language learners?* Washington, DC: Pew Hispanic Center.

Fry, R. (2008). *The role of schools in the English language learner achievement gap*. Washington, DC: Pew Hispanic Center.

Green, J., Yeager, B., & Castanheira, M. (2008). Talking texts into being: On the social construction of everyday life and academic knowledge in the classroom. In N. Mercer & S. Hodgkinson (Eds.), *Exploring talk in schools: Inspired by the work of Douglas Banres*. London: Sage.

Gutiérrez, K., Baquedano-López, P., & Tejeda, C. (1999). Rethinking diversity: Hybridity and hybrid language practices in the third space. *Mind, Culture, and Activity*, 6(4), 286–303.

Hollins, E.R. (1996). *Culture in school learning: Revealing the deep meaning*. Mahwah, NJ: Erlbaum.

Kopriva, R. (2008). *Improving testing for English Language Learners*. New York, NY: Routledge.

Koretz, D. (2008). *Measuring up: What educational testing really tells us*. Cambridge, MA: Harvard University Press.

Koretz, D., Stecher, B.M., Klein, S.P., & McCaffrey, D.F. (1994). The Vermont portfolio assessment program: Findings and implications. *Education Measurement: Issues and Practice*, 13(3), 5–16.

Lager, Carl A. (2006). Types of mathematics–language reading interactions that unnecessarily hinder algebra learning and assessment. *Reading Psychology*, 27(2), 165–204.

Linquanti, R. (2001). *The redesignation dilemma: Challenges and choices in fostering meaningful accountability for English language learners.* UC Berkeley: University of California Linguistic Minority Research Institute. Retrieved from: http://escholarship.org/uc/item/2hw8k347.

Luecht, R. (2006). Designing tests for pass–fail decisions using item response theory. In S. Downing & T. Haladayna (Eds.), *Handbook of test development.* New York, NY: Routledge, pp. 575–596.

No Child Left Behind (NCCB) Act (2002). Public Law No. 107–110, 115 Stat. 1425.

Payne, D.A. (2002). *Applied educational assessment.* Florence, KY: Centage Wadsworth.

Rothstein-Fisch, C., & Trumbull, E. (2008). *Managing diverse classrooms: How to build on students' cultural strengths.* Alexandria, VA: ASCD.

Ryan, J. (2006). Practices, issues, and trends in student test score reporting. In S. Downing & T. Haladayna (Eds.), *Handbook of test development.* New York, NY: Routledge, pp. 677–710.

Solano-Flores, G., & Trumbull, E. (2003). Examining language in context: The need for new research and practice paradigms in the testing of English language learners. *Educational Researcher*, 32(2), 3–13.

Solorzano, R. (2008). High stakes testing: Issues, implications, and remedies for English Language Learners. *Review of Educational Research*, 78(2), 260–329.

Tharp, R., & Gallimore, R. (1988). *Rousing minds to life: Teaching, learning, and schooling in social context.* New York, NY: Cambridge University Press.

Trumbull, E., Greenfield, P.M., Rothstein-Fisch, C., & Quiroz, B. (2007). Bridging cultures in parent conferences: Implications for school psychology. In G. Esquivel, E. Lopez, & S. Nahari (Eds.), *Handbook of multicultural school psychology: An interdisciplinary approach.* Mahwah, NJ: Erlbaum, pp. 615–636.

Valencia, R.R. (1997). *The evolution of deficit thinking: Educational thought and practice.* Bristol, PA: Falmer Press.

Winter, P., Kopriva, R., Chen, C., & Emick, J. (2006). Exploring individual and item factors that affect assessment validity for diverse learners: Results from a large-scale cognitive lab. *Learning and Individual Differences*, 16, 267–276.

# Chapter 7

# Promoting Cultural Validity in the Assessment of Bilingual Special Education Students

*John J. Hoover and Janette Klingner*

---

**Chapter Overview**

This chapter examines cultural validity in the assessment of bilingual students. It includes an overview of the response to intervention model and selected research results concerning its use with English language learners (ELLs) and a discussion of the overrepresentation of bilingual students in programs for students with disabilities and cultural responsive referral and assessment practices. Also, the chapter provides recommendations for practitioners to best understand and address cultural differences in making eligibility and referral decisions.

---

Assessment of culturally and linguistically diverse students requires the effective application of sound assessment principles applied in culturally responsive ways to reduce unnecessary referrals, the selection and use of appropriate assessment devices and practices, and the interpretation of assessment scores to best meet diverse needs in education. Concern with the proper assessment of diverse learners for special education has existed for decades, especially as related to referrals, eligibility, validity, and appropriate educational programming. Currently, educators attempting to develop and implement multi-tiered responses to intervention models struggle with how the assessment needs of culturally and linguistically diverse learners are best addressed within this structure.

## Overview of Multi-Tiered Response to Intervention

The contemporary structure for completing assessments in today's schools is found within a multi-tiered response to intervention (RTI) model (Fuchs & Fuchs, 2006). "The Response to Intervention (RTI) process is a multi-tiered approach to providing services and interventions to struggling learners at increasing levels of intensity" (Perangelo & Giuliani, 2008, p. 1). Therefore, RTI includes tiers or levels of instruction that increase in intensity and duration based on learners' progress toward defined educational benchmarks or standards. Most school systems have, or are in the process of developing, a multi-tiered response to intervention model (Hoover, Baca, Love, & Saenz, 2008) that generally includes three tiers of instruction:

Tier 1. Implementation of researched-based curriculum in general education for all learners.
Tier 2. Implementation of evidence-based interventions for struggling learners to support the research-based curriculum found within Tier 1.
Tier 3. Implementation of evidence-based interventions and/or alternate research-based curricula to meet significant needs of struggling learners, which may include students with special education needs.

Estimates are that 80–90% of all learners should be successful with Tier 1 instruction, while 15–20% will need some Tier 2 supplemental support and 1–5% will require intensive Tier 3 interventions (Yell, 2004). Three primary types of assessments are associated with the multi-tiered level of instruction (Hoover, 2009b).

- *Universal screening*—The general screening of all learners (e.g., screening three times per year) to identify students who may be showing signs of struggling to achieve annual benchmarks.
- *Progress monitoring*—The regular and systematic monitoring of learner progress toward benchmarks once they have been identified as struggling learners. Progress monitoring occurs more frequently than universal screening (e.g., monthly, bi-weekly) to more closely assess student progress as well as determine the effects of Tier 2 supplemental supports.
- *Diagnostic*—The use of assessment practices and devices to more clearly identify individual learner academic and social-emotional needs as well as clarify the existence of a disability. Diagnostic assessment may be completed to best determine needed Tier 3 intensive interventions and/or whether a disability exists requiring special education. However, diagnostic assessment may also be required to clarify progress monitoring scores obtained in Tiers 1 or 2 (Capizzi & Fuchs, 2005) or to supplement other assessment data (Riddle Buly & Valencia, 2002).

## RTI Research and ELLs

Recent projects have researched current practices seen in today's schools for educating ELLs within RTI models, some of which yield results that suggest less than desirable situations for meeting bilingual or ESL needs through response to intervention models. Orosco and Klinger (2007) found that the lack of vocabulary knowledge for some ELLs was a frustration to an elementary classroom teacher, leading to placing blame on the child for lack of progress. Hoover and Love (in press) found that in some schools, ELLs are provided

Tier 2 instruction based on one screening score with little or no consideration for "rate of progress" and related cultural and linguistic factors to initially adjust Tier 1 core instruction. In some instances, up to 50% of ELL students in the same classroom were targeted to receive Tier 2 instruction prior to adjusting Tier 1 instruction to better meet the majority of learner needs in the classroom (Hoover & Love, in press). In a national study, Hoover et al. (2008) found that state department directors of special education indicated that their statewide trainings in multi-tiered response to intervention placed the least amount of emphasis on culturally responsive RTI as compared to several other topical areas.

Additional research on the effectiveness of various interventions with Hispanic students or ELLs includes work completed by Calhoon and colleagues (Calhoon, Otaiba, Cihak, King, & Avalos, 2007; Calhoon, Otaiba, Greenberg, King, & Avalos, 2006) as well as McMaster, Kung, Han, and Cao (2008), who found that peer-assisted learning strategies worked well as a first-tier instructional approach in bilingual and Title 1 classrooms. Carlo et al. (2004) and Silverman (2007) focused on vocabulary instruction for ELLs in bilingual and mainstream classrooms. Denton, Anthony, Parker, and Hasbrouck (2004) examined the effects of two tutoring programs on the English reading development of Spanish–English bilingual students. In a series of well-designed studies, Vaughn and Linan-Thompson and their colleagues have tested the effectiveness of Spanish and English interventions for ELLs considered at risk for reading difficulties in kindergarten, first grade, and second grade, with positive results (Linan-Thompson, Bryant, Dickson, & Kouzekanani, 2005; Linan-Thompson, Vaughn, Hickman-Davis, & Kouzekanani, 2003; Linan-Thompson, Vaughn, Prater, & Cirino, 2006; Vaughn et al., 2006a; Vaughn et al., 2006b; Vaughn et al., 2006c). Gerber and his team of researchers (Gerber, Jimenez, Leafstedt, Villaruz, Richards, & English, 2004; Leafstedt, Richards, & Gerber, 2004) found that small-group interventions in phonological awareness in Spanish could be quite effective for K-1 ELLs. Haager and Windmueller (2001) and Kamps et al. (2007) successfully implemented second-tier interventions in English for ELLs, as did Gunn, Smolkowski, Biglan, Black, and Blair (2005) with Hispanic students. This body of research provides a valuable resource for practitioners searching for validated practices for their ELLs.

These and other similar studies underscore the need for more targeted professional development and onsite supports to more effectively prepare teachers to provide sufficient opportunities to learn for ELLs within response to intervention models. Additional discussions about issues pertaining to the successful education and assessment of ELLs are included in subsequent sections of this chapter. In summary, within multi-tiered response to intervention models, all learners are now required to be screened, have their progress monitored, and, if necessary, receive a comprehensive diagnostic assessment, should continued and pervasive lack of progress toward achievement of benchmarks be evident. Within each of the six aspects of multi-tiered RTI (i.e., universal screening, progress monitoring, diagnostic, Tier 1, Tier 2, Tier 3), specific issues arise relative to the effective implementation of each with culturally and linguistically diverse learners. The diverse issues discussed in this chapter and book pertain to all three aspects of assessment within RTI as well as to the appropriate implementation of each tier of instruction. While this chapter is targeting cultural and linguistic issues specific to assessment for possible special education, the issues must be considered in all aspects of multi-tiered response to intervention to ensure cultural validity for diverse learners.

A continuing source of controversy with the assessment of diverse learners is the misidentification leading to inappropriate placements. Sorrells, Webb-Johnson, and Townsend (2004) found that general and special educators' misperceptions of diverse needs contribute to a school's inability to meet cultural and linguistic needs in the classroom. Invalid assessment for diverse learners for special education results from several educational practices including the following, as discussed by Baca and Cervantes (2004), Hoover (2011), Klingner and Harry (2006), Klingner, Hoover, and Baca (2008), Patton (1998), and Salend and Garrick-Duhaney (2005):

1. Bias in assessment devices and practices;
2. Misperceiving various diverse behaviors as indicators of a disability;
3. Inequities in the distribution of school funding that limits access to appropriate education for many culturally and linguistically diverse learners;
4. Lack of support for and input from family/community in the assessment process; and
5. Inappropriate application and uses of assessment scores when making instructional decisions.

The ability of assessment teams to successfully address these and related issues directly affects culturally responsive and valid assessment for diverse learners. Several broad topics reflective of the above issues in the implementation of culturally valid assessment of diverse learners are discussed below. These include: (1) overrepresentation, (2) cultural influences in assessment, and (3) pre-referral and referral for special education of diverse learners. We begin with a discussion and overview of the misplacement and overrepresentation of culturally and linguistically diverse learners in special education.

### Overview of Disproportionate Representation of Diverse Learners in Special Education

The disproportionate representation of culturally and linguistically diverse students in special education is not a new problem. Ever since 1968, when Dunn first pointed out the extent to which culturally and linguistically diverse students were overrepresented in programs for students with mental retardation, educators, researchers, and policy-makers have tried to bring about changes that would reduce overrepresentation. The National Research Council (NRC) studied disproportionate representation in 1982 (Heller, Holtzman, & Messick, 1982) and again 20 years later (Donovan & Cross, 2002). Yet despite these two NRC reports as well as numerous resolutions, statements, and actions from major professional organizations, such as the Council for Exceptional Children (CEC) (1997, 2002), litigation (e.g., court cases such as Larry P. v. Riles, 1984 and Diana v. the California State Board of Education, 1970), policy changes (e.g., Individuals with Disabilities Education Act amendments), a federally funded technical assistance center (i.e., the National Center for Culturally Responsive Education Systems), pressure from parent groups, and efforts from a limited number of researchers, little has changed (see Table 7.1 for current risk ratios[1]) (Klingner et al., 2005). African American students are the most likely to be overrepresented, particularly in the high incidence disability categories of mental retardation and serious emotional disturbance (see Table 7.1). Yet other ethnic and linguistic groups are also overrepresented; this becomes especially apparent when examining variations in placement rates across states and even school districts and looking at population sub-groups (Artiles, Rueda, Salazar, & Higareda, 2005; MacMillan & Reschly, 1998; Oswald, Coutinho, Best, & Singh, 1999).

Overrepresentation is most prevalent in the "judgmental" categories of special education, or, in other words, those disabilities typically identified by school personnel rather than a medical professional after children have started school (i.e., learning disabilities, mental retardation,[2] and severe emotional disturbance). Research across three decades suggests that when determining whether students qualify for special education in one of these categories, school clinicians are influenced by a multitude of factors other than within-child characteristics and exercise wide latitude when making decisions (Gottlieb, Alter, Gottlieb, & Wishner, 1994; Harry & Klingner, 2006; Mehan, 1991; Mehan, Hartwick, & Meihls, 1986).

Placement rates among Hispanics and ELLs have changed substantially over the last four decades since Diana v. California Board of Education (1970) and Mercer (1973) pointed out that Hispanics were highly overrepresented in MR programs. It was common for psychologists to label ELLs as MR using English tests even when the students only spoke Spanish. Over time, the number of Hispanic students placed in MR programs has decreased to the point that Hispanic students are now about as likely to be labeled MR as White students (see Table 7.1). Hispanic students are now more likely to be identified as LD. Although the national risk ratio for Hispanic students is only a little over 1, at 1.10, meaning

*Table 7.1* Risk Ratios in High Incidence Special Education Categories, by Ethnicity

| Disability | American Indian/ Alaska Native | Asian/Pacific Islander | Black (not Hispanic) | Hispanic | White (not Hispanic) |
|---|---|---|---|---|---|
| LD | 1.53 | 0.39 | 1.34 | 1.10 | 0.86 |
| MR | 1.10 | 0.45 | 3.04 | 0.60 | 0.61 |
| SED | 1.30 | 0.28 | 2.25 | 0.52 | 0.86 |

Source: Adapted from the *26th Annual Report to Congress on the Implementation of Individuals with Disabilities Education Act, 2004* (Skiba et al., 2008).

Note
LD = learning disabilities; MR = mental retardation; SED = serious emotional disturbance.

that they are just slightly overrepresented in LD, in some states and among some sub-populations of Hispanic students, such as ELLs, the risk ratio is much higher (Klingner et al., 2005).

The identification of ELLs as LD is quite complex because linguistic and immigration factors compound cultural, socioeconomic, and other influences (Klingner, Artiles, & Méndez-Barletta, 2006). For instance, determining whether an ELL is struggling with reading because of LD or factors associated with the language acquisition process is notoriously challenging (Klingner et al., 2008). Artiles et al. (2005) investigated the special education placement patterns of sub-populations of ELLs in 11 urban districts in California and noted significant overrepresentation when they examined data by grade, special education category, and language program (straight English immersion, modified English immersion, bilingual), and level of English proficiency. They found that older ELLs were more likely to be overrepresented than younger students, ELLs in English immersion programs were more likely to be identified than their peers in modified English immersion or bilingual programs, and students whose language proficiency tests indicated they were limited in both Spanish and English were more likely to be placed than ELLs with higher scores in their native language.

For many reasons, in some schools and districts ELLs are actually under- rather than overrepresented in special education (USDOE & NICHD, 2003). One factor influencing placement rates is that many practitioners are hesitant to refer and/or place ELLs in special education before they seem to be fully proficient in English. It is not uncommon for teachers and support personnel to be confused about district policies and believe that ELLs must have acquired a certain level of English proficiency before the referral process can begin (Harry & Klingner, 2006). In part, this is because the characteristics of students who are in the process of learning a new language (i.e., English) can mirror those of students with learning disabilities, and it can be challenging even for experienced professionals to distinguish between the two. Thus, some ELLs' special educational needs are not being met while other ELLs are inappropriately receiving special education services. Our goal is to identify the right students.

Some might wonder why it is problematic to place students in special education who do not really have a disability. After all, students in special education presumably receive intensive instructional support tailored to meet their individual needs. Although there are benefits to receiving this kind of special education, there also are negative consequences. Disability labels stigmatize students as inferior and tend to result in lowered expectations by teachers, parents, and the students themselves. These lowered expectations can result in a self-fulfilling prophecy and learned helplessness. Also, special education programs potentially separate students from peers and restrict their access to the general educational curriculum. This seems to be especially true for ELLs placed in special education (Zehler, Fleischman, Hopstock, Stephenson, Pendzick, & Sapru, 2003). Also, ELLs in special education are more likely to receive fewer language support services and to be instructed only in English than ELLs who are not in special education (Zehler et al., 2003). Special education placement may lead to inappropriate services that do not match students' needs, and ultimately result in poor educational and life outcomes (Patton, 1998).

One of the more prominent realities that contribute significantly to the over-representation of diverse learners in special education is the lack of consideration of cultural and linguistic diversity within the assessment process. We continue our discussions about valid assessment by presenting critical cultural/linguistic considerations and practices that contribute to effective assessment for diverse learners in today's instructional environments.

### Culturally Valid Assessment

Culturally valid assessment refers to a process that considers cultural values and norms as well as English as a second language development in the selection and administration of assessment devices and practices, along with the scoring, interpretation, and uses of the assessment scores. Overall, culturally valid assessment is a process that is reliable, fair, and appropriate for diverse learners (Solano-Flores, Chapter 1, this volume). Valid assessment for diverse learners best occurs when cultural responsiveness exists for the following: (1) assessment instruments and practices; (2) assessment decision-making process; (3) educator cultural competence; and (4) use of assessment scores in instructional and eligibility decisions. Consideration of a variety of cultural and linguistic issues within each of these facilitates implementation of culturally valid assessment.

### Assessment Instruments and Practices

The most fundamental consideration associated with selection and use of an assessment device or practice is validity. This includes: (1) extent to which these measures assess that which they purport to measure for the population of learners being assessed (Abedi, Chapter 3, this volume), and (2) accurate interpretation and use of assessment scores or results (Durán, Chapter 6, this volume). Table 7.2 provides several items relevant to determining the cultural responsiveness of an assessment instrument. The table, developed from information found in Baca and Cervantes (2004), Hoover (2009a), and Klingner et al. (2008), provides educators with information necessary to evaluate the appropriateness of an assessment instrument for use with culturally and linguistically diverse learners.

As shown, the items reflect a variety of critical diversity topics such as appropriate content and examples, validation with diverse learners, discussion within the assessment manual reflecting appropriateness for use with diverse learners, necessary experiential background in test-taking, and English language proficiency levels required to complete the assessment. A positive response to each of the items in the table facilitates a more culturally responsive assessment by ensuring that proper assessment devices are selected and used with diverse learners.

In addition to assessment instruments, a variety of assessment practices are appropriate for use to assess needs of culturally and linguistically diverse students. These reflect the many authentic ways for gathering assessment data such

Table 7.2  Culturally Valid Assessment Devices

*A culturally valid assessment device includes the following ...*

Development, research, and validation of assessment devices include adequate numbers of diverse learners in the population sample.

Technical manual adequately describes and summarizes procedures and steps reflecting cultural and linguistic diversity among population included in the development and norming samples.

Translated assessment devices were developed adhering to proper translation procedures.

Device allows for accommodations of second language acquisition needs when used with English learners.

Assessment's technical manual describes appropriate uses and potential limitations for use with culturally and linguistically diverse learners.

If testing is completed in English, assessment manual clearly delineates necessary level of English language proficiency required for completion of the device (e.g., fluent English speaker).

Language of the assessment device is in the student's most proficient language and/or English when assessment results are used for making special education eligibility decisions.

as curriculum-based measurement, running records, performance-based assessment, functional behavioral assessment or work sample analysis, to name a few. Similar to the use of assessment devices, the proper implementation of authentic assessment practices requires consideration of cultural and linguistic factors to be of most relevance for use with diverse learners. Table 7.3 provides selected items that educators should consider when using various assessment practices with diverse learners. These items complement those presented in the previous table as a comprehensive assessment is completed (i.e., use of formal assessment instruments along with authentic, classroom-based assessment). The table, developed from information found in Hoover, Klingner, Baca, and Patton (2007), Hoover (2009a), Klingner et al. (2008), provides practical considerations when completing authentic assessment with diverse students.

As shown, items such as consideration of cultural values and norms, language proficiency, acculturation, and sufficient opportunities to learn ensure the proper implementation of authentic assessment practices with diverse learners. A strength in using authentic assessment for diverse learners is the ability of educators to adjust assessment conditions to address unique cultural and linguistic factors the learner brings to the classroom. Some of these factors are presented in Table 7.3, and adherence to these will facilitate a more culturally valid assessment. Therefore, as shown in both Tables 7.2 and 7.3, a variety of issues reflect culturally responsive assessment, and educators are encouraged to apply these items in the selection and use of the various assessment instruments and practices used with diverse learners to ensure cultural validity.

*Table 7.3* Culturally Responsive Assessment Practices

*Consideration of the following facilitates greater opportunities in assessment for culturally and linguistically diverse learners*

Assessment practice respects and values cultural and linguistic diversity.

Ecological information from the home and community is obtained and considered when implementing and interpreting screening and progress monitoring results gained from selected assessment practices.

Effects of acculturation on suspected area of need are accommodated when using the assessment practice.

Educator completing the assessment practice possesses cultural competence that is appropriately reflected in the assessment situation.

Native and/or English language instructional goals are considered when implementing and interpreting results obtained through use of the assessment practice.

Administration of the selected assessment practice is in the learner's most proficient language and/or English if the student is bilingual.

Properly trained translators/interpreters are used, if necessary, to more appropriately implement the assessment practice to meet the student's language needs.

Culturally and linguistically diverse learners are provided sufficient opportunities to demonstrate knowledge/skills assessed through the selected assessment practice.

Assessment practices are completed in authentic ways within proper classroom contexts to best reflect the learner's second language acquisition abilities and cultural diversity.

*Assessment Decision-Making Process*

A culturally valid assessment requires decision-making teams to reflect upon a variety of diverse needs as both instructional or special education eligibility decisions are made. Effective decision-making begins with ensuring that the most appropriate members are assembled, which in cases involving diverse learners must include educators who speak the native language of the student as well as possess an understanding of the cultural values and norms associated with the learner's home and community environments. Within today's multi-tiered response to intervention models, assessment problem-solving teams are required to make decisions within the following parameters. Examples include:

- Classroom performance data serve as the foundation for instructional decision-making;
- All learners must be taught using research-based curriculum and evidence-based interventions;
- Student progress is monitored on a regular basis and results charted to illustrate growth;

- Instruction is periodically adjusted, if necessary, based on the progress monitoring results;
- Referral for special education is made only after sufficient opportunities to learn have occurred based on adjusted instruction and progress monitoring results; and
- Assessment for special education must adhere to all provisions and safeguards identified with IDEA (2004).

While each of these above items relates to education of all learners within a multi-tiered response to intervention model, diverse students bring an added dimension to the assessment decision-making process. Specifically, assessment teams are challenged to consider each of the above items within the context of cultural and linguistic diversity. Table 7.4, developed from information found in Baca and Cervantes (2004), Hoover (2009a), and Klingner et al. (2008), provides several considerations to assist assessment teams to best interpret educational instructional progress and reduce bias associated with assessment decision-making for diverse learners.

As shown, several behaviors reflective of cultural and linguistic diversity may be misinterpreted as learning or behavior disorders by educators uninformed about a student's particular culture and/or linguistic needs. All assessment problem-solving teams should consider these behaviors relative to the learner's culture and English language development to avoid misinterpreting learning differences as disabilities. While assessment teams may function in various ways to meet struggling learner needs, consideration of items listed in Table 7.4 facilitates the implementation of a culturally valid assessment decision-making process for diverse students.

### Educator Cultural Competence

Among the many assessment skills necessary to provide a culturally valid assessment is the need for educators to possess a minimum level of cultural proficiency in instruction and assessment (Basterra, Chapter 4, this volume). Lack of cultural competence leads directly to potentially invalid assessment results and/or uses of the assessment scores for diverse students. Gay (2000), Hoover et al. (2007), Mason (1993), and Patton and Day-Vines (2002) discuss a process for assisting educators to develop cultural proficiency. According to these researchers, educators generally reflect one of six-stages. Stages 1–3 reflect debilitating educational situations for diverse learners, while Stages 4–6 reflect genuine efforts to acknowledge and accommodate diversity in education.

- Stage 1: Cultural Destructiveness—Existence of cultural diversity is denied along with a refusal to recognize its value in any aspect of education.
- Stage 2: Cultural Incapacity—Cultural diversity is ignored and provided little attention while being unsupportive in classroom instruction.
- Stage 3: Cultural Blindness—Cultural diversity is acknowledged while also being viewed as insignificant in classroom instruction.

- Stage 4: Cultural Pre-Competence—Cultural diversity is acknowledged as educators attempt to incorporate cultural values into the classroom (although infrequently) as well as improve own personal skills through professional development.
- Stage 5: Cultural Competence—Cultural diversity is regularly and systematically included in classroom instruction and activities.
- Stage 6: Cultural Proficiency—Cultural diversity is embedded into all aspects of education, including curriculum development and professional training.

While stages 1–3 represent attitudes and practices that do not reflect culturally responsive education, many teachers are found within Stages 4–6, which provide a solid foundation for implementing culturally valid assessment for diverse students. Assessment teams should ensure that a minimum level of cultural competence exists among their members to best implement effective assessment for culturally and linguistically diverse students educated in today's schools.

### Use of Assessment Scores in Instructional and Eligibility Decisions

Validity of assessment also reflects the manner in which assessment scores are interpreted and applied to make important instructional and/or special education eligibility decisions. McMillan (2001) discusses the "validity of the inference from test scores" (p. 17) (See also Durán, Chapter 6, this volume.). Therefore, once the proper selection and administration of assessment devices and/or practices have occurred, the assessment team is challenged to accurately interpret the assessment results. When addressing the needs of diverse learners, uses of assessment scores to base educational decisions on require consideration of an added element (i.e., role of cultural and linguistic diversity). The previous tables provide many ideas and issues that must be addressed to effectively use assessment scores for diverse learners. In particular, the following items should be considered to best apply assessment scores. Cultural validity in the use of assessment scores reflects:

- Selection of appropriate assessment devices and practices;
- Consideration of influences of cultural values and norms;
- Use of assessment language consistent with English language proficiency levels;
- Use of scores only for purposes for which the assessments were designed (e.g., reading fluency, math computation, functional behavior);
- Effective ESL/bilingual education implemented as necessary;
- Authentic assessment result in addition to/instead of norm reference comparisons; and
- Assessment completed by culturally competent/proficient educators.

According to Baca and Clark (1992), approximately 25% of assessment bias originates within the assessment devices, while 75% of bias reflects uses of assessment results. This underscores the significance of ensuring consideration of these various cultural and linguistic factors when interpreting assessment scores.

*Table 7.4* Assessment Considerations to Reduce Biased Decision-Making in Response to Intervention Models

*The following represent examples of behaviors that often reflect cultural/linguistic differences and should be considered from this perspective to avoid biased decision-making for diverse students*

**Assessment consideration 1**
The acquisition of a second language or adjustments to new cultural environments may temporarily result in increased anxiety that often subsides as language proficiency increases and adjustments to new environmental situations are made.

**Assessment consideration 2**
Acquisition of a second language and the uncertainties related to adjusting to new environments may temporarily result in students' exhibiting withdrawn behaviors that often subside over time as learners become more language proficient and familiar with the new environment.

**Assessment consideration 3**
Learning and behavioral expectations found in US schools and classrooms may be unfamiliar to many diverse learners resulting in the need for additional time to allow them to adjust to classroom instructional expectations.

**Assessment consideration 4**
Cultural and linguistic values and norms shape students' views and preferences toward learning; respect for this diversity should prevail to avoid conflicts between school and cultural expectations that often result in unnecessary referrals to special education.

**Assessment consideration 5**
Selected evidence-based interventions used in the classroom may be unfamiliar to some diverse learners; learner inexperience with teaching interventions should not be misinterpreted as evidence for special education eligibility.

**Assessment consideration 6**
Progress monitoring must include consideration of a learner's cultural and linguistic background to avoid misinterpreting lack of progress (resulting from learning differences) as evidence of a learning disability.

**Assessment consideration 7**
Some diverse learners may exhibit a quiet demeanor and/or extended periods of silence; oftentimes, these behaviors are reflective of cultural teachings, early stages of second language acquisition, and/or early stages of acculturation, and must be viewed in their proper contexts to avoid misinterpreting these behaviors as evidence of withdrawal requiring special education.

**Assessment consideration 8**
Cultural norms and values influence learner perceptions about what is or is not within one's own control (i.e., locus of control); learner preferences toward locus of control should not be misinterpreted as indicators of a disability simply because they differ between home and school cultures.

*continued*

*Table 7.4* Continued

**Assessment consideration 9**
Views toward different concepts such as time, space, and belongings may vary
by culture; these variations should not be viewed as problems or indications
of a disability for learners whose perspectives differ from those of educators
and other students in schools and classrooms.

**Assessment consideration 10**
Some diverse learners new to US schools may be unfamiliar with
expectations associated with independent, competitive learning and may
prefer cooperative and group ways of acquiring knowledge and skills.

**Assessment consideration 11**
Different cultures may teach students to respond more assertively than
expected by teachers to some social situations (i.e., stand up for oneself);
this social behavior may be more consistent with cultural values taught to the
learner rather than deviant behaviors requiring special education.

**Assessment consideration 12**
A test given in English for students who lack adequate English proficiency
becomes only an "English Test," and results must be interpreted relative to
English language proficiency levels; lower test performance may indicate level
of English proficiency rather than lack of acquired knowledge and skills which
may be best assessed in the native language.

## Culturally Responsive Referral of Diverse Learners for Special Education

The educational assessment environment in today's schools reflects a model
that is designed to be *preventative* rather than the more traditional *reactive*
model where students are provided intervention assistance sooner rather than
later in schooling. The contemporary model, multi-tiered response to intervention, replaces the previous pre-referral intervention model where students
were required to show significant needs prior to receiving necessary academic
or behavior supports (i.e., wait to fail). Currently, through multi-tiered
instructional models, struggling learners are provided needed academic or
social-emotional support as soon as indicated, thereby reducing unnecessary
referrals to special education. However, the need to provide and demonstrate
instructional efforts to address educational needs prior to a formal referral of
a struggling learner for special education is a requirement clearly described in
IDEA (2004) as "early intervening services." For several decades, these types
of efforts have been completed as pre-referral interventions leading to a
formal referral for special education, should pre-referral attempts be unsuc-
cessful. These same IDEA requirements for early intervention supports continue to be important in the overall special education referral process within
multi-tiered response to intervention models. The discussion below summarizes referral issues for culturally and linguistically diverse learners within
today's contemporary response to intervention models, beginning with pre-
referral interventions.

### Pre-Referral Interventions

Previously, pre-referral interventions were designed to provide necessary class-room supports to struggling learners; however, this assistance was general in nature, based primarily on teacher judgment and less on assessment data, and was not rigorously evaluated to clearly document student progress (Hoover & Patton, 2008). As a result, many students continued to struggle in school to a point where their needs became so significant that special education was deemed to be the only or best instructional choice. For many struggling students, the pre-referral stage was an extended period of time that contributed to their falling farther behind grade- or age-level peers in academics or social-emotional development, resulting in a formal referral.

The contemporary RTI models continue to emphasize pre-referral-type activities; however, these are conducted under significantly different conditions. Early efforts to assist struggling learners within multi-tiered RTI models are based on:

- Data from universal screening;
- Corroborated evidence that initial instruction includes use of a research-based curriculum;
- Results of various evidence-based differentiations;
- Periodic monitoring of progress toward academic benchmarks or standards; and
- Results from implementation of evidence-based interventions that increase in duration and intensity based on progress monitoring results.

For most learners, decisions concerning the need for a formal referral for special education occur after Tier 2 supplemental instruction is provided to support the Tier 1 research-based core curriculum. The results of those supplemental supports are monitored and documented, and the implementation of curriculum is completed in the manner in which it was designed (i.e., fidelity of implementation). Within response to intervention models, a student may eventually be referred for special education due to significant needs and/or lack of progress toward academic or behavioral benchmarks (Vaughn, 2003). As a result, should a referral occur, all educational efforts, interventions, and progress monitoring results become important pre-referral information (Hoover, 2009b).

### Culturally Responsive Referral

As previously discussed in this chapter, a culturally valid assessment for diverse learners requires specific consideration of cultural and linguistic needs to best understand and interpret assessment results and scores. Since a formal referral for special education requires documented prerequisite pre-referral interventions or early intervening services, the same cultural and linguistic considerations discussed above apply to all educational efforts prior to the referral. In particular, an assessment team's ability to discern a learning difference from a disability is essential to avoid the misinterpretations and misplacements of diverse students into special education (i.e., overrepresentation). Therefore, culturally valid assessment for special education begins with culturally responsive early intervening (i.e., pre-referral) services within the structure of multi-tiered response to intervention models. However, should insufficient progress be made, a formal referral to special education may be warranted. Table 7.5, developed from information found in Baca and Cervantes (2004), Hoover (2009a, b), Hoover et al. (2007), and Klingner et al. (2008), provides several items that should be addressed to ensure a culturally responsive referral.

As shown, many of the same items that ensure cultural validity in the overall assessment process for diverse learners are required to ensure cultural responsiveness of the initial formal tasks within special education assessment processes (i.e., pre-referral, referral). Educators on assessment teams should ensure that each item in Table 7.5 is satisfactorily addressed *prior* to acting on a formal referral of a diverse learner for possible special education.

*Table 7.5* Cultural and Linguistic Considerations in Referrals for Special Education

*The following are essential items to consider and address prior to a formal referral of a culturally and linguistically diverse learner for special education*

Learner's native and English language proficiency are considered.

Curriculum-based measures and practices are completed to ensure authentic assessment.

Parents/guardians' input is solicited and valued through regular contacts, home visits, and/or school meetings concerning learner's progress and needs.

Compatibility between teacher instructional style and learner preferences is determined and adjusted so instructional compatibility exists in the teaching and learning environment.

Learner is provided sufficient and appropriate opportunities to learn, reflecting understanding of cultural and linguistic diversity (i.e., Tier I Core Instruction is culturally responsive).

Evidence-based interventions used in the classroom are responsive to culture and linguistic needs.

Language of assessment is the same as the language of instruction, which may include native and/or English languages.

Learner's academic and social–emotional behaviors are interpreted relative to acculturation, experiential background, and cultural values.

Learner received a recent vision and hearing exam.

Assessments and classroom observations used to justify a potential referral for special education are completed by culturally responsive educators.

Learner's response to instruction (i.e., RTI) is monitored using culturally responsive progress-monitoring practices and measures, with results interpreted in culturally responsive ways.

Assessment tasks are familiar to the learner and consistent with cultural values and norms.

## Continued Challenges in Assessing Bilingual Students

In this section we discuss some of the many challenges that continue to confront educators in the assessment of bilingual students. These are associated with three contemporary issues previously introduced in this chapter: (1) linguistic and cultural bias in tests; (2) flawed assessment practices; and (3) response to intervention. We first provide additional discussion of linguistic and cultural bias in tests. Next we explain some of the challenges faced by the diagnosticians who test bilingual students and the other professionals who rely on test scores to make instructional and eligibility decisions about students. Then we discuss important assessment considerations when using response to intervention models with English language learners.

### Linguistic and Cultural Bias in Tests

Because of how they are developed, standardized tests typically possess strong psychometric properties for some students, particularly those who speak English as their first language and are from mainstream backgrounds. Yet these same tests tend to underestimate the intelligence and achievement of bilingual students and lack the same levels of predictive and construct validity they demonstrate with English-only students (Abedi, 2002, Chapter 3, this volume; MacSwan, Rolstad, & Glass, 2002; Valdés & Figueroa, 1994). For example, Figueroa and Sassenrath (1989) compared the grade point averages and standardized reading and mathematics scores of approximately 1,260 students in 1982 with their Full-Scale WISC-R scores from 1972. They found that Latino students who in 1972 had scored at or below the mean on the WISC-R were more likely than White students to show above-expected school grades and achievement. In other words, the WISC-R lacked predictive and construct validity for the Latino students.

Figueroa (1990) reviewed the literature on the assessment of bilingual students and found that bilingual students from various backgrounds tend to exhibit the same low verbal IQ and higher non-verbal IQ profile on standardized intelligence tests. It is common for diagnosticians as well as practitioners to misinterpret students' lack of full English proficiency as a broad-spectrum intelligence deficit (Oller, 1991) or as a language or learning disability (Langdon, 1989). Some psychologists and linguists have mistakenly inferred that bilingualism impedes verbal intelligence, even though substantial evidence suggests otherwise (August & Hakuta, 1997; Hakuta, 1990). One reason for this conclusion is that testers often assess bilingual students in English when the students appear to have acquired oral English proficiency, even though they are not yet ready to be assessed at higher cognitive levels in English (Cummins, 1984). Bilingual students' test performance is affected by: (1) differences in background knowledge and culture that affect how they interpret questions, (2) lack of familiarity with the vocabulary and language register used in the test, (3) limited English language proficiency, and (4) issues of language dominance (Garcia & Pearson, 1994; Solano-Flores, 2006).

### Flawed Assessment Practices

Over the years, several researchers have examined how bilingual students are evaluated and the ways in which psychologists and educators use assessment data to make decisions about students. There seems to be a disconnection between what is known about the need for non-biased assessment procedures and what actually happens in practice. This has been borne out by earlier studies as well as research conducted only a few years ago.

In perhaps the first investigation of its type, Maldonado-Colon (1986) examined special education placement decisions and found that psychologists followed many questionable practices. They tested most students in English, regardless of home language, and without using testing accommodations. They rarely administered Spanish measures and seemed to disregard issues of language difference when determining eligibility for special education. Similarly, Barrera Metz (1988) studied psychologists' assessment practices and found that they rarely considered home language information when making placement decisions.

In a set of related studies, all based on survey data, Ochoa and colleagues (Ochoa, González, Galarza, & Guillemard, 1996; Ochoa, Powell, & Robles-Piña, 1996; Ochoa, Rivera, & Powell, 1997) studied the assessment practices of psychologists who all indicated they had experience testing bilingual students. Ochoa et al. (1997) found that the psychologists overlooked several important considerations when making their determinations, including whether the student spoke another language than English in the home and the number of years of English instruction the student had received. Only 1% attempted to determine if students manifested a disability in both English and their home language.

More recently, Figueroa and Newsome (2006) examined several psychological reports to determine whether school psychologists tested English language learners in non-discriminatory ways when diagnosing LD. They noted numerous incidences when the psychologists did not follow legal or professional guidelines for conducting non-discriminatory assessments with bilingual children. In similar fashion, Wilkinson, Ortiz, Robertson, and Kushner (2006) looked at the eligibility decisions made for 21 Spanish-speaking English language learners determined to have LD. An expert panel independently reviewed the decisions made by school-level multidisciplinary teams and found that their determinations differed significantly from those of the multidisciplinary teams. The researchers noted many discrepancies associated with referral, assessment, and eligibility determinations for ELLs.

Harry, Klingner, and colleagues (Harry & Klingner, 2006; Harry, Klingner, Sturges, & Moore, 2002; Klingner & Harry, 2006) focused on factors that affected the assessment process and the decision to identify a student as qualifying for special education. They found that many factors affected the special education identification process, including teachers' informal diagnoses of children's problems, the influence of school personnel's impressions of the family, external pressures for identification and placement, the exclusion of information on classroom ecology, the choice of assessment instruments, and a disregard for written procedures and established criteria. Psychologists and multidisciplinary team members put undue emphasis on the results of English-language testing, sometimes excluding native language test results even when they were available, and not focusing enough on language acquisition issues as possible reasons for students' difficulties.

Each of these investigations reached a similar conclusion: psychologists and others responsible for evaluating ELLs for possible placement in special education frequently ignore or give insufficient attention to students' native language. They often administer English language tests even, when it would be more appropriate to test the child bilingually (Abedi, Chapter 3, this volume). Language differences are rarely given adequate consideration. To lessen these difficulties, Harry and colleagues (Harry et al., 2002; Harry & Klingner, 2006) suggest that we start by acknowledging the arbitrary nature of the assessment process. Like Donovan and Cross (2002), they recommend modifying the ways we support student learning and how we determine who is in need of special education services. These suggested changes are reflected in the reauthorization of the Individuals with Disabilities Education Improvement Act (IDEA, 2004) and its stipulation that states move to RTI as a way of providing students with early support and identifying students for special education.

## What Teachers Can Do

### Response to Intervention (RTI)

As previously discussed, RTI models potentially provide a way to address the disproportionate numbers of ELLs being placed in special education by making sure that those students who truly need the kinds of support special education provides, and only those students, are identified (Vaughn & Fuchs, 2003). The role of assessment in RTI is quite different from what it was in previous special education identification models. States now have the option of eliminating the use of IQ tests for making placement decisions. Instead, the focus is on determining how well a student "responds to intervention," with the idea that the intervention must be research-based and implemented with fidelity (Vaughn & Fuchs, 2003).

Though this approach potentially solves some of the problems associated with the biased assessment procedures used with bilingual students in the past, RTI raises new concerns. As with previous identification procedures, this model must be based on students' having received an adequate "opportunity to learn." When students do not seem to be making adequate progress, we must first examine the quality of instruction and the educational context rather than assuming that the students are not progressing because they have a disability. This requires observing in classrooms to note the appropriateness of instruction and of the learning environment. When the majority of ELLs in a class are struggling, the first step should be to improve instruction. Only when most ELLs are thriving and it is just a few students who do not seem to be progressing or reaching benchmarks should school personnel look specifically at those students. In other words, in

RTI it is important to compare students with their true peers (Fuchs & Fuchs, 2006).

Also, it is essential to make sure that interventions have been validated with students similar to those with whom they are being put into practice. It should not be assumed that research conducted with mainstream populations applies to ELLs. Factors such as students' levels of English proficiency can affect how suitable an instructional practice is for them. Finding appropriate interventions for ELLs has been challenging because until recently few studies had been conducted that focused on ELLs. Historically, ELLs have been left out of research samples in special education (Artiles, Trent, & Kuan, 1997), and researchers rarely disaggregated their findings to examine how factors such as language proficiency and ethnicity might differentially affect student outcomes.

The success of RTI for ELLs will depend on more than whether their teachers implement appropriate research-based practices. Teachers also must be able to adjust instruction for students who do not seem to be responding to a particular approach. After all, students do not all learn the same way. Research can help us determine which interventions are most likely to benefit the majority of students, but not which approach will work best for everyone. Some students may actually do better with an alternative approach (Klingner & Edwards, 2006). Also, the level of instruction might not be ideal for students; thus, teachers need to be able to differentiate instruction. In addition, teachers must establish a supportive learning environment in which students' cultural and linguistic attributes are valued and used to facilitate their learning (Baca, 2002; Nieto, 2004; Ortiz, 1997, 2002).

## Conclusions

As discussed throughout this chapter, several critical issues are embedded within various practices and devices used to assess culturally and linguistically diverse students. The emerging multi-tiered response to intervention framework provides unique opportunities as well as continuing challenges to educators who teach and assess diverse students. Below is a summary of key points to keep in mind to conduct effective assessments with English learners, including bilingual students, as discussed by Klingner et al. (2006) and Hoover (2009a).

- Use alternative ways of assessing students' strengths to determine the upper limits of their potential.
- Conduct observations of students in different settings as part of any evaluation.
- Pay greater attention to cultural and affective considerations when evaluating students (e.g., sources of potential conflict, motivation).
- Give greater attention to students' native language and the role of language acquisition when determining whether a student may have LD.
- Consider that weak auditory processing skills could indicate language acquisition issues rather than a cognitive processing disorder or LD.
- Evaluate students in their first language as well as English to determine predictors of reading achievement.

- Make certain that progress monitoring directly assesses that which is taught in the classroom.
- Utilize curriculum-based measurement techniques to accommodate diverse learning needs in the assessment process.
- Evaluate each assessment device prior to its use with diverse learners to make certain that it is appropriate for the population for which it is used.
- Interpret assessment scores relative to learners' experiential backgrounds and English language proficiency levels to put results into a meaningful and relevant context.
- Apply the various considerations presented in Table 7.4 to reduce assessment bias and increase the accuracy of assessment results for diverse learners.

Overall, educators who adhere to the guidelines and suggestions presented in this chapter to make certain that both assessment devices and practices are culturally responsive are best positioned to implement effective and relevant assessment of all learners educated within today's multi-tiered instructional framework.

## Notes

1. A risk ratio (also called an odds ratio) is calculated by dividing the risk index of one group by the risk index of another for comparative purposes. Risk ratios greater than 1.0 indicate greater risk of identification. The risk index is calculated by dividing the number of students in a given racial or ethnic category served in a given disability category by the total enrollment for that group in the school population. Donovan and Cross (2002) used Whites as the denominator when calculating risk ratios, as was common practice at the time. Now risk ratios are calculated with all other students (Whites plus students in other ethnic groups) as the denominator. See Donovan and Cross (2002) for a discussion of the pros and cons of different approaches to calculating disproportionate representation.
2. Now referred to as developmental disabilities or, more specifically, as intellectual disabilities.

## References

Abedi, J. (2002). Standardized achievement tests and English language learners: Psychometric issues. *Educational Assessment*, 8, 231–257.

Artiles, A.J., Rueda, R., Salazar, J., & Higareda, I. (2005). Within-group diversity in minority disproportionate representation: English Language Learners in urban school districts. *Exceptional Children*, 71, 283–300.

Artiles, A.J., Trent, S.C., & Kuan, L.A. (1997). Learning disabilities research on ethnic minority students: An analysis of 22 years of studies published in selected refereed journals. *Learning Disabilities Research & Practice*, 12, 82–91.

August, D., & Hakuta, K. (Eds.) (1997). *Improving schooling for language-minority children: A research agenda*. Washington, DC: National Academy Press.

Baca, L.M. (2002). Educating English language learners with special education needs: Trends and future directions. In A.J. Artiles & A.A. Ortiz (Eds.), *English language learners with special education needs: Identification, placement, and instruction* (pp. 191–202). Washington, DC: Center for Applied Linguistics.

Baca, L., & Cervantes, H. (2004). *The bilingual special education interface*. Columbus, OH: Merrill.

Baca, L.M., & Clark, C. (1992). *EXITO: A dynamic team assessment approach for culturally diverse students.* Minneapolis, MN: CEC.

Barrera Metz, I. (1988). The relative importance of language and culture in making assessment decisions about Hispanic students referred to special education. *The Journal for the National Association for Bilingual Education, 12*(3), 191–218.

Boulder-BUENO Center (n.d.). National Association of State Directors of Special Education (NASDSE) website: www.nasdse.org.

Calhoon, M.B., Otaiba, S.A., Cihak, D., King, A., & Avalos, A. (2007). Effects of a peer-mediated program on reading skill acquisition for two-way bilingual first-grade classrooms. *Learning Disability Quarterly, 30,* 169–184.

Calhoon, M.B., Otaiba, S.A., Greenberg, D., King, A., & Avalos, A. (2006). Improving reading skills in predominantly Hispanic Title 1 first grade classrooms: The promise of Peer-Assisted Learning Strategies. *Learning Disabilities Research & Practice, 21*(4), 261–272.

Capizzi, A.M., & Fuchs, L.S. (2005). Effects of curriculum-based measurement with and without diagnostic feedback on teacher planning. *Remedial and Special Education, 26,* 159–174.

Carlo, M.S., August, D., McLaughlin, B., Snow, C.E., Dressler, C., Lippman, D.N., Lively, T.J., & White, C.E. (2004). Closing the gap: Addressing the vocabulary needs of English-language learners in bilingual and mainstream classrooms. *Reading Research Quarterly, 39*(2), 188–215.

Cummins, J. (1984). *Bilingualism and special education: Issues in assessment and pedagogy.* San Diego, CA: College Hill.

Denton, C.A., Anthony, J.L., Parker, R., & Hasbrouck, J.E. (2004). Effects of two tutoring programs on the English reading development of Spanish–English bilingual students. *The Elementary School Journal, 104*(4), 289–305.

*Diana v. State Board of Education,* C.A. 70 RFT (N.D. Cal., Feb. 3, 1970, 1973).

Donovan, S., & Cross, C. (2002). *Minority students in special and gifted education.* Washington, DC: National Academy Press.

Figueroa, R.A. (1990). Assessment of linguistic minority group children. In C.R. Reynolds & R.W. Kamphaus (Eds.), *Handbook of psychological and educational assessment of children; Vol. 1. Intelligence and achievement.* New York, NY: Guilford.

Figueroa, R.A., & Newsome, P. (2006). The diagnosis of LD in English language learners: Is it nondiscriminatory? *Journal of Learning Disabilities, 39*(3), 206–214.

Figueroa, R.A., & Sassenrath, J.M. (1989). A longitudinal study of the predictive validity of the system of multicultural pluralistic assessment (SOMPA). *Psychology in the Schools, 26*(1), 5–19.

Fuchs, D., & Fuchs, L.S. (2006). Introduction to response to intervention: What, why, and how valid is it? *Reading Research Quarterly, 41*(1), 95–99.

Garcia, G.E., & Pearson, P.D. (1994). Assessment and diversity. In L. Darling-Hammond (Ed.), *Review of research in education, 20* (pp. 337–391). Washington, DC: American Educational Research Association.

Gay, G. (2000). *Culturally responsive teaching.* New York, NY: Teachers College Press.

Gerber, M., Jimenez, T., Leafstedt, J., Villaruz, J., Richards, C., & English, J. (2004). English reading effects of small-group intensive intervention in Spanish for K-1 English learners. *Learning Disabilities Research & Practice, 19*(4), 239–251.

Gottlieb, J., Alter, M., Gottlieb, B.W., & Wishner, J. (1994). Special education in urban America: It's not justifiable for many. *The Journal of Special Education, 27,* 453–465.

Gunn, B., Smolkowski, K., Biglan, A., Black, C., & Blair, J. (2005). Fostering the development of reading skill through supplemental instruction: Results for Hispanic and non-Hispanic students. *Journal of Special Education, 39*(2), 66–85.

Haager, D., & Windmueller, M.P. (2001). Early reading intervention for English language learners at-risk for learning disabilities: Student and teacher outcomes in an urban school. *Learning Disability Quarterly*, 24, 235–250.

Hakuta, K. (1990). *Bilingualism and bilingual education: A research perspective*. Washington, DC: George Washington University, Center for Applied Linguistics.

Harry, B., & Klingner, J.K. (2006). *Why are so many minority students in special education? Understanding race and disability in schools*. New York, NY: Teachers College Press.

Harry, B., Klingner, J., Sturges, K.M., & Moore, R.F. (2002). Of rocks and soft places: Using qualitative methods to investigate disproportionality. In D. Losen & G. Orfield (Eds.), *Racial inequity in special education* (pp. 71–92). Cambridge, MA: Harvard Education Press.

Heller, K.A., Holtzman, W.H., & Messick, S. (Eds.) (1982). *Placing children in special education: A strategy for equity*. Washington, DC: National Academy Press.

Hoover, J.J. (2011). *Response to intervention models: Curricular implications and interventions*. Boston, MA: Pearson Merrill.

Hoover, J.J. (2009a). *Differentiating learning differences from disabilities: Meeting diverse needs through multi-tiered response to intervention*. Boston, MA: Pearson, Allyn & Bacon.

Hoover, J.J. (2009b). *RTI assessment essentials for struggling learners*. Thousand Oaks, CA: Corwin.

Hoover, J.J. Klingner, J., Baca, L.M., & Patton, J.M. (2007). *Methods for teaching culturally and linguistically diverse exceptional learners*. Columbus, OH: Pearson.

Hoover, J.J., & Love. E. (in press). *Supporting school-based response to intervention: A Practitioner's model. Teaching exceptional children*.

Hoover, J.J., Baca, L.M., Love, E., & Saenz, L. (2008). *National implementation of response to intervention (RTI): Research summary*. University of Colorado.

Hoover, J.J., & Patton, J.R. (2008). Role of special educators in multi-tiered instructional programming. *Intervention in School and Clinic*, 43, 195–202.

IDEA (2004). *Individuals with Disabilities Education Act Amendments of 2004*, Washington, DC.

Kamps, D., Abbott, M., Greenwood, C., Arreaga-Mayer, C., Wills, H., Longstaff, J., Culpepper, M., & Walton, C. (2007). Use of evidence-based, small-group reading instruction for English language learners in elementary grades: Secondary-tier intervention. *Learning Disability Quarterly*, 30, 153–168.

Klingner, J.K., Artiles, A.J., Kozleski, E., Harry, B., Zion, S., Tate, W., Durán, G.Z., & Riley, D. (2005). Addressing the disproportionate representation of culturally and linguistically diverse students in special education through culturally responsive educational systems. *Education Policy Analysis Archives*, 13(38), 1–39. Available at http://epaa.asu.edu/epaa/v13n38/.

Klingner, J.K., Artiles, A.J., & Méndez-Barletta, L. (2006). English language learners who struggle with reading: Language acquisition or learning disabilities? *Journal of Learning Disabilities*, 39, 108–128.

Klingner, J.K., & Edwards, P. (2006). Cultural considerations with response to intervention models. *Reading Research Quarterly*, 41, 108–117.

Klingner, J.K., & Harry, B. (2006). The special education referral and decision-making process for English Language Learners: Child study team meetings and staffings. *Teachers College Record*, 108, 2247–2281.

Klingner, J.K., Hoover, J.J., & Baca, L. (Eds.) (2008). *Why do English Language Learners struggle with reading? Distinguishing language acquisition from learning disabilities*. Thousand Oaks, CA; Corwin Press.

Langdon, H.W. (1989). Language disorder or language difference? Assessing the language skills of Hispanic students. *Exceptional Children*, 56, 160–167.

Leafstedt, J.M., Richards, C.R., & Gerber, M.M. (2004). Effectiveness of explicit phonological-awareness instruction for at-risk English learners. *Learning Disabilities Research & Practice*, 19(4), 252–261.

Linan-Thompson, S., Bryant, D.P., Dickson, S.V., & Kouzekanani, K. (2005). Spanish literacy instruction for at-risk kindergarten students. *Remedial and Special Education*, 26(4), 236–244.

Linan-Thompson, S., Vaughn, S., Hickman-Davis, P., & Kouzekanani, K. (2003). Effectiveness of supplemental reading instruction for second-grade English language learners with reading difficulties. *Elementary School Journal*, 103, 221–238.

Linan-Thompson, S., Vaughn, S., Prater, K., & Cirino, P.T. (2006). The response to intervention of English language learners at risk for reading problems. *Journal of Learning Disabilities*, 39(5), 390–398.

McMaster, K.L., Kung, S.H., Han, I., & Cao, M. (2008). Peer-Assisted Learning Strategies: A "tier 1" approach to promoting English learners' response to intervention. *Exceptional Children*, 74(2), 194–214.

MacMillan, D.L., & Reschly, D.L. (1998). Overrepresentation of minority students: The case for greater specificity or reconsideration of the variables examined. *The Journal of Special Education*, 32, 15–24.

McMillan, J.H. (2001). *Essential assessment concepts for teachers and administrators.* Thousand Oaks, CA: Corwin Press.

MacSwan, J., Rosltad, K., & Glass, G.V. (2002). Do some school-age children have no language? Some problems of construct validity in the Pre-LAS Español. *Bilingual Research Journal*, 26, 395–420.

Maldonado-Colon, E. (1986). Assessment: Interpreting data of linguistically/culturally different students referred for disabilities or disorders. *Journal of Reading, Writing, and Learning Disabilities International*, 2(1), 73–83.

Mason, J.L. (1993). *Cultural competence self assessment questionnaire.* Portland, OR: Portland State University, Multicultural Initiative Project.

Mehan, H. (1991). The schools' work of sorting students. In D. Zimmerman & D. Boden (Eds.), *Talk and social structure.* Cambridge: Polity Press.

Mehan, H., Hartwick, A., & Meihls, J.L. (1986). *Handicapping the handicapped: Decision-making in students' educational careers.* Stanford, CA: Stanford University Press.

Mercer, J. (1973). *Labeling the mentally retarded.* Berkley, CA: University of California Press.

Nieto, S. (2004). *Affirming diversity: The sociopolitical context of multicultural education* (4th Edition). New York, NY: Longman.

Ochoa, S.H., González, D., Galarza, A., & Guillemard, L. (1996). The training and use of interpreters in bilingual psycho-educational assessment: An alternative in need of study. *Diagnostique*, 21(3), 19–22.

Ochoa, S.H., Powell, M.P., & Robles-Piña, R. (1996). School psychologists' assessment practices with bilingual and limited-English-proficient students. *Journal of Psychoeducational Assessment*, 14, 250–275.

Ochoa, S.H., Rivera, B.D., & Powell, M.P. (1997). Factors used to comply with the exclusionary clause with bilingual and limited-English-proficient pupils: Initial guidelines. *Learning Disabilities Research & Practice*, 12, 161–167.

Oller, J.W., Jr. (1991). Language testing research: Lessons applied to LEP students and programs. In *Proceedings of the first research symposium on limited English proficient students' issues: Focus on evaluation and measurement: Vol. 2* (pp. 42–123). Washington,

DC: U.S. Department of Education, Office of Bilingual Education and Minority Language Affairs.

Orosco, M., & Klingner, J.K. (2010). One school's implementation of RTI with English language learners: "Referring into RTI." *Journal of Learning Disabilities*, 43, 269–288.

Ortiz, A.A. (1997). Learning disabilities occurring concomitantly with linguistic differences. *Journal of Learning Disabilities*, 30, 321–332.

Ortiz, A.A. (2002). Prevention of school failure and early intervention for English language learners. In A.J. Artiles & A.A. Ortiz (Eds.), *English language learners with special education needs: Identification, placement, and instruction* (pp. 31–48). Washington, DC: Center for Applied Linguistics.

Oswald, D.P., Coutinho, M.J., Best, A.M., & Singh, N. (1999). Ethnic representation in special education: The influence of school-related economic and demographic variables. *The Journal of Special Education*, 32, 194–206.

Patton, J.M. (1998). The disproportionate representation of African-Americans in special education: Looking behind the curtain for understanding and solutions. *Journal of Special Education*, 32, 25–31.

Patton, J., & Day-Vines, N. (2002). A curriculum and pedagogy for cultural competence: Knowledge, skills and dispositions needed to guide the training of special and general education teachers. Unpublished manuscript.

Riddle Buly, M., & Valencia, S.W. (2002). Below the bar: Profiles of students who fail state reading tests. *Educational Evaluation and Policy Analysis*, 24, 219–239.

Salend, S.J., & Garrick-Duhaney, L.M. (2005). Understanding and addressing the disproportionate representation of students of color in special education. *Intervention in School and Clinic*, 40, 213–221.

Silverman, R. (2007). Vocabulary development of English-language learners and English-only learners in kindergarten. *The Elementary School Journal*, 107(4), 365–383.

Skiba, R.J., Simmons, A.D., Ritter, S., Gibb, A., Rausch, M.K., Cuadrado, J., & Chung, C.G. (2008). Achieving equity in special education: History, status, and current challenges. *Exceptional Children*, 74, 264–288.

Solano-Flores, G. (2006). Language, dialect, and register: Sociolinguistics and the estimation of measurement error in the testing of English-language learners. *Teachers College Record*, 108(11), 2354–2379.

Sorrells, A.M., Webb-Johnson, G., & Townsend, B.L. (2004). Multicultural perspectives in special education: A call for responsibility in research, practice, and teacher preparation. In A.M. Sorrells, H.J. Rieth, & P.T. Sindelar (Eds.), *Critical issues in special education: Access, diversity and accountability*. Boston, MA: Pearson.

U.S. Department of Education (2003). *Key indicators of Hispanic student achievement: National goals and benchmarks for the next decade*. Retrieved June 27, 2003, from www.ed.gov/pubs/hispanicindicators/.

U.S. Department of Education, Office of Special Education and Rehabilitative Services (2006). *26th Annual Report to Congress on the Implementation of Individuals with Disabilities Education Act, 2004*. Washington, DC: Westat.

Valdés, G., & Figueroa, R.A. (1994). *Bilingualism and testing: A special case of bias*. Norwood, NJ: Ablex.

Vaughn, S. (2003). *How many tiers are needed for response to intervention to achieve acceptable prevention outcomes?* Paper presented at the National Center on Learning Disabilities Responsiveness-to-Interventions Symposium, Kansas City, MO, December.

Vaughn, S., Cirino, P.T., Linan-Thompson, S., Mathes, P.G., Carlson, C.D., Cardenas-Hagan, E., et al. (2006a). Effectiveness of a Spanish intervention and an English intervention for English-language learners at risk for reading problems. *American Educational Research Journal*, 43(3), 449–487.

Vaughn, S., & Fuchs, L.S. (2003). Redefining learning disabilities as inadequate response to treatment: The promise and potential problems. *Learning Disabilities Research and Practice*, 18(3), 137–146.

Vaughn, S., Linan-Thompson, S., Mathes, P.G., Cirino, P.T., Carlson, C.D., Pollard-Durodola, S.D., Cardenas-Hagan, E., & Francis, D.J. (2006b). Effectiveness of Spanish intervention for first-grade English language learners at risk for reading difficulties. *Journal of Learning Disabilities*, 39(1), 56–73.

Vaughn, S., Mathes, P., Linan-Thompson, S., Cirino, P., Carlson, C., Pollard-Durodola, S., Cardenas-Hagan, E., & Francis, D. (2006c). Effectiveness of an English intervention for first-grade English language learners at risk for reading problems. *The Elementary School Journal*, 107(2), 153–180.

Wilkinson, C.Y., Ortiz, A.A., Robertson, P.M., & Kushner, M.I. (2006). English language learners with reading-related learning disabilities: Linking data from multiple sources to make eligibility determinations. *Journal of Learning Disabilities*, 39(2), 129–141.

Yell, M. (2004). *Understanding the three-tier model.* Presentation at the Colorado State Directors of Special Education annual meeting, Denver, February.

Zehler, A., Fleischman, H., Hopstock, P., Stephenson, T., Pendzick, M., & Sapru, S. (2003). *Policy report: Summary of findings related to LEP and SPED-LEP students.* Submitted by Development Associates, Inc. to U.S. Department of Education, Office of English Language Acquisition, Language Enhancement, and Academic Achievement of Limited English Proficient Students.

Chapter 8

# Overview of Current Federal Policies in Assessment and Accountability and their Impact on ELL Students

*Julia Lara and Magda Chia*

**Chapter Overview**

This chapter presents an overview of the No Child Left Behind (NCLB) assessment and accountability requirements that pertain to English language learners (ELLs) and reviews concerns that have been expressed regarding impact of assessment and accountability provisions on ELLs and schools they attend. In addition, this chapter outlines the positive outcomes of the law relative to ELLs; presents a brief discussion of accountability and assessment approaches offered as alternatives to the current system; and contains recommendations culled from the various reports that examined issues of assessment, accountability, and ELLs.

The chapter is directed at teachers and other school level practitioners; therefore, it excludes technical (measurement) considerations that are presented elsewhere in this book. Instead, we focus on ELL issues that have raised the most concern among interested stakeholders in the field of education. The authors acknowledge that these concerns have been presented in various reports focusing on NCLB. Nonetheless, the chapter strives for a balanced approach to a critique of the law. Also, it reinforces conclusions drawn elsewhere that, despite good intentions, many of actions taken to address the call for ELL inclusion in assessment are threats to the cultural validity of assessments for ELL students.

Much has been written about the impact of the NCLB Act of 2001 at various levels of the educational system. The law has been a powerful source of external accountability pressure on schools, districts, and states. The pressure to comply with the provisions of the law is felt at all levels of the educational system. However, it is at the school and in the classroom that the pressure is most felt since, at these levels, the consequences have the most direct impact on the adults in the system. The drive to obtain higher test scores has provoked behaviors that ultimately undermine the intent of the law. This has been well documented in reports focused on NCLB implementation. The most often cited behavior change is the over-emphasis on test preparation, which narrows the curriculum to subjects tested and concurrently reduces time allotted to non-tested subjects. But, as is the case with implementation of any federal law, there are also positive effects that have changed the system's response to the needs of students enrolled in needy schools. For example, there is now more programmatic coherence in the delivery of educational services than was the case prior to NCLB.

Like all students in the public schools, English language learners (ELLs) are affected by the educational system's response to the NCLB assessment and accountability requirements.[1] However, unlike other students, ELLs have a double burden—they are learning the language of instruction and subject matter content at the same time. This presents an added level of complexity to the implementation challenges educators face in their attempts to execute the provisions of the law.

## Historical Context

The lagging performance of students in U.S. public schools became a national concern in the 1970s and has generated increasingly demanding legislated reforms leading up to the current No Child Left Behind Act (NCLB), which requires states to assess student performance and improve achievement on a specified timetable. A part of the challenge has been the nation's increasing ethnic and cultural diversity and the complexities of measuring and valuing the achievement of second language learners, students from low-income and ethnic minority households, and students with disabilities.

Beginning in the 1970s, analysis of educational trends nationally and internationally showed that, nationally, students were not meeting standards as measured by the National Assessment of Educational Progress (NAEP), various standardized achievement tests, and college entrance examinations. The U.S. was far behind other industrialized countries and a few developing countries in some content areas, particularly mathematics. In addition, the private sector reported that workers were unable to meet skill requirements in many occupations. It was clear that the economic well-being of the country required a more educated citizenry. No longer could schools support the advancement of the top performers and leave the others behind, particularly when a demographic shift was taking place: the economic viability of the U.S. depended on all students, regardless of ethnic and cultural backgrounds or disabilities, receiving a strong education and the opportunity to become economically productive citizens of their communities.

Prior to the 1970s, the performance of students from low-income and ethnic minority households and students with disabilities was invisible from a policy perspective because of the assessment practices of the time. Performance data were aggregated at all instructional levels, but not disaggregated by student groups. At the school level, the scores were averaged for all students. Therefore, the performance of students who scored low on the tests was masked by that of the high performers. ELL students were often not included in assessments at either the state or local levels. Further, because school systems were not disaggregating by group (or including certain students), they frequently were not aware of the struggles of second language learners, students with disabilities, and students from low-income and ethnic minority households. Thus, they were not adapting instruction to meet their needs. In short, there were no accountability mechanisms in place.

These factors led to the reassessment of the federal government's role in education, and of the policy levers that it could use to advance education reform. Since the 1960s, the Elementary and Secondary Act of 1965 (ESEA) had been the mechanism the federal government used to assist states and districts with the education of poor students. These funds were directed to states and their subgrantees (school districts) based on a formula.[2] States need to account for the expenditures but the funds were not tied to results.

During 30 years of ESEA implementation (1965–1994), however, improvements were not occurring at the scale necessary to address the demands of an increasing technology based market economy. The first attempt to bring some level of policy coherence and accountability for the academic achievement of all students was the reauthorized ESEA, Improving America's Schools Act of 1994 (IASA). However, while IASA set expectations for improved student achievement, the federal policy instruments to achieve the goals were weak in terms of enforcement mechanisms. For example, by 2001, only 11 states were in compliance with the standards and assessment provisions of IASA, and 30 had obtained waivers from various provisions of the law (DeBray, 2003). Consequently, the intent of the statute to improve student achievement and close the achievement gap was far from being achieved when ESEA was reauthorized in 2001 and the nation's public schools were required to conduct statewide assessments whose scores were disaggregated by specific groups and to set and meet performance goals for these groups. No Child Left Behind, as the ESEA reauthorization is titled, makes the nation's public schools accountable for the performance for all students and, for the first time, includes students from low-income and ethnic minority households, second language learners, and students with disabilities.

## Overview of NCLB: Assessment and Accountability Requirements

The reauthorized Elementary and Secondary Act of 2001 (NCLB) contains a standards-based policy framework similar to that of its 1994 predecessor, the Improving America's Schools Act (IASA). However, NCLB differs significantly from IASA in the amount of testing, the accountability requirements, and the consequences for states, districts, and schools for not meeting state-defined performance standards. Also, it sets a timeframe for schools to move students to the "proficient" performance standard.[3] Under NCLB, the enforcement mechanism was strengthened. Expectations have been raised so that schools are no longer allowed to "plan to improve" without producing student achievement results.

NCLB requires testing of all students in Language Arts and Mathematics assessments in grades 3 through 5, at least once in 6 through 9, and 10 through 12;[4] inclusion of 95% of all students enrolled in a school; and disaggregating and reporting of scores by sub-groups. The sub-groups are: all students, economically disadvantaged, and students from major racial and ethnic groups, including ELL and special education students. These students can be members of multiple sub-groups and are often those that schools have found most difficult to serve.

The state-based assessments system is the underpinning of the accountability framework under NCLB. States, districts, and schools are held accountable for student achievement. The inability of schools to meet a performance level of "proficient" on the statewide tests can result in a designation of a school or district as "in need of improvement." Moreover, if students in a given school do not meet the standard over successive years, then the school is faced with consequences of increasing severity, depending on the number of years the school remains in school improvement. For example, a school that misses the adequate yearly progress (AYP) targets for one year is required to offer public school choice. If that same school misses AYP for three consecutive years, then the school must implement a corrective action plan and offer public school choice. The ultimate sanction is change in governance of the school or restructuring.

The uniqueness of the NCLB accountability framework is that schools are evaluated based on the average score of each sub-group relative to a fixed target a year at a time, not just on average scores of all students in a school.[5] Consequently, schools are no longer able to disguise gaps among groups of students by reporting average scores for all students. Schools must meet adequate yearly progress targets on the statewide assessments for all and for each sub-group. The performance target is defined as the percentage of students in a school achieving the proficient level that year, *as defined by the state*.[6] Thus, if disadvantaged students in a given school do not meet the AYP targets, the school is identified as "in need of improvement" even when all other students meet the standards. Although states have the discretion to set the performance targets, they must test at the specified grades in the subjects indicated and include all sub-groups.[7] This requirement has placed significant attention on students whose needs were not previously visible on the policy radar.

### Accountability Provisions and ELL Students

The accountability framework holds districts and schools accountable for the achievement of ELL students in English language arts and mathematics in the provisions of Title I of NCLB, and for making progress in learning English and reaching the English proficient status (attainment) through the provisions in Title III.

Title I requires testing of ELL students in statewide tests in English language arts, mathematics, and science at least once in grades 3 through 5, 6 through 9, and 10 through 12. Districts and schools must meet the state-established AYP targets for the ELL students along with other sub-groups in a school. Since the enactment of the law, there has been an adjustment to the accountability provisions of the law in relationship to ELL students.

Specifically, newly arrived students can be exempted from participating in the English Language Arts (ELA) assessment.[8] If they do participate, the ELA test scores are not counted in the AYP formula. Students are not exempted from mathematics assessment, but scores are not counted if the students are newly arrived. Since the composition of the ELL group changes as the students learn English and are consequently reclassified, the US Department of Education allowed states to include scores of former LEP students in the accountability formula for a period of two years. This was done because it became evident that schools would not be able to show progress if higher scoring students (former LEPs) were not counted in the AYP sub-group. This change gave schools credit for moving students out of the LEP status into the mainstream classroom. More important, it increased the possibilities that ELLs as a sub-group would meet the achievement standards under Title I. Thus, the two year rule was helpful from an accountability perspective but, as will be discussed below, it did not address a major weakness of the assessment system relative to ELL students.[9]

Title III of NCLB is a source of federal funding to states and their sub-grant-ees (districts and schools) to support the instructional needs of ELLs in the areas of English language development and the core academic subjects. Its account-ability requirements direct states to develop English language proficiency (ELP) standards, and measure the annual progress of students relative to the ELP stan-dards. States set targets for annual measurable achievement objectives (AMAOs) that gauge ELL students' improvement in learning English and attaining English proficiency. Thus, states and districts must show annual increases in the percent-age of ELL students who make progress, learn English, and meet core academic standards (Title I). However, unlike the accountability framework under Title I, there are no consequences at the school level for failing to meet the progress and attainment standards of Title III. Instead, the consequences apply to states and districts.[10] Also, Title III directs districts to improve instruction and assessment of ELL students by providing high quality professional development to teachers and other school personnel.

### Critical Issues

The reaction to the test-based accountability approach embodied by NCLB has engendered controversy across the educational spectrum and at all levels of the system. In this section, we discuss the critiques that have been most often articu-lated by the field.

It has been widely reported that teachers and administrators have negative views of NCLB. A recent poll commissioned by ETS (2007) reported that 77% of teachers had a negative view of the law, and 63% of administrators shared the teachers' opinion. While the general sentiment is unfavorable, it is not unani-mous within each stakeholder group, and there is a difference between teacher and administrator in degree of support. Moreover, despite a high level of disap-proval, the same ETS poll noted that both teacher and principal groups support reauthorization of the law, but with changes. The finding regarding difference between administrators and teachers is reflected in a study by the Urban Insti-tute (Chu, de Cohen, & Murray, 2007), which examined implementation in three high ELL districts and six schools. Researchers noted that staff perceptions about the impact of testing requirements differed depending on the level of implementation (state, district, school, and classroom). Administrators believed the requirements had a favorable effect because it propelled them in the direc-tion of aligning ELL programs with the general curriculum, state standards, and assessments (De Cohen & Chu, 2007). The Center on Education Policy (2006) reached a similar conclusion in a brief policy report summarizing the "big effects" of NCLB, which was based on four years of gathering information on the NCLB implementation. In the Urban Institute study, teachers reported less favorable views, asserting that the requirements imposed a burden on both students and schools and that the expectations were unrealistic. However, in a study conducted by the Rand Corporation (Hamilton et al., 2007), researchers noted that, while teachers reported negative effects (reduced morale, inadequate time, limited funding), they also acknowledged positive effects—greater efforts to align instruction with standards and improve teacher practice.

Clearly, the assessment and accountability requirements under both Title I and III have driven states and districts to rethink how they serve ELL students. States and districts have put in place a delivery system in which the needs of these students are no longer on the periphery of the core mission of schools. Along the way, there have been unintended negative consequences as systems have reacted and adjusted to the mandates. In the following section, we highlight key LEP specific arguments and a few that transcend ELL student considerations.

### Validity of ELL Student Inclusion in Statewide Assessments

The most compelling argument against inclusion in the assessment system is that ELLs are included before they have gained the level of English language proficiency to validly access the linguistic demands of the test. Even with the one-time exemption flexibility, it is highly unlikely that ELLs would have mastered sufficient English language skills to understand and adequately respond to the questions posed. On average, the number of years it takes for ELL students to reach the level of English language proficiency to handle the academic demands of the mainstream classroom is five-to-seven years (Collier, 1989). Therefore, when tested in English, ELLs may have knowledge of the subject matter, but not be able to understand the question or communicate knowledge of the concepts and skills in the test response. This means that judgments about what students do or do not know within a specific content domain might be incorrect (see Solano-Flores, Chapter 1, this volume). This analysis holds true in testing knowledge of both English language arts and mathematics. While ELL students generally perform better in mathematics than in English language arts, mathematics items have become increasingly more language-based. Thus, what students know (content knowledge, skills, and cognition) in the content area may be confounded with their English language proficiency level (Trumbull & Solano-Flores, Chapter 10, this volume).

In an attempt to minimize the effects of language on achievement scores and to strengthen validity of the assessment process, NCLB allows for assessment in a native language and the use of accommodations in tests administered to ELLs in the content areas. Although the law allows use of native language assessments, only 16 states use them to measure achievement in one or more content areas (GAO, 2007). However, the use of the native language assessments is not advisable when students are not instructed in their native language or are not literate in their first language (Abedi, Chapter 3, this volume). Moreover, at the state level, the use of native language assessments has been politically untenable. There appears to be no statewide support for the development of assessments in a language other than English. For that reason, it has been difficult to get legislative support to fund the development of assessments in languages other than English.

Almost all states offer some form of test accommodation. But, in some cases, the validity of the accommodations is uncertain. As a consequence, they may not be appropriate, or effective and may produce invalid assessment outcomes (Abedi, 2007, Chapter 3, this volume). This is partly because accommodations used and or recommended for ELLs were developed mostly for special education students. In recent years the body of knowledge on appropriate forms accommodations for ELLs has grown. The work by Abedi and others shows that some accommodations are supported by research and can be used with ELL students during the assessment process.[11] Unfortunately, states and districts are not limiting the use of "allowable accommodations" to those proven to be most appropriate to ELLs. Instead, the most frequently used are the least recommended, such as extra time, small group administration, and reading the test aloud. The least frequently used are those considered most appropriate, which include: modifying vocabulary of the test, providing additional examples or practice items, and modifying the linguistic complexity of the test. Moreover, the guidance for districts and schools has often been unclear (Wolf, 2008).

Another critique regarding the validity of the assessments relative to ELL students is the extent to which the tests have been "normed" on a representative sample of ELL students. Test creators often use data from cognitive interviews and initial pilot tests to verify one type of validity (norming process). However, if ELLs are not included during the cognitive interviews or pilot test, then test developers are unable to gather data about the way in which ELL students respond to items or to the entire test (Solano-Flores, Chapter 1, this volume). Best practice in test development dictates that, during the development phase, samples of students who will be eventually measured by the test be included. The sample should be representative of the language groups in the ELL population (Crawford, 2004). Although we do not know with certainty that state assessments have this flaw, researchers have noted that often ELLs are not included in the norming process. Therefore, it is important to consult the test manual to identify the student groups included in the norming process. If a group is not listed, then the assumption is that the group was not included in the norming process (La Celle-Peterson & Rivera, 1994).

Finally, there is the issue of cultural validity. Arguments presented from this perspective rest on a body of work that affirms that current state assessments have not considered the role that cultural background plays in shaping how a student approaches the assessment task and in how he or she responds to questions asked. This is particularly important when using large-scale measurement tools to assess ELL students' content knowledge. The concept of cultural validity helps educators and test creators to understand that knowledge is a social construction and that how a student thinks, learns, and solves problems are deeply connected to the actual socio-cultural and socio-economic conditions prevalent in the student's life

(Solano-Flores & Nelson-Barber, 2001). Without giving clear attention to the role of cultural world views, cultural communication, and socialization styles, assessments may not accurately measure student language proficiency or content knowledge and skills (Solano-Flores, Chapter 1, this volume; Basterra, Chapter 4, this volume; Trumbull & Solano-Flores, Chapter 2, this volume).

Researchers have looked at specific cases of test items that fail to address aspects of cultural validity and have shown how the items can be confusing to ELLs and consequently fail to measure accurately their content knowledge (Oakes, 1990; Solano-Flores & Nelson-Barber, 2001). For example, the item below comes from a state exam used to measure knowledge of eighth-grade science.[12] The assessment in which this item appears was last used in March of 2007 and released in the fall of 2007.

Michael studied the effects of temperature and pressure on the expansion rate of gases. When publishing the results of the experiment for others to study, which of the following would be **most** important for Michael to include?

A.  detailed steps in the procedures used
B.  cost of the materials used in the study
C.  acknowledgement of family members
D.  name of the building where the experiments were performed

In the above list of multiple-choice responses, option "C" is problematic for students who come from a community whose culture places high emphasis on family connections and approval. Although the question is trying to measure knowledge of the scientific method, the item has included a possible answer that, though incorrect, can be an important trigger for some students. For these particular students, option "C" has a specific and important meaning that is relevant to their home community, which can prove confusing when trying to respond to the item. It is possible that for these students the *most* important statement is an acknowledgement of the support received from family members. These students would naturally bring in cultural knowledge when reading, interpreting, and responding to the question. Elsewhere in this book, the issue of cultural validity is discussed in depth. In the context of this chapter, it is important to note that the criticism of statewide assessments based on the cultural validity arguments rests on an extensive body of work.

### Title III Provisions

Few concerns have been raised regarding the Title III requirements. Nonetheless, two issues have once again become visible on the policy radar—the definition of "fully English proficient" and standardization of the ELL exit criteria across states. Although discussions about these issues have taken place prior to NCLB, the use of a single ELP assessment across a state has prompted a reassessment of the problem and led state and local educators to seek guidance from the U.S. Department of Education (USDE) (cf., CCSSO, 1992). This is because some states have given districts flexibility in determining the definition of "fully English proficient" and in setting criteria for exiting ELL students from English language support programs.

Generally, the criteria include elements such as the exit score on the ELP, scores on content achievement tests, teacher observations, and local committee recommendations. Not all factors are uniform across districts, which has raised concerns about comparability of scores across districts (and states). The USDE has informed states of its preference for consistency across a state, but there has been no specific policy set forth by the USDE.

In addition to the modifications cited above, which apply to all states, individual states have requested changes in rules and regulations as they encountered implementation challenges. The mechanism for requesting and obtaining greater flexibility has been the state's accountability plans that must be approved by the USDE. Many of the requests have focused on those provisions related to inclusion of special education and ELLs. The requests generally sought to exempt ELLs from participating in statewide assessments until they had reached a number of years in English language schooling or reached a certain level of English language development. States also sought approval based on alternative assessments for ELL students. Almost all of the states' requests were denied by the USDE.

Thus, the USDE has shown some level of flexibility in interpreting the law in order to ease the implementation challenges at the state and local levels. However, the key areas of concern (inclusion in statewide assessments and the AYP formula) have remained points of contention at state and local levels.

## Impact of Accountability Provisions

The fundamental objection to the accountability provisions of NCLB is the use of an AYP formulation that holds schools accountable for students' progress and applies consequences to schools and districts when the performance targets are not met. School level staff view these provisions as unreasonable. The desire to avoid the labeling of schools and the consequences that accrue over time have resulted in institutional coping mechanisms that observers view as detrimental.

The institutional responses described below have a bearing on both ELL and non-ELL students. Since ELLs comprise a significant proportion of students enrolled in low performing schools, it is impossible to isolate impact solely to ELLs beyond those associated with delivery of language instruction and support cf. Kopriva & Sexton, Chapter 5, this volume). Nonetheless, the most salient issues related to the delivery of services to ELLs include the use of native language, identification of schools, and ELL student drop-out.

## Use of Native Language

There is evidence of a reduction in native language instruction as districts and schools push to meet the performance standards that are measured with English language assessments. The degree to which this reaction is prevalent across districts with significant ELL student enrollment is not known since few published reports have addressed this issue. Nevertheless, in a study of the use of bilingual education in New York City schools, Menken (2009) reported that enrollment in bilingual education programs dropped from 40% of total enrollment in 2003 to 25% by 2008. During the same period of time, there was an increase in enrollment in ESL programs from 53% of ELLs to 69%. The author attributed the decline in bilingual enrollment to a response to the testing demands. The pressure to reduce instruction in the native language was cited in an unpublished report of Dual Language Programs in the District of Columbia. Interviews of teachers in dual language programs revealed that the number of minutes used to teach content in the native language has decreased as school leadership sought to improve the schools' test scores.[13] A similar response was reported by Crawford (2004) in writing about the impact of the Reading First program on a dual language program outside of Washington, DC. He noted that in an attempt to comply with requirements of Reading First, the leadership disrupted the program by expanding the time allotted to the English language reading block. Reading First is a federally funded formula grant program (Part B of Title I) designed to strengthen the teaching of reading in grades kindergarten through third.

This response at the district and school levels undermines the intent of the law but is not illogical simply because it is based on unrealistic expectations. Specifically, it was expected that ELLs would be academically proficient in less than two years. It takes three-to-five years for students in bilingual programs to show progress in learning English. Yet, schools are held accountable for progress in the content areas in less than two years of English language instruction. Consequently, it would be understandable for schools to increase instructional time in English language arts or focus solely on content instruction in English. Although local staff may know that students receiving native language instruction ultimately meet grade level expectations in content areas, and often surpass non-ELLs, they cannot wait for the benefits to accrue, given the short time during which they need to show progress.

### Identification of Schools

The large number of schools that have been identified as in need of improvement has been another area of concern. Schools with high numbers of ELL students are "penalized" in the accountability system because ELLs are members of multiple AYP sub-groups (poor, ELL, special education), which increases the chances that schools will not meet the proficiency target. The more homogeneous the school, the less likely they are to be identified. Therefore, schools that have been traditionally under-resourced and diverse are more likely to be "penalized" under NCLB. During school year 2005–2006, there were approximately 10,000 schools in some phase of school improvement planning or restructuring (Stullich, Abrams, Eisner, & Lee, 2009). This represents 20% of all Title I schools. In urban districts, the proportion of schools in need of improvement is higher, given that they have a greater proportion of students at risk of and ELL learners.

While schools with higher concentration of students at risk are more likely to be identified, it is also the case that in schools with low concentrations of ELL students, the scores of ELLs may be excluded from the AYP formula. This is of concern to the advocacy community (Lukan, 2009). In this scenario, students are tested, but not counted for AYP.[14] For example, in an elementary school with 50 ELL students, scores would not be included for students tested at the third grade if they are 50 or fewer. Consequently, the school is not held accountable for the performance of the third-grade ELL students. This is because states determine the minimum number of students from each sub-group, per school, that can be included in the AYP calculation. The number of ELL students excluded per school across states is as low as five and as high as 50. The average number is 30 students. The larger the number, the more students a school can exclude (but only up to the number set by the state). The rationale for larger numbers, as presented by some states, is that schools need to protect the identity of the students—the smaller the number of ELLs in one school, the easier it is to identify individual students. Also, there is the issue of greater score instability as the number of sub-group members within a school becomes smaller. This means that test results can misrepresent actual student achievement when the group involved is too small (Durán, Chapter 6, this volume). The degree to which there are other ways of accounting for these students needs further examination. It is of value to know how states with smaller numbers of ELLs are addressing the issue of privacy and score instability.

Nonetheless, some would argue that the concentration of ELL and poor students in particular schools should not absolve adults in those schools from the responsibility for maximizing educational outcomes (and learning) of students. These are precisely the schools that have not served poor students well and ought to welcome the opportunity to focus attention on struggling students. Many agree that additional resources and guidance should be directed to these schools.

### Usefulness of Test Score Reports

Observers have noted that some test score reports do not provide meaningful information at the classroom level. Through a teacher interview used to discuss the Colorado State Assessment Program (CSAP) writing test, Chia (November 1, 2009) found that the test reports educators often use do not include curriculum-specific results that teachers can use to inform instruction. Although a teacher received a report on an individual student's proficiency level in writing mechanics, the educator receives no information regarding where specifically the student is doing well or poorly. Given the limited information on *what* students do not know, it would be difficult for teachers to determine, from these types of reports, *why* a student does not understand a particular aspect of a construct (standard). A similar finding was reported by the Center on Education Policy (CEP, 2009) in a recent case study of the impact of the accountability policies on curriculum and instruction. CEP interviewed district officials and members of the school community in three states and conducted classroom observations. They concluded that state test data were mainly used to "make broad district or school policy decision and not helpful for instruction."

Some would argue this is an appropriate use of state level data. This example makes evident the challenge of implementation, which often results in implementers going beyond the intent of the policy-makers. Reports compiled at the state level were not intended as diagnostic tools for classroom use (see Durán, Chapter 6, this volume). The intent was to provide information that, along with other indicators, could inform teacher decision-making.

### Narrowing the Curriculum

Much visibility has been given to reports about school level responses such as "teaching to the test," increasing instructional time on reading and mathematics, and reducing instructional time in non-tested subjects. This criticism has been echoed and documented in multiple reports and localities. Specifically, the Center on Education Policy (2009) reported that, while there is greater alignment between district and school curricula and state's standards, there is also evidence of a focus on test preparation, and more time devoted to subjects tested by the state. Moreover, English language arts and mathematics are the subjects most frequently chosen in professional development sessions. For example, over half of Title II professional development dollars (combined) focus on English language arts (29%) and Mathematics (25%) (Chambers, Mahitivanichcha, Esra, & Shambaugh, 2009). The expenditure is even higher when other federal funds (Title I) that target professional development are considered. The consequence of this is less time devoted to subjects such as social studies, science, and the arts.[15]

### Focus on Bubble Kids

Another undesirable consequence is focusing on students near the proficient cut score. This practice was publicized recently in a *Washington Post* article (Turque, 2009) about the District of Columbia Public Schools. The article noted that the school system had been focusing intensively on a "Saturday Scholars" program composed of students who required the least help. These are the students just below the proficient target. With intensive coaching, they are pushed over the threshold, thereby ensuring that the schools meet the performance target. While this practice is fairly common in school districts, it is viewed by some educators as insincere when implemented in isolation of a comprehensive and long-term strategy to improve achievement outcomes for struggling students.

### ELL Drop-Out Rate and NCLB

The relationship between the drop-out rate and NCLB testing requirements at the high school level is difficult to determine. Several reports have posited that the testing requirements are contributing to the drop-out rate of ELL students. But without separating the effect of high school exit tests from NCLB mandated tests, causation cannot be attributed to NCLB.[16] Nonetheless, some observers have noted that struggling students (including ELLs) become discouraged and drop out, or are "pushed out" of secondary schools by the testing policies (Darling-Hammond, 2006).

In his 2009 briefing, *The Condition of Education 2009*, the acting commissioner of the National Center for Education Statistics (NCES) reported that the high school drop-out rate for Whites, Blacks, and Hispanics had decreased between 1994 and 2007.[17] However, he noted that Hispanics and Blacks were more likely to drop out than Whites. He attributed the higher drop-out rate among Hispanics to percentage of foreign-born Hispanic students. The drop-out rate for foreign-born Hispanic students (proxy for ELL) was three-times the rate of Hispanics born in the United States. Looking at this in terms of high school completion rates, in 2007, 56% of foreign-born Hispanics aged 18–24 completed high school compared to 86% of Hispanics born in the U.S. At the national level, the completion rate for 2007 was 89%.

The magnitude of the problem is particularly stark when examining district level data. Researchers at the Mauricio Gastón Institute (Vaznis, 2009) examined the relationship between drop-out rates and the sheltered English instruction policy enacted in Massachusetts in 2003.[18] They found that the drop-out rate among students in Boston ELL programs rose from 6.3% in 2003 to 12.1% in 2006. The percentage of middle school LEP students who dropped out tripled from 0.8% in 2003 to 2.7% in 2006. Since 38% of Boston's enrollment is composed of non-native English speakers, the implication of the high drop-out rate for this city should be of concern to its citizenry. If the trend is not reversed, it will have a detrimental impact on the economic well-being of the city. Thus this program, which was the school system response to the English-only law in Massachusetts, apparently contributed to the drop-out rate in ELLs enrolled in the Boston school system.

These findings are consistent with those reported for the New York City Public School System. In a recent article, *El Diario La Prensa* states that only 23.5% of New York City's ELL students are graduating from high school. According to the newspaper, teenage newcomers and long-term ELLs make up a large portion of the 150,000 ELL students in the public schools. Though some may attribute the low high school completion rates to student-based issues, such as motivation, according to results of the National Research Center for College and University Admissions (NRCCUA) and the Hispanic Heritage Foundation (HHF) College Preparation 2007 study, nearly 98% of Latino high school students say they want to attend college, and nearly 95% say they realistically believe that they will graduate from college. These results mirrored those of high school students across all ethnic groups.[19]

The examples cited above substantiate further a long-term problem—high drop-out rates for ELL/Hispanic students at the high school level. The NCLB assessment requirements are not the only factor contributing to the increase in the drop-out rate. For example, all of the states that have experienced a significant influx of immigrants have passed English-only policies in the past 10–15 years. In many of these states, enrollment of ELL students is high (above 60,000). In addition, states enacted high school exit tests prior to NCLB. Consequently, it is likely that what is contributing to the drop-out rate is the combined effects of these policies rather than a single contributing factor such as the assessment policies under NCLB.

## Positive Effects of the Law

### Greater Policy Coherence

The positive views of the law previously attributed to a segment of administrators in high ELL schools is generally supported by many in the ELL advocacy community.[20] Disaggregation of scores by sub-groups is a feature of the law that has forever changed how data about student performance is reported. While recognizing the shortcomings of the law, supporters consider the increased attention to the needs of ELL learners as a positive outcome of the law. Moreover, they point to its impact in bringing greater policy and programmatic coherence at the state and district levels. There is now an infrastructure at these levels designed to support the education of ELLs. Specifically, since the enactment of NCLB, almost all states have developed English language development standards and ELP assessments aligned to the ELP standards. Prior to NCLB, only seven states had developed ELP standards and none had assessments aligned to those standards (CCSSO, 2007). In addition, many states have developed teacher standards for ELL instruction and guidance regarding how to select research based instructional programs of ELL students (Editorial Projects, 2009).

### Strengthening System of Delivery and Guidance to LEAs

The availability of ELL test scores by ELP proficiency and content areas has enabled educators to track student performance and direct interventions that have the potential of improving achievement outcomes for ELL students. In testimony to the US House of Representatives, the Superintendent from a district in California described how her district is one of six that developed a consortium to address the needs of ELL students.[21] The members of the consortium have developed a comprehensive plan and services delivery mechanism with necessary supports to ensure ELLs are given all opportunities to succeed. Moreover, professional development activities are now coordinated thereby ensuring that teachers are not working in isolation of one another.

### Data Informed Decision-Making

While the student assessment data is not consistently used as intended, and may not provide the level of specificity desired at the classroom level, it has become central to district-wide reform strategy, particularly when used along with other indicators. Federally supported technical assistance agencies (centers and regional laboratories) are expending resources in working with district and school staffs on data analysis to identify instructional gaps, establish district-wide goals, and adjust methods to meet students' ELL needs (*r&d alert* 8.1). All of the

10 centers have as their core strategy to work with schools and districts on data driven decision-making.

In a recent report focusing on districts on the path toward "improving," the Council of Great City Schools (2009) noted that student achievement data was instrumental in driving district level policy decisions in three of the four major school districts examined in the study (Dallas, New York City, and San Francisco). Data used not only to inform policy, but also to target instructional improvement efforts. Similarly, in their examination of three states (Georgia, Pennsylvania, and California), Hamilton and Berends (2006) found that teachers were using statewide assessments to guide their classroom decisions. They concluded that educators responsible for teaching grades in which a state assessment was administered used the results to search for more effective teaching methods, emphasized topics seen on the test, and dedicated time to teaching test style and format.

These findings stand in contrast to those previously reported, which point to the inadequacies of the test reports for the purposes of informing classroom instruction. Apparently, districts and school level staff are reporting both the value of these reports and their limitations. It may be that in cases where teachers find these data useful, there are other indicators supplementing their decision-making, or that the degree of specificity that is attached to the score reports differs across states. Whichever is the case, it is difficult to make generalizations regarding this issue. Thus, there is a need for a more careful examination of the nature of the reports provided to the schools by state officials.

## Achievement at the Elementary Level

Data on the impact of NCLB on ELL student achievement is sparse, difficult to interpret, and sometimes contradictory. Moreover, achievement outcomes can't be directly attributed to NCLB. Nonetheless, the long-term performance (2002–2007) of ELLs as measured by the National Assessment of Educational Progress (NAEP) shows a pattern of improvement at the elementary level.[22] Specifically, at the fourth-grade level, the percentage of ELL students scoring at or above basic on NAEP rose from about 30% in 2000 to 55% in 2007. While there is some improvement at the eighth-grade level, the percentage of students showing improvement was less significant (20%) in 2000 to about 30% in 2007. In addition, as reported in the USDE biennial report, ELL students made progress in learning English and reaching the "attainment" level on ELP tests.[23] Starting in 2005, the performance of former ELLs was tracked and, not surprisingly, over the two year period, former ELLs outperform their ELLs peers in math and reading, at the fourth- and eighth-grade level.

However, when looking at data on the achievement gap, the optimism is diminished. On statewide assessments and in NAEP, the gap between ELLs and non-ELLs is significant (Editorial Projects, 2009, p. 39). For 2006–2007, the gap in performance on the state assessments at the fourth- and eighth-grade levels in mathematics was 23% (averaged). In reading for the same year, it was 32%. On the NAEP 2007 mathematics and reading assessment, the gap was 25% in math and 25% in reading.[24] None of this is surprising. In both state and NAEP assessments, problems of accessibility and appropriateness exist: specifically, inclusion of ELLs in testing programs before they can access the language of the items and accommodations that may not be appropriate for ELLs.

## Alternatives to the Current Accountability Paradigm: Growth Model and Formative Assessments

Earlier in this chapter, we discussed the difficulties with implementation of assessment and accountability requirements of NCLB relative to ELL students. The reality is that the notion of holding schools accountable for the performance of all students is supported by the public and is likely to remain in future versions of ESEA.[25] The challenge as NCLB approaches reauthorization is to develop assessments and accountability systems that are defensible and bring to fruition the goals intended by the framers of the law. This means assessments that are valid and reliable and accountability systems that provide meaningful information to stakeholders at various levels of the educational system.

This cannot be accomplished with one test. Instead, there is a need for a balanced and coherent assessment system in which a number of tests are designed for different purposes and different contexts (Pellegrino, Chudowsky, & Glaser, 2001). In such a framework, assessments are staggered and developed for use at multiple levels (classroom, across classrooms, district, and state level).[26] Thus, large-scale assessments such as those used to satisfy NCLB requirements are acceptable for accountability purposes, as long as they meet the psychometrics standards set by the profession. Data from large-scale tests provide summative information that districts and schools can use to form judgments about student performance relative to standards and, similarly, school performance relative to state expectations at a point in time. This is valuable and necessary for program level decision-making. For the purpose of informing classroom instruction, culturally valid, formative assessments are highly recommended. Formative assessments can be used jointly with an accountability system that recognizes effort at the school level while still holding schools accountable for students' achievement results.

### The Growth Model Approach to Accountability

Over the eight-year implementation of the NCLB law, there appears to be consensus around the notion that a growth model approach to determining school progress for accountability purposes is highly desirable. In a growth model approach to educational accountability, the achievement scores of individual students are measured year to year to ascertain whether, on average, the students make progress. In addition, scores of the *same* students are compared to their previous year's performance (Goldschmidt, 2005). For example, the scores of individual fourth-graders are measured against the scores they previously received in the third grade. In contrast, the current system compares a group of students in one grade (third grade) against a different group of students in the previous year's third-grade class. It does not measure individual student growth. Instead, it measures the status of groups of students (third-graders) relative to a performance target over time.

The growth model approach is more acceptable to state and district level educators because it acknowledges effort at the individual student and school levels. However, it requires a sophisticated data system, yearly testing of students, consistent proficiency levels across grades, and the use of individual student identification numbers (Hoff, 2007). Not all states have such a system. However, given the level of support that has been provided to states to form these systems, it is likely that most states will soon have a data system that will enable them to adopt a growth model approach to accountability, should they choose to do so. Some advocates and scholars have voiced concern about the adoption of an accountability approach that does not measure growth against an achievement target. The concern is that low performing schools might become complacent with high levels of growth (which they are likely to show) and low expectations. On the other hand, high performing schools with pockets of low performing students might show slow growth and be identified as "in need of improvement." For high performing schools, this has been the primary source of disagreement with the accountability provisions. Specifically, that they have been identified as in need of improvement because one or more of their sub-groups have not met the performance targets. Some researchers assert that it is possible to have a system that has both growth and status components.

This dilemma will likely be resolved prior to the upcoming reauthorization of ESEA, particularly since states have already been allowed to test these approaches under NCLB. Partly in response to the outcry about the number of schools identified for school improvement, USDE introduced a growth model pilot program that allowed a limited number of states (10) to use growth models in their AYP calculations. Pilot project states are required to compare results from their growth model with status model results. Thus, the outcome of the pilot process will greatly inform the deliberations that take place around issues of accountability during reauthorization.

### Measuring Progress at the Classroom Level

NCLB has made the schools accountable for improving achievement; however, states have had difficulty developing assessments that provide meaningful information on performance at the classroom level, mostly because of the complexities and cost of scoring state level tests for use in the classroom. In addition, statewide assessments may not have the psychometric properties needed to yield the type of information required by decision-makers to judge the effectiveness of services at the program level. It is clear that both statewide assessments for accountability purposes and locally administered formative assessments for use diagnostically and to improve instruction types are necessary. Still, in recent years, some states have found the appropriate roles for a balance between summative vs. formative assessments.

The use of formative assessments has gained momentum partly in response to the prominence that summative assessments have attained at the state level. According to *EdWeek* (Cech, 2008), 30% of the $2.1 billion assessment revenue of testing companies are generated through the sale of formative assessments. There is a realization that large-scale assessments have limitations in terms of informing classroom practice. More important, research suggests that formative assessment can be a powerful tool to support teaching and learning (Phelan, Kang, Niemi, Vendlinski, & Choi, 2009). According to Popham (2006), "An assessment is formative to the extent that information from the assessment is used, during the instructional segment in which the assessment occurred, to adjust instruction with the intent of better meeting the needs of the students assessed." While there is disagreement about the characterization of formative assessments as process or product, there is agreement about the importance of their role as a key component of an overall assessment system.

Clearly, formative assessments can and should play an important role in improving the performance of ELL students. Promising examples of formative assessment efforts that have been designed for ELL students are the *Literacy Squared* project at the elementary level, and FLARE at the secondary level. While these represent positive trends in the assessment of ELLs, the outcome data are still being gathered and, therefore, no definitive statements can be made about program effectiveness.

The *Literacy Squared* project is an effort to bridge standards to instruction and formative assessment. The project, developed at the University of Colorado at Boulder, uses a strong formative assessment component designed for ELLs. Through it, students—with teacher guidance—can work toward full biliteracy. The program stresses the importance of assessing emerging biliterate students in both languages as part of language arts instruction, so that teachers are able to understand each student's proficiency level in each language (Escamilla, Soltero-Gonzalez, Butvilofsky, Hopewell, Sparrow, & Escamilla, 2009). The University of Colorado's School of Education provides writing prompts in English and Spanish and a scoring rubric (in English) that addresses writing conventions and content. By implementing detailed professional development, through which teachers learn how to use the rubric, *Literacy Squared* researchers help teachers gather specific information about student writing progress that they can use in a formative way. Teachers use information that they gather at the class and student level to inform daily lesson plans and one-on-one work that they do with individual students. Teachers working with *Literacy Squared* use modified explicit instruction for phonics, vocabulary, comprehension, and writing while focusing on productive language arts skills (speaking and writing) (Escamilla et al., 2007). The program helps educators to balance listening, reading, and metalinguistic awareness while working with students. Results from *Literacy Squared* research indicate that there is a positive relationship between increased attention to the teaching of writing and improvement in overall literacy achievement. Over 80% of each of the student cohorts participating in *Literacy Squared* throughout three years are on a positive trajectory towards biliteracy (Escamilla & Hopewell, 2009).

At the secondary education level, FLARE is a program designed to use benchmark exams, formative assessments, and student self-assessments to assist teachers working on literacy with English language learners. FLARE staff insist that, in order to be of high quality, formative assessments must be technically sound, embedded in classroom practice, and linked to learning goals. For formative assessments to be productive, educators need to provide meaningful exemplars, results should identify student proficiency level within the assessed construct, and test performance should allow teachers to indicate how the student can improve (Cook, 2009). Like *Literacy Squared*, FLARE connects formative assessment practices to classroom instruction. The program stresses the need to focus on vocabulary knowledge, grammatical control, comprehension skills, communication skills, and discourse capabilities (e.g., functional language abilities) (Cook, 2009). FLARE is in its pilot stages and, therefore, quantitative and qualitative results about student progress is forthcoming.

## Summary of Recommendations from Various Sources

The recommendations outlined below have been put forth by various sectors of the education community and are intended to address the drawbacks of the current assessment system relative to ELL students. In addition, there are recommendations directed at teachers, intended to support their work with ELL students while the broader policy issues related to assessment and accountability are debated and resolved at the state and local levels:

1. Exempt ELLs from meeting the state's proficient level standard in any subject matter—mathematics, language arts, science, and social science— until they have been deemed fully English proficient. However, continue to track student performance in English language development and content knowledge through administration of formative assessments.
2. Include former ELLs in the accountability system for a minimum of three years, or through their enrollment in the school district.
3. Address issues of language and culture at all stages of assessment, from development to implementation to data analysis to reporting. Using this perspective as a guide while creating assessment items can lessen problems with test score validity due to confounding linguistic complexity and content specific skills.
4. Support the development of primary language assessments for students in bilingual programs and students with a history of schooling in their countries' languages. This support should be informed by appropriate studies on the adequacy of language of testing at the local level (e.g., school or school district). Recent evidence shows that, even within the same broad linguistic group (e.g., native Spanish speakers), more dependable measures of academic achievement can be obtained for some groups of students when they are tested in their native language, whereas more dependable measures can be obtained for other groups when they are tested in English (see Solano-Flores, Chapter 1, this volume).

5. Encourage the development of a coordinated assessment system containing multiple measures, so that decisions about schools or individual students are not based on the results of a single assessment.
6. Support development of accountability systems that acknowledge "progress" while holding schools accountable for meeting set performance targets.
7. Focus more on English language proficiency than academic content assessment results when ELLs are in the beginning stages of learning English. As the student progresses through the education system and becomes more proficient in English, more weight would be given to the academic content assessment.
8. Give states flexibility in assessing identified ELLs during the first three years after school entry, while requiring specific achievement for students for up to three years. During the three year period, allow states to use USDE approved alternate assessments.

## What Teachers Can Do

1. Participate in the professional development opportunities supported by Titles I, II, and III, focusing on strengthening teacher content knowledge and aligning curriculum. Of particular value are those professional development opportunities in which ELL teachers collaborate with mainstream classroom teachers.
2. Deepen understanding of the second language development process in order to more effectively work with ELL students. This is particularly important for mainstream classroom teachers who are often faced with ELL students who are still in the process of learning English.
3. Advocate for fixes in the ESEA assessment and accountability requirements, but support the disaggregation provisions.
4. Advocate for increases in Title III funding to expand the ESOL teachers' pipeline and professional development opportunities.
5. Use various forms of formative assessment to assess ELL student progress, including benchmark assessments, interim, and common assessments.

## Conclusion

This chapter has provided an overview of the provisions of NCLB that are most problematic for educators at the local level and has presented the unintended consequences that have been the source of critiques of the law. These include inappropriate instruments to gauge ELL knowledge of content, reduction of instruction in native language, and over-emphasis on subjects tested on the state assessments. The discussion has also shown that policy and programmatic changes at the state and local levels regarding the establishment of a coherent policy and programmatic framework are likely to have a long-term positive effect on the education of ELL learners. In addition, the chapter presented two alternatives that are likely to be debated in policy conversations regarding reauthorization of ESEA—growth model approaches to accountability and formative assessments both of which hold promise for addressing problems raised by the opponents of the law. Finally, examples of promising formative assessment practices designed for ELL students were presented. While more evidence is needed to evaluate their success, preliminary results show positive effects for ELL students.

A major issue not addressed in the chapter, but in need of further exploration and analysis, is the issue of the teacher quality provision and its relationship to ELL students. NCLB has directed significant funds to teacher development at the preserve and in-service levels. How these funds are combined at the district level to strengthen the capacity of teachers of ELL students is not evident. There are also unanswered questions regarding the role of paraprofessionals in supporting ELL student education since enactment of NCLB. Paraprofessionals have played an important role in mediating ELL student access to the language of instruction. How NCLB has strengthened their capacity to assist with classroom instruction is not clear. There is limited research in these areas, and the available research is inconclusive in providing an understanding of how teacher quality provisions under Titles I, II, and III help to advance the education of ELL learners.

## Notes

1. In this chapter, "ELL" and "LEP" will be used interchangeably.
2. The formula is needs-based. The higher the level of poverty, the greater the amount of funds that are directed first to the states and then sub-granted to the districts.
3. This is the level at which students are considered to have mastery of content assessed.
4. In 2007 science was added as one of the subjects to be tested.
5. There must be a minimum number of sub-group students in the school to be included in the accountability formula. The number (N) varies across states. Moreover, this does relieve states from testing the students.
6. Policy analysts are troubled by the variability across states in the definition of proficient because it has resulted in lowering of expectations in some states in order to meet the performance target.
7. Setting the performance standards means that states define the performance standards (basic, proficient, advanced) in terms of rigor and cut-off scores on the test.
8. A newly arrived student means a year or less in the US school system.
9. The two year rule is to include the scores of former ELLs in the AYP formula for up to two years.
10. Failure to meet the measure of annual progress under Title III for two years requires districts to develop an improvement plan, and, if they fail to meet the measure for more than two years, this requires the modification of the education program. Also, states have the option of withholding Title III funds.
11. Those that have been cited in the research literature include reducing language complexity, glossary, extra time, simplifying test directions, and tests in native language.
12. According to a 2002 report by the US Department of Education, this state has a diverse student population: 10% of students were LEP and almost 50% of students were non-white.
13. Lara (2009).
14. As previously noted, 95% of students enrolled at the schools must be tested.
15. Center on Education Policy (2009).
16. The high school exit tests have been in place in many states prior to NCLB.
17. The high school drop-out rate measured for the briefing was defined as the percentage of 16-to-24-year-olds who, in a given year, are not enrolled in school and have not earned a high school credential such as a diploma or GED.

18. Massachusetts adopted an English-only law that severely curtailed the delivery of content instruction in the native language. Instead, districts were mandated to use a sheltered English approach.
19. www.impre.com/eldiariony/opinion/2009/7/22/shamefully-low-graduation-rate-1369 29- 2.html#top.
20. Organizations such as the Hispanic Education Coalition, MALDEF, and the National Council of LaRaza.
21. Impact of NCLB on English learners, testimony provided by Francisca Sánchez, San Bernardino County Superintendent of Schools.
22. Positive performance trend is defined as an increase in the percentage of students reaching at least basic proficiency.
23. This is the level at which ELLs are at the point of exiting the language assistance program. However, in most states, decisions regarding exiting the students involve more than the score on the ELP test.
24. These figures represent the average gap for state developed assessments in 50 states plus the District of Columbia and 33 states participating in NAEP.
25. Educational Testing Service (2007).
26. Such a framework was published by the *Journal of the National Staff Development Council* (Stiggins & Chappuis, 2006).

# References

Abedi, J. (2007). English language proficiency assessment and accountability under the NCLB Title III: An overview. In J. Abedi (Ed.), *English language proficiency in the nation: Current status and future practice*. Davis, CA: University of California, Davis.

*Biannual Report to Congress on the Implementation of Title III State Formula Grants, 2004–2006.*

CCSSO (1992). *Recommendations for improving the assessment and monitoring of students with limited English proficiency*. Council of Chief State School Officers, Washington, DC.

CCSSO (2007). *Statewide educational accountability systems under NCLB Act—A report on 2008 amendments to state plans*. Council of Chief State School Officers, Washington, DC.

Cech, S. (2008). Test industry split over formative assessment. *Education Week*, September 17.

Center on Education Policy (2006). Ten big effects of the No Child Left Behind Act on public schools. *Phi Delta Kappan*, 88(2), 1110–1113.

Center on Education Policy (2009). *How state and federal accountability policy have influenced curriculum and instruction in three states*. Center on Education Policy, Washington, DC.

Chambers, Lam, I., Mahitivanichcha, K., Esra, P., & Shambaugh, L. (2009). State of No Child Left Behind Act: Vol. VI. Targeting and uses of federal education funds. US Department of Education, Office of Planning, Evaluation and Policy Development et al.

Chu Clewell, B., Consentino de Cohen, C., & Murray, J. (2007). *Promise or peril? NCLB and the education of ELL students*. Washington, DC: The Urban Institute.

Collier, V.P. (1989). How long? A synthesis of research on academic achievement in second language. *TESOL Quarterly*, 23(3), 509–531.

Cook, H.G. (2009). *Formative assessment: Best practices part I*. Presented at Elluminate Session, Pennsylvania Department of Education.

Crawford, J. (2004). *No Child Left Behind: Misguided Approach to School Accountability for English Language Learners*. Washington, DC: National Association of Bilingual Education.

Darling-Hammond, L. (2006). *Powerful teacher education: Lessons From exemplary programs*. San Francisco, CA: Jossey-Bass Publishers.

DeBray, E. (2003). The federal role in school accountability: Assessing recent history and the new law. *Voices in Urban Education*, Spring. Annenberg Institute for School Reform, Brown University, RI.

DeCohen, C.C., & Chu Clewell, B. (2007). *Putting English language learners on the educational map*. Washington, DC: Urban Institute Brief.

Editorial Projects in Education (2009). Quality counts. *Education Week*, 28(17).

Educational Testing Service (2007). *Standards, accountability and flexibility: Americans speak on No Child Left Behind reauthorization*. Washington, DC: Peter D. Hart Research Associates, Inc. & The Winston Group.

Escamilla, K., & Hopewell, S. (2009). Transitions to biliteracy: Creating positive academic trajectories for emerging bilinguals in the United States. *International perspectives on bilingual education: Policy, practice, and controversy*, in press.

Escamilla, K., Soltero-Gonzalez, L., Butvilofsky, S., Hopewell, S., Sparrow, W., & Escamilla, M. (2009). *Transitions to biliteracy: Literacy Squared*, in press.

GAO (2007). *No Child Left Behind Act: Education assistance could help states better measure progress of students with limited English proficiency*. US Government Accountability Office.

Goldschmidt, P. (2005). *Policymakers' guide to growth models for school accountability: How do accountability models differ?* Washington, DC: Council of Chief State School Officers.

Hamilton, L.S., & Berends, M. (2006). *Instructional practices related to standards and assessments*. Working Paper, RAND Education.

Hamilton, L.S., Stecher, M.B., Marsh, A.J., Sloan McCombs, J., Robyn, A., Russell, J., Naftel, S., & Barney, H. (2007). *Standards based accountability under No Child Left Behind: Experiences of teachers and administrators in three states*. Santa Monica, CA: Rand Corporation.

Hoff, D. (2007). Growth models gaining in accountability debate. *Education Week*, December, 19.

Kieffer, Michael J., Lesaux, Nonie K., Rivera, Mabel, & Francis, David J. (2009). Accommodations for English language learners taking large-scale assessments: a meta-analysis on effectiveness and validity. *Review of Educational Research*, 79, July 1.

La Celle-Peterson, M.W., & Rivera, C. (1994). Is it real for the kids? A framework for equitable assessment policies for English language learners. *Harvard Educational Review*, 64(1), 1–23.

Lara, J. (2009). Unpublished report: Bancroft Elementary Dual Language Program, April.

Linquanti, R., & Carstens, L. (2006). *R&D alert: Timely knowledge for education and human development. Using data to drive reform*. 8(1). Retrieved December 18, 2009 from www.wested.org/online_pubs/rd-06-01.pdf.

Lukan, J. (2009). *Strengthening accountability to ensure Latino Success: An analysis of NCLB Title I Regulations*. White Paper, National Council of La Raza, Washington, DC.

McClure, P. (2004). Grassroots resistance to NCLB. www.earlyreadingplayschool.com.au/webarticles/theoreticalIssues.

Menken, K. (2009). No Child Left Behind and its effects on language policy. *Annual Review of Applied Linguistics*, 29, 103–117.

Oakes, J. (1990). Multiplying inequalities: The effects of race, social, class, and tracking on opportunities to learn mathematics and science. Santa Monica, CA: RAND.

Pellegrino, J.W., Chudowsky, N., & Glaser, R (Eds.) (2001). *Knowing what students know: The science and design of educational assessment*. Washington, DC: National Academy Press.

Phelan, J., Kang, T., Niemi, D.N., Vendlinski, T., & Choi, K. (2009). *Some aspects of the technical quality of formative assessments in middle school mathematics* (CRESST Tech. Rep. No. 750). Los Angeles, CA: University of California, National Center for Research on Evaluation, Standards and Student Testing (CRESST).

Popham, W.J. (2006). *Determining the instructional sensitivity of accountability tests.* Paper presented at the Annual Large-Scale Assessment Conference, Council of Chief State School Officers, San Francisco, CA.

Solano-Flores, G., & Nelson-Barber, S. (2001). On the cultural validity of science assessments. *Journal of Research in Science Teaching*, 38(5), 553–573.

Stiggins, R., & Chappuis, J. (2006). Learning teams can help teachers shift their understanding of assessment to realize how to assess for learning. *Journal of the National Staff Development Council*, 27(1), 46–51.

Stullich, S., Abrams, A., Eisner, E., & Lee, E. (2009). *Title I Implementation Update and Recent Evaluation Study (2009).* U.S. Department of Education, Office of Planning, Evaluation and Policy Development Policy and Program Studies Service.

Turque, B. (2009). Testing tactics fuel DC School gains. *Washington Post*, Friday July 17.

Vaznis, J. (2009). Boston students struggle with English-only rule: Many non-natives quit the system, *Boston Globe*, April 7, p. B.1.

Wolf, P.J. (2008). School voucher programs: What the research says about parental school choice. *Brigham Young University Law Review*, 2008(1), 415–446.

# Part III

# Field Efforts to Increase Cultural Validity in Assessment

Chapter 9

# Language Arts
## Designing and Using a Reading Assessment for Learners Transitioning to English-Only Instruction[1]

*Elise Trumbull and Nanette Koelsch*

---

**Chapter Overview**

Most, if not all, of the efforts to accommodate ELL students have been directed at those receiving special services. Yet students who have made the transition from bilingual, English as a Second Language (ESL), or English Language Development (ELD) programs to English-only instruction may also need modified assessments in order to demonstrate what they know and can do. This chapter describes a research and development effort to design valid literacy assessments for students who have just moved from bilingual instruction to English-only instruction. It entails researchers working with teachers to align assessment formats with instructional formats, identify ways to reduce unnecessary language load, and connect assessment content with students' cultural background knowledge and values.

---

As the federal government approaches the passage of a new Elementary and Secondary Education Act (ESEA), longstanding concerns about valid assessment practices vis-à-vis ELLs continue to abound (e.g., McCarty, 2008; Pappamihiel & Walser, 2009).

## The Challenge

It is widely agreed that it is inappropriate to use assessments designed for students whose native language is English with those who are still acquiring English as a new language (Gándara & Merino, 1993; Miramontes, Nadeau, & Commins, 1997; Solano-Flores & Trumbull, 2003; Valdés & Figueroa, 1994). As Valdés and Figueroa (1994) state:

> When a bilingual individual confronts a monolingual test, developed by monolingual individuals, and standardized and normed on a monolingual population, both the test taker and the test are asked to do something that they cannot. The bilingual test taker cannot perform like a monolingual. The monolingual test cannot "measure" in the other language.
>
> (p. 87)

This fact can hardly be stated too strongly: a bilingual student will never perform just like a monolingual student, and comparisons between the two on the basis of a test created for the monolingual student are always of questionable validity. To get at what a bilingual student knows and can do, he or she must be tested in both languages (Solano-Flores, Lara, Sexton, & Navarrete, 2001).

Professional organizations of educators and researchers have taken strong stands on the matter. According to a joint statement of the American Educational Research Association, American Psychological Association, and National Council on Measurement in Education, "If English language learners are tested in English, their performance should be interpreted in the light of their language proficiency. Special accommodations for English language learners may be necessary to obtain valid scores" (AERA, APA, & NCME, 1999, p. 5). They also state, "[W]hen there is credible evidence that a test score may not adequately reflect a student's true proficiency, alternative acceptable means should be provided by which to demonstrate attainment of the tested standards" (p. 3).

Achieving validity and equity in the assessment of ELLs requires addressing all of the elements of assessment: content (including language of instructions and any other text), format, administration, scoring criteria and procedures, score interpretation, and use (i.e., the decisions made on the basis of student scores) (Farr & Trumbull, 1997; Solano-Flores et al., 2001; Solano-Flores & Trumbull, 2003; Solano-Flores, Trumbull, & Nelson-Barber, 2002). To date, efforts to improve validity and equity have focused on accommodations such as increased time, provision of dictionaries or glossaries, translation or repetition of instructions, teachers reading questions aloud, and linguistic modifications of test prompts (e.g., Abedi, Leon, & Mirocha, 2003; Butler & Stevens, 1997; Heubert & Hauser, 1999; Shepard, Taylor, & Betebenner, 1998). As Kopriva (2000) notes, accommodations to make assessments fairer to English language learners should not be applied like band-aids after assessments are developed. They should be considered as assessments are developed.

## Promising New Approaches to Assessment of ELLs[3]

Several lines of research suggest some promising new methods for improving assessment development and practice. Among these are alternative methods of developing assessments in two languages (Solano-Flores, Nelson-Barber, & Trumbull, 2002), new techniques for estimating the linguistic load of a test item (Solano-Flores, Trumbull, & Kwon, 2003), approaches to translation that factor in students' particular linguistic and cultural contexts (Solano-Flores et al., 2002), and implementation of various kinds of linguistic modifications in test development (Abedi et al., 2003). The approach described in this chapter entails collaboration between two researchers and educators in a district to develop assessments aligned with local standards, instructional practices, and students' cultural and linguistic characteristics.

## Assessing Bilingual Students Newly Assigned to English-Only Instruction

Recent studies have shown that English language proficiency is correlated with students' performance on standardized achievement tests in English (Abedi, Leon, & Mirocha, 2000; Stevens, Butler, & Castellon-Wellington, 2000). The greatest discrepancy in performance between native English speakers and English language learners is on assessments of reading (Abedi, 2004). These findings are not surprising, but what may not be recognized by those not directly involved with English language learners (such as policy-makers) is the very fact that students who have been redesignated as "fully English proficient" on the basis of a test or other indicators are still not linguistically comparable to native speakers of English.

### Differences in Vocabulary and Prior Knowledge

The English vocabularies of many second language learners are not equivalent to those of their native English-speaking peers (García, 1991; Stevens et al., 2000; Wong Fillmore, 1989). Research on bilingual elementary students has shown that they are often less familiar with the background knowledge and vocabulary necessary for understanding English language texts than their monolingual peers (García, 1999; Jiménez, García, & Pearson, 1996; Kucer & Silva, 1995). Nor are these students likely to process the decontextualized and sometimes arcane language of the typical assessment so quickly or easily as their native English-speaking peers (Baker, 2000; Carrell, 1991; Heubert & Hauser, 1999; Shaw, 1997; Trumbull & Solano-Flores, Chapter 2, this volume).

### Cultural Factors

Students whose home language is not English nearly always come from cultural backgrounds whose values and beliefs differ from those of the dominant U.S. culture in important respects (Delgado-Gaitan, 1994; McCarty, 2002; Valdés, 1996). Culture is inherent not only in the content of assessment but also every other aspect of assessment. Knowledge itself is "personal, contextual, and cultural" (Goodwin & Macdonald, 1997, p. 217). Notions of how knowledge is acquired and shared differ from culture to culture. To take an example relevant to the assessment development effort that will be discussed here, students whose home culture is Mexican-American are likely to be less competitive than their dominant culture peers and more oriented toward cooperating with peers to learn and demonstrate learning (Isaac, 1999; Raeff, Greenfield, & Quiroz, 2000). It could be argued that the inherently competitive orientation of assessment in American schools already puts such students at a disadvantage. Reading passages on tests may be more or less appealing or comprehensible, depending on the cultural match for students. In fact, cultural familiarity of text has been shown to facilitate reading comprehension (Droop & Verhoeven, 1998; Pritchard, 1990).

# The Sequoia Valley Assessment Development Project

## Assessment Backdrop to the Project

In the early 1990s, the Sequoia Valley School District[4] began a process of developing standards detailing what students should know and be able to do in mathematics, language arts, and social studies for grades K-8. In line with this effort, the district worked with a publisher to develop its own performance-based assessments[5] (PBAs) in reading, writing, and mathematics. These PBAs are given at grades 2, 5, and 7. Yearly norm-referenced tests are given at all grades as well, for the purpose of state-level accountability. At the time of the assessment development described here, the district was administering the *Comprehensive Test of Basic Skills* (1990) and the Spanish language *Aprenda* (1997).

## The District: Its Students and Programs

The Sequoia Valley School District, to the south of San Francisco, is a K-8 district with about 8,500 students. The student population is ethnically mixed, with approximately 70% ethnic Hispanic students, mostly of Mexican background. Of these, 49% are designated "limited English proficient" (LEP). In 1997–1998, the year we focus on, the district's Spanish–English bilingual program was a "transitional" program in which LEP students were taught academics in their primary language and received daily English as a Second Language (ESL) instruction. As the LEP children became more proficient in English, academic instruction in English was added to their instructional program over the years. When these academic subjects are introduced in the child's second language, instruction is considered "transitional," and teachers who teach in English use instructional strategies appropriate for students who are learning English.[6] All LEP students are assessed yearly on the Idea Proficiency Test (IPT) (Dalton, 1979, 1982, 1991) to determine their level of English proficiency.

## Students in Transition

Fifth grade is designated a transitional year for most English language learners. It is when bilingual students who have met the criterion of F (fluent) or M (mastery) on the IPT move into an English-only program. They must also be at grade level in Spanish reading (according to teacher judgment) and have had four years of primary language instruction, along with English as a Second Language.

## Moving Toward a Transitional Performance-Based Reading Assessment

By the fourth year of its implementation, concerns about the validity of the PBA for students receiving transitional instruction in English had risen to a high level. Many non-native speakers of English did poorly, especially on the fifth-grade reading assessment; yet teachers believed that the low performances were attributable more to the assessment itself than to students' abilities or level of preparation. Students who were competent readers in Spanish and acquiring substantial literacy skill in English were unable to demonstrate their competence in their second language on the assessment. The Sequoia Valley Department of Bilingual Education became convinced that merely introducing special accommodations for transitional students, such as allowing them to read texts in Spanish as well as English, or take more time to complete the assessment if they so desired, would not address students' actual needs.[7] Rephrasing prompts or instructions or responding to student questions also seemed inadequate to solving what teachers saw as the real problems with the assessments.

Modification of the PBA was rejected on the basis that, since the texts would have to be changed, in effect the whole assessment would have to be rebuilt. Teachers wanted texts that were culturally and age-appropriate but at a lower grade level, assessment formats that paralleled familiar instructional formats, a student-friendly process of administration, and scoring and interpretation processes that took students' language issues into account (cf., Darling-Hammond & Falk, 1997; Hamayan & Damico, 1991; Thurlow, Liu, Quest, Thompson, Albus, & Anderson, 1998).

Persuaded that an alternative was needed, the district supported a team of teachers to work with outside researchers to develop a transitional performance-based reading assessment. A group composed of 13 resource teachers and transitional classroom teachers as well as the director of bilingual education was convened. It was this group, along with two researchers from WestEd who developed the new assessment.[8] Hereafter we refer to this group as the "assessment design group."

The intent of the project was to create an English reading assessment that would perform the same functions as the PBA, sample many of the same standards, and replicate the PBA in form to the degree possible. The TPBA would not be comparable to the PBA in the sense of equated assessments, but—for political reasons—neither would it look dramatically different from the PBA. Of course, it needed to be appropriate for English learners in their first year of English reading.

### Designing an Assessment Appropriate for Transitional Students

During an intensive two-day meeting, the assessment design group grappled with the question of how to make the TPBA a fair and useful assessment. Teachers believed that the TBPA should parallel the instruction delivered in the transitional classes so that it would maximize students' ability to transfer their knowledge of reading strategies and literary elements from Spanish to English texts (cf., August, Calderón, & Carlo, 2000; Durgunoglu, Nagy, & Hancin-Bhatt, 1993; Fitzgerald, 1995).

### Teachers' Definition of Reading

The first obstacle faced by the assessment design group was the requirement to link the assessment to district reading standards. The participating teachers'

---

(Note: Standards assessed by the TPBA are italicized)
**COMPREHENSION/Literary**
*II B I*

*Comprehend literal meanings by identifying details, main ideas, simple cause and effect, sequencing events, and contextual use of vocabulary*

*II B 2*

*Recognize details and sequence of a story through involvement in a variety of activities (e.g., webbing, weaving, story graphs and story lines)*

*II B 3*

*Comprehend inferred meaning by predicting outcomes, sensing emotions, and implying main ideas*

*II B 4*

*Develop and apply skills in classifying, categorizing and summarizing.*

---

*Figure 9.1* Sample Grade 5 Standards Assessed by PBA.

definition of literacy was more comprehensive and more socially and culturally situated than the definition implicit in the district's standards. (Figure 9.1 shows a sample of the district's standards.) They saw reading, writing, and speaking as integrated and reflected that perspective in their teaching (Braunger & Lewis, 1997; Earle & Zimmerman, 2003; Nelson & Calfee, 1998). They believed that reading is a process of making meaning, in which one's own personal experience and knowledge are brought to bear (Bloome, Champion, Katz, Morton, & Muldrow, 2001; Langer, 1991).

Teachers believed that students' home languages and cultures were valuable in their own right as well as resources for learning to read in a new language (Diaz, Moll, & Mehan, 1986; García, 2000; Langer, Bartolomé, Vasquez, & Lucas, 1990). So, when students brought their own cultural perspectives to the interpretation of literature, teachers saw this as a positive thing—even as they attempted to introduce new perspectives to them. When students' reading and writing showed evidence of influence from their first language, Spanish, teachers saw students as drawing on existing knowledge that could be built upon. Nevertheless, teachers believed they could construct an assessment that was consonant with their view of literacy and that assessed the reading standards of the district.

## Making the Purposes of Assessment Explicit

In the process of discussion, teachers deepened and made more explicit their notions of the purposes a new assessment could serve. They judged that the assessment could serve two primary purposes. One, it would provide data about individual performance on the district standards for students at the transitional level. Two, the aggregate data would be used to identify areas of strength and weakness in reading instruction in the transitional program.

### Scaffolding Assessment

In the transitional language arts classes, instructional practices provide a "scaffold" for students (Cazden, 1988; Peregoy & Boyle, 2001). That is, the instruction itself is designed to help students participate at their own developmental level and, through structured support, achieve what they might not be able to in a less supportive environment. Teachers may pre-teach vocabulary, model the reading process, and use visual supports or demonstrations to support language comprehension, for instance. A key question for the assessment design group was how much scaffolding was necessary and appropriate in the assessment process. The belief was that, to get maximum participation from students, some scaffolding during the pre-assessment activities would clearly be necessary. Teachers identified strategies for scaffolding performance, such as discussion about a text topic, introduction to new vocabulary, and activities to stimulate interest and trigger prior knowledge; and they came to a consensus about the overall design of the TPBA, which would effectively scaffold student performance through familiar response formats.

### Mediating Administration

The group agreed that students should be given time to prepare for an assessment. Students should be able to talk about their experiences with tests and ask questions about the test or the testing process. Step-by-step instructions, rather than extended instructions in a large block of text, would be important for transitional students. In addition, teachers should be allowed to re-phrase prompts if requested to do so by students, or if it was apparent that students were not able to get started on an item.

## Assessment Design Features

Here we review specific design features teachers recommended for types of assessment items and ways of scaffolding them.

### Use of Appropriate Texts

Prior to meeting with researchers, design group teachers had begun looking for texts that would be appropriate for their students. Their goal was to find a story (narrative) and a non-fiction text that were at a somewhat lower reading level (approximately third grade) and that reflected themes meaningful to their Latino immigrant students. Less-difficult texts were required because students' vocabularies and readiness to persevere with lengthy texts in English could not be expected to support use of grade-level texts (García, 1991; Stevens et al., 2000; Wong Fillmore, 1989). At the same time, they wanted these texts to be complex enough to engage students in thinking at a level appropriate to their age and developmental stage. Teachers realized that texts with themes related to important home values would likely make for greater engagement.

### Drawing on Multiple Modalities

Teachers emphasized that a good assessment needs to have multiple entry points for students—that is, it should have more than one way to assess knowledge (cf., Gardner, 1992; Gordon, 1992). For example, students could use multiple modalities—not only written responses, but drawing or oral responses. They wanted to incorporate opportunities for students to use art in their completion of the assessment because they had observed that many of their students express themselves well through art; but the idea was set aside because of the challenge of scoring artwork. Nevertheless, the question of whether to include a drawing activity arose again at the end of the process. Teachers came back to their original rationale: Drawing is good for (1) engagement, (2) alignment with instructional practices, (3) giving a break in the writing, (4) fun, and (5) letting some students shine on a task, even though it is not scored. For these reasons, the final TPBA included a drawing activity—but one that would not be scored.

### Using Graphic Organizers and Visually "Friendly" Formats

Visual supports are an accepted instructional tool in ESL instruction (Crandall, 1992; Perez & Torres-Guzman, 1996). The group believed that using graphic organizers would aid in assessing students' comprehension of the texts. In the realm of literacy instruction, a graphic organizer is a drawing or diagram that helps a student tap tacit knowledge of the structure of a text, construct a written response, or grasp the relationship among several elements in a text. Visual organizers can be used to get at comprehension and vocabulary knowledge as well as recall of details or understanding of relationships among concepts (e.g., the category "mammal" subsumes the category "cat"). "Thought bubbles," like those in cartoons, can be used to elicit students' understanding of a character's thoughts. Chart formats that help students construct written responses are especially helpful for students who are still developing fluency in written language. Such formats provide students with visual clues about types and lengths of expected responses. Figure 9.2 shows several graphic organizers used in the TPBA.

### Allowing Flexibility in Response

Teachers also thought that open-ended questions and activities were most likely to elicit the best student responses. If responses weren't heavily constrained or pre-determined, students could more readily draw upon their own experiences or knowledge to demonstrate reading comprehension (cf., García & Pearson, 1991; Gordon, 1992; Mitchell, 1992; Wiggins, 1993).

### Simplifying Instructions

For students still learning English, having to process and hold in mind a series of instructions (often dependent on very accurate comprehension of complex syntax) can unduly complicate their efforts to respond to assessment prompts (Durán, 1985;

1. Trevor did many things when he began to help the homeless. Using your pencil, underline 4 different things that Trevor did for the homeless after he saw the news report on television. Be sure to underline the entire sentence in your article.

2. Think about what you have read about Trevor and complete the chart below.

Below is a picture of the Rich Señora dropping into the sea of darkness. In the thought bubble coming from her head, write what she is thinking about the things she did in her life.

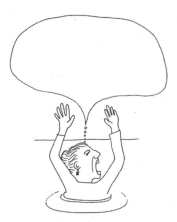

In the pictures below, write a conversation that you think Trevor might have with the Rich Señora if he had the chance to speak to her.

continued

*Figure 9.2* Graphic Organizers Used in the TPBA.

3. Complete the chart below.

|  | The Rich Señora | Trevor's Campaign for the Homeless |
|---|---|---|
| What is the main idea of each story | | |
| What did each story make you think about? | | |

*Figure 9.2* continued

Solano-Flores & Trumbull, 2003). The PBA's instructions were linguistically complex in terms of their syntax and length, and teachers thought they should be simplified. Research supports their thinking. A large study comparing limited English proficient students in grades 3–11 with native English-speaking peers found that the greater the English language complexity in the assessment, the greater the performance gap between LEP and non-LEP students (Abedi et al., 2000).

### An Associated Requirement: Expertise of Scorers

Teachers strongly urged that assessments of transitional learners be scored by those who have an understanding of the linguistic and cultural issues of the students taking an assessment (Darling-Hammond, 1994). For example, many spelling patterns of transitional bilingual students are understandable with reference to their primary language but almost inscrutable to a reader who does not know that language. "He geib ibriting" may not be read as "He gave everything" by such a reader. The problem extends to understanding students' syntax and their intended meaning. Confusion about how to mark the past tense ("he didn't wanted") may be understandable, but a phrase such as "of your form your act" may be unclear to a non-Spanish speaker. A Spanish speaker would likely recognize the parallel in form to the phrase "manera de ser," which can mean "form of being" and was the likely source of one writer's awkward syntax (Beaumont, de Valenzuela, & Trumbull, 2002). A character may be described as "shy" rather than "ashamed" by a student (as occurred on the TPBA), because the same word in Spanish (vergüenza) can mean both shame and shyness. An untrained scorer may conclude that a student has low comprehension rather than specific problems with spelling, syntax, or vocabulary.

## Comparing the PBA and the TPBA

As mentioned, one goal of the assessment development process was to design a reading assessment for transitional students that assessed as many of the same standards as the district PBA as possible and was parallel in structure. The time required for administration and administration procedures would also be similar to those of the PBA. The comparisons made below are between the TPBA and a released or "prototype" version of the PBA. Table 9.1 summarizes the points of comparison (but note that some categories discussed are collapsed in the table).

*Table 9.1* Comparison of District PBA and TPBA

|  | *District PBA prototype* | *Transitional PBA* |
|---|---|---|
| Text selection | • Two pieces on related topics (a girl learning about wildlife and a factual article on eagles), one fiction, one non-fiction.<br>• Fifth-grade reading level. | • Two pieces on the same topic (the importance of community and giving to others), one fiction, one non-fiction.<br>• Third- and fourth-grade reading level, fifth-grade content. |
| Assessment format | • Pre-assessment activities activate background knowledge.<br>• 15 items: three items graphically structure responses.<br>• Reading assessed through written responses.<br>• Fiction: no illustrations<br>• Non-fiction: illustrations of phenomena described. | • Pre-assessment activities provide key word definition, activate background knowledge, clarify directions.<br>• 10 items: five items include graphic organizers.<br>• Reading assessed through written responses.<br>• One drawing activity (unscored) provided.<br>• Fiction and non-fiction supported by illustrations. |
| Administration | • Matrix sampling—several forms assessing different combinations of standards.<br>• Three sessions (50 min. ea.). | • One form assessing same set of standards.<br>• Three sessions (50 min. ea.). |
| Scoring | • Item analysis.<br>• Mixed group of district teachers, primarily non-bilingual. | • Combination holistic/analytic.<br>• Bilingual and transition teachers. |
| Interpretation and use | • By item, by percent at each proficiency level, by *p* values, to schools, school board, press.<br>• An unintended use of scores is by realtors to sell houses.<br>• Scores are used (not always fairly) by the public to judge teachers and schools. | • By single score, percent at each proficiency level, to schools, school board, parents.<br>• Scores and performance patterns are used to plan instruction and improve program. |

## Pre-Assessment Activities

To activate students' prior knowledge and scaffold their reading of the texts, the TPBA includes pre-assessment activities for each of the two texts. The pre-assessment activities for the narrative text ("The Rich Señora," Lyons & Antal, 1972) include the teacher's reading aloud of the first paragraph of the story prior to giving the students the selection, clarification (through discussion) of a key vocabulary word (*stingy*), brainstorming predictions about what will happen, and a partner activity designed to draw upon students' personal knowledge and beliefs. For the partner activity, the teacher asks open-ended questions and does not interact with students to shape their responses. Thus, the pre-assessment activity paralleled sound instructional practice (cf., Brisk & Harrington, 2000). Teachers believed that using this technique in the assessment would also put students at ease and lower their anxiety about taking an important test.

The directions provided to teachers clearly describe each step of these activities and prescribe what teachers are to say. They also state the testing accommodations allowed: students may raise their hands to ask the teacher to clarify directions; teachers may not help students with the reading of text. The district PBA also includes extensive pre-assessment activities that build vocabulary, tap prior knowledge, and engage students in talking with each other about text-related experiences. The key points of difference between the pre-assessment activities on these two tests are the reading aloud of one paragraph and the ability to request clarification.

## The Text Selections

To parallel the PBA, the TPBA uses two reading selections, a fiction piece ("The Rich Señora," a Mexican folktale) and a non-fiction piece ("Trevor's Campaign for the Homeless," which appeared in a student magazine). The two texts are age-appropriate in terms of theme and content but easier than fifth-grade texts in terms of syntax and vocabulary. They are also shorter than the texts on the PBA.

Teachers believed that "The Rich Señora" would present a familiar genre (folk/morality tale) and theme (selfishness is punished) for their students. "Trevor's Campaign for the Homeless" would be appropriate both because of its values of community-mindedness and sharing and the topic of homelessness—a concern in their own town. They judged that the values represented in these texts were those emphasized in their students' homes.

One important difference between the reading selections included in the TPBA and the PBA is the degree to which the texts foreground key events or ideas, as opposed to embedding them in syntactically and structurally complex passages. The group determined that a text appropriate for transitional students would foreground key textual content rather than force students to hunt for it. Students would still be asked to infer meanings, but they would not be asked to comprehend text in which important ideas were deeply embedded in the discourse of the selection. The excerpts presented in Table 9.2—the first two paragraphs of "The Rich Señora" and "In the Shadow of the Eagle," the PBA text prototype provided to teachers—show differences between what

*Table 9.2* Samples of TPBA and PBA Texts

| The rich señora | In the shadow of the eagle |
|---|---|
| The people sometimes tell about a certain rich Señora, whose son was the Mayor of Motúl. Although she was very, very rich, this woman was also very stingy. Every day, the poor people came to her door to beg for food. Every day, she sent them away with nothing. | Anna breathed the cool, fresh air of spring. Winter was over, the snows were gone, the rivers ran free, and her traps had several squirrels. Now that Anna was twelve, she could have her own traps. She felt tall and proud as she reached up to her neck to touch the sun-warmed squirrel pelts that hung from a leather thong on her backpack. |
| One day the rich Señora was eating, when a very poor, very old woman came to the door and begged her for a little food. Quickly, the rich Señora threw a cloth over her plate to hide the food piled high there. Then she ordered the old woman away, slamming the door in her face. But when the Señora returned to her food and lifted the cloth from her plate—what do you think? It was crawling with snakes. | Anna's parents had come to Alaska from Lapland before Anna was born. They had come to teach the Eskimos how to herd reindeer. In turn, Anna's family had learned many skills from the Eskimos. |

might be called the "directness" of the texts. One can see that the syntax of "The Rich Señora" is simpler and that vocabulary meaning is more determinable from context. In addition, the sequence of text topics is in accordance with the actual sequence of story events, while that is not the case with "In the Shadow of the Eagle."

One concern of the district was that the texts proposed for the TPBA were not rated as "fifth-grade" level. Their concern was mitigated when it was made clear that any testing information released to the public would specify that the texts were at third- and fourth-grade level.

### Visual Elements of the Assessments

While both the regular PBA and the TPBA use illustrations and graphic organizers to engage students, the TPBA makes greater use of these elements. Illustrations based on "The Rich Señora" were added to the assessment to increase student engagement with text. The graphic organizers chosen for the TPBA range from the highly stylized "thought bubbles" and "cartoon sequences" to charts that help students organize their written responses and provide visual clues about the expected length of their written response (see Figure 9.2). Instead of asking students to list main ideas or events, the TPBA asks students to underline important ideas or events in the text. Five out of 10 items on the TPBA include graphic organizers. Only three items require more than a sentence or two of written response, and only one requires a written summary.

In contrast, the prototype PBA requires students to construct lengthy written responses and provides fewer visual cues about the length of response than the TPBA. Three of the 15 PBA items graphically structure and guide written responses. One item contains an "index card," on which students are to write. The visual is accompanied by eight lines of written directions and functions more as a text box than a graphic organizer. One item asks for words or phrases from the article. The other 11 items appear to ask students to respond at considerable length. The number of lines left for responses gives some cues to expected length. However, it is not clear whether students are expected to use the entire space or not. Thus, nearly three-quarters of the items on the prototype PBA require students to write extended prose and judge independently whether their written responses are complete.

## Administration: Assessment Instructions and Prompts

The standardized administration of the TPBA parallels that of the PBA. Directions for administration were drafted by a sub-committee of the design group and reviewed and revised by the whole group. The TPBA is intended to be given over a period of three class periods. Each section of the assessment includes directions for administration that specify materials, pre-assessment activities, oral directions to students, guidelines for handling student questions about directions, and collection procedures.

## Scoring Rubrics

During the development year (1996–1997), the researchers conducted a rubric design workshop for the assessment group. At this workshop, teachers reviewed item-specific, holistic, and analytic rubrics,[9] finally selecting a holistic rubric as the best choice. The teachers believed strongly that the holistic rubric, with its assessment of performance across items, was the most equitable scoring approach. Many of the teachers in the group had scored the PBA using the district's item-specific rubric, and they had noticed that their students' performance often improved over the course of the test. With the item-specific rubric, such improvement made little difference in the student's overall score. However, an analytic rubric would give more specific information. An iterative process of rubric creation and revision resulted in a combination holistic/analytic rubric with a five-point scale—allowing for both specific information and a cumulative score.

## Scoring Process, Interpretation, and Use

### Scoring

An eight-member scoring team of the participating teachers, the two researchers, and one former bilingual teacher scored 114 reading assessments. Each paper was scored independently by two people. If scorers disagreed on the final score, or if their analytic scores varied by two or more points on any item, they met to review and reconcile score points. If the two scorers could not reconcile a disagreement, or if a paper received a borderline total score (within a point or two of the range for the next score point on the rubric), the paper was read a third time by another reader. Inter-rater reliability was steady at 0.75.

Some 75 students, or 60%, received a score of 3 ("proficient") or higher; 24% attained a score of 2 ("limited proficiency"), and 7% of students scored a 1 ("minimal proficiency").[10]

### Interpretation and Use

In 1997 (the pilot year), teachers judged that some components of the assessment appeared more powerful than others at revealing students' comprehension. They cited (1) the summary students were asked to write of "Trevor's Campaign for the Homeless," (2) the thought bubble in which students have to imagine what the Rich Señora is thinking, and (3) the cartoon sequence showing dialogue between Trevor and the Rich Señora as excellent indices of understanding of the texts. Teachers noted that these assessment strategies were aligned with classroom practices and were ones that students themselves often chose when given the opportunity.

During the debriefing of the 1997 scoring session, teachers observed that students' performance suggested they needed more instruction in locating textual evidence for their inferences and conclusions. In fact, at the teachers' urging, the rubric had been modified after the first year in order to capture more detail related to these aspects of performance. From this outcome, we could see clearly that the rubric itself plays a key role in determining the usefulness of assessment data for the purpose of informing instruction.

## Outcomes and Discussion

### Increased Validity, Equity, and Utility

We believe that the TPBA is a more valid and equitable assessment of the reading skills of students newly-transitioned to English-only instruction for the following reasons: (1) It provides multiple entry points for students and elicits a range of performance; (2) It mirrors instruction in format, hence eliminating some of the cultural and linguistic barriers presented by tests like the PBA; (3) It appears to actually motivate participation—to support students' maximal performance; and (4) Overall student outcomes exchange with teachers' judgment of students' capabilities.

Unlike the PBA, the TPBA provided a lot of information that could be used to make some fairly fine-grained decisions about students' needs. Indeed, using the TPBA, teachers were able to identify specific patterns of performance that suggested the need to intensify or alter instruction. They recognized that the TPBA results could be used in combination with other information to improve decisions about students' readiness for transition programs and about the kinds of instruction they needed. Teachers determined that they needed to provide more explicit instruction on how to locate information in a text and use supporting details as evidence for an argument or conclusion. They also concluded that students' language needs might be better met by a longer period of transitional instruction. This observation reflects concerns expressed by Goldenberg, who has studied literacy development in immigrant Latino students (e.g., Goldenberg, 1996; Goldenberg, Gallimore, & Reese, 2003). He believes that a model of *gradual* transition providing primary language support for longer periods of time, along with a more gradual exposure to English, is likely to be better for second language reading development.

The process of scoring and subsequent analysis of performance also crystallized questions about how to distinguish normal language acquisition limitations from developmental immaturity and genuine cognitive or reading problems. Teachers realized the need for guidelines on how to make such distinctions in order to determine appropriate instructional goals and methods.

### Filling a Gap in the Range of Possibilities

The Sequoia Valley experience suggests that there are useful alternatives to mediation, accommodation, and assessment modification for English language learners. In addition, it underlines the need to recognize and address the special status of students in transition. It is reasonable to assess them in English, because their instruction is in English—with the acknowledgement that more information might be gathered by assessing them in their first language as well. But even if they are progressing very well in English, they are not likely to be able to demonstrate their skills on a test that is above their level. Educators are presented with a conundrum: Should such students be made to take the regular assessment, when they may not produce much—yielding little information and exposing students to a frustrating and possibly damaging experience? Accountability would be better served by an alternative assessment that elicits a range of student performance and can yield real information about students' development.

### Value for Professional Development Purposes

Teachers found the process of developing, administering, and scoring the TPBA a valuable professional development experience. In scoring the TPBA and interpreting the outcomes, the assessment design group realized what a powerful professional development tool the examination and discussion of student performance samples could be. In particular, these assessments provide innumerable examples of second language development issues for English language learners. But they also demonstrate the complexity of sorting out the contribution of cognitive developmental factors, linguistic factors, and other non-construct-related task factors (e.g., whether students were engaged by the assessment, clarity of instructions, etc.) to individual performances. The opportunity to review the work of so many transitional students reinforced the design group's belief that all teachers who work with bilingual students should have the benefit of training in special ESL (English as a second language) techniques. It is that training that gave these teachers the common core of knowledge and practice that underpins the TPBA.

The assessment data provide the district with a rich store of examples of the issues in instruction and assessment of students in transition. In addition, the assessment design group teachers now have an even greater understanding of these issues and how they play out for their students. If the district could tap these resources (the teachers and the data) to expand the knowledge base of teachers who will be teaching English language learners at some point in their development, it would undoubtedly be of great benefit to students and teachers.

### Is the Method Feasible?

One serious concern about many new methods of assessment development is whether they are feasible—i.e., practicable and cost-effective. The answer with regard to the method described here is, we believe, "Yes," if a district has a knowledgeable group of teachers. With approximately 30 days of researchers' support (the total for both researchers), this district developed a credible and useful tool that fills two important needs. In fact, this model of local develop-ment resulted in an assessment that meets the needs of both the district (for accountability) and teachers (for instructional planning), while engaging stu-dents in a process they actually enjoy.

## What Teachers Can Do

The assessment development process described here certainly demonstrates that there are many things teachers can do to contribute to cultural validity in assess-ment. Reading this chapter, any teacher who works with ELLs is likely to recog-nize issues as well as teacher strategies that apply in some form across a range of ages and contexts. Here are some of the things the Sequoia Valley teachers did that others facing similar concerns can do:

- Pursue opportunities to improve assessment practices in a school or district when that is needed.
- Collaborate across role groups with a district to maximize the knowledge base from which assessment development proceeds (in this case, bilingual teachers, bilingual administrators, general education teachers).
- Seek opportunities for outside support from assessment professionals. (Sometimes another agency will share costs.)
- In designing an assessment, draw upon knowledge of what has worked to engage students in instruction as well as knowledge of students' cultures and languages.

- Ensure that speakers of students' first language(s) are involved in the scoring process for any constructed response items, at least in the process of training scorers.
- Debrief assessment results as a group to make decisions about future instruction or program revisions.

## Conclusion

Just because a student has been classified as "fully English proficient" does not mean that he or she will perform in a manner similar to that of native English-speaking peers on a grade-level assessment. In the case of the Sequoia Valley fifth-graders, who had just been transitioned from bilingual education to English-only instruction, a group of savvy and dedicated teachers was able to intervene with assessment practices that were simply not working for their students. Teachers knew that the district reading assessment was not revealing the reading skills of these students. Fortunately, the administrators in charge of district assessment listened to them and were willing to give support to a process of alternative assessment development.

When the Sequoia Valley teachers worked in combination with researchers, they were able to make their knowledge explicit for the purpose of developing a more culturally valid reading assessment—one that had the potential to elicit students' knowledge and skills. The resulting assessment was linked to district reading standards *and* culturally responsive in that it (1) drew upon students' cultural values and culture-based experiences and (2) relied on formats and activities familiar to students and known to scaffold language comprehension. The work documented in this chapter is now more than a decade old, but its lessons for teachers and professional assessment developers are still applicable.

## Notes

1. The assessment development described in this chapter was conducted under the auspices of the Regional Educational Laboratory for the Western Region at WestEd, San Francisco, California.
2. An assessment is equitable if its administration and outcomes do not systematically underestimate or overestimate the knowledge or skills of a *particular* group; and it is valid if it can be shown to assess the constructs specified—and only those constructs (i.e., that inferences about a student's knowledge or ability are accurate).
3. Even within the group of students designated as "ELL," there is a considerable spread of English proficiency (Stevens et al., 2000).
4. Not the district's real name.
5. The district uses the term "performance-based assessment" in reference to assessments that have extended constructed response portions and rely on integration of multiple skills in a domain. Although we speak of "the PBA" in the singular, in fact there is more than one PBA per subject domain per grade assessed. A matrix sampling strategy is used, with different classes taking different forms of each domain test.
6. Accommodations are made for students who enter after kindergarten.
7. Translation introduces its own set of problems: Meaning is almost inevitably changed when tests are translated, because language and meaning (and culture) are inextric-

ably linked (van de Vivjer & Poortinga, 1997). When meaning is changed, construct validity is jeopardized.

8. Not every teacher attended every development session. On average, there were 10 people at each meeting.

9. An item-specific rubric is a scoring guide that yields a score for each item. A holistic rubric yields a single score for an entire assessment. An analytic rubric yields a score on two or more traits or skills, such as comprehension, decoding, and character analysis.

10. Nine percent could not be scored because they were incomprehensible in English or were written in Spanish.

# References

Abedi, J. (2004). The No Child Left Behind Act and English language learners: Assessment and accountability issues. *Educational Researcher*, 33(1), 4–14.

Abedi, J., Leon, S., & Mirocha, J. (2000). *Impact of students' language background on content-based performance: Analyses of extant data*. University of California, Los Angeles, National Center for Research on Evaluation, Standards and Student Testing.

Abedi, J., Leon, S., & Mirocha, J. (2003). *Impact of students' language background on content-based assessment: Analyses of extant data* (CSE Tech. Rep. No. 603). Los Angeles, CA: University of California, National Center for Research on Evaluation, Standards, and Student Testing.

American Educational Research Association, American Psychological Association, and National Council on Measurement in Education (1999). *Standards for educational and psychological testing*. Washington, DC: American Educational Research Association.

*Aprenda. La prueba de logros en español* (1997). San Antonio, TX: Harcourt Educational Measurement, Inc.

August, D., Calderón, M., & Carlo, M. (2000). *Transfer of skills from Spanish to English: A study of young learners*. Ed-98-CO-0071. Washington, DC: Office of Bilingual Education and Minority Language Affairs, U.S. Department of Education.

Baker, E. (2000). *Assessment and the English language learner*. Paper presented at the Annual Meeting of the California Association for Bilingual Education, San Francisco, CA, March.

Beaumont, C., de Valenzuela, J., & Trumbull, E. (2002). Alternative assessment for transitional bilingual readers. *Bilingual Research Journal*, 26(2), 241–268.

Bloome, D., Champion, T., Katz, L., Morton, M.B., & Muldrow, R. (2001). Spoken and written narrative development: African American preschoolers as storytellers and storymakers. In J.L. Harris, A.G. Kamhi, & K.E. Pollock (Eds.), *Literacy in African American communities* (pp. 45–76). Mahwah, NJ: Lawrence Erlbaum Associates.

Braunger, J., & Lewis, J.P. (1997). *Building a knowledge base in reading*. Portland, OR: Northwest Regional Educational Laboratory, Urbana, IL: National Council of Teachers of English, and Newark, DE: International Reading Association.

Brisk, M.E., & Harrington, M.M. (2000). *Literacy and bilingualism: A handbook for ALL teachers*. Mahwah, NJ: Lawrence Erlbaum Associates.

Butler, F.A., & Stevens, R. (1997). *Accommodation strategies for English language learners on large-scale assessments: Student characteristics and other considerations*. Los Angeles, CA: Center for the Study of Evaluation, Standards and Student Testing.

Carrell, P. (1991). Second language reading: Reading ability of language proficiency? *Applied Linguistics*, 12(2), 159–179.

Cazden, C. (1988). *Classroom discourse: The language of teaching and learning*. Portsmouth, NH: Heinemann.

*Comprehensive Test of Basic Skills* (1990). Monterey, CA: CTB/McGraw-Hill.

Crandall, J. (1992). Content-centered learning in the United States. *Annual Review of Applied Linguistics*, 13, 111–126.

Dalton, E.F. (1979, 1982, 1991). *IPT oral grades K-6 technical manual, IDEA oral language proficiency test forms C and D English*. Brea, CA: Ballard & Tighe, Publishers.

Darling-Hammond, L. (1994). Performance-based assessment and educational equity. *Harvard Educational Review*, 64(1), 5–30.

Darling-Hammond, L., & Falk, B. (1997). Supporting teaching and learning for all students: Policies for authentic assessment systems. In A.L. Goodwin (Ed.), *Assessment for equity and inclusion* (pp. 51–75). New York, NY: Routledge.

Delgado-Gaitan, C. (1994). Socializing young children in Mexican-American families: An intergenerational perspective. In P.M. Greenfield & R.R. Cocking (Eds.), *Cross-cultural roots of minority child development* (pp. 55–86). Hillsdale, NJ: Lawrence Erlbaum Associates.

Diaz, S., Moll, L.C., & Mehan, H. (1986). Sociocultural resources in instruction: A context-specific approach. In Bilingual Education Office (Ed.), *Beyond language: Social and cultural factors in schooling language minority students* (pp. 187–230). Los Angeles, CA: Evaluation, Dissemination and Assessment Center, California State University.

Droop, M., & Verhoeven, L. (1998). Background knowledge, linguistic complexity, and second-language reading comprehension. *Journal of Literacy Research*, 30(2), 253–271.

Durán, R. (1985). Influences of language skills on bilinguals' problem solving. In J.W. Segal, S.F. Chipman, & R. Glaser (Eds.), *Thinking and learning skills* (pp. 287–207). Hillsdale, NJ: Lawrence Erlbaum Associates.

Durgunoglu, A., Nagy, W.E., & Hancin-Bhatt, B.J. (1993). Cross-language transfer of phonological awareness. *Journal of Educational Psychology*, 85(3), 453–465.

Earle, C.B., & Zimmerman, C. (2003). *The reading/writing connection*. New York, NY: Longman.

Farr, B., & Trumbull, E. (1997). *Assessment alternatives for diverse classrooms*. Norwood, MA: Christopher-Gordon.

Fitzgerald, J. (1995). English-as-a-second language learners' cognitive processes: A review of the research in the United States. *Review of Educational Research*, 65(2), 145–190.

Gándara, P., & Merino, B. (1993). Measuring the outcomes of LEP programs: Test scores, exit rates, and other mythological data. *Educational Evaluation and Policy Analysis*, 15(3), 320–338.

García, G.E. (1991). *Factors influencing the English reading test performance of Spanish-speaking Hispanic children*. Technical Report No. 539. Champaign, IL: Center for the Study of Reading.

García, G.E. (1999). Bilingual children's reading: An overview of recent research. *ERIC News Bulletin*, 23(1), 1–9.

García, G.E. (2000). Bilingual children's reading. In M.L. Kamil, P.B. Mosenthal, P.D. Pearson, & R. Barr (Eds.), *Handbook of reading research, Vol. III*. Mahwah, NJ: Lawrence Erlbaum Associates.

García, G.E., & Pearson, P.D. (1991). The role of assessment in a diverse society. In E.H. Hiebert (Ed.), *Literacy for a diverse society: Perspectives, practices, and policies* (pp. 253–278). New York, NY: Teachers College Press.

Gardner, H. (1992). Assessment in context: The alternative to standardized testing. In B.R. Gifford & M.C. O'Connor (Eds.), *Changing assessments: Alternative views of aptitude, achievement and instruction* (pp. 37–76). Boston, MA: Kluwer.

Goldenberg, C. (1996). The education of language minority students: Where are we, and where do we need to go? *Elementary School Journal*, 96(3), 353–361.

Goldenberg, C., Gallimore, R., & Reese, L. (2003). Using mixed methods to explore Latino children's literacy development. In T. Weisner (Ed.), *Discovering successful pathways in children's development: New methods in the study of childhood and family life.* Chicago, IL: University of Chicago Press.

Goodwin, A.L., & Macdonald, M. (1997). Educating the rainbow: Authentic assessment and authentic practice for diverse classrooms. In A.L. Goodwin (Ed.), *Assessment for equity and inclusion* (pp. 210–227). New York, NY: Routledge.

Gordon, E.W. (1992). *Implications of diversity in human characteristics for authentic assessment.* CSE Technical Report 341. Los Angeles, CA: National Center for Research on Evaluation, Standards, and Student Testing.

Hamayan, E.V., & Damico, J.S. (1991). *Limiting bias in the assessment of bilingual students.* Austin, TX: Pro-Ed.

Heubert, J.P., & Hauser, R.M. (Eds.) (1999). *High stakes testing for tracking, promotion, and graduation.* Committee on Appropriate Test Use, Board on Testing and Assessment, Commission on Behavioral and Social Sciences and Education, National Research Council. Washington, DC. National Academy Press.

Isaac, A.R. (1999). How teachers' cultural ideologies influence children's relations inside the classroom: The effects of a cultural awareness teacher training program in two classrooms. Psychology Honors Thesis. Unpublished manuscript, University of California, Los Angeles, CA.

Jiménez, R.T., García, G.I., & Pearson, P.D. (1996). The reading strategies of bilingual Latina/o students who are successful English readers: Opportunities and obstacles. *Reading Research Quarterly*, 31(1), 90–112.

Kopriva, R. (2000). Ensuring accuracy in testing for English language learners. Presentation to the California Department of Education High School Exit Examination Panel, April.

Kucer, S.B., & Silva, C. (1995). Guiding bilingual students "through" the literacy process. *Language Arts*, 72(1), 20–29.

Langer, J. (1991). Literacy and schooling: A sociological perspective. In E. Heibert (Ed.), *Literacy for a diverse society: Perspectives, practices, and policies* (pp. 9–27). New York, NY: Teachers College Press.

Langer, J.A., Bartolomé, L., Vasquez, O., & Lucas, T. (1990). Meaning construction in school literacy tasks: A study of bilingual students. *American Educational Research Journal*, 70, 350–354.

Lyons, G., & Antal, A. (1972). *Tales the people tell in Mexico.* New York, NY: J. Messner.

McCarty, T.L. (2002). *A place to be Navajo: Rough Rock and the struggle for self-determination in indigenous schooling.* Mahwah, NJ: Lawrence Erlbaum Associates.

McCarty, T.L. (2008). The impact of high-stakes accountability policies on Native American learners: Evidence from research. *Teaching Education*, 20(1), 7–29.

Miramontes, O., Nadeau, A., & Commins, N. (1997). *Restructuring schools for linguistic diversity: Linking decision making to effective programs.* New York, NY: Teachers College Press.

Mitchell, R. (1992). *Testing for learning: How new approaches to evaluation can improve American schools.* New York, NY: Free Press.

Nelson, N., & Calfee, R.C. (1998). *The reading–writing connection: Ninety-seventh year-*

*book of the national society for the study of education, part II.* Chicago, IL: University of Chicago Press.

Pappamihiel, N.E., & Walser, T.N. (2009). English language learners and complexity theory: Why current accountability systems do not measure up. *Educational Forum,* 73(2), 133–140.

Peregoy, S., & Boyle, O. (2001). *Reading, writing, & learning in ESL.* New York, NY: Addison Wesley Longman.

Perez, B., & Torres-Guzman, M.E. (1996). *Learning in two worlds: An integrated Spanish/English biliteracy approach* (2nd edition). New York, NY: Longman.

Pritchard, R.H. (1990). The effects of cultural schemata on reading processing strategies. *Reading Research Quarterly,* 25, 273–295.

Raeff, C., Greenfield, P.M., & Quiroz, B. (2000). Conceptualizing interpersonal relationships in the cultural contexts of individualism and collectivism. In S. Harkness, C. Raeff, & C. Super (Eds.), *New directions in child development* (pp. 59–74). San Francisco, CA: Jossey-Bass.

Shaw, J. (1997). "The test was explein with secretly words": Reflections on performance assessment of English language learners. In B.P. Farr & E. Trumbull (Eds.), *Assessment alternatives for diverse classrooms* (pp. 334–342). Mahwah, NJ: Lawrence Erlbaum Associates.

Shepard, L., Taylor, G., & Betebenner, D. (1998). *Inclusion of limited-English proficient students in Rhode Island's grade 4 mathematics assessment performance assessment* (CSE Technical Report 486). Boulder, CO: Center for the Study of Evaluation, Standards and Student Testing.

Solano-Flores, G., Lara, J., Sexton, U., & Navarrete, C. (2001). *Testing English language learners: A sampler of student responses to science and mathematics test items.* Washington, DC: Council of Chief State School Officers.

Solano-Flores, G., & Trumbull, E. (2003). Examining language in context: The need for new research and practice paradigms in the testing of English language learners. *Educational Researcher,* 32(2), 3–13.

Solano-Flores, G., Trumbull, E., & Kwon, M. (2003). *The metrics of linguistic complexity and the metrics of student performance in the testing of English-language learners.* Paper presented at the Annual Meeting of the American Educational Research Association, Chicago, IL.

Solano-Flores, G., Trumbull, E., & Nelson-Barber, S. (2002). Concurrent development of dual language assessments: An alternative to translating tests for linguistic minorities. *International Journal of Testing,* 2(2), 107–129.

Stevens, R.A., Butler, F.A., & Castellon-Wellington, M. (2000). *Academic language and content assessment: Measuring the progress of English language learners (ELLs).* CSE Technical Report 552, Los Angeles, CA: Center for the Study of Evaluation/National Center for Research on Evaluation, Standards, and Student Testing.

Thurlow, M.L., Liu, K.K., Quest, C., Thompson, S.J., Albus, D., & Anderson, M. (1998). *Findings from research on accommodated statewide assessments for English language learners.* Paper presented at the conference of National Center for Research on Evaluation, Standards and Student Testing, Los Angeles, CA, September.

Valdés, G. (1996). *Con respeto.* New York, NY: Teachers College Press.

Valdés, G., & Figueroa, R.A. (1994). *Bilingualism and testing: A special case of bias.* Norwood, NJ: Ablex Publishing Corporation.

Van de Vijver, F., & Poortinga, Y.H. (1997). Towards an integrated analysis of bias in cross-cultural assessment. *European Journal of Psychological Assessment,* 13(1), 29–37.

Wiggins, G.P. (1993). *Assessing student performance: Exploring the purpose and limits of testing*. San Francisco, CA: Jossey-Bass.

Wong Fillmore, L. (1989). Language learning in social context. The view from research in second language learning. In R. Dietrich & C.F. Graumann (Eds.), *Language processing in social context* (pp. 277–301). North-Holland: Elsevier Science Publisher B.V.

Chapter 10

# Addressing the Language Demands of Mathematics Assessments

## Using a Language Framework and Field Research Findings

*Elise Trumbull and Guillermo Solano-Flores*

---

**Chapter Overview**

In Chapter 2, we discussed the role of language in teaching and learning and how the linguistic features of tests influence the performance of students on tests. We showed how these influences are particularly important for students who are not proficient in the language in which tests are administered. In this chapter, we focus on a specific content area—mathematics. We discuss the relationship between language and mathematics and present a framework for comprehensively analyzing the language of assessments from three perspectives, structural (formal), functional, and cultural. We use the framework to discuss findings from a series of research projects on assessment development and adaptation for English language learners (ELLs) that show the critical role that teachers can play in ensuring more culturally valid assessment for these students.

---

## Language Issues in Mathematics Assessments

It is often believed that ELLs should have little difficulty learning and demonstrating their skills and knowledge in mathematics. Underlying this belief is the perception of mathematics as a "universal language" or a "language-less content area." However, an overwhelming body of evidence from the field of mathematics education discredits such a belief. As with any discipline, mathematics has its own register—a specialized language that includes, among other features, a specific set of terms, notation conventions, and discursive forms (e.g., ways of building arguments or asking questions).

No wonder performance on mathematics is greatly influenced by language skills (see Durán, 1989; Francis, Lesaux, & August, 2006; Secada, 1992). While, on mathematics computation tasks, ELLs tend to perform more like their native English-speaking peers than on other academic assessments (Kiplinger, Haug, & Abedi, 2000), in problem-solving—arguably the heart of mathematics functioning (Kabasakalian, 2007)—language becomes critical (Durán, 1985). Mathematics word problems, for instance, depend greatly upon language skills (Barwell, 2009a; Mestre, 1988).

While mathematics is not a language, some of its properties can be examined using the reasonings from linguistics (see Pimm, 1987). To a large extent, the linguistic challenges of learning and being assessed in mathematics stem from the fact that, while there is some overlap between mathematics and natural language, the correspondence between them is far from perfect. For example, the arrangement of the components in the expression "A = 3 + 8," parallels the syntax of the expression, "A is equal to 3 plus 8." In contrast, whereas in ordinary language, the word "multiplication" is used to imply an increase in number, in mathematics the product of a multiplication can be either an increase or a decrease in number (e.g., the product of 10 by 0.5 is 5).

Learning mathematics involves meaning negotiation—making sense of concepts and ideas across different contexts (e.g., everyday life experiences and the classroom)—through social interaction (Gee, 1992). Meaning negotiation is intrinsic to the process of learning specialized language, regardless of the level of general proficiency in the language of instruction. For example, Gardner (1977, cited in Wellington & Osborne, 2001) found that native English-speaking children in New Zealand experienced considerable difficulty understanding over 70 logical connectives (e.g., *consequently, essentially, conversely, hence, similarly, thus*) that are more frequent in textbooks and in the context of science than in everyday life outside the school.

In the case of ELLs, the challenges are even bigger because of the fact that meaning negotiation also takes place across languages and cultures. For example, ELLs need to identify and deal with false cognates (e.g., *actually* and *actualmente*, which means *currently* in Spanish; *billion* means *one million millions* in Spanish). Also, they need to grapple with the fact that knowledge is organized and taught differently in different cultures (e.g., *square* in many countries is taught as a coordinate category of the geometric shape category called *rectangle*, while in the U.S. it is taught as a subordinate category of the category *rectangle*).

While these cognitive, linguistic, and cultural conflicts can be viewed as sources of rupture, innovation, and change that may lead to learning (see Gutiérrez, Baquedano-López, & Tejeda, 1999), rarely is this diversity noticed or seen as a valuable pedagogical resource, which limits the opportunity to properly address language and culture in mathematics instruction and assessment. Standards and other normative documents overemphasize formal vocabulary and dismiss the importance of natural language (see Solano-Flores, 2010), thus limiting the linguistic resources students can use to construct mathematical knowledge (see Moschkovich, 2006), and the linguistic resources that test developers and educators can use to construct or review assessments.

Academic assessment can become a test of an individual's language proficiency (including reading skills) as much as his or her knowledge and understanding of the content assessed (American Educational Research Association, National Council of Mathematics Educators, & American Psychological Association, 1999; Heubert & Hauser, 1999; Solano-Flores & Trumbull, 2003; Valdés & Figueroa, 1994). A recent study showed that high school ELLs' mathematics problem-solving skills, as measured by several assessments, increased with their proficiency in English reading (Beal, Adams, & Cohen, 2010). Another study conducted with

9,000 secondary students in South Africa found that English proficiency was the most important factor associated with performance on a large-scale mathematics test (Howie, 2002, 2003, cited in Barwell, 2009a). Also, Hofstetter (2003) found that both ELLs and native English-speaking students who were poor readers performed better on mathematics standardized tests in which the language was simplified (thus lowering the reading level of the tests) than their control counterparts who were given the tests without modifications.

In summary, critical to culturally valid assessment for ELLs is how assessment developers and educators address the following: the nature of the mathematics register and its differences and commonalities with everyday language, the particular demands of different genres of mathematics discourse (word problems, procedural explanations, etc.), the reliance of mathematics problem-solving on language (including reading skills), the intersection of language and culture in language use, and the examinees' previous exposure to mathematics instruction in English or another language.

## A Comprehensive Conceptual Framework for Examining Language in ELL Mathematics Assessment

In the course of any given week, a teacher is likely to engage in activities such as: (1) deciding when to use an assessment, (2) creating a new assessment, (3) selecting an existing assessment, (4) modifying an existing assessment (either teacher-made or commercial), (5) administering an assessment and (6) making sense of students' performance on an assessment. All of these activities can benefit from the ability to examine language from multiple perspectives—not only in terms of language arts modalities that call upon particular skills but also in terms that linguists, sociolinguists, and cultural anthropologists use. These different, complementary approaches to language can assist teachers in their reasoning about the role of language in both instruction and assessment.

Teachers can use these different views of language to guide their understanding of how the language of particular assessment types and particular mathematics problems interacts with students' strengths, needs, and learning preferences. They can use them to examine the assessments they design or modify for ways to improve their accessibility to students. And they can apply these different perspectives on language to the process of making inferences about the meanings of student responses to assessment.

Educators tend to conceptualize language in terms of *language arts*, as the four modalities of listening, speaking, reading, and writing (Table 10.1). A teacher is likely to look to a student's proficiency with oral and written English as a source of higher or lower performance on a test. At times, he or she may consider how the reading level of a test matches a student's reading level or how writing demands are in sync with students' writing proficiencies. A teacher may also think in terms of a student's *language status* (monolingual, bilingual, or ELL; second dialect learner) and how that might be a factor influencing their learning and performance on assessments.[1]

*Table 10.1* Language Arts View of Language: Focus on Language as a Developmental Skill and Tool for Learning and Teaching

**Listening**
Following directions, comprehending oral academic and social language.

**Speaking**
Engaging in social and academic conversation, using appropriate vocabulary and sentence structures, pronouncing words clearly enough that others understand them.

**Reading**
Identifying words (with increasing accuracy and speed as student matures); accessing constructing word, sentence, and text meanings.

**Writing**
Expressing meaningful ideas via appropriate vocabulary as well as sentence, paragraph, and text structures; using devices of coherence and cohesion; spelling words correctly (with increasing accuracy as student matures); observing punctuation conventions of English.

While these approaches to language are useful, we believe that valid mathematical assessment is more likely to be achieved by using a comprehensive, multi-disciplinary approach to language.

Professional test developers and teachers alike face the challenge of selecting linguistic forms that are developmentally appropriate for the students who are to be assessed. They need to consider also what language is appropriate for those students who are still learning English. They may ask, "Is this vocabulary that a fifth-grader ought to know?" or "Are most third-graders fluent with this kind of syntactic construction?" or "Can an English language learner be expected to read this lengthy, complex sentence accurately?" They may revise the wording of a question so as to simplify vocabulary or grammar. They may use their knowledge of the students' culture to change the background context of a word problem.

When linguistic simplification is provided as a form of testing accommodation for ELLs, test developers need to be careful that it does not reduce the level of mathematical reasoning that the tasks are intended to elicit. For example, replacing important mathematical language with everyday language may have the undesirable consequence of distorting the concepts assessed. When teachers avoid the technical language of mathematics, they may end up using ambiguous language that expresses little mathematical meaning (Schleppegrell, 2004, p. 155). For instance, by asking a student to reduce the fraction 16/10 (in an effort to elicit 8/5 or, eventually, 1 3/5), a teacher may say, "Can you go down any lower?" (Schleppegrell, 2004, p. 155, citing Khisty, 1993, p. 646). In the context of either instruction or assessment, such simplification often does not help students to learn mathematics.

In the following paragraphs, we present a comprehensive conceptual framework for examining mathematics assessment for ELLs. This conceptual framework integrates three aspects of language: structure (form), function (use), and culture. The cultural aspect of language is often implicit in functionalist views;

however, for the purposes of analyzing issues in assessment development and use, we believe it is helpful to examine it separately. We contend that, in order to properly address the linguistic needs of ELLs, assessment developers and educators should use the three views in combination.

### A Structural View of Language—Language as Form

Language can be thought of as a structure built of units (e.g., phonemes, words, sentences). Sounds (phonemes, syllables) are structured to form words, which are combined to form sentences. This approach to language entails focusing on linguistic forms and relations among them without immediate consideration for the context in which the language is used. From this perspective, one may examine how morphemes are combined in multi-syllabic words (respect-ful-ly; base-ball; in-vis-ible) or how sentences are combined through the use of connectives (Kim made the salad *and* Jason made the main course), or by embedding (Mike and Susan, *who are Kim's parents*, brought the dessert). A structural view of language is concerned with which parts of speech can be combined in which ways with each other. In English, it is grammatically correct to say, "The circus came to town yesterday" but not "Circus the came to town yesterday."

Analysis of language forms can be done without regard for meaning or the social context of the use of the language under analysis, and without reference to the age of a speaker or reader. Such analysis will be most useful to the teacher when it is understood in light of how it is to be used and with whom (e.g., for a discussion question or test item with ELLs). However, form, meaning, and usage can be examined independently in the process of assessment development and critique.

### A Functional View of Language—Language in Use

The functionalist view of language comes from the field of sociolinguistics, or the study of language as it is used in social contexts to accomplish particular purposes (Hymes, 1974;[2] Schleppegrell, 2004). This perspective on language is described as "functionalist" because it examines language in use, as a dynamic phenomenon. In the classroom, language is used both for transactions (to share ideas and information) and interactions (to develop and maintain relationships) (cf., Brown & Yule, 1983). Students use language transactionally to engage in mathematics with others. We would expand the definition of the transactional aspect of language to include its function of formulating or constructing knowledge, whether internally (mentally) or "out loud," alone or with others. Students use language interactionally when they apologize to the teacher for behavior, compliment a fellow student, or recount an event to a friend (cf., Schleppegrell, 2004).

Language in use is characterized by differences in the actual grammatical systems used by speakers, depending upon which variety (dialect) of a language they speak or what the social circumstances are. Implicit rules for pronunciation, syntax, and discourse (creating extended spoken or written texts) vary from dialect to dialect. In addition, speakers use different "registers," or versions of language specialized for different contexts—for example, when discussing mathematics, visiting the doctor, talking to a child, and the like. Whereas dialect is associated with the language user (based on social and geographic background), register is associated with the context of use—the classroom, the doctor's office, at home with a child.

## A Cultural View of Language—Language as Reflector and Vehicle of Culture

Language can also be viewed as a cultural phenomenon. From the perspective of cultural anthropology, each language is a cultural creation that is continuously re-created, as the lives of its speakers change and present new communicative needs. It is also a vehicle of culture, in that it records and transmits the values, beliefs, knowledge, and experience of the people who speak it across generations. "[L]anguage and communication styles are systems of cultural notations and the means through which thoughts and ideas are expressively embodied" (Gay, 2000, p. 81). Within the classroom, choices of topics for conversation and discussion as well as reading and writing are situated within cultural perspectives on what knowledge is, what counts as important knowledge, and how it is constructed and assessed in students (Greenfield et al., 2006). The particular context in which a mathematics assessment task is set may affect how a student interprets the core problem presented and how to solve it (cf., Koelsch & Estrin, 1996). Linguist Wallace Chafe says:

> I believe that understanding depends on the ability to place ordinary, particular experiences, whether they are derived through the sense or through events in ourselves, within some larger picture where they "make sense"; that is, where they are recognized as at least partly familiar, and where expectations already partly established can provide ways of reacting to them and interacting with them.
>
> (1992, p. 81)

In reading through a word problem on a mathematics test, to understand the context, a student must be able to make some kind of personal connection to it. Given cultural variation in students' backgrounds, a teacher cannot safely assume that a context familiar to him or her will be so for students. The same may be true for the actual format used to pose a mathematics problem (Barwell, 2009a; Nelson-Barber & Trumbull, 2007). For example, multiple-choice items present frustration to some students who have been socialized to respect all possible answers to a question and avoid "exclusive" thinking (Nelson-Barber & Trumbull, 2007). Others may have had no experience with multiple-choice tests before entering U.S. schools (Trumbull, 2003). This is reportedly the case of immigrant students from the Dominican Republic who attended public schools there (Trumbull, 2002).

We mentioned the concept of genre earlier, referring to a type of mathematical problem or task that has particular features and is characterized by a specific language usage. Examples are word problems, procedural questions, and explanations (Chval & Khisty, 2009). Each mathematical genre entails a set of assumptions about how a problem is framed in language. Barwell (2009a) uses the following word problem (Figure 10.1) from a Year 5 (fifth-grade) classroom in England to illustrate the kinds of assumptions associated with that genre.[3]

---

Mrs. Patel buys **4 milkshakes** costing **65p** each and **3 sandwiches** costing £1.70 each.
   Work out the **total cost**.

---

*Figure 10.1* Fifth Year English problem (source: Barwell, 2009a, p. 63).

In order to make sense of this problem, a student needs a fair amount of knowledge about the word problem genre. Those of us who have spent a lifetime reading such problems may not appreciate the linguistic demands and the inferences a student has to make in order to solve the problem correctly, or the cultural assumptions behind the story context provided. As Barwell notes, we don't know who Mrs. Patel is, where she is, why she is buying four milkshakes and three sandwiches (or for whom), and why the milkshakes are so cheap! Much is left implicit in word problems.

Inferring the meaning of the context requires both linguistic and cultural knowledge. Word problems are often difficult for native speakers (Verschaffel, Greer, & deCorte, 2000), but they are likely to be more difficult for students who are still learning English and whose cultures are not the same as that of the assessment developer. Such students may overlook the context entirely and proceed directly to what they perceive as the mathematics task at hand. Without reading the "story," they are likely to simply add the two figures, as was the case of a Chinese–English bilingual child cited by Barwell (2009a). Teachers in an assessment development research project with students whose home language was Spanish noted that, when reading word problems in English, their students had a tendency to want to skip over the words and go directly to what they expected the mathematical operation to be. One said, "Kids may look at the two numbers and start to add or subtract versus reading the problem" (Trumbull, 2002). Another teacher said, "Students have to learn to read the whole item— read the directions. Get used to multiple steps, versus start working when you see the first piece of information" (Trumbull, 2002).

Other cultural issues that are made manifest in language (though not always open to conscious inspection) have to do with how "each language brings the potential for thinking about the supposedly universal ideas of mathematics in a variety of ways" (Barwell, 2009b, p. 166). There is not time or space to explore this topic adequately, but it raises the question of how students' cultural and linguistic knowledge can be tapped in the course of mathematics instruction and assessment. One approach is to allow—even encourage—ELLs to engage in code-switching (Halai, 2009; Jones, 2009). Different kinds of information are likely to be available to students in their different languages. For instance, bilingual

English–Welsh students (whose education is, indeed, bilingual) may more easily recognize the mathematical meaning of *cyflun* than of "similarity" because the Welsh word is not usually used in a non-mathematical sense (Jones, 2009, p. 125). Likewise, the term for "right-angles" in Welsh (*onglau sgwâr*) literally reads as "square angles." The Somali word for "inequality" (*dheeli*) may be more transparent to a Somali student than "inequality" is to an English speaker because of its everyday language meaning, "unbalanced load on a donkey or camel" (Staats, 2009).

Table 10.2 describes these three perspectives on language and suggests their possible implications for mathematics assessment. No matter what lens a teacher uses to examine language in the classroom, he or she needs to always bear in mind that language is a cultural phenomenon. Both language forms and uses are influenced greatly by the cultural contexts in which students have been nurtured to learn language. Hence, even as one examines a structural element of language, in order to formulate credible hypotheses about the demands it places on the ELL (or any student), one needs to draw upon sociolinguistic and cultural information.

## Learning to Speak Mathematically

For all students, language is at the heart of mathematics learning and performance. To learn mathematics concepts, solve mathematical problems, and demonstrate their mathematical knowledge in a range of ways, students rely on both everyday language and the mathematics register (Halliday, 1978; Solano-Flores, 2010). The mathematics register is the set of specific vocabulary, syntactic, and discourse structures used to express mathematical ideas. One might think of this as the mathematical version of academic language (see Trumbull & Solano-Flores, Chapter 2, this volume). Often, the meaning of a term in everyday language overlaps with its mathematic meaning—but is not equivalent to it. For instance, "slope" in everyday language often refers to the steepness of a hill or mountain. In the plural, it may simply refer to a mountain without implying anything about its steepness ("She's on the ski slopes for the weekend"). But in the mathematics classroom, "slope" refers very specifically to the ratio of the vertical change to the horizontal change between two points on a line. Likewise, the word "area" is used very flexibly in everyday language to refer to a region of some sort (or a topic of interest or study—"His area is computational linguistics"). But it has a very constrained meaning in mathematics: the extent of a two-dimensional surface within a set of lines (cf., www.merriam-webster.com/dictionary/area).

Perhaps even greater challenges are presented by small words, such as "by," "for," "through," and "in" (Mitchell, 2001). In the sentence, "A room is 40 by 20 feet," the meaning of "by" does not overlap in any obvious way with its usual meanings in everyday language. Word combinations, both phrases and sentences, have special meanings as well. (Figure 10.2 lists some words and phrases of the mathematics register.) In everyday language, "degree of freedom," for instance, could refer to a person's latitude for social interactions. It has different meanings in the fields of mathematics, physics, and mechanics.

Table 10.2 Three Other Perspectives on Language: Language as Structure, Language in Use, and Language as a Cultural Phenomenon

| | Language as Structure: Focus on Language Components Out of Context | Language in Use: Focus on Language Use in Context | Language as a Cultural Phenomenon: Focus on Cultural Content of Language |
|---|---|---|---|
| **Listening/speaking** | Vocabulary/semantics (word meanings and meaning relations among words). Pronunciation. Phonology (sounds and sound patterns). Syntax (sentence grammar). Discourse organization (structure of conversation, discussion, etc.). | Social communication. Communication for teaching and learning (constructing and showing knowledge). Use of language, dialect, register appropriate to purpose and context. Language (L1, L2, D1, D2)* choice to signal group identity. | Choice of topics for conversation, classroom discussion, assessment. Choice of vocabulary and style consonant with participation in a particular cultural community and the topic at hand. |
| **Reading/writing** | Word recognition: syllable structure, prefixes, suffixes. Semantics: word meaning, ways relationships among words are signaled. Phonemic structure of words. Phoneme–grapheme relations, orthography. Syntax. Text genres and their organization. | Reading for different purposes: using strategies/processes appropriate to purpose. Constructing meaning from written text, based on own knowledge and perspective and construal of writer's intent. Writing for different purposes, using strategies/processes appropriate to purpose. Selecting appropriate language, dialect, register for writing, depending upon purpose and audience. | Content/cultural orientation of texts (teacher and student choices). Student and teacher choices in topics for writing. Student and teacher interpretation of texts, influenced by cultural perspectives and experience (including education). |

continued

*Table 10.2* Continued

| **Implications for mathematics assessment** | Students' proficiency with the vocabulary, syntax, and text organization of mathematics problems will influence their comprehension, solutions, and explanations. Teachers should investigate to see whether performance problems are in part attributable to students' gaps in knowledge of structural features of language. | Students' familiarity with the ways the mathematics register differs from other registers will affect their ability to make sense of mathematics problems and express solutions and explanations. Teachers should assess how students use the mathematics register, e.g., whether they use it successfully orally to explain a problem solution. | Students' cultural familiarity with particular content and vocabulary may influence interpretation of mathematics problems and ways of solving them. Educational experience in another country may influence students' interpretation of assessment formats. Mathematics vocabulary knowledge in another language can facilitate understanding English terms; code-switching may invoke germane cultural knowledge. |

---

**Words**

result • prove • establish • simplify • negative • solution • identity • image • relation • universal • chord • face • index • multiple • network intersection • mean • mode • operation • origin • multiple • plane • prime • range • variable • rational • product • real • reciprocal • closed • average • fraction • exponent • sine • cosine • theorem • polygon

**Phrases**

degree of freedom • identity mapping • cumulative frequency • frequency diagram • direct route • prime factor • right angle • ordered pairs • highest common factor • rounding off • empty set • square root • identity element • lowest common denominator • missing leg • x-axis • total cost • divide by

---

*Figure 10.2* Sample Vocabulary from the Mathematics Register (source: Adapted from: Chapman, 1993).

Mathematical language is not, however, always precise (Barwell, 2005). As in any domain, there can be ambiguity in mathematical discourse. One source of ambiguity is the fact (cited above) that the same terms can be used in mathematical and non-mathematical ways, even in the mathematics classroom. One might expect that, in mathematics instruction and assessment, a term such as "diagonal" would be used in its technical, mathematical sense most of the time. However, a study by Monaghan of instances of the use of "diagonal" and related words ("diagonally," "diagonals") in a large body of elementary mathematics materials showed that, out of 66 instances across 35 activities, only 32 were in the technical mathematical sense (Monaghan, 2009). Other research has shown that this may make good sense in instruction: When teachers strive to use terms precisely only in the strictest mathematical sense, and to have their students do the same, they may be depriving students of learning opportunities afforded by using natural language (Leung, 2005; Raiker, 2002).

English language learners are faced with the task of continuing to refine their understanding and use of everyday language while acquiring the mathematics register in English. If they have learned some mathematics in their first language, this is no doubt useful for conceptual understanding. But it may be of little use in fostering acquisition of the English mathematics register, particularly with regard to these small words and how they are used. Native Spanish speakers may have difficulty with the distinction between "in" and "on," for instance. The Spanish word "en" may be translated as either "in" or "on," and learning the distinctions between the English terms may take longer than is evident to a teacher. English is not so consistent as it might seem. Consider the differences between "in time" and "on time" or "in public" and "on the QT."

At the same time, one should be cautious about assuming that ELLs will be deficient in learning the mathematics register and dealing with multiple meanings of words. Moschkovich (2007) gives an interesting example of native Spanish-speaking middle school students in a bilingual (English–Spanish) summer school classroom. Students were engaged in the study of area and perimeter issues involving rectangles. Those participating in a lesson in Spanish did not know the word for "rectangle" in Spanish (though they were fluent in everyday

Spanish) or English. Moschkovich notes that the fact that students used the term "rangulo" instead of "rectangulo" or "rectangle" should not (and did not, in this case) blind the teacher to their mathematical understanding.

With regard to promoting acquisition of the mathematics register, a teacher will need to engage students in mathematical discourse and carefully observe students' strengths and weaknesses so as to target particular mathematical language for further instruction. Similarly, students whose home dialect is not the same as the dialect of school may make different kinds of errors as they learn the mathematics register. These should not be taken as indicators of learning problems but as information about where everyday language and the language of mathematics may cause difficulties for them (Rickford, 1999).

## Sources of Linguistic Interference on Mathematics Assessments

As has been discussed in various ways within this volume, assessment of ELLs (and perhaps others whose English is "non-standard") in any domain risks confusing English language proficiency with subject area proficiency. The challenge to any assessment developer—professional psychometrician or classroom teacher—is to lessen the degree to which successful assessment performance depends on language that is not necessary to the understanding of the content being assessed. Difficult vocabulary has been shown to be the biggest source of linguistic challenge on assessments (e.g., Shaftel, Belton-Kocher, Glasnapp, & Poggio, 2006). But there is a point past which vocabulary cannot be simplified and the integrity of a problem or question maintained. The mathematics register, no doubt the greatest source of vocabulary complexity, cannot be avoided. However, many items on large-scale tests (and, no doubt, end-of-unit tests and teacher-created assessments) use language that is unnecessarily syntactically complex. The test item shown in Figure 10.3 illustrates this problem.

This item has been analyzed in previous research and shown to be linguistically complex from several perspectives (Solano-Flores & Li, 2009; Solano-Flores & Trumbull, 2003). (See a discussion about the sociocultural aspect of this item in Basterra, Chapter 4, this volume.) For now, let's just look at the last sentence, "What is the least number of $1.00 bills that his mother should give him so he will have enough money to buy lunch for 5 days?" Sentence length is a good indicator of sentence complexity (they are highly related), and at 26 words, this sentence is lengthy for a fourth-grade test item prompt. This sentence actually

---

Sam can purchase his lunch at school. Each day he wants to have juice that costs 50¢, a sandwich that costs 90¢, and fruit that costs 35¢. His mother has only $1.00 bills. What is the least number of $1.00 bills that his mother should give him so he will have enough money to buy lunch for 5 days?

---

*Figure 10.3* The Lunch Money Item: A Fourth-Grade NAEP Mathematics Item (source: National Assessment of Educational Progress, 1996).

has four different sentences (noun–verb sets) rolled into one: (1) What is the least number of $1.00 bills, (2) that his mother should give him, (3) so he will have enough money, (4) to buy lunch for 5 days. The student reading this question has to be able to parse all that syntax and understand the relationships among the idea units or propositions communicated.

In addition, the phrase "$1.00 bills" is itself very complex. The noun "$1.00" acts as an adjective describing another noun—bills. It could also be written, "one-dollar bills," which to a practiced reader (but maybe not a fourth-grader) would indicate the relationship better. Or, it could be written, "bills of one dollar." That would not be idiomatic usage in English, i.e., a student is not likely to ever have heard that phrase in the speech of adults or older children. But it does have certain virtues, as we will discuss shortly. Numerous students responding to the item were found to have interpreted "His mother has only $1.00 bills" as meaning, "His mother has only $1.00." A possible alternative to the item is offered in Figure 10.4. Sentence length, vocabulary (purchase/buy), and structural complexity have been simplified without compromising item difficulty, we believe.[4] The phrase "bills of one dollar," by fronting the plural word "bills," may cue a young reader to the fact that Sam's mother has more than one dollar. We hypothesize, further, that the use of words alone rather than the symbolic representation ($1.00) may elicit a more careful reading. When a student sees "$1.00," he or she may fix on that as providing all of the mathematical information necessary—when, in fact, it does not.

---

Sam can buy his lunch at school. Each day he buys juice for 50¢, a sandwich for 90¢, and fruit for 35¢. His mother has only bills of one dollar—no fives or tens. What is the least number of one-dollar bills Sam needs in order to buy lunch for 5 days?

---

Figure 10.4 Possible Alternative to the Item in Figure 10.2.

In Chapter 2 (this volume) we identify known sources of structural complexity that can most often be eliminated in assessment items. Lengthy sentences, complex tenses, relative clauses, and multiple prepositional phrases are to be avoided if possible. Consider the NAEP (National Assessment of Educational Progress) fourth-grade mathematics item:

---

The length of a dinosaur was reported to have been 80 feet (rounded to the nearest 10 feet). What length other than 80 feet could have been the actual length of this dinosaur?

Answer_____

---

Figure 10.5 The Dinosaur Item (source: National Assessment of Educational Progress, 2000).

The complex verb forms "reported to have been" and "could have been" might be unnecessary sources of difficulty for ELLs. In fact, they are probably not common in the speech of most fourth-graders. The use of the passive in the first sentence ("was reported") adds linguistic difficulty that could be avoided; and the phrase "length other than 80 feet" is also unduly complex for a nine- or ten-year-old student.

As suggested above, some of the most difficult language for ELLs may well be the small words that signal relationships among parts of a mathematical sentence, such as "by," "through," "with," "if ... then." Another issue is that the small words often have multiple meanings. Monaghan (2009, p. 27) gives a list of 19 different instances of the use of the word "about" in a mathematics curriculum. Some uses of the word are clearly part of the mathematics register, and some are not. Examples:

"toppled first about line x and then about line y ..."

"blood cells have a diameter of about 0.00075 centimeters"

"What do you notice about the power of 10 ...?"

"Think about the number line as it passes below ..."

"Fibonacci was born about 1175 in Pisa ..."

Teachers need to consider how these kinds of linguistic factors and others may affect students' comprehension (orally and in writing) and ways of expressing mathematical ideas on formal assessments and in classroom discussion. The ease with which students deal with language demands like these will vary according to many factors, including students' English proficiency in the four modalities, their mathematics knowledge in another language (and the degree to which they are free to bring it to bear), the social climate of the classroom, and the teacher's skill in interpreting students' meanings and fostering mathematical and language learning (Chval & Khisty, 2009; Halai, 2009; Moschkovich, 2009).

## Research on New Ways of Developing, Adapting, and Reviewing Mathematics Assessments

We, and others, have been involved in several research collaborations on assessments with teachers in school districts in various regions of the United States (see, e.g., Solano-Flores & Li, 2009; Solano-Flores & Trumbull, 2008; Solano-Flores, Trumbull, & Kwon, 2003; Solano-Flores, Trumbull, & Nelson-Barber, 2002). All of the districts serve large numbers of ELLs—some of them recent immigrants, some second- or third-generation speakers of languages other than English. These projects have in common that researchers and teachers worked together to adapt existing assessment tasks or create new ones that were judged by teachers to be culturally and linguistically appropriate for the students served by their schools. This can be thought of as an alternative form of accommodation (Solano-Flores, Li, Speroni, Rodriguez, Basterra, & Dovholuk, 2007).

At the outset of each project, researchers helped lay down conceptual frameworks about language and developing assessments for ELLs, and teachers educated researchers about the linguistic and cultural contexts in which they taught. In all cases, the process of participation in collaborative research gave teachers an opportunity to develop a more sophisticated understanding of language in ways that linguists and sociolinguists have characterized it. And it gave researchers a chance to deepen their understanding of the actual issues faced by students and teachers in very different sociocultural contexts.

As we discuss the processes researchers and teachers used to develop new assessment items or modify existing ones for ELLs, we will examine how different views of language came into play and how language and culture were evidently intertwined.

## Designing Mathematics Assessments for Mexican-Origin Students in the Northwest

### The Context

This K-12 district in the Northwest serves many families whose origins, both immediate and in previous generations, are in Mexico or Central America. Some families still migrate between the Northwest and Michoacán, Mexico, following the seasonal work associated with the fruit orchards. Spanish is the home or heritage language of many students. Students are bilingual to differing degrees. For recent immigrants and those whose families continue to migrate between Mexico and the U.S., Spanish is still a primary language. At the time the research was conducted, the district had a transitional bilingual program for elementary-grade students, who moved into English-only instruction at fourth grade. At middle and high school, students had access to an English as a second language (ESL) program. This latter program was necessary for newly arriving older students and others who still needed language support.

### The Assessment Development Process

Every few weeks for a period of more than a year, two teams of three-to-five teachers worked with two researchers via the "concurrent assessment development method" to develop fourth-grade constructed response mathematics items in English and Spanish (Solano-Flores & Trumbull, 2003). Each team was responsible for developing one language version—English or Spanish—of the same items. The Spanish team consisted of three Latino teachers fluent in Spanish and English. The English team consisted of four non-Latino teachers, all of whom spoke Spanish.

The two teams came together to discuss progress on each item and how the two versions could be revised to align most closely. Once an item was completed in both Spanish and English, teachers administered it to students and then interviewed them to find out why they solved it as they did and how they might reword it, if they thought that would improve the item. Items were then revised through a process involving negotiation across languages and tried out again with students. This process is very different from the usual way of developing a bilingual assessment in which most time is devoted to developing the assessment in one language (e.g., English), and far less time is given to translating it into another language (e.g., Spanish) (Solano-Flores & Nelson-Barber, 2001).

## Linguistic and Cultural Issues in Assessment Identified by Teachers

In the course of the project, teachers identified many structural, functional, and cultural issues related to language choice, content, and formatting of each assessment item. Table 10.3 shows examples of these issues. The functional and cultural aspects have been kept separate in the table but collapsed in the following discussion because they are considerably interrelated.

### Structural Issues

The interrelationships among the structural, functional, and cultural perspectives on language are clear in many of the examples used here. In fact, the examples can be coded in multiple ways, as will be evident below. Word choice discussions among the Northwest teachers occurred both within a team and across teams, so that word difficulty could be kept at approximately equal levels across language versions of an assessment item. Some discussions about terms were revisited multiple times. This process was a clear indicator of the limitations of a simple translation process. Teachers argued at length over specific words. At times, they would return to a word issue—supposedly settled—in the context of a new mathematics item. Should it be *"precio"* (price) or *"costo"* (cost) in certain situations? Should "tetherball" be left as "tetherball" in Spanish or translated as *"pelota para pegar"* or some similar term? (See Figure 10.6.) Related to "tetherball," they wondered whether Spanish speakers' problems with pronouncing the word would add to item difficulty.

Teachers struggled with whether to keep sentence structure parallel in the English and Spanish versions of an assessment task or to go for what sounded better in each language. If the English version of an item says, "With the information above, find the total price of the ingredients, (Figure 10.7)," can the Spanish version say, *"Calcula el costo total de los ingredientes con la información de arriba"* [Calculate the total cost of the ingredients with the information above]?

### Functional and Cultural Issues

The new assessments were based on mathematics tasks on statewide assessments, in large part because teachers wanted their students to gain more experience with the types of items they would encounter on those tests later. But teachers

*Table 10.3* Examples from the Northwest Teachers: Structural, Functional, and Cultural Perspectives

## Structural perspective

### Word
- A word in English may have no equivalent in Spanish, so the English word may be preferable e.g. "tetherball."

### Pronunciation/spelling
- It is hard to pronounce (e.g., "tetherball") and may raise anxiety or take up processing time, as students try to read/pronounce the word. Should the English word be used?
- A Spanish-speaking student notes that "taco" and "tortilla" are easy for him to spell (in the context of assessment item). Should assessment developers actively look for words that cross languages this way?

### Syntax
- In instructing students to calculate the cost of ingredients for a recipe, should one say, "Obten el resultado" ("Get the result") or "Calcule el precio total" ("Calculate the total price") or "Encuentra el precio total de la gelatina" ("Find the total cost of the jello")? Are any of the differences among these sentences important?
- Adding an explanation of a term adds to language processing demands—length of an item, e.g., explaining what "tetherball" means. How can one decide whether to clarify and lengthen or keep the language of an item brief?
- Do sentences in English and Spanish versions of an assessment task have to be structurally parallel? Are the two following versions appropriate?
- "Find the total cost of the jello from the ingredients shown above." "Calcula el costo total de la gelatina con los ingredientes de arriba." Or can the Spanish sentence begin, "Con la información de arriba ...?" (with the information above ...)

### Discourse
- Spanish-speaking students seem to find text broken up by visuals confusing. Should the assessment developer consider putting all text in an item together, in one block of language, rather than interrupted with visuals?
- Immigrant students may be less goal-oriented (competitive) than dominant culture students. How does this affect solving a lengthy problem presented in many segments/complex format? Should the bottom-line question be posed at the very beginning vs. end after context is established?

*continued*

Table 10.3 Continued

## Functional perspective

- Latino students have never seen a particular kind of problem before. Scanning the format to determine what they are supposed to do presents challenges. How should the item be modified to accurately assess such students' learning?

- Latino students appear to be more focused on the task (e.g., making a birdhouse or piñata) presented as context for a math problem than the math involved. Dominant culture students appear to focus more on solving the math problem than engaging with the activity? Should the math question be posed up front: "How much money will you need to …?" vs. "The class is going to build a birdhouse" or "La familia Lopez va hacer una piñata" ("The Lopez family is going to make a piñata").

## Cultural perspective

- Latino students are not used to standardized testing. Speaking English is not equivalent to understanding the premise behind testing or behind a given test item. How can teachers orient students to assessments and how to parse the language of assessment?

- Solving the problem of determining quantities of ingredients for a dish "correctly" means overlooking cultural knowledge (prepare for more guests than invited). How can assessment design anticipate such cultural issues?

- Some students are familiar with the metric system (e.g., recent immigrant from Honduras) but not the English system. Which should be used, kilograms or pounds?

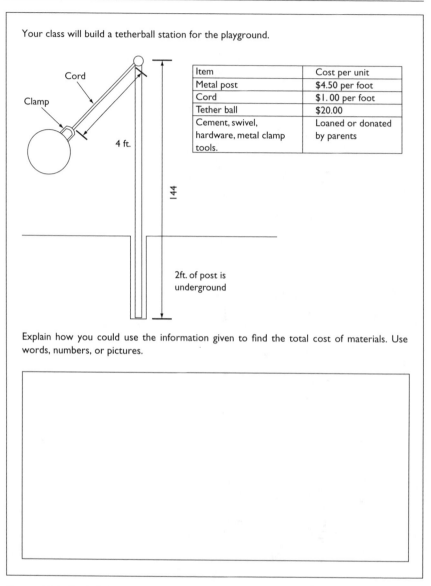

Your class will build a tetherball station for the playground.

| Item | Cost per unit |
|---|---|
| Metal post | $4.50 per foot |
| Cord | $1.00 per foot |
| Tether ball | $20.00 |
| Cement, swivel, hardware, metal clamp tools. | Loaned or donated by parents |

4 ft.

144

2ft. of post is underground

Explain how you could use the information given to find the total cost of materials. Use words, numbers, or pictures.

*Figure 10.6* English Version of the Tetherball Task.

questioned whether the organization of discourse and visual formats of some items were best for their students. Regarding one task, a teacher said:

[My students] would never be able to do it even in English or in Spanish because they have never seen a problem like this before. The American students ... have seen it before, and so that would be the difference. My students would not have a clue ...

You are going to make jello for 12 people.

| Ingredients | Price per unit |
|---|---|
| Fruit | $2.00 total |
| 2 cups of hot water | from the sink |
| 2 cans of juice | $1.50 per can |
| 2 packages of jello | $1.00 per package |

Water

Heat the water for 3 minutes

With the information above, find the total price of the ingredients. You can use pictures, numbers, and/or words.

Explain how you used the information above to find the total price of the ingredients.

Figure 10.7 English Version of the Jello Task (source: Solano-Flores, Trumbull, & Nelson-Barber, 2002).

A discussion of whether to translate English measurement terms (inch, foot) into Spanish or use metric terms in one assessment item showed the intersection of word choice and sociocultural background. Students who had been educated for some time in Mexico or Central America would be more likely to know metric system terms; those who spoke Spanish but had been educated in the U.S. would be more likely to know the English system terms. This could also be considered a functional/ use issue from the perspective of the mathematics register. What might be the nature of the mathematics register of a student schooled in two different cultural settings?

Another teacher described the frustration that one of his ELL students exhibited when trying to navigate a multi-step task that combined linguistic and visual information, with a box for explaining one's problem solution:

> [H]e seemed really stuck on what was the question, what to do, where to write the answer, and I pointed to the space—"*Usa ese espacio para explicar*" [Use this space to explain ...]. He said, "Oh," and then he started. It was like he couldn't find his way down to the space ... and Carlos[5] was the same way. He was stuck on where to put his answer. He said, "I don't get it. I don't get it. What do I have to do? Do I have to put the answer? Where do I put the answer? I don't get it. I don't get it."

This teacher asked his fellow teachers whether their native English-speaking students had the same problems with the item and was told, "No, they knew right where to go." "They knew the answer ... had taken the [State Test], so they have seen this. They were not confused about what to do or where to put [their answer]."

At a meeting some weeks later, teachers talked about possible cultural differences between their Latino students and the native English-speaking students (whom they called "Anglos"). A case in point is the piñata task:

> *The López family is going to make a piñata for their son Antonio's birthday. With the information above* [a table with the cost of different materials], *find the total cost of the piñata. You can use pictures, numbers and/or words.*

When faced with the Piñata task, teachers hypothesized that the Latino students focused on the task of making the piñata, whereas the Anglo students focused on the mathematics of the problem. A teacher said, "[The way the Latino students approach the task] is almost the reverse of the Anglo kids, isn't it? Because we're working so hard to get them to go beyond just doing math [to communication]. 'Would you please talk about ...'" Another teacher, speaking of the Latino students, said:

> You start right off by saying, "*La familia Lopez va hacer una piñata*," you're saying right there they're going to make a piñata, so that locks in ... their minds that the ... activity itself, that is the problem itself.

Further discussion led to a suggestion to reformat the problem to highlight the mathematics problem up-front.

## Multiple Issues in Interplay

In analyzing the demands of such tasks, teachers examined the clarity of the words and sentences themselves, the ways the discourse was formatted (all in one paragraph or interrupted by illustrations), the ways students were asked to use language (explain, calculate, show, describe, etc.), and the ways students' cultural backgrounds and educational experiences might intersect with those demands.

At times, teachers made observations about the overall role of language in assessment. One teacher noted that, on a standardized test, her students did well overall, although not as well as she thought they could have. She examined the pattern of sub-scores, thinking she might identify an area to target for instruction. However, her ELL students' scores seemed to be depressed in all areas rather than higher in some strands (e.g., algebra or geometry) and lower in others. She suspected that linguistic challenges in English might be affecting their performance on all math areas.

## Deepening Analysis

As the development process wore on, the teachers reached increasingly deeper levels of analysis in their discussions of language, culture, and assessment design. They moved beyond a focus on accurate translation of terms to a realization that what presents itself as a simple vocabulary issue might actually be a larger linguistic and cultural issue. The discussion excerpted above, related to how the overall format and discourse of a task might present unwanted difficulties because of students' educational experiences, represented a high level of awareness on the part of the teachers. Even the discussion of the appropriateness of the word "tetherball" in the Spanish item was an opportunity to examine several language issues. The question was revisited several times throughout the development process (as teachers came back to items in order to design rubrics, etc.) and seemed to lead from a simple question of vocabulary to many other issues:

- Can Spanish-speaking students identify the written word "tetherball?"
- Can they arrive at a reasonable phonological representation of the word, given that it is hard for a Spanish speaker to pronounce? (Some students referred to it as "teacherball.")
- Do they equate that word with the game of tetherball?
- Will the complexity of the word make some students anxious just as they approach the problem?
- Will trying to decode the word slow students down or take attention away from actually solving the tetherball problem?
- Is "tetherball" an appropriate context for a mathematics problem for immigrant Latino students? Would soccer be better? Basketball (as a Latina student suggested)?
- How important is a "cultural match" for engaging students in problem solution? (Is a problem based on tacos better than a problem based on hamburgers or pizza?)

- What do we know about students' experiences and how they might affect their interpretation of an assessment item? One must take into account that some families still migrate, others are recent immigrants, and yet others have lived in the area for two or more generations. Some were partially educated in another country.

Given the opportunity to engage in intensive, facilitated conversations about the language of assessments, teachers rapidly moved beyond any overgeneralizations about the experiences, language proficiency, and cultural backgrounds of their students. We believe that deep reasoning about the students' language and culture occurs because throughout the entire process of concurrent assessment development, two languages are treated with the same respect and are given the same chance to shape the characteristics of a task. Every action assessment developers take is with a specific population of students in mind and within a specific cultural context. The complexity of the cultural context is thus appropriately recognized (Solano-Flores & Nelson-Barber, 2001).

## Designing Mathematics Assessments in Two Dialects of Spanish

Spanish—the home or heritage language of the majority of ELLs in the U.S.—has many dialects, associated with different geographic origins. The Spanish of the Dominican Republic spoken by Dominican-American students is different in some ways from the Spanish spoken by Mexican-American students. The goal of this research project was to determine whether mathematics assessment items written in students' particular dialect of Spanish would function differently from those written in another dialect of Spanish (i.e., whether students' performance would vary according to the dialect version of an assessment). Researchers hypothesized that ELLs would perform better on assessment items phrased in their local dialect of Spanish. (See Solano-Flores et al., 2007, for a discussion of results.)

### The Contexts

Two sites, both serving high numbers of ELLs whose home language was Spanish, participated in this project. One site was in New York City. The other was composed of two neighboring districts in Southern California. The students in New York City had their roots in the Dominican Republic. The California students were primarily of Mexican origin or ancestry. A large majority of the teachers at each site came from the same backgrounds as their students; all spoke Spanish.

### The Assessment Adaptation Process

The groups of teachers, facilitated by researchers, adapted 12 released NAEP constructed response mathematics items to reflect the language usage of students in their district (National Assessment of Educational Progress, 1996, 2000). The term "adapted" rather than "translated" is used because the items were not directly translated but interpreted and rendered in Spanish through a process that allowed for maintaining meaning without literally matching words. The teams of teachers varied from five to seven, depending upon the scheduling of meetings. We refer to the two groups of teachers here as the "Dominican dialect group" and "Mexican dialect group." As in the Northwest teacher project, researchers facilitated a series of all-day meetings on-site. Teachers often spent the better part of a day adapting an item; at times they returned to an item when discussion about another item shed new light on an old issue. Because the items were being adapted and not developed from scratch, there was less latitude for teachers to bring their deeper linguistic and cultural knowledge to bear. However, in the adaptation process, they applied a very thorough and detailed analysis to each item.

## Linguistic and Cultural Issues in Assessment Identified by Teachers

As in the project with teachers from the Northwest, teachers identified issues related to vocabulary choice, sentence and discourse structure, use of language to convey particular intentions, and cultural factors that might influence comprehension of a test item. Linguistic and cultural issues arising from two items (Figures 10.8 and 10.9) are discussed. Tables 10.4 and 10.5 present examples, respectively,

---

George buys two calculators that cost $3.29 each. If there is no tax, how much change will he receive from a $10 bill?

Answer_____

---

Figure 10.8 The Calculator Task (source: National Assessment of Educational Progress (1996)).

---

Think carefully about the following question. Write a complete answer. You may use drawings, words, and numbers to explain your answer. Be sure to show all of your work.

Jose ate ½ of a pizza.

Ella ate ½ of another pizza.

José said that he ate more pizza than Ella, but Ella said that they both ate the same amount. Use words and pictures to show that José could be right.

---

Figure 10.9 The Pizza Task (source: National Assessment of Educational Progress (1996)).

*Table 10.4* Examples from the Dominican Spanish Dialect Group: Structural, Functional, and Cultural Perspectives

---

**Structural Perspective**

---

**Word**
- An English name (George) can/should be changed to a Spanish name (*Jorge*) for Spanish speaking students.
- Students may not recognize the notation "$3.29." Should *pesos* be used rather than dollars?
- *Impuesto* (tax) is not a common word and probably not known by some students. Should "tax" be used?
- *Cuidadosamente* (carefully) is a long word. *Piensa bien* (think well/hard) is simpler.

**Pronunciation/spelling**
- Students from the D.R. likely pronounce "pizza" as "pisa" (others as "pidza"). How should it be spelled?
- *Asegúrate* requires an accent over the "u" because of its pronunciation pattern.

**Syntax**
(No observations made)

**Discourse**
- Order of clauses in the question may matter—"If there is no tax, how much change ..." vs. "How much change will he receive, if there is ..." Which order works better in Spanish?

**Functional perspective**
- Usage of past tense grounds story better—students will understand better (*compró*—bought vs. *compra*—buys) better than present tense. Is there a reason the item has to remain in present tense?
- The word *cuidadosamente* is used in different contexts in Spanish, i.e. more associated with "neatness."
- Speakers of the Dominican dialect of Spanish do not use *usted* (formal form of "you"). They use *tú* (familiar form of "you"). For imperatives, use the verb form associated with tú (*piensa* vs. *piense*—"think").
- Dominican students are likely to be more familiar with the word *menudo* than *cambio* for "change" (money). An alternative phrasing can eliminate the need to choose between words.

**Cultural perspective**
- Students who have immigrated from the D.R. may not know what taxes/ *impuestos* are, since there is no sales tax in the D.R. Is the item biased if "tax" is left in?
- The choice of *tú* (the familiar form of "you") in assessment items is also a cultural issue.
- Knowledge of pizza and its spelling is tied to cultural experience. D.R. students have likely seen pizza parlors, with the "pizza" spelling on a sign.

---

of issues the Dominican dialect teacher group and the Mexican dialect teacher group addressed in their adaptation of the 12 items. Figures 10.10 through 10.13 show the final versions of the two adapted items discussed here. In the paragraphs below, structural, functional, and cultural issues raised and resolved by the two groups are discussed together to show where they overlapped and diverged.

*Table 10.5* Examples from the Mexican Spanish Dialect Group: Structural, Functional, and Cultural Perspectives

## Structural perspective

### Word
- Change an English name (George) to a Spanish name (*Jorge*).
- "Ella" is not a good choice for a girl's name in Spanish because *ella* is the pronoun "she." Change to "Eva."
- *Impuesto* may be too difficult a word for fourth-graders. But "tax" may be inappropriate. Use *impuesto*?

### Pronunciation/spelling
- Place accent on "a" in *cuanto* (*cuánto*) when it is used as an interrogative at the beginning of a question.
- The article *el* (the) is different from the pronoun *él* (he).

### Syntax
- How should the phrase "$10 bill" be rendered in Spanish?
- Choice of tense forms can be challenging: *pudo haber tenido razón* ("could have been right"—simple past) vs. *pudiera tener razón* ("could have been right"—imperfect subjunctive). Is either appropriate or preferable for fourth-graders?
- Choice of verb form—reflexive (*se comió*, "ate") or non-reflexive (*comió*).

### Discourse
- If a test item were broken up into *dos pedazos* (two pieces), would that facilitate comprehension? Would it over-simplify the item?
- Changing a sentence from "You may use drawings, words, and numbers to explain your answer" to "Explain your answer, using ..." could make the direction to "explain" more salient.

### Functional perspective
- Should *dólares* be spelled out? Will students know what $ means?
- "Question" has a broader meaning than its closest equivalent in Spanish— *pregunta*. In some cases on a test, *situación* is more appropriate.
- The verbs *enseñar* (teach) and *mostrar* (show/demonstrate) may elicit different responses from students. The distinction in Spanish is not the same as in English. *Enseñar* can mean "show" as well.
- The phrase *en lo cierto* is more idiomatic than *en lo correcto* to render the English phrase "be right."

### Cultural perspective
- One cannot assume a student knows about U.S. context *or* his or her country of origin (e.g., tax/*impuesto* issue). Avoid context that is so specific?
- The culture of the school supports formal language in the classroom. Shouldn't the assessments mirror the formal mathematical register?

## Structural Issues

In the process of adapting the calculator item, both groups of teachers automatically changed "George" to the Spanish *Jorge*. Both groups questioned whether their students would be able to read "$3.29" as three dollars and twenty-nine cents. They questioned whether they needed to change dollars to pesos or to write out *dolares*. The Mexican dialect group entertained the idea of providing a

Jorge compra dos calculadoras que cuestan $3.29 cada una. ¿Cuánto le sobrará si paga con un billete de $10.00?

Respuesta:_____

Close translation: George bought two calculators that cost $3.29 each. How much will be left over [to him] if he pays with a bill of $10.00?

*Figure 10.10* Dominican Spanish Dialect Version of the Calculator Task.

Jorge compra dos calculadoras que cuestan $3.29 cada una. Si no cobran impuestos, ¿cuánto cambio recibirá de un billete de $10?

Respuesta:_____

Close translation: George buys two calculators that cost $3.29 each. If [they] do not collect taxes, how much change will he receive from a bill of $10?

*Figure 10.11* Mexican Spanish Dialect Version of the Calculator Task.

Piensa bien antes de contestar la siguiente pregunta. Escribe una respuesta completa. Puedes usar dibujos, palabras, y números para explicar tu respuesta. Asegúrate de mostrar todo tu trabajo.

Jose se comió ½ de una pizza.

Ela se comió ½ de otra pizza.

José dijo que el comió más pizza que Ela, pero Ela dijo que los dos comieron la misma cantidad. Usa palabras y dibujos que muestran que José puede estar en lo cierto.

*Figure 10.12* Dominican Spanish Dialect Version of the Pizza Task.

Piensa cuidadosamente en la siguiente situación. Escribe una respuesta completa. Puedes usar dibujos, palabras, y números para explicar tu respuesta. Asegúrate de enseñar todo tu trabajo.

Jose se comió ½ de una pizza.

Eva se comió ½ de otra pizza.

José dijo que se comió más pizza que Eva, pero Eva dijo que los dos comieron la misma cantidad. Usa palabras y dibujos para explicar que José pudo haber tenido razón.

*Figure 10.13* Mexican Spanish Dialect Version of the Pizza Task.

key at the bottom of the item: $ = dollar. However, they decided against adding another segment to the item. The phrase "$10 bill" is a complex noun phrase, like "$1.00 bill" in the lunch money problem mentioned earlier (Figure 10.2) that is known to cause processing difficulties in young students. Both groups identified that phrase as a potential source of difficulty. One teacher from the Mexican dialect group said of the English version, "Why did they even use '$10 bill?' They're not asking what form the change will be in!" In the end, they maintained the structure. The Dominican dialect group wrote it as "*un billete de $10.00*," whereas the Mexican dialect group wrote it as "*un billete de $10.*" It would seem that the Spanish version of the item in either case is a bit more transparent than the English version by virtue of putting the word *billete* ("bill") first.

Both the Dominican dialect group and the Mexican dialect group identified a problem in translating the word "tax." They judged the equivalent in Spanish— *impuesto*—to be a difficult word for fourth-graders to read. The Dominican dialect group, in translating the word "carefully" in the pizza item, thought that the Spanish equivalent, *cuidadosamente*, would be too difficult for fourth-graders to read. They changed "Think carefully" to *Piensa bien* ("think well/hard").

Tensions between choosing the "best" word and one that fourth-graders would be familiar with and be able to identify in print arose several times. The Mexican dialect group went back and forth between *enseñar* ("to teach"—and perhaps less commonly – and … – "to show") and *mostrar* ("to show") for the word "show" in the pizza item sentence, "Be sure to show all of your work." They thought *demostrar* was a better choice meaning-wise but too long a word. Both groups also explored several different ways of rendering the phrase "José could be right" at the end of the pizza item. Possibilities offered were:

(1) *Pudo haber tenido razón*—could have been right (a past tense form of the idiom *poder haber razón*)
(2) *Pudiera tener razón*—could be right (an imperfect subjunctive form of the same idiom)
(3) *Puede estar en lo cierto* (can be certain)
(4) *Puede estar en lo correcto* (can be correct)

The Dominican group decided that *en lo correcto* was too literal and that *en lo cierto* was more appropriate. They chose option (3). The Mexican dialect group finally chose option (1).

Whereas punctuation is not typically a part of formalist linguistic focus, it is certainly an issue of written language form. In both groups, structural-level discussion concerned placement of accents in Spanish words. For example, the Mexican dialect group discussed the difference between *el* (Spanish article meaning "the" in the masculine form) and *él* (Spanish pronoun meaning "he") in the process of adapting the pizza item. The Dominican dialect group noted that *asegúrate* requires an accent over the "u" because it is *una palabra esdrújula*—a word that is accented on the third from the last (antepenultimate) syllable.

There was not much discussion about discourse—how to organize text. The Dominican dialect group did discuss order of clauses in the second sentence of the calculator item (see Table 10.4). However, in the end they jettisoned the clause about tax. The Mexican dialect group briefly entertained restructuring the calculator item but decided against it lest they over-simplify the item. The same group also considered reversing the order of clauses in the pizza item sentence, "You may use drawings, words, and numbers to explain your answer" so it would read, "Explain your answer, using drawings, words, and numbers." But that change would make it awkward to convey the aspect of choice about using draw-ings, words, and numbers.

### Functional and Cultural Issues

The word "tax" also brought up functional and cultural issues: It is not a fre-quently used word, particularly in the company of children. Moreover, students who have immigrated from the Dominican Republic may not know what a "tax" is, since there are no sales taxes in the Dominican Republic. There are other kinds of taxes—real estate and the like—but not something one deals with on a frequent basis. Hence this word presents problems of structural difficulty, usage, and cultural lack of relevance. A teacher said, "In their experience here for a child, a lot of the time they won't come across this term because of their culture, social class, and background, and they wouldn't know what *impuesto* is." As they talked about this topic, the Dominican dialect group noted that those who would be tested in Spanish and not English would have arrived in the U.S. any time from the recent past to one-and-a-half years ago; so none would have extensive experience with their new language and the wider cultural context. As can be seen in Figure 10.9, the Dominican dialect group eliminated the mention of tax entirely in their final version of the item. In the same fashion, the group dis-cussed whether *menudo* or *cambio* would be the appropriate word for "change" (money remaining). That question was finessed by phrasing the question, ¿Cuánto le sobrará … ("How much will be left over …?") and leaving out explicit mention of change.

The Dominican dialect group spent well over an hour discussing whether to change "George buys" to *Jorge compra* (present tense) or *Jorge compró*. Arguing for past tense, one of the teachers said, "[T]he purpose of this is to see if it is more understandable for the Dominican child." Another said, "In English it [buys] sounds good, but in Spanish it doesn't sound good." All agreed that the students could probably make sense of the problem if "buy" were translated in the present tense (*compra*), but they didn't like the sound of it. Another teacher, said, "[I]n the way that we are saying this, is it that the Dominican child only understands past tense? They are supposed to be able to understand anything." The discussion proceeded to clarify that refining the item in Spanish was for the purpose of arriving at something that was most like what students would expect to hear/read in such a problem context. However, the item was finally written with *compra*, more parallel to the English version.

Another concern that could be characterized as "functional" has to do with what the test item developers intended when they designed an item. Teachers wondered whether their alterations in the form of an item would alter its level or difficulty or what it was actually assessing. One Mexican dialect teacher questioned whether providing a key to terminology would change the item too much: "If you break it down, it gives them a clue. [How do we] know what the test author intended?" Another said, "To translate, you need to know the original intent." A teacher observed that many students see the way a test item is written "as a trick"—something that alters the way they might go about reading and responding to it. When students view an assessment as trying to trick them, what does this mean in terms of how they approach it—the language of its directions and prompts? The issue clearly becomes more than just one of comprehending a second language.

The pizza item brought up the issue of using *tú* (familiar form of "you," singular) versus *usted* (polite form of "you," singular) and the verb forms associated with either pronoun. Remarking on a proposed form of the Spanish sentence, "Think carefully about the following question," one Dominican dialect group teacher said, "The first word—*piense* [polite form of "think," imperative]—we have *piensa* [familiar form of "think," imperative] because in our culture, *nosotros tuteamos a todo el mundo* [we use *tú* with the whole world]. *Hablamos de tú*, not *de usted* [We use *tú*, not *usted*]. So that would throw them off if you write "*piense.*" This is the perfect example of a discrete structure chosen on the basis of social/cultural usage. A Dominican dialect group teacher said that he was examining the resulting items to be sure that they were "understandable to the Dominican child." "I'm taking into consideration the Dominican child, because I studied their whole life practically."

As mentioned above, the word *cuidadosamente* was flagged by the Dominican dialect group as too difficult (though not all agreed). One teacher said, "[It's] a very long vocabulary word for the kids that are very low level academically speaking in Spanish." Another teacher questioned the same word on the grounds of its connotation as referring to neatness: "I think *cuidadosamente*, I think of erasures. I am thinking of that type of *cuidadosamente.*"

Another discussion in the Mexican dialect group about terms centered around differences between "question" in English and *pregunta* ("question" in Spanish). According to the teachers, *pregunta* has a narrower meaning in Spanish than in English. In English, "question" can refer to a general problem—the question of the efficacy of antibiotics for the common cold, for instance. The pizza item asks students to "think about the following question," but it does not pose a question anywhere in the item. It instructs students to solve a problem. So, the Mexican dialect group chose *situación* (situation) over the word *pregunta*. The Dominican dialect group did not identify the same issue; they used the word *pregunta* without discussion, beyond deciding whether it should be singular or plural.

## What Teachers Can Do

Perhaps the best actions teachers can take in their assessment related activities is to cultivate ways to collaborate with colleagues and engage in a process of surfacing the knowledge they collectively have about language, culture, and assessment of students in mathematics—or any subject domain. Teachers very often know intuitively whether presenting a problem to their students in a certain way will likely elicit what students know. They know more than any outside expert can know about their own students and the conditions under which they are exposed to the enacted curriculum. Making their knowledge explicit and sharing it with others are powerful strategies for improving assessment practices. An ideal situation is one in which collaboration takes place among teachers from different linguistic and cultural backgrounds that reflect students' backgrounds. If the opportunity to work with professional researchers on an assessment project arises, a teacher should try to make use of it. Many teachers find such collaborations gratifying and helpful to their own practice.

Another powerful step teachers can take is to learn from students' families about the ways language is used in their communities and about the experiences students are having that may bear on classroom mathematics. Students can be asked to contribute their own analyses of mathematics tasks and test items through cognitive interviews (Basterra, Chapter 4, Solano-Flores, Chapter 1, this volume). Teachers can ask even very young students, "What was easy about a problem?" "What was hard?" "Was there a word or sentence you didn't understand?" "How did you solve it?" (with probes such as, "What did you do next?") "Why did you do it that way?" "Would you change the language in any way to make it clearer?" Students can also create their own mathematics word problems, a process that can be revealing to both teachers and students (Barwell, 2009a). Such activities can yield information about how students construe mathematical problems and, arguably, promote metacognitive awareness of their approaches to mathematics assessments.

Some of the specific steps teachers can take as they use existing mathematics assessments, modify those assessments for their students, or design new ones, are:

- Examine the language demands of those assessments, and consider how appropriate those demands are for the students they teach. (See Figure 2.1, Trumbull & Solano-Flores, Chapter 2, this volume.)
- Check students' knowledge of the mathematics register, not only in terms of vocabulary but in ways of forming and interpreting mathematical expressions/sentences.
- Consider the cultural assumptions embodied in word problems or performance tasks. Are they appropriate? Is the resulting problem or task likely to be meaningful?
- Consider whether students grasp the expectations of different kinds of assessment formats (multiple-choice, word problem, etc.).
- Recognize that any mathematics assessment is not going to elicit every student's mathematical knowledge, and be skeptical of results that do not make sense based on what he or she knows about a student.

## Conclusion

Conventional approaches to addressing language issues in ELL testing are based on using a few professionals who work in isolation or who spend a limited amount of time examining potential sources of language bias. The potential bias is seldom discussed beyond the structural properties of items (mainly vocabulary and syntax), without addressing functional and cultural issues. If efforts are made to address culture, they are often guided by simplistic (if not stereotypical) assumptions about cultural groups and neglect the important role that the context of the local communities plays as a cultural factor.

In this chapter, we have discussed in detail multiple examples that illustrate the structural, functional, and cultural linguistic issues in the testing of ELLs that arise when teachers engage collaboratively in developing, translating, adapting, or reviewing tests. As our discussion shows, the linguistic features of the same items may pose different sets of challenges for educators of ELLs in different contexts. Or, the same challenge may be addressed in different ways by educators in different contexts. It is only through detailed discussion among educators from the same communities as their ELL students that issues of language and culture can be identified. Designing mathematics assessments does, indeed, present many challenges in terms of ensuring accessibility to students from a great range of ethnolinguistic backgrounds. Teachers are continuously assessing their students, formally and informally; and they can benefit from frameworks, guidelines, and examples that illuminate the linguistic and cultural issues inherent in mathematics assessment.

Based both on literature in the field of ELL testing and our own assessment research, we have attempted to characterize the language demands of mathematics instruction and assessment and elucidate the abstract picture with many kinds of concrete examples. The assessment development studies cited in the second half of the chapter showcase the importance of teacher involvement in assessment development—both for improving the quality of assessments and for the opportunity for professional development such an activity can provide (see, also, Trumbull & Solano-Flores, Chapter 2, this volume). All of the teachers we worked with had a tremendous wealth of knowledge about their students' histories, social environments (in and out of school), languages, and cultures—the kind of nuanced knowledge that is highly beneficial to the assessment development process. As is evident from the very abbreviated account of teachers' discussions during assessment development, attention is given to every layer of language in the process—from punctuation (e.g., accents) to word length (e.g., *cuidadosamente*), to sentence and discourse structure (whether to reverse the order of clauses), to vocabulary meaning (*pregunta* vs. *situación*), usage (*tú* vs. *usted*), and cultural meanings (tax/*impuesto*). There is simply no substitute for teacher involvement in the assessment development process; and collaborations with researchers stand to serve as professional development in both directions: Teachers can make their knowledge more explicit and accessible to other professionals involved in assessment, and in the process they can continue to develop their understanding of assessment and how to apply their knowledge more effectively in their own settings.

## Notes

1. In research on ELLs, language status is often treated as a *factor* that differentially affects the performance of native English speakers and English language learners on assessments (see, e.g., Abedi, Bailey, Butler, Castellon-Wellington, Leon, & Mirocha, 2000/2005; Abedi, Chapter 3, this volume). In this case, language is seen as "something that needs to be controlled or accounted for in order to obtain accurate measures of … achievement" (Solano-Flores, 2010).
2. Using a term from cultural anthropology, Hymes called the study of language in social context the "ethnography of communication."
3. Bolding is present in original, exactly as replicated here.
4. To test this hypothesis, we would have to design an experiment involving the original and modified versions of the item.
5. A pseudonym.

## References

Abedi, J., Bailey, A., Butler, F., Castellon-Wellington, M., Leon, S., & Mirocha, J. (2000/2005). *The validity of administering large-scale content Assessments to English language learners: An investigation from three perspectives.* CSE Report 663. Los Angeles, CA: National Center for Research on Evaluation, Standards, and Student Testing (CRESST). Graduate School of Education and Information Studies (GSEIS), University of California.

American Educational Research Association, National Council of Mathematics Educators, & American Psychological Association (1999). *Standards for educational and psychological testing.* Washington, DC: Author.

Barwell, R. (2005). Ambiguity in the mathematics classroom. *Language and Education,* 19(2), 118–126.

Barwell, R. (2009a). Mathematical word problems and bilingual learners in England. In R. Barwell (Ed.), *Multilingualism in mathematics classrooms: Global perspectives* (pp. 63–77). Bristol: Multilingual Matters.

Barwell, R. (2009b). Summing up: Teaching and learning mathematics in a multilingual world. In R. Barwell (Ed.), *Multilingualism in mathematics classrooms: Global perspectives* (pp. 161–168). Bristol: Multilingual Matters.

Beal, C.R., Adams, N.M., & Cohen, P.R. (2010). Reading proficiency and mathematics problem solving by high school English language learners. *Urban Education,* 45(1), 58–74.

Brown, G., & Yule, G. (1983). *Discourse analysis.* Cambridge: Cambridge University Press.

Chafe, W. (1992). The importance of corpus linguistics to understanding the nature of language. In J. Svartik (Ed.), *Directions in corpus linguistics,* Proceedings of Nobel Symposium 82, Stockholm, August 4–8.

Chapman, A. (1993). Language and learning in school mathematics: A social semiotic perspective. *Issues in Educational Research,* 3, 35–46.

Chval, K.B., & Khisty, L.L. (2009). Bilingual Latino students, writing and mathematics: A case study of successful teaching and learning. In R. Barwell (Ed.), *Multilingualism in mathematics classrooms: Global perspectives* (pp. 128–144). Bristol: Multilingual Matters.

Durán, R.P. (1985). Influences of language skills on bilinguals' problem solving. In S.F. Chipman, J.W. Segal, & R. Glaser (Eds.), *Thinking and learning skills* (pp. 187–207). Hillsdale, NJ: Lawrence Erlbaum Associates.

Durán, R.P. (1989). Testing of linguistic minorities. In R. Linn (Ed.), *Educational measurement* (3rd edition) (pp. 573–588). New York, NY: Macmillan.

Francis, D.J., Lesaux, N.K., & August, D.L. (2006). Language of instruction for language minority learners. In D.L. August & T. Shanahan (Eds.), *Developing literacy in second-language learners* (pp. 365–414). Mahwah, NJ: Erlbaum.

Gardner, P.L. (1977). Logical connectives in science: A summary of the findings. *Research in Science Education*, 7, 9–24.

Gay, G. (2000). Culturally responsive teaching: Theory, research, & practice. New York, NY: Teachers College Press.

Gee, J. (1992). *The social mind: Language, ideology and social practice.* New York, NY: Bergin & Garvey.

Greenfield, P.M., Trumbull, E., Keller, H., Rothstein-Fisch, C., Suzuki, L., Quiroz, B., & Maynard, A. (2006). Cultural conceptions of learning and development. In P.A. Alexander and P.H. Winne (Eds.), *Handbook of educational psychology* (2nd edition) (pp. 675–692). Washington, DC: American Psychological Association.

Gutiérrez, K.D., Baquedano-Lopez, P., & Tejeda, C. (1999). Rethinking diversity: Hybridity and hybrid language practices in the third space. *Mind, Culture, and Activity*, 6(4), 286–303.

Halai, A. (2009). Politics and practice of learning mathematics in multilingual classrooms: Lessons from Pakistan. In R. Barwell (Ed.), *Multilingualism in mathematics classrooms: Global perspectives* (pp. 47–62). Bristol: Multilingual Matters.

Halliday, M.A.K. (1978). *Language as social semiotic: The social interpretation of language and meaning.* London: Edward Arnold.

Heubert, J.P., & Hauser, R.M. (Eds.) (1999). *High stakes testing for tracking, promotion, and graduation.* Committee on Appropriate Test Use, Board on Testing and Assessment, Commission on Behavioral and Social Sciences and Education, National Research Council. Washington, DC: National Academy Press.

Hofstetter, C.H. (2003). Contextual and mathematics accommodation test effects for English-language learners. *Applied Measurement in Education*, 16(2), 159–188.

Hymes, D. (1974). *Foundations in sociolinguistics: An ethnographic approach.* Philadelphia, PN: University of Pennsylvania Press.

Jones, D.V. (2009). Bilingual mathematics classrooms in Wales. In R. Barwell (Ed.), *Multilingualism in mathematics classrooms: Global perspectives* (pp. 113–127). Bristol: Multilingual Matters.

Kabasakalian, R. (2007). Language and thought in mathematics staff development: A problem probing protocol. *Teachers College Record*, 109(4), 837–876.

Kiplinger, V.L., Haug, C.A., & Abedi, J. (2000). *Measuring math—not reading—on a math assessment: A language accommodations study of English language learners and other special populations.* Paper presented at the Annual Meeting of the American Educational Research Association, New Orleans, LA, April.

Koelsch, N., & Estrin, E.T. (1996). Cross-cultural portfolios. In R.G. Calfee & P. Perfumo (Eds.), *Writing portfolios in the classroom* (pp. 261–284). Mahwah, NJ: Lawrence Erlbaum Associates.

Leung, C. (2005). Mathematical vocabulary: Fixers of knowledge or points of exploration? *Language and Education*, 19(2), 127–135.

Mestre, J.P. (1988). The role of language comprehension in mathematics and problem solving. In R.R. Cocking & J.P. Mestre (Eds.), *Linguistic and cultural influences on learning mathematics: The psychology of education and instruction* (pp. 201–220). Hillsdale, NJ: Erlbaum.

Mitchell, J.M. (2001). Interactions between natural language and mathematical structures: The case of "wordwalking." *Mathematical Thinking and Learning*, 3(1), 29–52.

Monaghan, F. (2009). Mapping the mathematical landscape. In R. Barwell (Ed.),

*Multilingualism in mathematics classrooms: Global perspectives* (pp. 14–31). Bristol: Multilingual Matters.

Moschkovich, J. (2006). Using two languages when learning mathematics. *Educational Studies in Mathematics,* 64(2), 121–144.

Moschkovich, J. (2007). Beyond words to mathematical content: Assessing English learners in the mathematics classroom. *Assessing Mathematical Proficiency,* 53, 345–352.

Moschkovich, J. (2009). How language and graphs support conversation in a bilingual mathematics classroom. In R. Barwell (Ed.), *Multilingualism in mathematics classrooms: Global perspectives* (pp. 78–96). Bristol: Multilingual Matters.

National Assessment of Educational Progress (1996). *Mathematics items public release.* Washington, DC: Author.

National Assessment of Educational Progress (2000). *Mathematics items public release.* Washington, DC: Author.

Nelson-Barber, S., & Trumbull, E. (2007). Making assessment practices valid for Native American students. *Journal of Indian Education,* Special Issue.

Pimm, C. (1987). *Speaking mathematically: Communication in mathematics classrooms.* London: Routledge & Kegan Paul Ltd.

Raiker, A. (2002). Spoken language and mathematics. *Cambridge Journal of Education,* 32(1), 45–60.

Rickford, J.R. (1999). Language diversity and academic achievement in the education of African American students—an overview of the issues. In C.T. Adger, D. Christian, & O. Taylor (Eds.), *Making the connection: Language and academic achievement among African American students* (pp. 1–29). McHenry, IL: Center for Applied Linguistics and Delta Systems.

Schleppegrell, M.J. (2004). *The language of schooling: A functional linguistics perspective.* Mahwah, NJL Erlbaum.

Secada, W.G. (1992). Race, ethnicity, social class, language, and achievement in mathematics. In D.A. Grouws (Ed.), *Handbook of research on mathematics teaching and learning* (pp. 623–660). New York, NY: Macmillan.

Shaftel, J., Belton-Kocher, E., Glasnapp, D., & Poggio, G. (2006). The impact of language characteristics in mathematics test items on the performance of English language learners and students with disabilities. *Educational Assessment,* 11(2), 105–126.

Solano-Flores, G. (2010). Function and form in research on language and mathematics education. In J. Moschkovich (Ed.), *Language and mathematics education: Multiple perspectives and directions for research.* Charlotte, NC: Information Age Publishing.

Solano-Flores, G., & Li, M. (2009). Language variation and score variation in the testing of English language learners, native Spanish speakers. *Educational Assessment,* 14(3–4), 180–194.

Solano-Flores, G., Li, M., Speroni, C., Rogriguez, J., Basterra, M. del R., & Dovholuk, G. (2007). *Comparing the properties of teacher-adapted and linguistically-simplified test items for English language learners.* Paper presented at the Annual Meeting of the American Educational Research Association, Chicago, IL, April.

Solano-Flores, G., & Nelson-Barber, S. (2001). On the cultural validity of science assessments. *Journal of Research in Science Teaching,* 38, 553–573.

Solano-Flores, G., & Trumbull, E. (2003). Examining language in context: The need for new research and practice paradigms in the testing of English language learners. *Educational Researcher,* 32(2), 3–13.

Solano-Flores, G., Trumbull, E., & Kwon, M. (2003). *The metrics of linguistic complexity and the metrics of student performance in the testing of English language learners.*

Symposium paper presented at the 2003 Annual Meeting of the American Evaluation Research Association, Chicago, IL, April 21–25.

Solano-Flores, G., Trumbull, E., & Nelson-Barber, S. (2002). Concurrent development of dual language assessments: An alternative to translating tests for linguistic minorities. *International Journal of Testing*, 2(2), 107–129.

Staats, S. (2009). Somali mathematics terminology: A community exploration of mathematics and culture. In R. Barwell (Ed.), *Multilingualism in mathematics classrooms: Global perspectives* (pp. 32–46). Bristol: Multilingual Matters.

Trumbull, E. (2002). Field Notes, October 17.

Trumbull, E. (2003). Field Notes, February 11.

Valdés, G., & Figueroa, R. (1994). *Bilingualism and testing: A special case of bias.* Norwood, NJ: Ablex Publishing Company.

Verschaffel, L., Greer, B., & deCorte, E. (2000). *Making sense of word problems.* Lisse: Swets & Zetitlinger.

Wellington, J., & Osborne, J. (2001). *Language and literacy in science education.* Buckingham, UK: Open University Press.

# Chapter 11

# Science and Literacy Assessments with English Language Learners

*Okhee Lee, Alexandra Santau, and Jaime Maerten-Rivera*

---

**Chapter Overview**

In this chapter we highlight our current research and development efforts to promote exemplary science instruction and assessment with ELL students in a large urban school district. This research is motivated by the goal of improving science and literacy instruction and achievement of ELL students, especially in the context of high-stakes testing in science that is implemented in many states and reported for formative purposes according to NCLB. The research project we describe represents an effort to develop science instruction and assessment protocols that are inquiry-based, aligned with state standards, and culturally responsive to ELL students.

---

Educational reform in general, and the No Child Left Behind (NCLB) Act of 2001 in particular, requires that *all* students achieve high academic standards in core subject areas. Teachers of English language learning (ELL) students have the added challenge of promoting English language and literacy development as well as academic achievement in content areas. A powerful vision of reform to support the academic achievement of ELL students requires integrating instruction in academic disciplines with efforts to develop students' English language and literacy proficiency. The need for such integration is especially urgent, given the policy context of high-stakes assessment and accountability facing today's schools, teachers, and students.

A crucial issue in the assessment debate is how to effectively address linguistic and cultural factors to ensure valid and equitable science assessments for all students. With ELL students, science assessment development should distinguish among science content, English language proficiency, and general literacy. That is, assessments must be designed to avoid confounding English language proficiency and general literacy proficiency with science knowledge and understanding. This topic is also addressed in Abedi, Chapter 3, this volume.

An equally critical issue involves the demands of high-stakes assessment and accountability for students who have traditionally been underserved in the science classroom. Students without access to adequate instruction cannot be expected to perform as well on assessments as students who have received high quality instruction.

The emphasis of this chapter is on the assessments developed through the project. These assessments reflect attention to sociocultural influences that affect students' thinking and meaning-making, as well as the ways in which they make sense of and respond to assessment items (cf., Basterra, Chapter 4, this volume). These sociocultural influences include the values, beliefs, experiences, communication patterns, teaching and learning styles, epistemologies originating in students' home communities, and the socioeconomic conditions in which they live. The sociocultural influences also include alternative ways of expressing ideas based on the students' diverse cultural backgrounds, which may mask their knowledge and abilities in the eyes of teachers unfamiliar with students' linguistic and cultural norms.

Solano-Flores and Nelson-Barber (2001) have synthesized these sociocultural influences into a set of five factors that must be taken into account to ensure *cultural validity* in science assessments: (1) student epistemology, (2) student language proficiency, (3) cultural worldviews, (4) cultural communication and socialization styles, and (5) student life context and values. Consistent with the notion of cultural validity, science instruction and assessment in our intervention articulated linguistic and cultural knowledge of ELL students with scientific practices and science content standards. In addition, our intervention offered multiple forms of assessment for ELL students to demonstrate their knowledge and abilities in their home language as well as English in both home and school contexts. It is noted that, as language and culture are intricately related ("languaculture," Agar, 1996), the intervention focused on both home language and culture of ELL students. It is also noted that since science instruction and assessment were integrally related in our intervention, we describe connections between instruction and assessment.

In this chapter, we first describe our intervention focusing on inquiry-based science instruction and simultaneous English language and literacy development. Second, we describe multiple approaches to assessments in science and literacy with ELL students within the project. Third, we describe our efforts to align our intervention with high-stakes science assessments for ELL students. Finally, based on our work and other research findings, we offer suggestions for what teachers can do to assess science and literacy achievement of ELL students using both academically rigorous and culturally valid approaches (readers may visit the project website, www.education.miami.edu/psell).

## Effective Science Instruction with ELL Students

What classroom practices can support increased science and literacy achievement of ELL students? In what ways can classroom practices in instruction and assessment relate science to students' linguistic and cultural experiences? Empirical research has demonstrated success with inquiry-based science for all students, especially ELL students (Lee, 2005). However, there is a huge variation in what science inquiry looks like in today's science classrooms. With science content standards setting expectations for curriculum content and science inquiry being established as the cornerstone of instruction, teachers are still faced with the question of how to meet the learning needs of ELL students in their classrooms.

Through university and school district collaborative research, "Promoting Science among English Language Learners (P-SELL) in a High-Stakes Testing Policy Context," we designed and tested an instructional intervention to promote ELL students' science and literacy achievement in the context of high-stakes testing and accountability. Our intervention involved teachers and students at grades 3 through 5 in 14 elementary schools in a large urban district. The intervention consisted primarily of curriculum units for teachers and students and teacher professional development. These schools enrolled greater-than-district proportions of ELL students and students from low socioeconomic status (SES) backgrounds, and had performed poorly according to the state's accountability system. The research addressed two questions: (1) Can ELL students learn academic subjects, such as science, while also developing English proficiency? (2) Can ELL students, who learn to think and reason scientifically, also perform well on high-stakes assessments?

Our intervention was grounded in the research literature indicating key features of effective science instruction with ELL students in the context of high-stakes testing and accountability policy: (1) state content standards and assessment in the context of accountability policy in science with ELL students, (2) reform-oriented practices to promote students' science inquiry and understanding, and (3) English language and literacy with ELL students to enhance both science and language learning.

## State Science Content Standards and High-Stakes Science Assessment

We developed a series of curriculum units comprising the entire science curriculum for grades 3 through 5 mandated by the State of Florida science content standards (Florida Department of Education, 1996), which were aligned to standards recommended by the National Science Education Standards (National Research Council, 1996). We gave special consideration to science test item specifications (Florida Department of Education, 2002) to ensure alignment between each curriculum unit and the benchmarks tested by the state assessment in science. Science assessment was factored into school accountability for the first time in 2006.

During teacher workshops, we described how the curriculum units from grades 3 through 5 aligned to state science content standards and specific science benchmarks. Teachers were introduced to the state-defined content clusters, including those benchmarks that were annually assessed as well as those assessed every three years. Teachers became familiar with the benchmark clarifications for those standards assessed at grade 5. Teachers also became aware of assessment item formats and the probable impact of high-stakes science test results on school grades according to the state's accountability system. Perhaps most important, we helped teachers recognize how students' science inquiry, as described next, could enhance performance on state science assessment.

The workshops emphasized challenges facing ELL students with state science assessment. Teachers discussed how such assessment, primarily designed for mainstream students and native speakers of English, might present obstacles and pitfalls to ELL students and low performing students in science (Solano-Flores & Trumbull, 2003). They also discussed how to distinguish ELL students' science knowledge from English proficiency and assist the students to demonstrate their science knowledge.

### Inquiry-based Science

Research on science instruction with ELL students identifies hands-on, inquiry-based science as a means of enabling the students to develop scientific understanding and acquire English language proficiency simultaneously (Amaral, Garrison, & Klentschy, 2002; Lee, Maerten-Rivera, Penfield, LeRoy, & Secada, 2008; Rosebery, Warren, & Conant, 1992). There are several likely reasons for the success of such an approach. First, hands-on activities are less dependent on formal mastery of the language of instruction, thus reducing the linguistic burden on ELL students. Second, hands-on activities through collaborative inquiry foster language acquisition in the context of authentic communication about science knowledge and practice. Third, inquiry-based science promotes students' communication of their understanding in a variety of formats, including written, graphic, oral, and gestural. Fourth, by engaging in the multiple components of science inquiry, ELL students develop their grammar and vocabulary, as well as their familiarity with scientific genres of speaking and writing. Finally, language functions (e.g., describing, hypothesizing, explaining, predicting, and reflecting) develop simultaneously with science inquiry and process skills (e.g., observing, describing, explaining, predicting, estimating, representing, inferring). By engaging in inquiry-based science, ELL students learn to think and reason as members of a science learning community.

To promote science inquiry with ELL students and other diverse student groups, our intervention employs the Science Inquiry Framework (see Figure 11.1). Although some advocates of more open-ended, student-centered inquiry would argue against a framework for organizing and planning inquiry, our practical experience as urban science educators with ELL students has demonstrated the importance of a structured framework as an initial step for teachers and students to begin the process of science inquiry. While making the inquiry process explicit, the framework also allows for flexibility to foster students' initiative and responsibility for their own learning. Thus, the process is not to be followed as a lock-step procedure, but to be considered as a guide.

Our intervention also scaffolds student initiative and responsibility in conducting science inquiry, as teachers gradually reduce their level of guidance. The National Research Council (2000) presents a teacher-directed to learner-directed continuum as it relates to the essential features of science inquiry. Initially, students may need a great deal of assistance to engage in inquiry. As they develop inquiry skills, they will need less and less assistance. Eventually, they can explore and conduct inquiry on their own. While engaging in multiple components of

| 1. Questioning | **State the problem**<br>• What do I want to find out? (Written in the form of a question)<br><br>**Make a hypothesis**<br>• What do I think will happen? |
|---|---|
| 2. Planning | **Make a plan by asking these questions (think, talk, write)**<br>a. What materials will I need?<br>b. What procedures or steps will I take to collect information?<br>c. How will I observe and record results? |
| 3. Implementing | **Gather the materials**<br>• What materials do I need to implement my plan?<br><br>**Follow the procedures**<br>• What steps do I need to take to implement my plan?<br><br>**Observe and record the results**<br>• What happens after I implement my plan?<br>• What do I observe?<br>• How do I display my results? (Using a graph, chart, table) |
| 4. Concluding | **Draw a conclusion**<br>• What did I find out?<br>• Was my hypothesis correct or incorrect? |
| 5. Reporting | **Share my results (informal)**<br>• What do I want to tell others about the activity?<br><br>**Produce a report (formal)**<br>• Record what I did so others can learn.<br>• Consider different ways to express my information. |

*Figure 11.1* Science Inquiry Framework.

inquiry, students learn to engage in some areas more easily (e.g., implementing activities and reporting results), while they may require more assistance and experience in other areas (e.g., developing testable questions). The Science Inquiry Matrix (see Table 11.1) illustrates this continuum, as teachers gradually relinquish authority and encourage students to assume responsibility for their own inquiry.

*Table 11.1* Science Inquiry Matrix

| Inquiry levels | Questioning | Planning | Implementing | Concluding | Reporting |
|---|---|---|---|---|---|
| 0 | Teacher | Teacher | Teacher | Teacher | Teacher |
| 1 | Teacher | Teacher | Students | Teacher | Students |
| 2 | Teacher | Teacher | Students | Students/ teacher | Students |
| 3 | Teacher | Students/ teacher | Students | Students | Students |
| 4 | Students/ teacher | Students | Students | Students | Students |
| 5 | Students | Students | Students | Students | Students |

### English Language and Literacy

The intervention focused on five aspects of English language development in science instruction with ELL students. First, the intervention focused on various strategies for developing literacy (reading and writing) in English for all students. Science learning and literacy development reinforce each other in a reciprocal process (Casteel & Isom, 1994; Douglas, Klentschy, Worth, & Binder, 2006; Lee & Fradd, 1998), and some of the strategies include:

- Using short stories or narrative vignettes to activate students' prior knowledge on science topics;
- Using comprehension strategies to understand science information in expository texts;
- Using a variety of language functions (e.g., describing, explaining, reporting, drawing, concluding) in the context of science inquiry;
- Having students write an expository paragraph to develop scientific genres of writing;
- Having students create Venn diagrams, concept maps, or graphic organizers using science vocabulary; and
- Incorporating trade books or literature with scientific themes into instruction.

Second, the intervention focused on language support strategies with ELL students, typically identified as ESOL strategies (Fathman & Crowther, 2006). Some of these strategies include:

- Engaging ELL students in hands-on inquiry;
- Using realia (real objects or events);
- Using multiple modes of representation through non-verbal (gestural), oral, graphic, and written communication;
- Guiding students to comprehend and use a small amount of key science vocabulary; and
- Introducing key vocabulary in the beginning of lessons and encouraging students to practice the vocabulary in multiple contexts (e.g., introduce, write, repeat, highlight).

Third, the intervention highlighted discourse strategies focusing on the teacher's role in facilitating ELL students' participation in classroom discourse (Gibbons, 2006). The challenge is how to modify classroom discourse while maintaining the rigor of science content and process. Some of the strategies include:

- Adapting language load for students at varying levels of English proficiency and adjusting the language load required for their participation (e.g., slower rate of speech, clearer enunciation, or longer periods of wait time);
- Using language that matches students' levels of communicative competence in length, complexity, and abstraction (e.g., using synonyms, paraphrasing difficult language, repeating and rephrasing main ideas, or recasting and elaborating on students' responses); and
- Communicating at or slightly above students' level of communicative competence (i.e., comprehensible input).

Fourth, it is important to draw a distinction between home language instruction (i.e., bilingual education) and home language support (Goldenberg, 2008). Even in the absence of bilingual education programs, ELL students' home language can be used as instructional support for their learning of academic content in English. Some of the strategies include:

- Introducing key science vocabulary in students' home language as well as in English;
- Allowing code-switching;
- Highlighting cognates as well as false cognates between English and the home language (for example, Spanish and the other Romance lexicons are often derived from Latin, the primary language of science);
- Encouraging bilingual students to assist less English proficient students in their home language as well as in English; and
- Allowing ELL students to write about science ideas or experiments in their home language.

Finally, since science has traditionally been regarded as "culture-free," incorporation of home culture into science instruction has not been adequately studied (Lee & Fradd, 1998). Teachers need to consider ELL students' cultural experiences in relation to science (for specific examples, see Luykx, Lee, Mahotiere, Lester, Hart, & Deaktor, 2007). Some of the strategies include:

- Highlighting funds of knowledge, the lived experiences of students at home and in the community that can serve as intellectual resources for academic learning (Moll, 1992);
- Using students' cultural artifacts, culturally relevant examples, and community resources in relation to science topics; and
- Exploring culturally based ways students communicate and interact in their home and community (i.e., cultural congruence).

## Multiple Approaches to Science and Literacy Assessments with ELL Students

In our research, we used multiple approaches to science and literacy assessments with ELL students: (1) assessment to support instruction, (2) performance assessment to measure students' scientific reasoning, and (3) paper-and-pencil tests to examine the impact of the intervention on students' science and literacy achievement. For each type of assessment, we incorporated students' home language and culture to establish cultural validity. Assessment approaches in our intervention, along with high-stakes science assessment (to be discussed in the next section), are summarized in Table 11.2.

### Assessment to Support Instruction

Assessment is integral to the instructional process (i.e., assessment "for" learning, as compared to assessment "of" learning). In our intervention, we built in various ways for teachers to monitor the progress of student learning as formative assessments for each lesson, for each unit, and from one grade to the next.

- We linked science learning to ELL students' home languages and cultures. For each lesson in the curriculum, we introduced science vocabulary in students' home languages and continued with assessment of students' prior knowledge in their home and community contexts. This practice is also addressed in Basterra, Chapter 4, this volume.

*Table 11.2* Science and Literacy Assessments with ELL Students

| Purpose | Type of Assessment |
| --- | --- |
| Assessment to support instruction | Assessment as part of class activities<br>End-of-lesson assessment<br>End-of-unit assessment<br>Prior knowledge assessment at fifth grade to measure specific science content and inquiry covered in grades 3 and 4 |
| Performance assessment to measure scientific reasoning | Reasoning interview tasks for measurement (third grade) forms of energy (fourth grade), and seasons (fifth grade) |
| Paper-and-pencil tests to examine the impact of the intervention on students' science and literacy achievement | Science tests for third, fourth, and fifth grades |
| | Writing test for third grade |
| High-stakes science assessment | State science assessment at fifth grade |

- As students engaged in science inquiry and discussion in small groups or the whole class for each lesson, we provided ample opportunities to assess students' knowledge of science concepts and inquiry in oral and written (including various graphic) formats.
- We provided multiple-choice, short-answer, and extended response items at the end of each lesson.
- We provided a comprehensive assessment at the end of each unit, which could be scored on a software program used district-wide.
- At the start of fifth grade, we provided a prior knowledge assessment to measure specific science content and inquiry covered in grades 3 and 4. Teachers used this assessment information as they prepared their fifth-grade students for high-stakes science assessments. Overall, the majority of the items came from public-release items from the National Assessment of Educational Progress (NAEP) and the Third International Mathematics and Science Study (TIMSS).

### Performance Assessment to Measure Scientific Reasoning

We have developed a reasoning interview task for each grade level to measure students' scientific reasoning. In addition to measuring students' reasoning of each science topic, reasoning interviews measure students' ability to apply measurement concepts using scientific tools at third grade, to conduct a scientific experiment on a force and motion task at fourth grade, and to engage in scientific discourse on an earth systems task at fifth grade. The three reasoning tasks represent critical elements of students' ability to engage in science inquiry (National Research Council, 2000). Additionally, these tasks address students' reasoning in the contexts of school activities and home and play connections. This topic is also addressed by Basterra (Chapter 4, this volume).

Reasoning interviews asked students to reflect on ways that they had engaged in tasks in the school and home contexts. For example, reasoning interviews for measurement tasks with third-grade students were composed of four parts, with each part addressing four topical areas covered in the measurement curriculum unit: length, weight, volume, and temperature. The first part asked students to discuss experiences they had had with measurement in the home context. For example, the interview asked questions about length ("Have you ever seen anyone in your family measure how long or how tall something is? What were they measuring? How did they do it? What did they do it with?"), followed by probes ("How tall are you? How do you know?"). The second part asked students to perform measurement tasks using a ruler, kitchen scale, graduated cylinder, measuring cup, and thermometer. The third part asked students to make estimates about each of the four topical areas of measurement. The final part asked students to discuss experiences they had had with measurement in the context of playing with their peers. For example, the interview asked questions, "Can you think of a time playing with your friends that you might need to measure something?" followed by probes, "Have you ever wanted to figure out how far something goes? How heavy something is?" Together, parts one and four were taken to represent the home context and parts two and three to represent the school context.

Based on a set of criteria, students were purposefully selected to provide for equal (or near equal) representation of gender, home language (Spanish and Haitian Creole), and participation in English to Speakers of Other Languages (ESOL) programs. Third- and fourth-grade interviews were conducted with students individually to examine their independent reasoning and inquiry, whereas fifth-grade interviews were conducted with students in pairs to examine their reasoning and discourse with peers. All interviews were conducted in English, since that was the language of classroom instruction. The interviewers used ESOL strategies to help ensure student comprehension of the reasoning tasks. During the fifth-grade task with pairs of students, the students were permitted to discuss the task with each other in their home language, but then must attempt to provide answers to the interviewer in English.

### Paper-and-Pencil Tests to Measure Science and Literacy Achievement

In addition to the performance-based reasoning interviews with a small sample of individual students (described above), we used paper-and-pencil tests in science and literacy with all students participating in the research as summative assessment of the impact of our intervention.

### Science Tests

We developed a pre–post science test for each grade level. The tests measured students' knowledge of key concepts and the "big ideas" of patterns, systems, models, and relationships for the science topics of the curriculum units during the school year. The tests also measured students' understanding of science inquiry by asking them to construct graphs and tables using the data provided, develop procedures for scenarios involving science experiments, offer explanations for the data, and draw conclusions. The tests consisted of project-developed items and public release items from the state science assessment, NAEP, and TIMSS. Item formats included multiple-choice, short-answer, and extended response. Four criteria guided the development of test items and selection of public release items from NAEP and TIMSS: (1) a range of high, medium, and low item difficulty, (2) a range of high, medium, and low cognitive complexity (according to Norman L. Webb on "Depth of Knowledge" adopted by the state), (3) appropriateness of language load and grammar for ELL students and students with limited literacy development, and (4) contexts of the items that would be familiar to students.

The test was administered in English to maintain continuity between the language of instruction and the language of assessment. Teachers followed standard procedures for test accommodations with ELL students and students with limited literacy, as follows. If students have difficulty reading the test, teachers read the test items out loud to the entire class. Teachers who speak the home language of their ELL students translate the items into the students' home language, whereas teachers who do not speak their students' home language solicit help from a colleague or use the translated science terms in Spanish and Haitian Creole provided in the teachers' guide for each curriculum unit. ELL students are allowed to write their answers in either English or in their home language. There is no time limit for completing the test.

For the project-developed items, we designed a scoring rubric to assess the conceptual accuracy of responses, completeness of responses, and use of science terms. For public-release items from the state science assessment, NAEP, and TIMSS, we used the available scoring rubrics. The maximum possible score for each specific item or item sub-components depends on the level of item difficulty or cognitive complexity. We accepted responses in ELL students' home languages. Also, we did not penalize linguistic aspects of student responses, such as spelling or grammar.

## Writing Test

We developed a pre–post expository writing prompt on the water cycle for third-grade students to assess both literacy (writing) and science content knowledge. Teachers followed standard procedures for administration of the writing prompt, as described for the science tests above. Based on a scoring rubric developed in our research, students received two scores on the writing prompt: (1) a score for *form*, based on students' use of conventions, organization, style, and voice; and (2) a score for *content*, based on students' ability to give scientific explanations and to use scientific vocabulary (see the scoring rubric in Appendix 11.1). This distinction between form and content allowed for assessments of science learning and English language proficiency separately (Shaw, 1997).

## Assessment Results

The three assessments (i.e., reasoning interviews, science tests, and writing tests) enabled us to examine the first research question—Can ELL students learn academic subjects, such as science, while also developing English proficiency?

## Performance-Based Reasoning Interviews

Across all three grade levels, student responses during reasoning interviews were analyzed with regard to reasoning complexity and science content knowledge. Additionally, the fourth-grade responses were analyzed with regard to scientific inquiry, and the fifth-grade responses were analyzed with regard to scientific argumentation.

To date, the results of reasoning complexity with third- and fourth-grade students point to several patterns across demographic sub-groups of ESOL level, home language, and gender in the contexts of school activities and home connections. First, across home and school contexts, students were capable of sharing their ideas and giving multiple predictions about science activities (representing lower reasoning abilities) but had difficulty offering justifications of their speculations or explanations about underlying scientific principles or mechanisms (representing higher reasoning abilities).

Second, across all demographic groups, reasoning about measurement in the home context was consistently more developed than reasoning in the school context. This result points out the importance of acknowledging the "funds of knowledge" that ELL students from low SES backgrounds brought about science topics from their home and play experiences into the school setting (Gonzalez & Moll, 2002; Moll, 1992). It also points out that students may not automatically transfer knowledge from out-of-school contexts to the school context (cf., Nunes, 1992; Saxe, 1988). In the following two examples, students demonstrated elaborate reasoning complexity about measurement in their home contexts:

> My mom she has to measure it [medicine] by looking at the label because it tells you how much if you weigh this much or that much. And so she puts it in the little cup and it has lines … one tablespoon, two tablespoon. And so I have to take one tablespoon so she pours it and gives it to me.
>
> (ESOL 5, Haitian Creole speaker)

> We were trying to get some people to do some work in our backyard. My dad measures. He puts like rails down and he measures the rails from end to end. And he uses a ruler 'cause the rails are split into squares. He measures the squares and then he adds them up.
>
> (ESOL 5, Spanish speaker)

Finally, in contrast to the modest differences across home language and gender, there were more pronounced differences across ESOL levels. The overall pattern of order from the highest to the lowest performance was as follows: (1) ESOL level 5 (i.e., those exited from ESOL programs within the past two years), (2) ESOL levels 3 and 4 (i.e., those at intermediary levels in ESOL programs), (3) ESOL exited (i.e., those exited from ESOL programs more than two years ago) and native speakers of English, and (4) ESOL levels 1 and 2 (i.e., those at entry levels in ESOL programs). It is notable that students at ESOL levels 3, 4, and 5 performed better than ESOL exited and native speakers of English. Our initial hypothesis for this result is that our intervention supports ELLs' reasoning development, which might not be readily available in regular classrooms.

### Paper-and-Pencil Science Tests

We examined achievement gains of grades 3 through 5 students and achievement gaps by English proficiency each year over the five-year implementation of the intervention (Lee & Penfield, 2010). Students' science achievement was measured using one project-developed science test at each grade level. Across the three grade levels, students demonstrated significant achievement gains on the project-developed science tests. ELL students made gains comparable to non-ELL students.

## Writing Test

We examined third-grade ELL students' writing achievement that included "form" (i.e., conventions, organization, and style/voice) and "content" (i.e., specific knowledge and understanding of science) in expository science writing (Lee, Mahotiere, Salinas, Penfield, & Maerten-Rivera, 2009). Writing samples were collected from three different groups of students over three separate years. Students displayed a statistically significant increase each year, and the gains were incrementally larger over the three-year period. Students at ESOL levels 1 to 4 made gains comparable to those who had exited from ESOL or never been in ESOL. These results indicate that students overall made noticeable improvements, as shown in the example below (prompt is shown in Appendix 11.1). It is noted that each writing sample was scored from 0 to 4 points for form and content respectively.

> *Pre-instruction writing:* First, you start being a solid with is [sic] and Ice, then you turn into a drop of water witch [sic] is a liquid and last you turn into gas witch [sic] is air and that's the water cycle (form, 1 point; content, 1 point).

> *Post-instruction writing:* If I were a drop of water, I would change my way of living. I would change from a gas to a liquid, a liquid to a gas also liquid to solid and solid to liquid. I would travel to many places when it rains. I would fall in a podle [sic] of water when it rains, the sun would evaporate me into the clouds, I would condense in the cloulds [sic] and then I would precipitate, I would fall back to where I started, and I would get ready to start again in the water cycle. While I go through the water cycle, I change to three stages, they are, liquid, solid and gas. While I travel through the different stages, I become water for liquid, air for gas and an ice cube for solid. In the water cycle I would evaporate into gas to go up in the air, then, I would condense in little drops in the clouds and then when the drops are in the clouds they get big and fat and when the clouds can't hold they rain drops they are ready to precipitate and fall. That's how the water cycle is created (form, 4 points; content, 3 points).

## High-Stakes Science Assessments with ELL Students

The state assessments are administered in reading, writing, mathematics, and science. Reading and mathematics are assessed in grades 3–10; and writing and science are assessed once each at the elementary, middle, and senior high levels. Science assessments began factoring into school accountability in 2006. Science tests measured student proficiency in the physical and chemical sciences, the earth sciences, the life and environmental sciences, and scientific thinking. Science tests required students to reason, plan, analyze, and use scientific thinking. Science tests included multiple-choice, short response, and extended response items.

Our research enabled us to examine the second research question—Can ELL students, who learn to think and reason scientifically, also perform well on high stakes assessments? We examined achievement gains of grade 5 students and achievement gaps by English proficiency each year over the three-year implementation of the intervention (Lee & Penfield, 2010). Students' science achievement was measured using state science tests at fifth grade that counted toward school accountability. When the fifth-grade students in the treatment group were compared to those in the comparison group, students in the treatment schools demonstrated significantly higher scores on the state science tests.

## What Teachers Can Do

An important aspect of classroom assessment includes the use of meaningful and relevant topics, tasks, and activities. Teachers can employ assessment practices for ELL students that may serve to benefit all students in a classroom. Next, we review some of the most important strategies that have been discussed in the chapter.

### Become More Knowledgeable About Students' Languages and Cultures

If teachers are aware of linguistic and cultural influences on ELL students' responses, they can support the assessment process in more culturally valid ways. Whereas efforts have traditionally focused on eliminating these influences, an emerging approach advocates understanding how home language and culture can be incorporated to guide the entire assessment process (Solano-Flores & Trumbull, 2003). In our intervention, we focused on ELL students' home languages and cultural experiences in teaching reform-based science. We also emphasized challenges facing ELL students with state science assessment. Teachers should think about various ways to consider ELL students' home languages and cultures to enhance cultural validity in science assessment.

### Use Separate Scoring Criteria

Consider using two separate sets of scoring criteria for writing prompts (see Appendix 11.1) or for short- and extended-response science tasks. One set of criteria is used to assess English language proficiency, and the other is used to assess science knowledge. This assessment practice can enable teachers to identify strengths and weaknesses of ELL students in each area. It may help teachers understand the learning needs of non-ELL students better as well. It is all-too-easy to score a well-written answer higher than a poorly written one. However, if a student's science knowledge is accurate and complete, the student should not be scored down on a science assessment for poor spelling or grammar. This scoring method can help teachers clarify whether an ELL student's learning difficulty is due to language learning or science learning.

## Assess in Both Languages

If at all possible, teachers can create opportunities to assess ELL students in their home languages as well as in English. Allowing students to communicate their science knowledge and abilities in their home languages—in oral or written form—may tap into knowledge and skills unavailable or underdeveloped in English. In addition, it can contribute to both general literacy and academic learning which, in turn, can promote English language proficiency. Achievement in these three areas develops simultaneously (Lee & Fradd, 1998).

## Use Multiple Modalities

We encourage teachers to promote the use of multiple representational formats in assessments, keeping in mind that the goal is to move ELL students toward established literacy standards. Students who cannot write in either their home language or English can express ideas in drawings, graphs, and tables, as well as in oral communication. When students realize that they are expected to produce meaningful representations of their knowledge in assessment settings, they engage in science learning activities and tasks in more meaningful ways. Through frequent formative assessments in addition to regular summative assessments, teachers can gauge student progress in academic content and language learning simultaneously.

Hands-on science activities, which depend less on language than many other kinds of classroom activities, can be valuable sources of information about student learning. Observation of how a student goes about carrying out such an activity, alone or in concert with others, can complement other more formal assessment methods without necessarily depending on oral or written communication by the student.

## Seek Professional Development Opportunities

Teachers can build their knowledge by collaborating with other professionals, taking workshops or courses, and participating in research projects (like ours) that bring teachers and researchers together (see Trumbull & Koelsch, Chapter 9, and Trumbull & Solano-Flores, Chapter 10, this volume). In our intervention, we shared the results of multiple measures of science and literacy achievement with participating teachers and school administrators. A primary purpose of sharing the results was to enhance teachers' knowledge, beliefs, and practices in promoting students' scientific reasoning, mastery of science content standards, and performance on high-stakes science assessment, along with English language proficiency. Beyond impacting classroom practices, we shared the achievement results to change school practices in terms of fostering administrator leadership, enhancing science programs at the school, and supporting school improvement plans for the state and NCLB requirements. As ELL students can now be found in virtually every school in the nation, it is incumbent on teachers to understand the learning needs of ELL students; to provide support for academic learning and English language development simultaneously; and to design and implement appropriate and culturally valid assessments.

# Conclusion

Since instruction and assessment complement and reinforce each other, it is essential to provide high quality instruction for ELL students and to assess their achievement outcomes in a manner that can guide subsequent instruction. Likewise, assessment "for" learning and assessment "of" learning, while serving different purposes, provide insights to improve both instruction and learning through a feedback loop.

In this chapter, we described our research and development on science intervention for instruction and assessment with ELL students in a large urban school district. Our intervention through curriculum units and teacher workshops was aimed at promoting science learning while also supporting English language development of ELL students. The results indicate that (1) ELL students can learn science while developing English proficiency, and that (2) ELL students can engage in science inquiry and reasoning while performing well on high-stakes assessments. These results contribute to the emerging literature in this field that can offer insights for science assessment of ELL students, which, in turn, can be used to further enhance science instruction for all students.

In our research, we addressed students' home languages and cultures using multiple measures of science and literacy assessments. Assessments of ELL students present both promises and challenges for science learning and English language development. The results of the performance assessments to measure students' scientific reasoning reveal ELL students' science abilities. Across all demographic groups, reasoning about measurement in the home context was consistently more developed than reasoning in the school context. In addition, ELL students at the intermediary levels (ESOL levels 3 and 4) and the advanced level (ESOL level 5) of English proficiency performed better than non-ELL students.

In spite of these promising findings, the challenges of assessing ELL students' science knowledge and abilities continue to be a critical issue. Their knowledge may not be measured accurately if assessment is not valid with regard to the students' home languages and cultures. Such problems arise when assessment is conducted in the language (i.e., English) that students are still acquiring (Solano-Flores & Trumbull, 2003), when the English-only policy does not allow the use of students' home languages (Wiley & Wright, 2004), and when accommodations are limited due to large-scale assessments that employ standardized procedures without consideration of cultural experiences of diverse student groups (Abedi, Hofstetter, & Lord, 2004). The results of such assessments underestimate ELL students' science knowledge and abilities, which, in turn, underestimate the effectiveness of educational interventions.

As science becomes a part of accountability measures in many states and is required for formative reporting purposes according to NCLB, cultural validity will become a more serious concern. Unfortunately, research on science assessments with ELL students is insufficient to guide large-scale or high-stakes assessments (Abedi et al., 2004). As a result, those students who have traditionally been underserved in the science classroom might be at an even greater risk by the impending accountability policy in science.

## Appendix 11.1

---

**Writing Prompt: The Water Cycle**

Pretend you are a drop of water. Before you begin writing, think about how water changes form in the water cycle. Explain to the reader how you are changed as you go through the water cycle.

---

## Writing Scoring Rubric for *Form*

The writing scoring rubric for *form* considers the following components.

Convention
- Spelling.
- Correct plurals and comparisons.
- Capitalization and punctuation.
- Subject/verb agreement and verb and noun forms.

Organization
- Indentation for new paragraphs.
- Idea development.

Style/Voice
- Sentence structures to communicate ideas.
- Coherence from sentence to sentence.

4: Complete/Comprehensive
- Spells all high frequency and most irregular words correctly with up to three errors.
- Uses correct plurals and comparisons (e.g., good, better, best).
- No errors in capitalization and punctuation.
- Subject/verb agreement and verb and noun forms are generally correct with up to two errors.
- Uses accurate indentation for each new paragraph.
- Ideas are presented logically.
- Uses a variety of sentence structures to communicate ideas.
- Writing is highly coherent.

3: Adequate
- Spells most high frequency (up to three errors) and many irregular words (with up to five errors) correctly.
- Generally uses correct plurals and comparisons (e.g., good, better, best) (with up to one error).
- Few errors (up to three) in capitalization and punctuation.
- Occasional errors in subject/verb agreement, which do not impede communication (with up to three errors).

- Generally uses accurate indentation for the majority of each new paragraph.
- Ideas are developed fairly logically.
- Uses a variety of sentence structures to communicate ideas, although most (more than half of all sentences) are simple constructions.
- Writing is fairly coherent.

2: Emerging/Expanding
- Some errors in spelling (up to eight errors).
- Some errors in plurals and comparisons (e.g., good, better, best) (up to three errors).
- Some errors in capitalization and punctuation (up to five).
- Errors in subject/verb agreement may somewhat impede communication.
- Writing may not be organized into paragraphs.
- Ideas are partially developed.
- Sentence structures are limited to simple constructions with little attempt at variety.
- Writing is partially coherent.

1: Minimal/Inaccurate
- Frequent errors in spelling (nine or more errors).
- Frequent errors in plurals and comparisons (e.g., good, better, best) (four or more errors).
- Frequent errors in capitalization and punctuation (more than five errors).
- Lacks subject/verb agreement; verb and noun forms are incorrect and impeded communication.
- No attempt to organize writing into paragraphs.
- Ideas are not developed.
- Sentence structure is fragmented/incomplete; lack of proper sentence structure may impede communication.
- Writing lacks coherence.

0: No response/Unscorable
- The response is simply a rewording of the prompt.
- The response is simply a copy of published work.
- The student refused to write.
- The response is illegible.
- The response contains an insufficient amount of writing to determine if the student was addressing the prompt.

## Writing Scoring Rubric for Science Content

### Elements of Writing

Since the prompts require expository writing, the scoring rubric considers science vocabulary and explanation. Use of science vocabulary and a comprehensive explanation include the following components:

- Scientific vocabulary.
- Three states of water (solid, liquid, gas, ice water, water vapor).
- Three processes of change during the water cycle (evaporation, condensation, and precipitation).
- Heating and cooling related to the water cycle.
- Concept of a cycle (continuous, ongoing, repetitive).
- Sequence of events.

## Ratings

4: Complete/Comprehensive
- Accurate use of science vocabulary with adequate explanations.
- Correctly names all three states of water as related to the water cycle.
- Accurately describes all three processes of change during the water cycle.
- Mentions process of both heating and cooling.
- Mentions concept of a cycle and the ongoing, repetitive nature of the process.
- Does not demonstrate sequencing errors.

3: Adequate
- Accurate use of science vocabulary with adequate explanations.
- Correctly names all three states of water as related to the water cycle.
- Accurately describes all three processes of change during the water cycle.
- May mention process of heating or cooling but does not include both elements.
- Mentions the concept of a cycle.
- Does not demonstrate sequencing errors.

2: Emerging/Expanding
- Expanding accurate use of scientific vocabulary with some explanation.
- Correctly names two of three states of water as related to the water cycle.
- Accurately describes two of three processes of change during the water cycle.
- Does not mention process of heating or cooling.
- Does not mention the concept of a cycle.
- May demonstrate sequencing errors.

1: Minimal
- Inaccurate use of scientific vocabulary or minimal accurate use of scientific vocabulary without explanation.
- Accurately names only one of three states of water as related to the water cycle.
- Accurately describes one of three processes of change during the water cycle.
- Does not mention process of heating or cooling.
- Does not mention the concept of a cycle.
- Inaccurate description of sequence of events.

0: No response, unidentifiable, and/or irrelevant content.

# Note

This work is supported by the National Science Foundation (NSF Grant #ESI–0353331). Any opinions, findings, conclusions, or recommendations expressed in this publication are those of the authors and do not necessarily reflect the position, policy, or endorsement of the funding agencies.

# References

Abedi, J., Hofstetter, C.H., & Lord, C. (2004). Assessment accommodations for English language learners: Implications for policy-based empirical research. *Review of Educational Research*, 74(1), 1–28.

Agar, M. (1996). *Language shock: Understanding the culture of conversation.* New York, NY: William Morrow.

Amaral, O.M., Garrison, L., & Klentschy, M. (2002). Helping English learners increase achievement through inquiry-based science instruction. *Bilingual Research Journal*, 26, 213–239.

Casteel, C.P., & Isom, B.A. (1994). Reciprocal processes in science and literacy learning. *The Reading Teacher*, 47, 538–545.

Douglas, R., Klentschy, M.P., Worth, K., & Binder, W. (Eds.) (2006). *Linking science and literacy in the K-8 classroom.* Arlington, VA: National Science Teachers Association.

Fathman, A.K., & Crowther, D.T. (Eds.) (2006). *Science for English language learners: K-12 classroom strategies.* Arlington, VA: National Science Teachers Association.

Florida Department of Education (1996). *Florida curriculum frameworks in science.* Tallahassee, FL: Department of State.

Florida Department of Education (2002). *Science grade 5 test item and performance task specifications.* Tallahassee, FL: Department of State.

Gibbons, P. (2006). *Bridging discourses in the ESL classroom.* New York, NY: Continuum.

Goldenberg, C. (2008). Teaching English language learners: What the research does—and does not—say. *American Educator*, 8(23), 42–4.

Gonzalez, N., & Moll, L. (2002). Cruzando el puente: Building bridges to funds of knowledge. *Educational Policy*, 16(4), 623–641.

Lee, O. (2005). Science education and English language learners: Synthesis and research agenda. *Review of Educational Research*, 75(4), 491–530.

Lee, O., & Fradd, S.H. (1998). Science for all, including students from non-English language backgrounds. *Educational Researcher*, 27(3), 12–21.

Lee, O., Maerten-Rivera, J., Penfield, R., LeRoy, K., & Secada, W.G. (2008). Science achievement of English language learners in urban elementary schools: Results of a first-year professional development intervention. *Journal of Research in Science Teaching*, 45(1), 31–52.

Lee, O., Mahotiere, M., Salinas, A., Penfield, R.D., & Maerten-Rivera, J. (2009). Science writing achievement among English language learners: Results of three-year intervention in urban elementary schools. *Bilingual Research Journal*, 32(2), 153–167.

Lee, O., & Penfield, R.D. (2010). *Science achievement of English language learners in urban elementary schools: Multi-year intervention across multiple grades.* Manuscript submitted for publication.

Luykx, A., Lee, O., Mahotiere, M., Lester, B., Hart, J., & Deaktor, R. (2007). Cultural and home language influence in elementary students' constructed responses on science assessments. *Teachers College Record*, 109(4), 897–926.

Moll, L.C. (1992). Bilingual classroom studies and community analysis: Some recent trends. *Educational Researcher*, 21(2), 20–24.

National Research Council (1996). *National science education standards.* Washington, DC: National Academy Press.

National Research Council (2000). *Inquiry and the national science education standards: A guide for teaching and learning.* Washington, DC: National Academy Press.

No Child Left Behind Act of 2001. Public Law No. 107–110, 115 Stat. 1425 (2002).

Nunes, T. (1992). Ethnomathematics and everyday cognition. In D. Grouws (Ed.), *Handbook of research on mathematics teaching and learning* (pp. 557–574). New York, NY: Macmillan.

Rosebery, A.S., Warren, B., & Conant, F.R. (1992). Appropriating scientific discourse: Findings from language minority classrooms. *Journal of the Learning Sciences, 21,* 61–94.

Saxe, G.B. (1988). Candy selling and math learning. *Educational Researcher, 17*(6), 14–21.

Shaw, J.M. (1997). Threats to the validity of science performance assessments for English language learners. *Journal of Research in Science Teaching, 34*(7), 721–743.

Solano-Flores, G., & Nelson-Barber, S. (2001). On the cultural validity of science assessments. *Journal of Research in Science Teaching, 38*(5), 553–573.

Solano-Flores, G., & Trumbull, E. (2003). Examining language in context: The need for new research and practice paradigms in the testing of English-language learners. *Educational Researcher, 32*(2), 3–13.

Wiley, T.G., & Wright, W.E. (2004). Against the undertow: Language-minority education policy and politics in the "age of accountability." *Educational Policy, 18*(1), 142–168.

# Part IV

# Conclusion

# Chapter 12

# Reflections on the Promise of Cultural Validity in Assessment

*Elise Trumbull, María del Rosario Basterra, and Guillermo Solano-Flores*

---

**Chapter Overview**

In this short chapter, we reflect on what has been presented in the book. For those readers who start at the back of a book, let us say that this chapter will not offer you a perfect backwards map to the book but will orient you to some of its important themes.

---

## The Goal of Cultural Validity in Assessment

The goal of cultural validity in assessment arises from the desire for (1) better information about how well our schools are doing in educating students (accountability); (2) information about student progress that can inform teachers and students (instructional planning); and (3) policies and practices that are fair and do not wrongly foreclose opportunities for students (equity). As Solano-Flores (Chapter 1, this volume) says, accounting for how sociocultural influences affect the way students learn and make sense of the world (and assessments are part of our world!) is not a simple task—perhaps a task never fully achieved—yet we do have theory and research from several domains to guide us in the effort.

Many, if not most, researchers and psychometricians working on improving the assessment of diversity of populations believe that the performance gap between culturally and ethnically "mainstream" students who speak English as a home language and other students is due at least in part to the failure to achieve cultural validity. Abedi (Chapter 3, this volume) notes that despite a rigorous process intended to avoid bias, standardized assessments are still less sound for ELLs—implicating linguistic and cultural differences. Of course, opportunity to learn is also an important source of performance differences; it, in turn, is associated with other factors, particularly socioeconomic status (SES). Lower SES families are disproportionately from racial, ethnic, and linguistic "non-mainstream" backgrounds; and their children often attend the schools least able to provide rich opportunities to learn. That is not a deterministic reality, however. As Lee, Santau, and Maerten-Rivera (Chapter 11, this volume) show, when strong instruction appropriate for the specific population of students is combined with well-designed assessment, the gap between ELLs and non-ELLs can disappear.

## Some Approaches to Improving Assessment for ELLs

Assessment experts have tried from many vantage points to improve the validity of assessments for ELLs. Translating existing assessments into other languages has long been thought to be one solution, but translation is fraught with problems; and assessment translations have often been highly flawed linguistically. In addition, decisions about the language in which a given ELL student should be assessed are not straightforward although there are some accepted guidelines. Determining a student's relative proficiency in his or her various languages is not so easy as imagined. Language proficiency tests often lack an academic language component; are tremendously context-bound; and are not comparable because they assess different aspects of language (and so they yield different measures of language proficiency). Also, for some languages, there are either no tests or no adults available to administer them.

The role of language looms large in all types of assessment (Trumbull & Solano-Flores, Chapter 2, this volume). Recent research has investigated the impact of linguistic modification to reduce language demands (Kiplinger, Haug, & Abedi, 2000), a range of other testing accommodations (Kopriva, 2008), and the application of new theoretical paradigms and statistical procedures (Solano-Flores & Trumbull, 2003). At the same time, public policy (especially the No Child Left Behind Act) has forced states and districts to include virtually all students in large-scale testing and hold systems accountable for serving all students. Despite many unwanted outcomes, the law can be credited with bringing attention to (while not necessarily effectively addressing) inequities in the assessment of ELLs, promoting interest in formative assessment (Lara & Chia, Chapter 8, this volume), and, in many ways, spurring attention to cultural validity in assessment.

## Recognizing and Addressing the Real Complexity of Student Populations

This book is not only about "English language learners" in the usual sense of the term. A teacher who takes into account all that has been said about language in the book will quickly realize that variations in students' experiences associated with socioeconomic class, ethnicity, race, geographic origin, and other aspects of human identity are often associated with differences in language, particularly the ways language is *used*. There are many students who have been exposed to another language and whose variety of English is colored by that language. Prominent among these are American Indian students, many of whom do not speak their heritage languages but whose English is nevertheless influenced by them (McCarty, 2009). Statistics on ELLs do not take into account the numbers of other students whose home dialects of English differ substantially from the "preferred" dialect of English (White, middle-class) valued in schools.

The ELL population itself is highly diverse and, for test developers and teachers alike, a recognition of the complexity of that population is a requirement for even beginning to approach the goal of cultural validity. How long have students been in the United States? What is their oral proficiency in a home language? What is their literacy proficiency in a home language? Are they familiar with test question formats? Do they know how to "bubble in" on multiple-choice questions? Do they know strategies for eliminating options in multiple-choice items (the preferred test format in assessment systems)? Is it reasonable to expect them to know fine shades of meaning in text passage vocabulary?

## Achieving Cultural Validity: Drawing from Many Disciplines

A multidisciplinary perspective must be brought to the ongoing creation of assessment theory and research, as well as to the whole enterprise of assessment development—at both large-scale and classroom levels. Educators naturally look to developmental psychology, cognitive psychology, and educational psychology to understand how students learn. But those domains concerned more directly with language and culture are also essential: linguistics (including sociolinguistics), cross-cultural psychology, and anthropology. To interrogate the cultural validity of a given assessment, one may ask whether what is known from these various disciplines has been considered in the development of that assessment.

## Assessment as a Cultural Enterprise

Any assessment is and will always be a cultural tool, one that reflects the perspectives, assumptions, goals, and values of those who create it.[1] The whole notion of assessment—what forms it may take and when and how it should occur—is cultural. For instance, in some cultural settings students may help each other on a final science exam as long as they do not actually write each other's answers (Rothstein-Fisch, Trumbull, Isaac, Daley, & Pérez, 2003). There is no single way of knowing or expressing a concept. As the primary vehicle for socializing children, teaching, learning, and assessment, language is a cultural creation.

As Basterra (Chapter 4, this volume) and others (e.g., Heath, 1983; Labov, 1972; Swisher & Deyhle, 1992) have observed, the way a student responds to a teacher's question or a test item will always reflect that student's own culture-based experience in some way. Students connect with assessment questions and problems in multiple ways—none necessarily more legitimate than another, yet judged more or less so based on standards (that are also cultural artifacts). Ideas of whether it is appropriate to exhibit one's knowledge or judge one's own work have a cultural foundation (cf., Trumbull, Greenfield, Rothstein-Fisch, & Quiroz, 2007). What counts as knowledge or knowing, ways of learning, ways of displaying one's knowledge, methods of teaching, and means of evaluating students' learning, are all culturally situated (Hollins, 1996; Nucci, Saxe, & Turiel, 2000; Rogoff & Chavajay, 1995). Likewise, ways of communicating and interacting in the classroom have a cultural foundation.

There is no easy way to account for how students will encounter an assessment depending on their cultural orientation. But awareness of some of the cultural demands entailed in various types of assessment will allow teachers to anticipate how students may respond, remind them to "mix it up" by using a range of assessments, and prompt them to identify ways they may support students to engage in assessments that are not perfectly matched to their comfort level (as Kopriva & Sexton, Chapter 5, this volume, suggest).

## Examining Language in Assessment from Multiple Perspectives

The role of language—itself a cultural phenomenon—in assessment must be appreciated in deeper and more complex ways, both in terms of its role in teaching, learning, and assessment, and in terms of the ways in which it can be characterized or analyzed. The vast majority of assessment is conducted through the medium of language, yet few teachers or professional assessment developers have a background in language development, sociolinguistics, psycholinguistics, or anthropological linguistics.

We tease language apart from culture at times in order to examine it and talk about it, but it does not function independently of culture. There is great cultural variation not only in language form but also in the ways it is used (the sociolinguistic aspect), with implications for both social and academic functions of language.

Language can be thought of as a set of cultural practices—a repertoire of expected ways of interacting with others through language in a variety of social contexts. This has implications for how a student interacts in the classroom and approaches different kinds of assessments, as Trumbull and Solano-Flores (Chapter 2 and Chapter 10, this volume) discuss. At times, shifting to this perspective will be more helpful to teachers than evaluating a student's knowledge of vocabulary or syntax.

Privileging only certain ways of using language in the classroom often forecloses use of linguistic resources students have developed elsewhere. For instance, the use of home languages or dialects and code-switching (moving back and forth between home language and school language) is sometimes forbidden by teachers. But these resources can certainly be used among students engaged in joint problem-solving during activities that teachers may use as opportunities for informal assessment (Halai, 2009). When all flexibility in language use is removed, assessment can become a restrictive activity that yields far less information about student learning than it might.

## Language, Culture and Cognition: Intertwined in Assessment

Although language can be examined in some ways apart from culture, it is truly a part of culture. Cognition can be investigated and characterized apart from culture; but it develops in a cultural context that shapes it (Greenfield, 2009). To interpret people's ways of thinking without reference to the cultural contexts in which they have developed is to miss a fundamental component of their mental processes (as Basterra, Chapter 4, this volume, illustrates in multiple ways). Culture should not be thought of as something to "control for" in assessment but, rather, as an intrinsic part of assessment—from its conceptualization and design to the interpretation of student performance.

Failure to recognize the interrelationships among language, culture, and cognition can lead to inappropriate diagnoses of "non-mainstream culture" students as learning disabled or mentally retarded. As Hoover and Klingner (Chapter 7, this volume) discuss, African-American students have long been disproportionately represented in classes for the mentally retarded (or "developmentally delayed"). Dialect differences, different patterns of interacting via language, and differences in language use (e.g., ways of recounting events, telling a story) can readily be mistaken for learning problems by an ill-informed teacher (Heath, 1983). And low performance on tests not culturally valid for the population with which they are being used is, of course, not grounds for being judged mentally retarded.

ELLs may exhibit behaviors that originate in different cultural patterns (e.g., remaining quiet to show respect), or are based on their stage of English language development (e.g., remaining quiet for fear of making mistakes). They may respond to criticism or praise in unexpected ways (Basterra, Chapter 4, this volume; Rothstein-Fisch & Trumbull, 2008). Teachers are cautioned to withhold judgment about such behaviors until they have investigated their possible linguistic and cultural sources.

## Knowing Who Our Students Are and What They Need: Considerations When Assessing ELLs for Special Education

Developing a culturally valid assessment depends upon knowing the populations to be served by the assessment. Knowledge of students' home language proficiency is essential to understanding what resources they bring to the learning process and to making decisions about what students need instructionally. But determining a student's proficiency in English or another language is not so straightforward as some may believe. As mentioned earlier, assessments of English vary in the language constructs they measure; and many do not address academic language, something important to gauging a student's ability to participate in instruction in English. A full assessment of language proficiency in any language includes observations of the student in a range of situations, a parent interview, and assessment of both oral and written language (Langdon, 1992). Language specialists capable of performing such an assessment (in English or the home language) may be in short supply, and much is likely to fall to the judgment of the teacher—whether or not he or she has adequate training.

Use of scores on an achievement tests can contribute to labeling a student as having a learning problem when, in fact, the assessment itself was not culturally valid. The history of testing of ELLs is one in which inappropriate assessments have been used to yield specious results that lead to inappropriate decisions. Determining whether an ELL has a learning disability is difficult and complicated by the interplay of many factors, as Hoover and Klingner (Chapter 7, this volume) explain. Schools risk not only over-identifying ELLs as learning disabled but also failing to identify the students who truly need intervention. In any population, 15–20% of students will benefit from instructional modification; and 1–5% will need very specialized help (Hoover & Klingner, Chapter 7, this volume). Teachers who have an awareness of the issues and response strategies discussed in the book will, at the very least, be alert to the potential for misdiagnosis of ELLs and other "non-mainstream culture" students, and be able to ensure that all possible information about a student is brought to bear on important decisions about such students. Hoover and Klingner (Chapter 7, this volume) offer a list of 12 considerations that can be applied to avoid biased decision-making about diverse students (see Table 7.4).

## Attending to Language and Culture at All Stages of Assessment

Assessment developers—be they large testing companies or teachers—need to plan for diversity, as Kopriva and Sexton (Chapter 5, this volume) indicate. Inclusion is good, but it needs to happen at the outset of the assessment development process and continue throughout that process. Assessment design depends upon knowledge of the student population with which an assessment will be used. In large-scale assessment, this means including representative numbers of relevant populations in the initial phases of item development, during item try-out, and in the process of reviewing the resulting assessment for linguistic load and cultural bias as Solano-Flores, Chapter 1, this volume, notes). It also means bringing linguistic and cultural knowledge to bear in the process of administering assessments, scoring, as well as interpreting scores and making decisions on the basis of those scores (Durán, Chapter 6, this volume).

## Collaboration Within and Across Role Groups

Whether as designers of classroom assessment or participants in assessment research projects, teachers play a key role in promoting cultural validity in assessment. Because they know their students and are in a position to learn more about them, teachers can contribute invaluable information about students and the community to an assessment development project affecting a school or district. Collaborations with researchers can be rich professional development opportunities and result in assessments that are more culturally valid (see Trumbull & Koelsch, Chapter 9; Trumbull & Solano-Flores, Chapter 10, this volume).

Collaborations between general education teachers and language specialists can also be very fruitful: Teachers learn about language issues and how to address them, and language specialists learn about the real-world of the classroom and are then in a better position to help ELLs and their teachers (Arkoudis, 2006).

## Using Large-Scale Assessment Results Judiciously

Teachers can benefit from understanding how psychometricians develop tests, how scores are derived, how to interpret scores, and ways of using standardized assessment information. As Durán (Chapter 6, this volume) observes, scores from large-scale assessments have important but constrained value for teachers. They can provide some information about how students are doing vis-à-vis cultural and linguistic peers in similar districts; they can offer one perspective on what students may need more support to learn. But, Abedi (Chapter 3, this volume) cautions, scores obtained by ELLs are less reliable indicators of their learning than scores obtained by non-ELLs, and they must always be regarded in light of other information on student learning collected through other means. The issue is further complicated when different cohorts of ELLs are compared on year-to-year large-scale assessments. A "growth model" approach (Lara & Chia, Chapter 8, this volume) has been proposed so that the progress of individual students—not groups—can be tracked over time.

Large-scale assessments present problems because they cannot be responsive to context (student characteristics as well as the taught curriculum) in the way that classroom assessments can be. ELLs and those still learning the language and ways of school may not interpret the stripped-down language of the *test register* accurately. Teachers and others need to refer to background knowledge about students to put large-scale and other standardized assessment information in appropriate context. Another issue in large-scale assessments, as well as other assessments, is the qualifications of scorers for constructed response items. Scorers need to have enough familiarity with students' home languages to make sense of unconventional spelling patterns (that make sense from the point of view of the phonology of the home language).

Adaptations and accommodations are actions taken after an assessment has been developed to make it more appropriate for particular students. However, the best hope for cultural validity is to consider the diversity of the population to be assessed at the very beginning of the development process—whether for large-scale or classroom assessment. Lara and Chia, Chapter 8 this volume, remind us of this in the context of statewide assessment; as do Basterra (Chapter 4, this volume) and Kopriva and Sexton (Chapter 5, this volume) in the context of classroom assessment. The first test of the cultural validity of any assessment development effort is the answer to the question: "To what extent does the process of test development take into consideration the ways in which students from different cultural backgrounds interpret items?"

Solano-Flores (Chapter 1, this volume) offers criteria for cultural validity in the development and use of large-scale assessments. He suggests that certain questions be posed to examine the degree to which cultural validity has been addressed for a given assessment. These questions concern the adequacy of population selection for trying out the test during the development process, the degree to which an item makes sense to students from all backgrounds (the "item view"), and the review process that vets assessment items before test implementation.

## Using Multiple Measures to Address Multiple Purposes and Student Diversity

It is a maxim that a good assessment program uses multiple measures—different kinds of assessments capable of revealing different aspects of and perspectives on student learning. Assessments can serve a range of purposes. Choice of assessment should be based on the purpose of assessing, the nature of the content to be assessed, the kind of cognitive activity of interest, and the nature of the students to be assessed. Depending upon their background and language proficiency, students may be able to demonstrate their knowledge and skills better through one assessment method than another. Strategies borrowed from English as a second language instruction can be used to make assessments of any stripe more accessible to ELLs.

Lee, Santau, and Maerten-Rivera (Chapter 11, this volume) show the power of linking strong instruction that uses techniques appropriate for ELLs with assessments of different types for different purposes: (1) assessment to support instruction, (2) performance assessment to measure students' scientific reasoning, and (3) paper-and-pencil tests to examine the impact of the intervention on students' science and literacy achievement. In their research, they used knowledge of students' linguistic and cultural backgrounds to address cultural validity in these assessments.

## Assessment *for* Learning and *of* Learning

For most teachers, the overriding goal of assessment is to gain information about student learning in order to plan future instruction (assessment of learning) and, often, to give students feedback. Planning assessment entails specifying what one wants to assess at what level of cognitive demand and selecting methods to match, while considering the cultural and linguistic profiles of students. Good classroom assessment begins with good instructional planning—identifying the big constructs that may be addressed by one or more instructional units. Kopriva and Sexton (Chapter 5, this volume) and Durán (Chapter 6, this volume) have both mentioned "learning progressions" (Heritage, 2008), a concept that has gained increasing currency in the past several years, as educators recognize that standards and curriculum units may not provide enough coherence to guide instruction. A learning progression is a sequence of skills, knowledge, and understanding that one might expect to see develop in a student over time (Heritage, 2008; National Research Council, 2001). To plan instruction and assessment, a teacher determines what the learning progression might be for a top-level construct. Without this kind of big-picture view, assessment does not have a meaningful focus. A question that remains to be answered is, "Do learning progressions look different depending upon a student's cultural–linguistic background?"

Classroom assessments to evaluate learning can take many forms, from observation of students as they work to formal end-of-unit tests. As Kopriva and Sexton (Chapter 5, this volume) and Trumbull and Koelsch (Chapter 9, this volume) suggest, on such tests the use of instructional tools that students are familiar with can help students make connections between instruction and assessment. Once teachers become more conversant with principles for achieving cultural validity, they are likely to reject packaged assessments "as is" and either modify them or create new ones. A temptation that should be resisted is oversimplifying assessments to accommodate student diversity. Use of techniques from the English as a second language instructional repertoire such as scaffolding and linguistic simplification is recommended, but over-cueing students and dumbing-down questions are to be avoided.

## Engaging Students

Teachers can involve students in gathering data about their own learning. Teacher-guided debriefing of an assessment, either as a group or individuals, can promote students' understanding of their own mental processes (metacognition), their self-evaluation of learning progress, and goal-setting for future learning, with the guidance of the teacher.

Students can also be cultural informants—sharing funds of knowledge from their out-of-school experiences. This can help students connect in- and out-of-school lives but also can help the teacher to understand students' lives. Teachers should consider using flexible assessment tools such as portfolios that can be responsive to student differences. Cognitive interviews can be used after an assessment to investigate how students interpreted questions and why they answered as they did, as several authors in the book suggest. Sample assessment items containing tasks couched in complex language can be used to point out test register or academic register examples; teachers can walk students through these examples, deconstructing and demystifying them (Abedi, Chapter 3, this volume).

These kinds of student-centered activities intended to promote autonomy and reflection need to be taught or fostered in culturally knowledgeable ways. Students from some backgrounds are likely to have been socialized to regard evaluation of student learning as the purview of the teacher, not the student, for example (e.g., Trumbull et al., 2007).

## Ethical Issues in Assessment

All of us involved in striving for cultural validity in assessment have ethical concerns. It is fundamentally unjust to perpetuate educational practices of any kind that do students more harm than good. Abedi (Chapter 3, this volume) raises the question of how students' motivation is affected when they do poorly on test after test. They may be inclined to avoid trying so as to have an excuse for poor performance. Low motivation is, of course, a potential source of measurement error; hence, a vicious circle is created. Besides emotional damage, culturally invalid assessment can lead to loss of opportunities (gifted or advanced placement education, graduation) or misplacement in a program for the learning disabled. These potential outcomes must be weighed against the positive value of accountability through inclusion.

## Conclusion

Cultural validity in assessment is an ideal that can be approached through policies and practices that are based on a deep understanding of the role of language and culture in the teaching and learning processes. Both classroom assessment and large-scale assessment must be planned with diversity in mind, with attention to what has been learned through research in the disciplines concerned with language, culture, and cognition. This sounds like a daunting task, but it is far more approachable now that we have a considerable body of theory and research to support our efforts to reach the goal of cultural validity in assessment.

## Note

1. As Solano-Flores says in Chapter 1, the term "culture" is used as though everyone knows what it is, without defining it. There are two ways of thinking about culture that seem germane and appropriate to the content of this book: (1) as a set of values, beliefs, and practices encompassing the daily life of a group; (2) as the participation of a group of people in a set of common practices. "Worldview," a cultural concept, is the result of participation as part of a cultural group.

## References

Arkoudis, S. (2006). Negotiating the rough ground between ESL and mainstream teachers. *International Journal of Bilingual Education and Bilingualism*, 9(4), 415–434.

Bailey, A.L. (2000/2005). Language analysis of standardized achievement tests: Considerations in the assessment of English Language Learners. In J. Abedi, A. Bailey, F. Butler, M. Castellon-Wellington, S. Leon, & J. Mirocha (Eds.), *The validity of administering large-scale content assessments to English Language Learners: An investigation from three perspectives*. CSE Report 663. Los Angeles, CA: National Center for Research on Evaluation, Standards, and Student Testing Graduate School of Education and Information Studies, University of California.

Greenfield, P.M. (2009). Linking social change and developmental change: Shifting pathways of human development. *Developmental Psychology*, 45(2), 401–418.

Halai, A. (2009). Politics and practice of learning mathematics in multilingual classrooms: Lessons from Pakistan. In R. Barwell (Ed.), *Multilingualism in mathematics classrooms: Global perspectives* (pp. 47–62). Bristol: Multilingual Matters.

Heath, S.B. (1983). *Ways with words: Language, life, and work in communities and classrooms*. New York, NY: Cambridge University Press.

Heritage, M. (2008). *Learning progressions: Supporting instruction and formative assessment*. Center on Continuous Instructional Improvement. Assessment and Accountability Comprehensive Center. Los Angeles, CA: National Center for Research on Evaluation, Standards, and Student Testing. Presentation at the Meeting on Advancing Research on Adaptive Instruction and Formative Assessment. Philadelphia (February 21–22). Retrieved May 30, 2010 from www.cpre.org/ccii/images/stories/ccii_pdfs/learning%20progressions_heritage.pdf.

Hollins, E.R. (1996). *Cultures in school learning: Revealing the deep meaning*. Mahwah, NJ: Lawrence Erlbaum Associates.

Kiplinger, V.L., Haug, C.A., & Abedi, J. (2000). *Measuring math—not reading—on a math assessment: A language accommodations study of English language learners and other special populations*. Paper presented at the Annual Meeting of the American Educational Research Association, New Orleans, LA, April 24–28.

Kopriva, R.J. (2008). *Improving testing for English language learners*. New York, NY: Routledge.

Labov, W. (1972). *Language in the inner city: Studies in the black English vernacular*. Philadelphia, PA: University of Pennsylvania Press.

Langdon, H.W., with Cheng, L.L. (1992). *Hispanic children and adults with communication disorders*. Gaithersburg, MD: Aspen.

McCarty, T.L. (2009). The impact of high-stakes accountability policies on Native American learners: Evidence from research. *Teaching Education*, 20(1), 7–29.

National Research Council (2001). *Knowing what students know*. Washington, DC: National Academies Press.

Nucci, L.P., Saxe, G.B., & Turiel, E. (2000). *Culture, thought, and development*. Mahwah, NJ: Lawrence Erlbaum Associates.

Rogoff, B., & Chavajay, P. (1995). What's become of research on the cultural basis of cognitive development? *American Psychologist*, 50(10), 859–877.

Rothstein-Fisch, C., & Trumbull, E. (2008). *Managing diverse classrooms: How to build on students' cultural strengths*. Alexandria, VA: Association for Supervision and Curriculum Development.

Rothstein-Fisch, C., Trumbull, E., Isaac, A., Daley, C., & Pérez, A. (2003). When "helping someone else" is the right answer: Teachers bridge cultures in assessment. *Journal of Latinos and Education*, 2(3), 123–140.

Solano-Flores, G., & Trumbull, E. (2003). Examining language in context: The need for new research and practice paradigms in the testing of English language learners. *Educational Researcher*, 32(2), 3–13.

Swisher, K., & Deyhle, D. (1992). Adapting instruction to culture. In J. Reyhner (Ed.), *Teaching American Indian students* (pp. 81–95). Norman, OK: University of Oklahoma Press.

Trumbull, E., Greenfield, P.M., Rothstein-Fisch, C., & Quiroz, B. (2007). Bridging cultures in parent conferences: Implications for school psychology. In G. Esquivel, E. Lopez, & S. Nahari (Eds.), *Handbook of multicultural school psychology: An interdisciplinary approach* (pp. 615–636). Mahwah, NJ: Erlbaum.

# Contributors

**Jamal Abedi** is a Professor at the School of Education of the University of California, Davis and a research partner at the National Center for Research on Evaluation, Standards, and Student Testing (CRESST). Abedi's research interests include studies in the area of psychometrics and test and scale developments. His recent works include studies on the validity of assessments, accommodations and classification for English language learners (ELLs) and students with disabilities, issues concerning comparability of alternate assessments for students with significant cognitive disabilities, opportunity to learn for ELLs, and measurement of creativity. Abedi is the recipient of the 2003 national Professional Service Award in recognition of his "Outstanding Contribution Relating Research to Practice" by the American Educational Research Association. He is also the recipient of the 2008 Lifetime Achievement Award by the California Educational Research Association. He holds a Master's and a Ph.D. degree from Vanderbilt University in Psychometrics.

**María del Rosario (Charo) Basterra** is an educational psychologist and independent educational consultant with over 28 years of experience on issues related to English language learners, language minority students, parental involvement, and preschool education. She worked as the Director of Language Minority Programs at the Mid-Atlantic Equity Center, Mid-Atlantic Equity Consortium (MAEC) for 15 years. As the Director of the Language Minority Programs, she provided technical assistance and training to states, school districts, and schools to assist them in their efforts to promote the academic achievement of language minority students K-12. She recently served as the Mid-Atlantic Equity Consortium (MAEC) Director of Informed Parents—Successful Children, a project funded by the Maryland State Department of Education. The project provided training and information on early childhood development to non-English speaking parents and caregivers throughout the state of Maryland. She also worked for five years at the Smithsonian Institution as Manager of Multicultural Programs at the Smithsonian Office of Education. She is the editor of the book *Excellence and Equity for Language Minority Students: Critical Issues and Promising Practice* (1999) and co-author of the *Family Involvement Information and Training Kit* (2000), developed in collaboration with the Delaware State Department of Education.

She has received awards from the Delaware State Department of Education and the District of Columbia Public Schools for her contributions toward the achievement of language minority students. She holds an M.A. in Educational Psychology from Temple University, Philadelphia, PA. She has been a recipient of a Fulbright Scholarship and a Ford Foundation Research grant.

**Magda Chia** is a third-year doctoral student in the School of Education at the University of Colorado at Boulder. She has participated in research projects regarding international summative assessments, formative assessments for Emerging Bilinguals, the evaluation of federal government programs, test translation practices, and gender bias in mathematics and science education. Her research interests include reliability, validity, and fairness in summative and formative assessments—particularly for Emerging Bilingual Students. Born in Bogota, Colombia, she and her family moved to New York City. She completed her B.A. at the University of Maryland, her M.A. at New York University and her Fulbright studies in Peru.

**Richard P. Durán** is a Professor at the Gevirtz Graduate School of Education, University of California Santa Barbara. He holds a Ph.D. in Psychology from the University of California, Berkeley, where he was trained as a cognitive scientist and measurement methodologist. He worked as a Research Scientist at Educational Testing in Princeton prior to joining the faculty of the University of California, Santa Barbara, in 1984. Durán has conducted and published research on assessment validity and education policy, and on educational interventions serving English language learners, and served as a member of the National Research Council Board on Testing and Assessment. Durán was also a member of the National Research Council Committee on Appropriate Test Use that authored a congressionally mandated report on the validity of tests for high school graduation purposes. He currently serves as a member of the NAEP Validity Studies Panel and the Technical Advisory Committees for the state assessment systems of New York, Texas, Washington, and California. Durán is author of many publications, including: "Do multiple representations need explanations? The role of verbal guidance and individual differences in multimedia mathematics learning" (with Roxana Moreno, 2004, *Journal of Educational Psychology*), "Assessment of English-language learners in the Oregon statewide assessment system: National and state perspectives" (2002, in *Large-Scale Assessment Programs for All Students: Validity, Technical Adequacy, and Implementation*), "Assessing English-language learners' achievement" (2008, *Review of Research in Education*).

**John J. Hoover** is currently a Research Associate and Adjunct Faculty in the Graduate School of Education at CU-Boulder. He holds a Ph.D. in Curriculum, Administration and Supervision with an emphasis in Special Education from the University of Colorado at Boulder, and an M.A. degree in Learning Disabilities/Emotional Disorders with an emphasis in Reading for Northern Arizona University. He is a former K-12 special education teacher and supervisor, working with students with learning disabilities and emotional disorders. He also has numerous years of administrative and supervisory experiences in research and teacher training in multicultural and special education accrued over the past 30 years. His work in the field of education is well documented, as he has over 60 publications ranging from university texts and textbook chapters to refereed journal articles in multicultural, special, and general education. He regularly teaches graduate level multicultural special education assessment courses and provides consulting expertise to New York City schools on assessment of English language learners and special education. Some of his forthcoming and recent publications include the article: "Special education eligibility decision making in response to intervention models" (in press); and books: *Response to intervention models: Curricular Implications and Interventions* (2010), *RTI Assessment Essentials for Struggling Learners* (2009), and *Differentiating Learning Differences from Disabilities: Meeting Diverse Needs Through Multi-Tiered Response to Intervention* (2009). He is also co-author of a recent book titled: *Methods for Teaching Culturally and Linguistically Diverse Exceptional Learners* (Hoover, Klingner, Baca, & Patton, 2008). His current line of research focuses on the implementation of response to intervention in elementary and secondary schools, including the application of RTI models in the assessment of diverse learners.

**Janette Klingner** is a Professor in Bilingual, Multicultural Special Education in the Department of Educational Equity and Cultural Diversity at the University of Colorado at Boulder. She was a bilingual special education teacher for 10 years before earning a Ph.D. in Reading and Learning Disabilities at the University of Miami. Currently, she is a co-Principal Investigator on two research projects funded by the Institute of Education Sciences, U.S. Department of Education, and a co-Principal Investigator for an Equity Assistance Center (Region VIII). To date, she has authored or co-authored 100 articles, books, and book chapters. In 2004 she won the American Educational Research Association's Early Career Award. Her research interests include reading comprehension strategy instruction for culturally and linguistically diverse students and for students with learning disabilities, Response to Intervention (RTI) for English language learners, and the disproportionate placement in special education of culturally and linguistically diverse students.

**Nanette Koelsch** is a Senior Research Associate in the Teacher Professional Development Program at WestEd. Her areas of expertise include professional development for teachers of English learners, literacy education, and portfolio assessment. She has led district-level projects that focused on developing culturally relevant assessments that inform instruction and meet state standards, including a nine-year collaboration with a public school district located in the Navajo Nation. Koelsch has taught graduate courses addressing literacy and the education of linguistically and culturally diverse students in the Department of Bilingual and Multicultural Education at the Northern Arizona University. She taught at the elementary and middle school levels before entering the doctoral program in the Language, Literacy, and Culture division of the School of Education at University of California, Berkeley, where she is completing her doctoral work. Koelsch is the author of many publications, among them a *Guide to Analyzing Linguistic and Cultural Assumptions in Assessment* (WestEd), a chapter on cross-cultural portfolios in *Writing Portfolios in the Classroom* (1996, Erlbaum), *Improving Literacy Outcomes for English Language Learners in High School: Considerations for States and Districts in Developing a Coherent Policy Framework* (2006, WestEd), *Selected States' Responses to Supporting High School English Language Learners* (2009,WestEd), and *What Are We Doing to Middle School English Learners? Findings and Recommendations for Change from a Study of California EL Programs* (2010, WestEd).

**Rebecca Kopriva** is a Senior Scientist with the Center for Education Research at the University of Wisconsin, Madison. She focuses on the psychometric properties of items and issues related to access to items by English language learners through workshop training sessions and ongoing consultation. Formerly she was Associate Professor in the California State University System, state testing director, and consultant for test publishers, the U.S. Department of Education, national legal and policy groups, and a variety of states and districts. She is a researcher who publishes and presents regularly on the theory and practice of improving large-scale test validity and comparability. She is a leader in addressing these topics as they relate to the measurement of academic knowledge and skills in racial, cultural, and ethnic minority students and students with disabilities.

**Julia Lara** has over 30 years of experience in the field of education, K-12, and higher education. Her most recent role has been as President of JLara Educational Consulting, LLC. In this capacity she managed various contracts focusing on the Education of ELL students or interventions designed to improve the delivery of instruction for students in public schools. Prior to her most recent work experience, she worked at the office of the Deputy Mayor for Education in the District of Columbia as the early childhood content specialist. For over 20 years, she held various assignments at the Council of Chief State School Officers (CCSSO) including Director of the Division of State Services and Technical Assistance (SSTA), center director, program director, and senior project associate. As Director of SSTA, she supervised over 30 professional and support staff and over 12 projects. Key areas of strength include: program management, policy research, analysis and writing, fundraising, and establishing and maintaining networks of state officials, researchers, community members. Ms. Lara was the lead staff on over six projects in various content areas of education, including education and assessment of ELL students, high school reform, early childhood, special education, school reform and education of students enrolled in low performing schools. Finally, Ms. Lara has written extensively on matters related to the education of English language learners and students enrolled in low performing schools.

**Okhee Lee** is a Professor in the School of Education, University of Miami, Florida. Her research areas include science education, language and culture, and teacher education. She was awarded a 1993–1995 National Academy of Education Spencer Post-Doctoral Fellowship. She received the Distinguished Career Award from the American Educational Research Association (AERA) for Scholars of Color in Education in 2003. She has directed research and teacher enhancement projects funded by the National Science Foundation, U.S. Department of Education, Spencer Foundation, and other sources.

**Jaime Maerten-Rivera** is a Research Associate in the School of Education, University of Miami, Florida. She researches various educational issues including science achievement, diversity in education, and teacher professional development. Her focus is in the area of applied methodological issues with a secondary focus on investigating the efficacy of large-scale interventions.

**Alexandra Santau** is an Assistant Professor of Science Education in the School of Education at Duquesne University in Pittsburgh, Pennsylvania. Her educational background is in microbiology and molecular biology, followed by a Ph.D. in Science Education from the University of Miami in 2008. Her research interests include elementary and secondary in-service and pre-service teachers' knowledge and practices in teaching science to English language learners in urban classrooms, as well as student achievement in science. She also conducts research in self-study and has recently been awarded a Barbara Sizemore Fellowship for research in urban settings.

**Ursula Sexton** is a Senior Research Associate at WestEd (Redwood City, CA) in the Center for the Study of Culture and Language in Education in the Science, Technology, Engineering and Mathematics program. Sexton manages projects investigating the roles that cultural diversity and language play in mathematics and science curriculum, assessment, and instructional practices. She works with districts serving high numbers of English language learners as well as indigenous communities in Arizona, New Mexico, Alaska, and the Pacific Rim. As a former Spanish–English bilingual science teacher, she led professional development and curriculum and assessment reform, and was recognized as a Teacher of the Year nationally. Sexton is the author of numerous articles and has co-authored science curricula (Scholastic, 1995), book chapters, and education guides. Among these are, *Teaching Science for All Children* (Allyn & Bacon, 1995), *Guide to Scoring LEP Student Responses to Open-Ended Science Items* (Chief Council of School State Officers—CCSSO, 1999), *Testing English Language Learners: A Sampler of Student Responses to Science and Mathematics Test Items* (CCSSO, 2000), and *Science for English Language Learners K-12 Classroom Strategies* (NSTA Press, 2005). She also co-authored *Making Science Accessible to English Learners: A Guide for Teachers* (WestEd, 2007).

**Guillermo Solano-Flores** is Associate Professor of Bilingual Education and English as a Second Language at the School of Education of the University of Colorado at Boulder. He specializes in educational measurement and the linguistic and cultural issues that are relevant to testing. A psychometrician by formal training, his work focuses on the development of alternative, multidisciplinary approaches that address linguistic and cultural diversity in testing. His main contributions to the field of testing include: a theory of test translation error that allows improved practice in test translation and test translation review; the use of generalizability theory—a psychometric theory of measurement error—as an approach for examining language as a source of measurement error in the testing of English language learners (ELLs); the use of illustrations as a form of testing accommodations for ELLs; and the concept of cultural validity—the subject of this book. Current research projects examine academic language load in tests for ELLs, the effectiveness of vignette illustrations in ELL testing (a project funded by the National Science Foundation), and the issues that are critical to providing technical assistance on test translation and test adaptation to countries participating in international test comparisons.

**Elise Trumbull** is an applied linguist and independent educational consultant specializing in relations among language, culture, learning, and schooling. She is a part-time faculty member at California State University, Northridge, where she has taught a course on Language, Culture, and Human Development several times. A former teacher and assessment coordinator for a K-3 public school, Trumbull completed an Ed.D. in Applied Psycholinguistics at Boston University in 1984. She has studied seven languages other than English and has conducted naturalistic and experimental research in cultural settings ranging from California, Washington, Florida, New York, and Arizona to various entities in Micronesia. Trumbull has co-authored numerous articles and book chapters, as well as seven books, including: *Assessment Alternatives for Diverse Classrooms* (Christopher-Gordon, 1997), *Bridging Cultures: A Guide for Teachers* (Erlbaum, 2001), *Language and Learning: What Teachers Need to Know* (Christopher-Gordon, 2005), and *Managing Diverse Classrooms: How to Build on Students' Cultural Strengths* (ASCD, 2008).

# Index

Page numbers in *italics* denote tables, those in **bold** denote figures.